THE INDISPENSABLE ZINN

D0048334

ALSO BY HOWARD ZINN

La Guardia in Congress (1959)

SNCC: The New Abolitionists (1964)

The Southern Mystique (1964)

New Deal Thought (editor, 1966)

Vietnam: The Logic of Withdrawal (1967)

Disobedience and Democracy: Nine Fallacies of Law and Order (1968)

The Politics of History (1970)

The Pentagon Papers: Critical Essays (co-edited with Noam Chomsky, 1972)

Postwar America, 1945–1971 (1973)

Justice in Everyday Life: The Way It Really Works (editor, 1974)

A People's History of the United States, 1492–1980 (1980)

Declarations of Independence: Cross-Examining American Ideology (1990)

Failure to Quit: Reflections of an Optimistic Historian (1993)

You Can't Be Neutral on a Moving Train: A Personal History of Our Times (1994)

A People's History of the United States: The Wall Charts (with George Kirschner, 1995)

A People's History of the United States: Abridged Teaching Edition (1997)

The Zinn Reader: Writings on Disobedience and Democracy (1997)

The Future of History: Interviews with David Barsamian (1999)

Marx in Soho: A Play on History (1999)

Howard Zinn on History (2001)

Howard Zinn on War (2001)

Three Strikes: Miners, Musicians, Salesgirls, and the Fighting Spirit of Labor's Last Century (with Dana Frank and Robin D.G. Kelley, 2001)

Emma (2002)

Terrorism and War (with Anthony Arnove, 2002)

Artists in Times of War (2003)

Passionate Declarations: Essays on War and Justice (2003)

A People's History of the United States: 1492 to the Present (2003)

A People's History of the United States: Abridged Teaching Edition (2003)

A People's History of the United States, Volume I: American Beginnings to Reconstruction (2003)

A People's History of the United States, Volume II: The Civil War to the Present (2003)

The Twentieth Century: A People's History (2003)

The People Speak: American Voices, Some Famous, Some Little Known (2004)

Voices of a People's History of the United States (co-edited with Anthony Arnove, 2004)

A Just War (with Moises Saman and Gino Strada, 2006)

Original Zinn: Conversations on History and Politics (with David Barsamian, 2006)

A Power Governments Cannot Suppress (with Donald Macedo, 2007)

Howard Zinn on Democratic Education (2008)

Uncommon Sense from the Writings of Howard Zinn
(selected and introduced by Dean Birkenkamp and Wanda
Rhudy, 2009)

The Unraveling of the Bush Presidency (2009)

*A Young People's History of the United States: Columbus to the War
on Terror* (with Rebecca Stefoff, 2009)

The Bomb (2010)

Three Plays: The Political Theater of Howard Zinn (2010)

The Indispensable Zinn

The Essential Writings
of the "People's Historian"

HOWARD ZINN

Edited by
Timothy Patrick McCarthy

Requests for permission to reproduce selections from this book should be mailed to:
Permissions Department, The New Press, 38 Greene Street,
New York, NY 10013.

Pages 377–79 constitute an extension of this copyright page.

Published in the United States by The New Press, New York, 2012
Distributed by Perseus Distribution

LIBRARY OF CONGRESS CATALOGING-IN-PUBLICATION DATA

Zinn, Howard, 1922–2010.
The indispensable Zinn: the essential writings of the "people's historian" /
Howard Zinn ; edited by Timothy Patrick McCarthy.
p. cm.
Includes bibliographical references.
ISBN 978-1-59558-622-3 (pbk. : alk. paper)   1. United States—History.
2. United States—Politics and government.   3. United States—Social conditons.
4. Social movements—United States—History.   5. Zinn, Howard, 1922–2010.
I. McCarthy, Timothy Patrick.   II. Title.
E178.6.Z555 2012
973—dc23
2011052775

Now in its twentieth year, The New Press publishes books that promote and enrich public discussion
and understanding of the issues vital to our democracy and to a more equitable world. These books are
made possible by the enthusiasm of our readers; the support of a committed group of donors, large and
small; the collaboration of our many partners in the independent media and the not-for-profit sector;
booksellers, who often hand-sell New Press books; librarians; and above all by our authors.

www.thenewpress.com

Composition by Westchester Book Composition
This book was set in Fournier

Printed in the United States of America
10 9 8 7 6 5 4 3 2 1

This book is dedicated to the memory of
HOWARD ZINN (1922–2010) and
MANNING MARABLE (1950–2011)
and to all those who speak truth to power

CONTENTS

FOREWORD

Noam Chomsky

It is not easy for me to write a few words about Howard Zinn, the great American activist and historian who passed away a few days ago. He was a very close friend for forty-five years. The families were very close too. His wife Roz, who died of cancer not long before, was also a marvelous person and close friend. Also somber is the realization that a whole generation seems to be disappearing, including several other old friends: Edward Said, Eqbal Ahmed, and others, who were not only astute and productive scholars but also dedicated and courageous militants, always on call when needed—which was constant. A combination that is essential if there is to be hope of decent survival.

Howard's remarkable life and work are summarized best in his own words. His primary concern, he explained, was "the countless small actions of unknown people" that lie at the roots of "those great moments" that enter the historical record—a record that will be profoundly misleading, and seriously disempowering, if it is torn from these roots as it passes through the filters of doctrine and dogma. His life was always closely intertwined with his writings and innumerable talks and interviews. It was devoted, selflessly, to empowerment of the unknown people who brought about great moments. That was true when he was an industrial worker and labor activist, and from the days, fifty years ago, when he was teaching at Spelman College in Atlanta, Georgia, a black college that was open mostly to the small black elite.

Originally appeared in *Resist Newsletter*, March/April 2010.

While teaching at Spelman, Howard supported the students who were at the cutting edge of the Civil Rights Movement in its early and most dangerous days, many of whom became quite well known in later years—Alice Walker, Julian Bond, and others—and who loved and revered him, as did everyone who knew him well. And, as always, he did not just support them, which was rare enough, but also participated directly with them in their most hazardous efforts—no easy undertaking at that time, before there was any organized popular movement and in the face of government hostility that lasted for some years. Finally, popular support was ignited, in large part by the courageous actions of the young people who were sitting in at lunch counters, riding freedom buses, organizing demonstrations, facing bitter racism and brutality, sometimes death. By the early 1960s a mass popular movement was taking shape, by then with Martin Luther King Jr. in a leadership role, and the government had to respond. As a reward for his courage and honesty, Howard was soon expelled from the college where he taught. A few years later he wrote the standard work on SNCC (the Student Nonviolent Coordinating Committee), the major organization of those "unknown people" whose "countless small actions" played such an important part in creating the groundswell that enabled King to gain significant influence, as I am sure he would have been the first to say, and to bring the country to honor the constitutional amendments of a century earlier that had theoretically granted elementary civil rights to former slaves—at least to do so partially; no need to stress that there remains a long way to go.

On a personal note, I came to know Howard well when we went together to a civil rights demonstration in Jackson, Mississippi, in (I think) 1964, even at that late date a scene of violent public antagonism, police brutality, and indifference or even cooperation with state security forces on the part of federal authorities, sometimes in ways that were quite shocking.

After being expelled from the Atlanta college where he taught, Howard came to Boston and spent the rest of his academic career at Boston University, where he was, I am sure, the most admired and loved faculty member on campus and the target of bitter antagonism and petty cruelty on the part of the administration—though in later years, after his retirement, he gained the public honor and respect that was always overwhelming among students, staff, much of the faculty, and the general community. While there, Howard wrote the books that brought him well-deserved fame. His 1967 book *Vietnam: The Logic of Withdrawal* was the first to express clearly and powerfully what many were then beginning barely to contemplate: that the United States had no right even to call for a negotiated settlement in Vietnam, leaving Washington with power and substantial control in the country it had invaded and by then already largely destroyed. Rather, the United States should do what any aggressor should: withdraw; allow the population to somehow reconstruct as they could from the wreckage; and, if minimal honesty could be attained, pay massive reparations for the crimes that the invading armies had committed, vast crimes in this case. The book had wide influence among the public, although to this day its message can barely even be comprehended in elite educated circles, an indication of how much necessary work lies ahead.

Significantly, by the war's end, 70 percent regarded the war as "fundamentally wrong and immoral," not "a mistake," a remarkable figure considering the fact that scarcely a hint of such a thought was expressible in mainstream opinion. Howard's writings—and, as always, his prominent presence in protest and direct resistance—were a major factor in civilizing much of the country.

In those same years, Howard also became one of the most prominent supporters of the resistance movement that was then developing. He was one of the early signers of the Call to Resist Illegitimate Authority and was so close to the activities of Resist that he was practically one of the organizers. He also took part at once in the sanctuary actions that had a remarkable impact in galvanizing antiwar protest. Whatever was needed—talks, participation in civil disobedience, support for resisters, testimony at trials—Howard was always there.

Even more influential in the long run than Howard's antiwar writings and actions was his enduring masterpiece, *A People's History of the United States*, a book that literally changed the consciousness of a generation. Here he developed with care, lucidity, and comprehensive sweep his fundamental message about the crucial role of the people who remain unknown in carrying forward the endless struggle for peace and justice, and about the victims of the systems of power that create their own versions of history and seek to impose it. Later, his *Voices of a People's History of the United States*, now an acclaimed theatrical and television production (*The People Speak*), has brought to many the actual words of those forgotten or ignored people who have played such a valuable role in creating a better world.

Howard's unique success in drawing the actions and voices of unknown people from the depths to which they had largely been consigned has spawned extensive historical research following a similar path, focusing on critical periods of American history, and turning to the record in other countries as well, a very welcome development. It is not entirely novel—there had been scholarly inquiries of particular topics before—but nothing to compare with Howard's broad and incisive evocation of "history from below," compensating for critical omissions in how American history had been interpreted and conveyed.

Howard's dedicated activism continued, literally without a break, until the very end, even in his last years, when he was suffering from severe infirmity and personal loss, though one would hardly know it when meeting him or watching him speaking tirelessly to captivated audiences all over the country. Whenever there was a struggle for peace and justice, Howard was there, on the front lines, unflagging in his enthusiasm; inspiring in his integrity, engagement, eloquence, and insight; his light touch of humor in the face of adversity; his dedication to nonviolence; and his sheer decency. It is hard even to imagine how many young people's lives were touched, and how deeply, by his achievements, both in his work and his life.

There are places where Howard's life and work should have particular resonance. One, which should be much better known, is Turkey. I know of no other country where leading writers, artists, journalists, academics, and other intellectuals have compiled such an impressive record of bravery and integrity in condemning crimes of state, and going above and beyond to engage in civil disobedience to try to bring oppression and violence to an end, facing and sometimes enduring severe repression, and then returning to the task. It is an honorable record, unique to my knowledge, a record of which the country should be proud. And one that should be a model for others, just as Howard Zinn's life and work are an unforgettable model, sure to leave a permanent stamp on how history is understood and how a decent and honorable life should be lived.

INTRODUCTION
THE PEOPLE'S HISTORIAN
Timothy Patrick McCarthy

Few historians write *and* make history. For more than half a century, Howard Zinn did both.

Like so many young people of my generation, I first encountered Howard in the opening pages of *A People's History of the United States*. The book did indeed knock me on my ass, as Matt Damon's title character exclaims in the 1997 Oscar-winning film *Good Will Hunting*. Howard's groundbreaking revisionist work was first published in 1980, just as the revolutionary spirit of the 1960s and 1970s was about to be steamrolled by the Reagan counterrevolution. I will never forget those opening paragraphs, unleashed without any introduction or warning:

> Arawak men and women, naked, tawny, and full of wonder, emerged from their villages onto the island's beaches and swam out to get a closer look at the strange big boat. When Columbus and his sailors came ashore, carrying swords, speaking oddly, the Arawaks ran to greet them, brought them food, water, gifts. . . .
>
> These Arawaks of the Bahama Islands were much like Indians on the mainland, who were remarkable (European observers were to say again and again) for their hospitality, their belief in sharing. These traits did not stand out in the Europe of the Renaissance, dominated as it was by the religion of popes, the government of kings, the frenzy of money that marked Western civilization and its first messenger to the Americas, Christopher Columbus."[1]

Here was Howard flipping the script on history, making it known that the narrative we had all been taught to revere and recite as schoolchildren—of Columbus's "heroic" "discovery" of the so-called New World—could be told from a radically different point of view. Indeed, it must.

No one who reads the first chapter of this book can miss the point: that this view of history, "a people's history," is the best antidote we have to the nationalist mythmaking that so often serves to justify the interests of the privileged and the powerful. And that's the thing about Howard Zinn—he wore his politics on his sleeve. For him, history was not merely an investigation or illumination of some distant past, but also an intervention in the present for the sake of our collective future. "If history is to be creative," Howard wrote, "to anticipate a possible future without denying the past, it should, I believe, emphasize new possibilities by disclosing those hidden episodes of the past when, even if in brief flashes, people showed their ability to resist, to join together, occasionally to win."[2] At the core of Howard's writing was a relentless critique of those who hold and abuse power, but also a stubborn optimism about the capacity of ordinary people to make history.

His optimism was firmly rooted in and shaped by his own life experiences. For Howard, the personal and political were always deeply intertwined with the historical. Born in Brooklyn in 1922 to hardworking Jewish immigrant parents, Howard was the product of a modest upbringing in which he was exposed early on to the everyday struggles of laboring people. As a young man coming of age during the Great Depression, Howard was deeply influenced by the protest literature of Charles Dickens, Upton Sinclair, Langston Hughes, Richard Wright, and John Steinbeck. When he was eighteen, he began working in a naval shipyard. In his celebrated memoir, *You Can't Be Neutral on a Moving Train*, he described this experience as "three years working on the docks, in the cold and heat, amid deafening noise and poisonous fumes, building battleships and landing ships in the early years of the Second World War."[3] In 1943, having just turned twenty-one, he enlisted in the Air Force and flew bomber missions in Europe, an experience that would later lead him to question the morality of war. Indeed, his subsequent antiwar activism—which reached a fever pitch during the Vietnam era and continued through the contemporary wars in Afghanistan and Iraq—was deeply informed by the feelings of regret he had from being a bombardier. After the war, Howard went to New York University and Columbia University on the G.I. Bill (he liked to brag that he

"never paid a cent" for his education).[4] While a graduate student in
American history, he worked the night shift in a warehouse and taught
part-time day and evening classes at several nearby schools to make
ends meet. Newly married, Howard lived with his wife Roz and two
small children in a housing project in lower Manhattan while he wrote
his Columbia dissertation, a well-regarded study of Fiorello LaGuardia, whose legendary congressional career during the 1910s and 1920s
was, Howard argued, "an astonishingly accurate preview of the New
Deal."[5] In 1956, before completing his doctorate, Howard secured a faculty position at Spelman College in Atlanta, Georgia, where he taught
a number of remarkable black women, including Alice Walker, the
award-winning writer and activist, and Marian Wright (later Edelman),
the founder and president of the Children's Defense Fund. His seven
years at Spelman—he was fired for "insubordination" in 1963 because of
his activism—coincided with the emergence of the black freedom
struggle in the South. The rest, we might say, is history. Howard's deep
involvement with movement work inspired a lifelong commitment to
civil rights and racial and socioeconomic justice. During the 1960s and
1970s, he was one of the leading voices of opposition to the Vietnam
War; in 1967, he called for the "immediate withdrawal" of troops from
Vietnam.[6] From 1964 to his retirement in 1988, Howard was a professor
of political science at Boston University, where he earned a reputation—
richly deserved—as a beloved teacher, a prolific scholar, and first-class
troublemaker.

Howard's troublemaking—pedagogically, intellectually, politically—
is now the stuff of legend, in large part because he was so consistently
willing to speak truth to power throughout his life, no matter the stakes.
The following excerpt from his memoir powerfully underscores the
fact that Howard's political commitments were always at least as important to him as his academic ambitions:

> [T]he beginning of my teaching at Boston University coincided
> almost exactly with the steep escalation of the United States' war
> in Vietnam, after the hazy incident in the Gulf of Tonkin. I be-
> came immediately involved in the protests against the war: rallies,
> teach-ins, demonstrations, articles—one of these, for the *Nation*,
> arguing the case for withdrawal from Vietnam.
>
> When I was hired, I was promised tenure after a year, which is
> a fairly strong guarantee of lifetime employment. But following
> that first year I was still without a tenure contract. A secretarial

error, I was told. Another year passed (in which my antiwar activity increased) and another excuse was given.

Finally, in early 1967, the Department of Political Science held a meeting to vote on my tenure. There were a few professors opposed, saying flatly that my actions against the war were embarrassing to the university. On the other hand, student evaluations of my teaching were enthusiastic, and my fifth book was being published that spring. The department voted for tenure.

Approval came soon from the dean and the president. (This was four years before John Silber became president of the university.) All that remained was a vote of the Board of Trustees.

That spring of 1967, some students came to my office saying that the trustees were going to have their annual meeting, to coincide with a Founders Day dinner, and that the guest speaker would be Dean Rusk, secretary of state, in a splendid affair at the Sheraton Boston Hotel. Rusk was one of the strategists of the Vietnam War, and the students were going to organize a demonstration in front of the hotel. They wanted me to be one of the speakers.

I hesitated as I thought of my tenure decision in the hands of the trustees. But I could hardly say no—hadn't I always maintained that risking your job is a price you pay if you want to be a free person? I must confess that my courage was not absolute; I envisioned that I would be one of the many speakers and perhaps not be noticed.

When the evening of the big event came, I made my way to the Sheraton Boston and joined several hundred demonstrators circling in front of the hotel. Soon one of the organizers came to escort me to the microphone, which was set up near the hotel entrance. I looked around. "Where are the other speakers?" I asked. He looked puzzled. "There are no other speakers."

And so I held forth to the crowd assembled in front of the hotel, talking about the war and why the United States did not belong in Vietnam. As I spoke, limousines drew up, one by one, and tuxedoed guests, including Dean Rusk, the trustees, and others, stepped out, stopped for a moment to take in the scene, and went into the hotel.

A few days later I received a letter from the Office of the President. As I opened it, I thought of that other letter of 1963 from the office of another president [when he was fired from Spelman College because of his involvement in the Civil Rights Movement]. But this one said, "Dear Professor Zinn, I am happy to inform you that you have been awarded tenure by a meeting of the Board of Trustees on the afternoon of. . . ." So the trustees had voted me tenure in the afternoon, then arrived in the evening for the

Founders Day dinner to find their newly tenured faculty member denouncing their honored guest.[7]

On the one hand, this episode speaks to just how lucky Howard was to have gotten tenure at that moment in history. Had his tenure not gone through, his increasingly vocal antiwar activism—as well as the hiring of John Silber as president of Boston University in 1971—would have surely led to his firing. As Howard has written, "Silber and I clashed almost immediately."[8] (This is something of an understatement!) On the other hand, Howard's professional life offers a powerful moral lesson to those of us in the academy—especially a younger generation of scholars—who would subordinate or silence our principles for the sake of promotion, rank, or job security. Indeed, whenever I'm feeling the treacherous tug-of-war between ambition and principle, I ask myself: "What would Howard do?" The answer is always the same: the right thing, not the safe thing.

Though Howard certainly had loyal defenders, including many of the leading intellectuals, artists, and activists of our time, his academic pursuits and political commitments also earned him harsh critics. One need only look at the 423 pages of his FBI files, released under the Freedom of Information Act in 2010, to understand what a threat he posed to the powers that be.[9] An unapologetic radical, his civil rights and antiwar activism made him a prime target for federal surveillance, starting in the late 1940s, when the FBI sought to "obtain additional information concerning this subject's membership in the Communist Party or concerning his activities in behalf of the party," and continuing through at least the 1970s.[10] (For the record, Howard always denied membership in the Communist Party and preferred to describe himself as "something of an anarchist, something of a socialist. Maybe a democratic socialist."[11]) His academic work, especially *A People's History of the United States*, likewise attracted fierce opposition. In an article titled "The Left's Blind Spot," historian Rick Shenkman, editor of the History News Network, indicted Howard for playing "the role in a self-satisfied often-uncritical mainstream culture of the seemingly attractive dangerous rebel."[12] Daniel J. Flynn, executive director of Accuracy in Academia, a conservative nonprofit that monitors college campuses because it "wants schools to return to their traditional mission—the quest for truth," accused the "unreconstructed, anti-American Marxist Howard Zinn" of having a "captive mind long closed by ideology." For Flynn, *A People's History* was "little more than an 800-page libel against his country."[13]

Not all of Howard's critics came from the right. In a searing critique published in *Dissent* in 2004, the distinguished social historian Michael Kazin wrote, "*A People's History* is bad history, albeit gilded with virtuous intentions. Zinn reduces the past to a Manichean fable and makes no serious attempt to address the biggest question a leftist can ask about U.S. history: why have most Americans accepted the legitimacy of the capitalist republic in which they live?"[14] The award-winning Columbia historian Eric Foner was more sympathetic. In his *New York Times* review of *A People's History*, Foner praised Howard for "an enthusiasm rarely encountered in the leaden prose of academic history" and predicted that "historians may well view it as a step toward a coherent new version of American history."[15] Still, in a *Nation* tribute to Howard the week after his death, Foner also acknowledged that "[s]ometimes, to be sure, his account tended toward the Manichean, an oversimplified narrative of the battle between the forces of light and dark."[16] In a February 2010 *New Yorker* blog post titled "Zinn's History," Harvard historian Jill Lepore compared the experience of reading *A People's History* in high school to reading J.D. Salinger's *The Catcher in the Rye* at the same age: "it's swell and terrible and it feels like something has ended, because it has."[17]

While Foner and Lepore (though not Kazin) could forgive these limitations as perhaps a natural consequence of writing the first comprehensive "bottom up" social history of the United States, others saw in Howard's work clear evidence of ideological manipulation—or worse, political treason. In an article published the day after Howard's death in January 2010, Ron Radosh, professor of history emeritus at the City University of New York, seemed to delight in dancing on Howard's grave, writing, "Zinn ransacked the past to find alternative models for future struggles."[18] The right-wing pundit David Horowitz went even further the same day on National Public Radio, calling the book a "travesty" and arguing that "there is absolutely nothing in Howard Zinn's intellectual output that is worthy of any kind of respect."[19] Two days later, concerned that NPR had edited his interview down to an inadequate sound bite, Horowitz used his blog to elaborate on his main point: "Zinn's wretched tract, *A People's History of the United States*, is worthless as history, and it is a national tragedy that so many Americans have fallen under its spell. . . . All Zinn's writing was directed to one end: to indict his own country as an evil state and soften his countrymen up for the kill. Like his partner in crime, Noam Chomsky, Zinn's life work was a pernicious influence on the young and ignorant, with destructive consequences for people everywhere."[20]

Truth be told, I am among the "young and ignorant" who have fallen prey to Howard's "pernicious influence." But I prefer to characterize myself, as Foner has elsewhere, as one of those "many excellent students of history" who "first had their passion for the past sparked by reading Howard Zinn."[21] The numbers, of course, speak for themselves. To date, *A People's History of the United States* has sold upward of 2 million copies, making it the bestselling work of American history *in* American history. According to Hugh Van Dusen, Howard's editor at HarperCollins, the book has increased its sales every year since its original publication in 1980, a trend that has only continued since his death. Writes Van Dusen: "I have never heard of another book, from any publisher, fiction or nonfiction, on any subject, of which that can be said—and I have asked a lot of people at other publishers whether they have heard of such a book."[22] There are many factors that have contributed to the runaway popularity of *A People's History*: it was the first "bottom up" history of the United States; it embodied the revolutionary spirit of the 1960s while eschewing the reactionary soullessness of the Reagan counterrevolution; its lively narrative style served as a refreshing alternative to traditional academic scholarship; it articulated a bold point of view about the power of history; and it advanced a blistering critique of powerful people and institutions. More than anything else, however, it was a book that allowed so many Americans—workers and women, farmers and feminists, socialists and students, immigrants and indigenous people, communists and civil rights activists—to see themselves as agents of history for the first time. The book is by no means perfect. In a later edition, Howard admitted that he "neglected groups in American society that had always been missing from orthodox histories," including, crucially, Latinos and queer people. As an openly gay man, I remember talking to Howard about these omissions, and I appreciated his forthright acknowledgment that "my own sexual orientation . . . accounted for my minimal treatment of the issue of gay and lesbian rights," something he tried to make up for in the 1995 edition of the book.[23] That was the thing about Howard—as with history, he saw himself as a work in progress. He was neither static nor set in his ways. As the title of his memoir suggests, though never neutral or "objective," he was always on a moving train.

Howard's critics—and there are many—have voiced three principal objections to his work. First, they accuse him of *ideological extremism*, of allowing his leftist politics to corrupt the more noble pursuit of historical "objectivity." Second, they accuse him of *oversimplification*, of

inverting "heroes" and "villains," "winners" and "losers," to construct
a Manichean narrative of the American past. And third, they accuse
him of *celebrity*, as if his entire career were driven more by the stroking
of ego than the struggle for equality. Let me address each one of these
criticisms in turn, beginning with the last.

In his later years, Howard was indeed something of a celebrity.
Nothing helped to underscore this more forcefully than the scene in
Good Will Hunting where Matt Damon's working-class character in-
voking *A People's History* in *Good Will Hunting*. Following the film's
runaway success, Damon, who shared the 1997 Academy Award for
best original screenplay with costar Ben Affleck, was determined to
bring Howard's bestselling book to the big screen. After Rupert Murdoch's Twentieth Century Fox withdrew from a potential deal, Damon
worked with Howard to get the film made through other channels,
culminating in the 2009 History Channel documentary *The People
Speak*, featuring an impressive list of A-list collaborators. Still, critics
of Howard's relatively recent "celebrity" miss several key points. First,
Howard knew Damon when he was a young kid growing up in Cambridge, and their relationship predates either man's celebrity. Second,
Howard was infamous long before he was famous. One could easily
make the case that his "celebrity," such as it is, was forged not in the
late-in-life embrace by liberal actors but in the relentless attacks of his
conservative critics—from J. Edgar Hoover, who called him a "communist," to Boston University president John Silber, who considered
him a "menace." If Howard became a media darling—and a lifetime of
public caricature and criticism tends to constrain such a thesis—it is
because he eventually earned a more favorable reputation by being on
the right side of history for more than half a century. Finally, it is worth
remembering that Howard spent half his life toiling away—as a worker,
soldier, student, and adjunct instructor—in relative obscurity before he
ever garnered any fame or fortune. He understood poverty because he
came from it, and he appreciated the struggles of ordinary people because he was one of them. He may have achieved celebrity later in life,
but he certainly didn't start with or expect it.

The charge of oversimplification is a more credible criticism, one
that we hear most often from professional historians committed to more
traditional academic careers and credentials. Then again, as the radical
historian Staughton Lynd, Howard's friend and colleague during the
early days at Spelman, has written, Howard was never principally concerned with impressing the academic elite: "the most remarkable thing

about Howard as an academician was that he was always concerned to speak, not to other academicians, but to the general public. Soon after arriving in Atlanta, I asked him what papers he was preparing for which academic gatherings. This was what I supposed historians did. Howard looked at me as if I were speaking a foreign language. He was one of two adult supervisors to the Student Nonviolent Coordinating Committee and was preoccupied with the question of how racism may be overcome."[24] That said, Howard did indeed juxtapose the experiences of "the people" against the interests of "the powerful" in much of his writing. As Foner rightly acknowledged in his *New York Times* review, "[t]hose accustomed to the texts of an earlier generation, in which the rise of American democracy and the growth of national power were the embodiment of Progress, may be startled by Professor Zinn's narrative. From the opening pages, an account of the 'European invasion of the Indian settlements in the Americas,' there is a reversal of perspective, a reshuffling of heroes and villains. The book bears the same relation to traditional texts as a photographic negative does to a print: the areas of darkness and light have been reversed."[25] Then again, the same could be said of much early revisionist social history, where scholars interested in African American history, immigrant history, labor history, women's history, social movement history, and gay and lesbian history sought to expand traditional interpretations of the American past beyond the experiences and perspectives of wealthy, straight white men. As with much of Howard's work, *A People's History* amplified and synthesized the contributions of ordinary Americans who had been left out of more traditional histories. The book was meant to be transformative, not definitive, an opening salvo rather than the final word. Still, as Howard knew as well as anyone, those who break the mold are often criticized for doing so.

The loudest criticisms of Howard's work, both his scholarship and his activism, come from his political detractors—some of them conventional liberals, others far more conservative. One could easily produce another entire anthology (or several!) of writings denouncing Howard for his "pessimism," his "left-wing bias," his "Marxism," his "lack of patriotism," you name it. That he was called everything in the book, however, does not diminish the importance or influence of the books he produced. The root of the problem is that Howard committed the worst of sins: he was a historian who rejected objectivity, an activist who refused to sit down and shut up, a soldier who hated war, and a citizen who dared to criticize his country. In other words, he understood—and insisted that we understand—that the denial of one's politics is a politics of its own. Those who hated Howard did so because they couldn't stand the fact that he was always forthcoming about his values and beliefs.

The audacity of Howard's political honesty became evident to me the first time I invited him to be a guest lecturer in one of my Harvard courses, "American Protest Literature from Tom Paine to Tupac," in the spring of 2002. I had asked him to come speak on the 1960s to help my undergraduates understand the connections between the civil rights and antiwar movements. Though he certainly didn't need one—his reputation far preceded him at that point—I gave him a glowing introduction. My students were thrilled to have him there, and he was eager to engage with them after his remarks. Unfortunately, word had gotten out about his visit, and we had a number of people in attendance that we had not invited to the class. I was keen to have this be a special experience for those enrolled in the course, rather than a public event. When Howard finished his lecture, one of the uninvited visitors—a misanthropic graduate student who had already earned something of a reputation among undergraduates for being a crank—piped up with a question. Unceremoniously, he launched into a direct criticism of me, particularly my introduction, which he likened to a "coronation." He ended his comments with this question: "Professor Zinn, don't you think it's irresponsible to display such overt politics in a classroom setting?" I was furious. Notwithstanding the fact that this graduate student had hogged the limited airtime reserved for my undergraduates, I felt that I had offered a sincere and gracious introduction, one that displayed my gratitude to Howard for his influence on me, as well as his generosity with my students. Before I could interject (a good thing, too), Howard smiled and responded with this gem: "No, I don't think it's irresponsible at all. Politics are in every classroom. As far as I'm concerned, my life has been devoted to rolling my little apple cart into the marketplace of ideas and hoping that I don't get run over by a truck." The point was clear. The students laughed. And I felt a measure of vindication. Howard really had become my hero.

The Indispensable Zinn is a collection of Howard's essential writings from the 1960s to the present day. It is meant to be representative rather than comprehensive; anything attempting the latter would require a multivolume set. Shortly after Howard passed away on January 27, 2010, my longtime friend and New Press editor Marc Favreau approached me with the idea for this book. Marc knew that Howard had been a dear friend and mentor to me, and he understood the fact that he was also a hero to generations of students and activists, an iconic public intellectual and freedom fighter who had used his many gifts to transform the way we think about American history, culture, and politics. This book was a no-brainer for The New Press, which has been a beacon of progressive publishing since the early 1990s. I was deeply flattered by the invitation to produce such an anthology, but I was also overwhelmed at the prospect. After all, Howard had written or edited nearly thirty books, including several plays. *A People's History* alone has inspired a documentary film, a graphic comic adaptation, a musical album, teaching guides, and other cultural forms. He published dozens of articles and essays, produced hundreds of editorials, and recorded countless interviews. His tenacious activism on behalf of radical causes was legendary, inspiring its own opus of FBI surveillance documents, beginning in 1949, amid the crucible of American anticommunist zealotry. By the time of his death, Howard had outlasted most of the critics and conspiracy theorists to become a household name whose books continue to fly off the shelves. Love him or hate him, more than any scholar of his generation he was undeniably the people's historian.

How, then, to do justice to Howard's life and legacy? I began by reading his entire body of work. I started with his first monograph, *La Guardia in Congress*, published in 1959 (based on his Columbia dissertation). Over the course of a year or so, I made my way through his other twenty-eight books, his decade of columns from *The Progressive*, and other writings and interviews. I reread—for the third time—*A People's History of the United States*, and familiarized myself with its various cultural offshoots. I also read his plays and his FBI files. With Marc's help and a considerable degree of agony, I narrowed the table of contents down to twenty-one selections, including his third and final play, *Marx in Soho*, and four excerpted interviews with David Barsamian, the pioneering alternative radio journalist with whom Howard shared a longstanding friendship. Again with Marc's assistance, we were able to secure additional short tributes from Noam Chomsky and Alice Walker, two of Howard's closest friends. These appear as the foreword and the afterword, respectively. Taken together, *The Indispensable Zinn* is a thoroughly collaborative volume. Howard wouldn't have had it any other way.

I have divided the book into five main sections, each corresponding to a major theme in Howard's writing (the Barsamian interviews, recorded between 1992 and 2004, appear as Interludes between each section). Part One: The People's History showcases Howard's "bottom up" approach to the writing of American history. Beginning with that famous first chapter from *A People's History*, this section includes writings on the Colorado coal strike of 1913–14, the early work of the Student Nonviolent Coordinating Committee (SNCC) during the 1960s, and the popular resistance to the conservative counterrevolution of the Reagan era. Here we see the history of the United States told through the experiences and voices of native peoples, workers, women, civil rights activists, and other ordinary people who have protested the abuses of those in power throughout history. Part Two: The Politics of History examines the contentious relationship between political ideology and historical representation. Rejecting the myth of "objectivity," Howard uses his personal experiences as a scholar, teacher, and activist to show the influence of radical politics on the writing of history, as well as the ways in which conservative politics—especially during the 1950s and 1980s—served to suppress more democratic forms of scholarship and citizenship. Part Three: Protest Nation explores the long tradition of civil disobedience, both in American society and throughout the globe. Beginning with the social and political unrest that gave rise to the American Revolution and continuing through the Vietnam era and subsequent battles for freedom and democracy in Latin America, South Africa, and Eastern Europe, Howard documents how popular protest against authoritarianism, racism, and militarism constitutes a form of "ultimate power" against state tyranny. Part Four: On War and Peace takes up the perennial challenge of finding peaceful alternatives to unjust wars. With stirring essays that span World War II, Vietnam, Afghanistan, and Iraq, Howard charts the long history of American imperialism and challenges his readers to embrace a different moral ethos in the hopes of creating a world where war is no longer the default option for American affairs throughout the globe. Finally, Part Five reprints Howard's acclaimed play *Marx in Soho* in its entirety. Taken together, these representative texts highlight both the critical and creative sensibilities that were the hallmarks of Howard's work and life.

Though Howard was best known for his prolific writing and tireless activism, those of us who spent time with him beyond his more public persona knew him to be an exceedingly humble and generous man. The first time I met Howard, in the spring of 1999, I was still a graduate student. After defending my dissertation prospectus at Columbia, Howard's alma mater, I moved back to Cambridge to become the guardian of a young man I had been mentoring since my days as an undergraduate at Harvard. This was a risky decision for me at that point in my graduate career. More than a few of my colleagues warned that it would derail my "professional progress" (they were right, of course, but sometimes life gets in the way of one's more selfish ambitions). I was lucky enough to secure a part-time teaching gig as a tutor in Harvard's undergraduate program on history and literature, but I was still anxious about the daunting prospect of balancing dissertation writing with my new teaching and parenting duties. Whatever the reason, I sent Howard an e-mail, totally out of the blue, asking if he'd be willing to have lunch with me. Having been radicalized at Columbia, I suppose I was looking for a suitable mentor who could stand in for Eric Foner and Manning Marable, my graduate advisers, in their absence. Within forty-eight hours, Howard responded with a date and time to meet at a favorite spot of his in Harvard Square. I brought my tattered first edition copy of *A People's History* for him to sign, along with a bundle of nerves. Howard was, after all, something of a hero to me, but he owed me nothing. I worried that he would find me annoying or pathetic, or both. As it turned out, he was immediately disarming, listening carefully and patiently to my manic ramblings about history, politics, life, and graduate school. He was kind enough to affirm that there was room for yet another study of American abolitionism (my dissertation topic), and even kinder to affirm my decision to move back to Cambridge to help raise this young boy, to live life on my own terms. In retrospect, I was slightly embarrassed to have dominated the conversation so much, which made me even more grateful for his friendship that day. He even paid for my sandwich and iced tea. I left our lunch with a renewed sense of energy and purpose, as well as a deeper appreciation for the fact that some heroes have the capacity to be both human and humane. This was a vital lesson for me to learn at such an early age, and I haven't forgotten it.

Over the years, our personal, professional, and political friendship deepened. Howard was a regular guest lecturer in my undergraduate course on "American Protest Literature," and we spoke on several panels together. He helped me and my co-editor John McMillian obtain our first book contract with The New Press for *The Radical Reader* (2003), and then wrote a generous blurb. It would be difficult to overstate how much that meant to us at such an early stage in our careers. Over the years, Howard and I often found ourselves at the same protests—for a living wage, peace, and the like—and we were both cited by Lynn Cheney's American Council of Trustees and Alumni (ACTA) for being "short on patriotism" because of our outspoken opposition to war in Afghanistan and later Iraq. In November 2001, when ACTA first published its report "Defending Civilization: How Our Universities Are Failing America and What Can Be Done About It"—which included a list of more than one hundred "campus responses" in the wake of 9/11—I called Howard to joke with him about the fact that my protests had gotten me ranked number 32, two spots higher than him. "Well," he quipped, "it's about time your generation stepped up." Such laughter felt good, even liberating, especially during those dark times. As a young scholar-activist with no job security, I was comforted and strengthened to know that Howard was also on the front lines during a time when precious few Americans were willing to speak out against the accelerating pace of American imperialism in the first decade of this century. Then again, Howard was *always* on the front lines when and where it mattered.

As committed as Howard was to political activism—or perhaps because of it—he always found time for young people. Several years ago, I asked him to come speak to a group of students I was taking down south to help rebuild an African American church that had been destroyed by arson. Each spring break for the last fifteen years, I've organized trips like these, and they always inspire deep conversations about race, religion, civil rights, and social justice. In an effort to provide an opportunity for education and reflection on these issues, I thought Howard would be a great person to talk with my students about how this work connected to the long history of civil rights activism in the United States. We settled on a Sunday afternoon, and I promised to buy him brunch beforehand. Howard was late to meet us; he had been trying to find parking in Harvard Square. After circling the block several times, he decided to park illegally. "A little civil disobedience never hurt anybody," he joked as I introduced him to the student leaders of the trip. During brunch, my students listened intently as Howard regaled them with stories of his involvement in the Civil Rights Movement, war and peace, history and activism, and his friendships with Alice Walker and Noam Chomsky. After brunch, we joined the rest of the group, and he spent nearly two hours talking with them, answering their questions, and posing for some photographs (it turns out he was a hero of theirs as well). As I was walking him to his car, I thanked him for his generosity and offered to pay for his parking ticket. "They never give me a ticket," he said devilishly. Turns out he was right. If only they knew it was Howard Zinn's car!

I share these stories to underscore several things about Howard's character that his critics never really seemed to take the time to understand or appreciate: his tireless commitment to teaching and mentoring, his uncommon generosity, and his quick wit. (The rebellious spirit, of course, is amply documented!) These were the things I most adored in him. Another quality I came to cherish was his love for the arts. When given the chance, Howard was always quick to acknowledge the crucial role of artists—musicians, filmmakers, playwrights, poets, novelists, and the like—in representing and promoting social change. He was fond of quoting literature, especially the poets of the Harlem Renaissance, as inspiration for his own political and cultural orientation. He believed that artists help us to understand more deeply the human condition in all its variations. A playwright himself (I once accompanied him to a performance of *Marx in Soho* at Jimmy Tingle's Theater in Somerville, Massachusetts), Howard was also a patron of the arts. He regularly attended poetry readings, plays, films, and opera performances all over Boston. He spoke with great pride about his son Jeff, who runs the Wellfleet Harbor Actors Theater on Cape Cod. And, as I've already mentioned, his writing, especially *A People's History*, inspired its own art forms. "Artists play a very special role in relation to social change," Howard argued in a 2004 interview with David Barsamian. "I thought art gave them a special impetus through its inspiration and through its emotional effect that couldn't be calculated. Social movements all through history have needed art in order to enhance what they do, in order to inspire people, in order to give them a vision, in order to bring them together, make them feel that they are part of a vibrant movement." Howard, too, made us feel "part of a vibrant movement" by insisting that art, history, and activism could be each other's muse. He believed this in his bones.

It is altogether fitting, then, that the last time I saw Howard—on Thursday, January 7, 2010—was at a play. We were sitting in the front row of the Underground Railway Theater in Central Square in Cambridge. We had been asked to take part in a public humanities program to coincide with the production of Lydia R. Diamond's stunning new play *Harriet Jacobs*, inspired by the 1861 slave narrative *Incidents in the Life of a Slave Girl*. This was the first time the autobiography had been adapted for the stage, and Howard and I were both eager to take part in a series of events that would help bring the remarkable story of Harriet Jacobs's life in and escape from slavery to a broader audience. My colleague John Stauffer and I were slated to lead a post-performance "talk back" with the audience on opening night; Howard was scheduled to do a similar event the next week. The play itself was brilliantly written and conceived, superbly staged and acted, and profoundly moving. During the lengthy standing ovation at the end of the performance, I remember worrying that I would have little to add to what was obviously a great triumph of the stage and of history. As John and I moved to take our seats in the middle of the black box theater, Howard turned to me and apologized for having to leave early. He was not feeling well. I told him that I had been meaning to get in touch to invite him to speak again at Harvard, and he said that he would come do an event with me as soon as he was on the mend. Then he put on his coat, reached out his long arm, and squeezed my shoulder. "Carry on," he said, before turning and exiting through the left-hand door at the back of the theater. Howard died three weeks later.

"Carry on." Those words still haunt me. In retrospect, I suppose I should have seen then that he was very weak, showing his age like never before. I'd gotten so used to Howard being so strong, almost invincible, that I was incapable of imagining an alternative, to say nothing of the inevitable. What I wouldn't do to go back in time, to have that moment once more, to hug him and thank him and make sure he knew that I, too, was part of that great democratic chorus that had found its voice—and its roots—because of his life. That's the thing about death: we never get a second chance. Howard knew that, and he lived accordingly. The people's historian may be gone, but there is more history to write and more history to make. It is our turn now to do what he taught us to do: "Carry on."

Notes

1. Howard Zinn, *A People's History of the United States* (New York: HarperCollins, 1980), 1–2.
2. Ibid., 10–11.
3. Howard Zinn, *You Can't Be Neutral on a Moving Train: A Personal History of Our Times* (Boston: Beacon Press, 1994), 6.
4. Ibid., 15.
5. Howard Zinn, *La Guardia in Congress* (Ithaca: Cornell University Press, 1959), 267.
6. Howard Zinn, *Vietnam: The Logic of Withdrawal* (Boston: Beacon Press, 1967).
7. Zinn, *You Can't Be Neutral*, 183–85.
8. Ibid., 185.
9. Howard Zinn (File # 100-360217), Federal Bureau of Investigation, 2010.
10. Letter, March 30, 1949 (File # 100-360217), Federal Bureau of Investigation, 2010.
11. Paul Glavin and Chuck Morse, "War Is the Health of the State: An Interview with Howard Zinn," *Perspectives on Anarchist Theory* 7, no. 1 (Spring 2003).
12. Rick Shenkman, "The Left's Blind Spot," History News Network, June 2, 2008, hnn.us/articles/50997.html.

13. Daniel J. Flynn, "Master of Deceit," FrontPageMagazine.com, June 3, 2003, archive
.frontpagemag.com/readArticle.aspx?ARTID=17914.
14. Michael Kazin, "Howard Zinn's History Lessons," *Dissent*, Spring 2004.
15. Eric Foner, "Majority Report," *New York Times Book Review*, March 2, 1980.
16. Eric Foner, "Zinn's Critical History," *The Nation*, February 4, 2010.
17. Jill Lepore, "Zinn's History," *New Yorker* Book Bench blog, February 3, 2010, www
.newyorker.com/online/blogs/books/2010/02/zinns-history.html.
18. Ron Radosh, "America the Awful—Howard Zinn's History," Minding the Campus,
January 28, 2009, www.mindingthecampus.com/originals/2010/01/america_the
_awfulhoward_zinns.html.
19. Allison Keyes, "Howard Zinn Remembered," National Public Radio, January 28,
2009, www.npr.org/templates/story/story.php?storyId=123081519.
20. David Horowitz, "Spitting on Howard Zinn's Grave," NewsRealBlog.com, January
30, 2009, www.newsrealblog.com/2010/01/30/spitting-on-howard-zinns-grave/.
21. Foner, "Zinn's Critical History."
22. William B. Higgins, "The Surprising Success of Howard Zinn's *A People's History of
the United States*" (unpublished junior essay, Harvard University, 2005), 4. Special
thanks to my former student Bill Higgins for his excellent research and analysis, as
well as his gracious permission to quote from his essay.
23. Howard Zinn, "Afterword," in *A People's History of the United States*, 2nd rev. ed.
(New York: HarperCollins, 1995), 686–87.
24. Staughton Lynd, "The Howard Zinn I Remember," History News Network, February 8, 2010, hnn.us/articles/123066.html.
25. Foner, "Majority Report."

ACKNOWLEDGMENTS

Every book is a collaborative affair, and this one is no different. I'd like to thank my friend and editor, Marc Favreau, for the honor and opportunity of doing this book, and for his helpful counsel and heroic patience along the way. Special thanks, too, to the amazing editorial team at The New Press—especially Azzurra Cox and Sarah Fan—for ushering the manuscript to publication. This is my fourth book with The New Press, and I continue to enjoy our collaboration beyond measure. I am grateful to my reliable team of radical historian friends—John McMillian, Jeremy Varon, Mike Foley, and Ian Lekus—for their excellent suggestions on Howard's Vietnam-era writings early on in the process. These friendships continue to inspire and sustain me. Eric Foner and Martin Duberman also provided wise counsel during the process, and I am grateful, as ever, for their ongoing friendship and mentorship. Laura Felpo, my former colleague at the Harvard Kennedy School's Carr Center for Human Rights Policy, performed crucial research assistance, especially in helping me track down and distill Howard's FBI files. Several other Carr Center colleagues—Elliott Prasse-Freeman, Sarah Bouchat, Steven Brzozowski, and Charlie Clements—provided additional support and friendship while I was working on this book. I am especially grateful to Alice Walker and Noam Chomsky for agreeing to be part of the effort, and for their radical example of how to live a just and meaningful life. I'd like to offer special thanks to all my students over the years—especially the Protest Lit and ASB crews—for listening to my stories about Howard and for sharing their own diverse reactions to his life and work.

I am grateful to Howard's children, Myla and Jeff, for taking such a keen interest in this book, and for supporting my efforts to do justice to their father's indispensable legacy. Special thanks also go to Rick Balkin, Howard's longtime agent, both for supporting this book and for helping us overcome many hurdles along the way.

My own family—Tom and Michelle McCarthy; Malcolm Green; and my husband, C.J. Crowder—provided all the usual love and support. C.J. was especially forgiving during the writing process, when late nights and early mornings ruined any hope for a normal routine. I'm not sure he bargained for all this when he married me, but I'm very lucky to have such a patient, loving, and generous partner for life. Finally, I dedicate this book to Howard and Manning Marable, two beloved mentors who have recently passed away. It's never easy to say good-bye, especially to these folks, who were rare in the world. I count myself among the luckiest of men to have had the chance to learn from them and walk by their side in this lifetime. I hope this book does some justice to the radical spirit that guided both of these intellectual freedom fighters while they were with us. May they rest in peace—and may the rest of us take up the torch.

Timothy Patrick McCarthy
Cambridge, Massachusetts

Part 1
THE PEOPLE'S HISTORY

COLUMBUS, THE INDIANS, AND HUMAN PROGRESS

from *A People's History of the United States* (1980)

Many readers were first introduced to Howard Zinn by reading *A People's History of the United States*, his sweeping revision of American history, first published in 1980. The book's opening pages take us back to the island shores of the Caribbean in the late fifteenth century, where we experience the arrival of Christopher Columbus and his sailors "carrying swords, speaking oddly" from the perspective of the Arawaks and other native peoples who were already living in the so-called New World long before Columbus landed there. Howard's story of "discovery" is not one of innocent encounter, but rather of violent conflict over land, riches, and culture. As he writes, "These Arawaks of the Bahama Islands were much like Indians on the mainland, who were remarkable (European observers were to say again and again) for their hospitality, their belief in sharing. These traits did not stand out in the Europe of the Renaissance, dominated as it was by the religion of popes, the government of kings, the frenzy for money that marked Western civilization and its first messenger to the Americas, Christopher Columbus." In this first chapter of *A People's History*, Howard sets out to upend the version of American history so many of us learned in our high school and college textbooks, to mess with the myths and puncture the perceptions that lie—literally—at the foundation of our national identity and our Western ideals of "progress." He rejects "rational" objectivity for a more radical optic, giving us American history "from the bottom up." In the process, he lays his politics on the line: "This book will be skeptical of governments and their attempts, through politics and culture, to ensnare ordinary people in a giant web of nationhood pretending to a common interest. I will try not to overlook the cruelties that victims inflict on one another as they are jammed together in boxcars of the system. I don't want to romanticize them. But I do remember (in rough paraphrase) a statement I once read: 'The cry of the poor is not always just, but if you don't listen to it, you will never know what justice is.' " So begins the first synthetic narrative of American history told principally from the perspective of the people rather than the powerful. To paraphrase Matt Damon's character in the award-winning film *Good Will Hunting*: Howard Zinn's *A People's History of the United States* will knock you on your ass!

———

ARAWAK MEN AND women, naked, tawny, and full of wonder, emerged from their villages onto the island's beaches and swam out to get a closer look at the strange big boat. When Columbus and his sailors came ashore, carrying swords, speaking oddly, the Arawaks ran to greet them, brought them food, water, gifts. He later wrote of this in his log:

> They . . . brought us parrots and balls of cotton and spears and many other things, which they exchanged for the glass beads and hawks' bells. They willingly traded everything they owned . . . They were well-built, with good bodies and handsome features. . . . They do not bear arms, and do not know them, for I showed them a sword, they took it by the edge and cut themselves out of ignorance. They have no iron. Their spears are made of cane. . . . They would make fine servants. . . . With fifty men we could subjugate them all and make them do whatever we want.

These Arawaks of the Bahama Islands were much like Indians on the mainland, who were remarkable (European observers were to say again and again) for their hospitality, their belief in sharing. These traits did not stand out in the Europe of the Renaissance, dominated as it was by the religion of popes, the government of kings, the frenzy for money that marked Western civilization and its first messenger to the Americas, Christopher Columbus.

Columbus wrote:

> As soon as I arrived in the Indies, on the first Island which I found, I took some of the natives by force in order that they might learn and might give me information of whatever there is in these parts.

The information that Columbus wanted most was: Where is the gold? He had persuaded the king and queen of Spain to finance an expedition to the lands, the wealth, he expected would be on the other side of the Atlantic—the Indies and Asia, gold and spices. For, like other informed people of his time, he knew the world was round and he could sail west in order to get to the Far East.

Spain was recently unified, one of the new modern nation-states, like France, England, and Portugal. Its population, mostly poor peasants, worked for the nobility, who were 2 percent of the population and owned 95 percent of the land. Spain had tied itself to the Catholic Church, expelled all the Jews, driven out the Moors. Like other states of the modern world, Spain sought gold, which was becoming the new mark of wealth, more useful than land because it could buy anything.

There was gold in Asia, it was thought, and certainly silks and spices, for Marco Polo and others had brought back marvelous things from their overland expeditions centuries before. Now that the Turks had conquered Constantinople and the eastern Mediterranean, and controlled the land routes to Asia, a sea route was needed. Portuguese sailors were working their way around the southern tip of Africa. Spain decided to gamble on a long sail across an unknown ocean.

In return for bringing back gold and spices, they promised Columbus 10 percent of the profits, governorship over newfound lands, and the fame that would go with a new title: Admiral of the Ocean Sea. He was a merchant's clerk from the Italian city of Genoa, part-time weaver (the son of a skilled weaver), and expert sailor. He set out with three sailing ships, the largest of which was the *Santa Maria*, perhaps 100 feet long, and thirty-nine crew members.

Columbus would never have made it to Asia, which was thousands of miles farther away than he had calculated, imagining a smaller world. He would have been doomed by that great expanse of sea. But he was lucky. One-fourth of the way there he came upon an unknown, uncharted land that lay between Europe and Asia—the Americas. It was early October 1492, and thirty-three days since he and his crew had left the Canary Islands, off the Atlantic coast of Africa. Now they saw branches and sticks floating in the water. They saw flocks of birds. These were signs of land. Then, on October 12, a sailor called Rodrigo saw the early morning moon shining on white sands, and cried out. It was an island in the Bahamas, the Caribbean sea. The first man to sight land was supposed to get a yearly pension of 10,000 maravedis for life, but

Rodrigo never got it. Columbus claimed he had seen a light the evening before. He got the reward.

So, approaching land, they were met by the Arawak Indians, who swam out to greet them. The Arawaks lived in village communes, had a developed agriculture of corn, yams, cassava. They could spin and weave, but they had no horses or work animals. They had no iron, but they wore tiny gold ornaments in their ears.

This was to have enormous consequences: it led Columbus to take some of them aboard ship as prisoners because he insisted that they guide him to the source of the gold. He then sailed to what is now Cuba, then to Hispaniola (the island which today consists of Haiti and the Dominican Republic). There, bits of visible gold in the rivers, and a gold mask presented to Columbus by a local Indian chief, led to wild visions of gold fields.

On Hispaniola, out of timbers from the *Santa Maria*, which had run aground, Columbus built a fort, the first European military base in the Western Hemisphere. He called it Navidad (Christmas) and left thirty-nine crewmembers there, with instructions to find and store the gold. He took more Indian prisoners and put them aboard his two remaining ships. At one part of the island he got into a fight with Indians who refused to trade as many bows and arrows as he and his men wanted. Two were run through with swords and bled to death. Then the *Nina* and the *Pinta* set sail for the Azores and Spain. When the weather turned cold, the Indian prisoners began to die.

Columbus's report to the Court in Madrid was extravagant. He insisted he had reached Asia (it was Cuba) and an island off the coast of China (Hispaniola). His descriptions were part fact, part fiction:

> Hispaniola is a miracle. Mountains and hills, plains and pastures, are both fertile and beautiful . . . the harbors are unbelievably good and there are many wide rivers of which the majority contain gold. . . . There are many spices, and great mines of gold and other metals. . . .

The Indians, Columbus reported, "are so naïve and so free with their possessions that no one who has not witnessed them would believe it. When you ask for something they have, they never say no. To the contrary, they offer to share with anyone. . . ." He concluded his report by asking for a little help from their Majesties, and in return he would bring them from his next voyage "as much gold as they need . . . and as many slaves as they ask." He was full of religious talk: "Thus the eternal God, our Lord, gives victory to those who follow His way over apparent impossibilities."

Because of Columbus's exaggerated report and promises, his second expedition was given seventeen ships and more than twelve hundred men. The aim was clear: slaves and gold. They went from island to island in the Caribbean, taking Indians as captives. But as word spread of the Europeans' intent they found more and more empty villages. On Haiti, they found that the sailors left behind at Fort Navidad had been killed in a battle with the Indians, after they had roamed the island in gangs looking for gold, taking women and children as slaves for sex and labor.

Now, from his base on Haiti, Columbus sent expedition after expedition into the interior. They found no gold fields, but had to fill up the ships returning to Spain with some kind of dividend. In the year 1495, they went on a great slave raid, rounded up fifteen hundred Arawak men, women, and children, put them in pens guarded by Spaniards and dogs, then picked the five hundred best specimens to load onto ships. Of those five hundred, two hundred died en route. The rest arrived alive in Spain and were put up for sale by the archdeacon of the town, who reported that, although the slaves were "naked as the day they were born," they showed "no more embarrassment than animals." Columbus later wrote: "Let us in the name of the Holy Trinity go on sending all the slaves that can be sold."

But too many of the slaves died in captivity. And so Columbus, desperate to pay back dividends to those who had invested, had to make good his promise to fill the ships with gold. In the province of Cicao on Haiti, where he and his men imagined huge gold fields to exist, they ordered all persons fourteen years or older to collect a certain quantity of gold every three months. When they brought it, they were given copper tokens to hang around their necks. Indians found without a copper token had their hands cut off and bled to death.

The Indians had been given an impossible task. The only gold round was bits of dust garnered from the streams. So they fled, were hunted down with dogs, and were killed.

Trying to put together an army of resistance, the Arawaks faced Spaniards who had armor, muskets, swords, horses. When the Spaniards took prisoners they hanged them or burned them to death. Among the Arawaks, mass suicides began, with cassava poison. Infants were killed to save them from the Spaniards. In two years, through murder, mutilation, or suicide, half of the 250,000 Indians on Haiti were dead.

When it became clear that there was no gold left, the Indians were taken as slave labor on huge estates, known later as *encomiendas*. They were worked at a ferocious pace, and died by the thousands. By the year 1515, there were perhaps fifty thousand Indians left. By 1550, there were five hundred. A report of the year 1650 shows none of the original Arawaks or their descendants left on the island.

The chief source—and, on many matters the only source—of information about what happened on the islands after Columbus came is Bartolomé de las Casas, who, as a young priest, participated in the conquest of Cuba. For a time he owned a plantation on which Indian slaves worked, but he gave that up and became a vehement critic of Spanish cruelty. Las Casas transcribed Columbus's journal and, in his fifties, began a multivolume *History of the Indies*. In it, he describes the Indians. They are agile, he says, and can swim long distances, especially the women. They are not completely peaceful, because they do battle from time to time with other tribes, but their casualties seem small, and they fight when they are individually moved to do so because of some grievance, not on the orders of captains or kings.

Women in Indian society were treated so well as to startle the Spaniards. Las Casas describes sex relations:

> Marriage laws are non-existent: men and women alike choose their mates and leave them as they please, without offense, jealousy or anger. They multiply in great abundance; pregnant women work to the last minute and give birth almost painlessly; up the next day, they bathe in the river and are as clean and healthy as before giving birth. If they tire of their men, they give themselves abortions with herbs that force stillbirths, covering their shameful parts with leaves or cotton cloth; although on the whole, Indian men and women look upon total nakedness with as much casualness as we look upon a man's head or at his hands.

The Indians, Las Casas says, have no religion, at least no temples. They live in

> large communal bell-shaped buildings, housing up to 600 people at one time . . . made of very strong wood and roofed with palm leaves. . . . They prize bird feathers of various colors, beads made of fishbones, and green and white stones with which they adorn

their ears and lips, but they put no value on gold and other precious things. They lack all manner of commerce, neither buying
nor selling, and rely exclusively on their natural environment for
maintenance. They are extremely generous with their possessions
and by the same token covet the possessions of their friends and
expect the same degree of liberality. . . .

In Book Two of his *History of the Indies*, Las Casas (who at first urged
replacing Indians by black slaves, thinking they were stronger and would
survive, but later relented when he saw the effects on blacks) tells about
the treatment of the Indians by the Spaniards. It is a unique account
and deserves to be quoted at length:

> Endless testimonies . . . prove the mild and pacific temperament
> of the natives. . . . But our work was to exasperate, ravage, kill,
> mangle and destroy; small wonder, then, if they tried to kill one
> of us now and then. . . . The admiral, it is true, was blind as those
> who came after him, and he was so anxious to please the King that
> he committed irreparable crimes against the Indians. . . .

Las Casas tells how the Spaniards "grew more conceited every day"
and after a while refused to walk any distance. They "rode the backs of
Indians if they were in a hurry" or were carried on hammocks by Indians
running in relays. "In this case they also had Indians carry large leaves
to shade them from the sun and others to fan them with goose wings."
    Total control led to total cruelty. The Spaniards "thought nothing of
knifing Indians by tens and twenties and of cutting slices off them to
test the sharpness of their blades." Las Casas tells how "two of these so-
called Christians met two Indian boys one day, each carrying a parrot;
they took the parrots and for fun beheaded the boys."
    The Indians' attempts to defend themselves failed. And when they
ran off into the hills they were found and killed. So, Las Casas reports,
"they suffered and died in the mines and other labors in desperate silence,
knowing not a soul in the world to whom they could turn for help." He
describes their work in the mines:

> . . . mountains are stripped from top to bottom and bottom to top
> a thousand times; they dig, split rocks, move stones, and carry dirt
> on their backs to wash it in the rivers, while those who wash gold
> stay in the water all the time with their backs bent so constantly it
> breaks them; and when water invades the mines, the most arduous

task of all is to dry the mines by scooping up pansful of water and throwing it up outside. . . .

After each six or eight months' work in the mines, which was the time required of each crew to dig enough gold for melting, up to a third of the men died.

While the men were sent many miles away to the mines, the wives remained to work the soil, forced into the excruciating job of digging and making thousands of hills for cassava plants.

> Thus husbands and wives were together only once every eight or ten months and when they met they were so exhausted and depressed on both sides . . . they ceased to procreate. As for the newly born, they died early because their mothers, overworked and famished, had no milk to nurse them, and for this reason, while I was in Cuba, 7000 children died in three months. Some mothers even drowned their babies from sheer desperation. . . . In this way, husbands died in the mines, wives died at work, and children died from lack of milk . . . and in a short time this land which was so great, so powerful and fertile . . . was depopulated. . . . My eyes have seen these acts so foreign to human nature, and now I tremble as I write. . . .

When he arrived on Hispaniola in 1508, Las Casas says, "there were 60,000 people living on this island, including the Indians; so that from 1494 to 1508, over three million people had perished from war, slavery, and the mines. Who in future generations will believe this? I myself writing it as a knowledgeable eyewitness can hardly believe it. . . ."

Thus began the history, five hundred years ago, of the European invasion of the Indian settlements in the Americas. That beginning, when you read Las Casas—even if his figures are exaggerations (were there 3 million Indians to begin with, as he says, or less than a million, as some historians have calculated, or 8 million as others now believe?)—is conquest, slavery, death. When we read the history books given to children in the United States, it all starts with heroic adventure—there is no bloodshed—and Columbus Day is a celebration.

Past the elementary and high schools, there are only occasional hints of something else. Samuel Eliot Morison, the Harvard historian, was the most distinguished writer on Columbus, the author of a multivolume biography, and was himself a sailor who retraced Columbus's route across the Atlantic. In his popular book *Christopher Columbus, Mariner,* written in 1954, he tells about the enslavement and the killing: "The cruel policy initiated by Columbus and pursued by his successors resulted in complete genocide."

That is on one page, buried halfway into the telling of a grand romance. In the book's last paragraph, Morison sums up his view of Columbus:

> He had his faults and his defects, but they were largely the defects of the qualities that made him great—his indomitable will, his superb faith in God and in his own mission as the Christ-bearer to lands, beyond the seas, his stubborn persistence despite neglect, poverty and discouragement. But there was no flaw, no dark side to the most outstanding and essential of all his qualities—his seamanship.

One can lie outright about the past. Or one can omit facts which might lead to unacceptable conclusions. Morison does neither. He refuses to lie about Columbus. He does not omit the story of mass murder; indeed he describes it with the harshest word one can use: genocide.

But he does something else—he mentions the truth quickly and goes on to other things more important to him. Outright lying or quiet omission takes the risk of discovery which, when made, might arouse the reader to rebel against the writer. To state the facts, however, and then to bury them in a mass of other information is to say to the reader with a certain infectious calm: yes, mass murder took place, but it's not that important—it should weigh very little in our final judgments; it should affect very little what we do in the world.

It is not that the historian can avoid emphasis of some facts and not of others. This is as natural to him as to the mapmaker, who, in order to produce a usable drawing for practical purposes, must first flatten and distort the shape of the earth, then choose out of the bewildering mass of geographic information those things needed for the purpose of this or that particular map.

My argument cannot be against selection, simplification, emphasis, which are inevitable for both cartographers and historians. But the mapmaker's distortion is a technical necessity for a common purpose shared by all people who need maps. The historian's distortion is more than technical, it is ideological; it is released into a world of contending interests, where any chosen emphasis supports (whether the historian means to or not) some kind of interest, whether economic or political or racial or national or sexual.

Furthermore, this ideological interest is not openly expressed in the way a mapmaker's technical interest is obvious ("This is a Mercator protection for long-range navigation—for short-range, you'd better use a different projection"). No, it is presented as if all readers of history had a common interest which historians serve to the best of their ability. This is not intentional deception; the historian has been trained in a society in which education and knowledge are put forward as technical problems of excellence and not as tools for contending social classes, races, nations.

To emphasize the heroism of Columbus and his successors as navigators and discoverers, and to deemphasize their genocide, is not a technical necessity but an ideological choice. It serves—unwittingly—to justify what was done.

My point is not that we must, in telling history, accuse, judge, condemn Columbus *in absentia*. It is too late for that; it would be a useless scholarly exercise in morality. But the easy acceptance of atrocities as a deplorable but necessary price to pay for progress (Hiroshima and Vietnam, to save Western civilization; Kronstadt and Hungary, to save socialism; nuclear proliferation, to save us all)—that is still with us. One reason these atrocities are still with us is that we have learned to bury them in a mass of other facts, as radioactive wastes are buried in containers in the earth. We have learned to give them exactly the same proportion of attention that teachers and writers often give them in the most respectable of classrooms and textbooks. This learned sense of moral proportion, coming from the apparent objectivity of the scholar, is accepted more easily than when it comes from politicians at press conferences. It is therefore more deadly.

The treatment of heroes (Columbus) and their victims (the Arawaks)—the quiet acceptance of conquest and murder in the name of progress—is only one aspect of a certain approach to history, in which the past is told from the point of view of governments, conquerors, diplomats, leaders. It is as if they, like Columbus, deserve universal acceptance, as if they—the Founding Fathers, Jackson, Lincoln, Wilson, Roosevelt, Kennedy, the leading members of Congress, the famous Justices of the Supreme Courts—represent the nation as a whole. The pretense is that there really is such a thing as "the United States," subject to occasional conflicts and quarrels, but fundamentally a community of people with common interests. It is as if there really is a "national interest" represented in the Constitution, in territorial expansion, in the laws passed by Congress, the decisions of the courts, the development of capitalism, the culture of education and the mass media.

"History is the memory of states," wrote Henry Kissinger in his first book, *A World Restored*, in which he proceeded to tell the history of nineteenth-century Europe from the viewpoint of the leaders of Austria and England, ignoring the millions who suffered from those statesmen's policies. From his standpoint, the "peace" that Europe had before the French Revolution was "restored" by the diplomacy of a few national leaders. But for factory workers in England, farmers in France, colored people in Asia and Africa, women and children everywhere except in the upper classes, it was a world of conquest, violence, hunger, exploitation—a world not restored but disintegrated.

My viewpoint, in telling the history of the United States, is different: that we must not accept the memory of states as our own. Nations are not communities and never have been. The history of any country, presented as the history of a family, conceals fierce conflicts of interest (sometimes exploding, most often repressed) between conquerors and conquered, masters and slaves, capitalists and workers, dominators and dominated in race and sex. And in such a world of conflict, a world of victims and executioners, it is the job of thinking people, as Albert Camus suggested, not to be on the side of the executioners.

Thus, in that inevitable taking of sides which comes from selection and emphasis in history, I prefer to try to tell the story of the discovery of America from the viewpoint of the Arawaks, of the Constitution from the standpoint of the slaves, of Andrew Jackson as seen by the Cherokees, of the Civil War as seen by the New York Irish, of the Mexican war as seen by the deserting soldiers of Scott's army, of the rise of industrialism as seen by the young women in the Lowell textile mills, of the Spanish-American war as seen by the Cubans, the conquest of the Philippines as seen by black soldiers on Luzon, the Gilded Age as seen by southern farmers, the First World War as seen by socialists, the Second World War as seen by pacifists, the New Deal as seen by blacks in Harlem, the postwar American empire as seen by peons in Latin America. And so on, to the limited extent that any one person, however he or she strains, can "see" history from the standpoint of others.

My point is not to grieve for the victims and denounce the executioners. Those tears, that anger, cast into the past, deplete our moral energy for the present. And the lines are not always clear. In the long run, the oppressor is also a victim. In the short run (and so far, human history has consisted only of short runs), the victims, themselves desperate and tainted with the culture that oppresses them, turn on other victims.

Still, understanding the complexities, this book will be skeptical of governments and their attempts, through politics and culture, to ensnare ordinary people in a giant web of nationhood pretending to a common interest. I will try not to overlook the cruelties that victims inflict on one another as they are jammed together in the boxcars of the system. I don't want to romanticize them. But I do remember (in rough para-phrase) a statement I once read: "The cry of the poor is not always just, but if you don't listen to it, you will never know what justice is."

I don't want to invent victories for people's movements. But to think that history-writing must aim simply to recapitulate the failures that dominate the past is to make historians collaborators in an endless cycle of defeat. If history is to be creative, to anticipate a possible future with-out denying the past, it should, I believe, emphasize new possibilities by disclosing those hidden episodes of the past when, even if in brief flashes, people showed their ability to resist, to join together, occasion-ally to win. I am supposing, or perhaps only hoping, that our future may be found in the past's fugitive moments of compassion rather than in its solid centuries of warfare.

That, being as blunt as I can, is my approach to the history of the United States. The reader may as well know that before going on.

THE COLORADO COAL STRIKE, 1913–1914

from *Three Strikes: Miners, Musicians, Salesgirls, and the Fighting Spirit of Labor's Last Century* (2001)

In 2001, Howard published a provocative essay on the Colorado Coal Strike of 1913–14, "one of the most dramatic and violent events in the history of the country," in a slim volume called *Three Strikes*. His essay appears alongside two others—one on the protest of New York City artists against mass-produced music by Robin D.G. Kelley, and one on the 1937 Woolworth's sit-down strike in Detroit by Dana Frank. Taken together, they illuminate some of the diverse if largely overlooked expressions of labor's discontent during the first half of the twentieth century. In making the case for a deeper examination of the strike, Howard writes, "It deserves to be recalled, because embedded in the events of the Colorado strike are issues still alive today: the class struggle between owners of large enterprises and their workers, the special treatment of immigrant workers, the relationship between economic power and political power, the role of the press, and the way in which the culture censors out certain historical events." Howard positions the story of the fourteen-month Colorado coal miner strike that culminated in the Ludlow Massacre within the long history of labor struggles and economic transformation in the United States, dating back to the nineteenth century. Here, iconic figures come alive—labor radicals like Mother Jones and Eugene Debs, political and business elites like Woodrow Wilson and John D. Rockefeller, and protest writers like Upton Sinclair and John Reed—to illuminate the growing tensions and contradictions within capitalism at the dawn of the modern era. Though historians who have written about the Colorado strike have tended to see it as "defeat for the workers," Howard, true to form, takes a different view: "At the same time, we are inspired by those ordinary men and women who persist, with extraordinary courage, in their resistance to overwhelming power. It is a story that continues in our time."

———

THE COLORADO STRIKE took place in a physical setting of vast proportions and staggering beauty. Down the center of the rectangle that is Colorado, from north to south, march an array of huge, breathtaking mountains—the Rockies—whose naked cliffs merge, on their eastern edge, with low hills covered with cedar and yellow pine. To the east of that is the plain—really a mile-high plateau—a tawny expanse of pasture grass sprinkled with prairie flowers in the spring and summer, and gleaming here and there with yellow-blossomed cactus.

Beneath the tremendous weight of the Rockies, in the course of countless centuries, decaying vegetation gradually mineralized into the black rock known as coal. The constantly increasing proportion of carbon in this rock transformed it from vegetable matter to peat, then to lignite and bituminous coal, and finally to anthracite.

Three great coalfields, consisting chiefly of bituminous coal, were formed in Colorado. One of them was contained within two counties in southern Colorado, Las Animas and Huerfano counties, just east of the mountains. This field was made up of about forty discontinuous seams, ranging from a few inches to fourteen feet thick. These seams were from two hundred and fifty to about five hundred feet deep.

The mining of these fields became possible on a large scale only in the 1870s, when the railroads moving west from Kansas City, south from Denver, and north from New Mexico, converged on the region. At about this time, settlers moving down the old Santa Fe trail built a town on the banks of the Purgatory River (*el Rio de las Animas Perdidas Purgatorio*— the river of lost souls), just east of the Sangre de Cristo (blood of Christ) mountains and about fifteen miles north of the New Mexican border.

The town was called Trinidad, and it became the center of the southern mining area. By 1913 it had about ten thousand people—miners, ranchers, farmers, and businessmen. From the main highways and railroad lines leading north out of Trinidad, branch railways and old wagon roads cut sharply west into the foothills of the mountains, into the steep-walled canyons where the mining camps lay. Scattered in these narrow canyons, on the flat bands of earth running along the canyon bottoms, were the huts of the miners, the mine buildings, and the mine entries.

It was a shocking contrast: the wild beauty of the Colorado countryside against the unspeakable squalor of these mining camps. The miners' huts, usually shared by several families, were made of clapboard walls and thin-planked floors, with leaking roofs, sagging doors, broken windows, and layers of old newspapers nailed to the walls to keep out the cold. Some families, particularly Negro families, were forced to live in tiny squares not much bigger than chicken coops.

Within sight of the huts were the coke ovens and the mine tipple, where coal was emptied from the cars that carried it to the surface. Thick clouds of soot clogged the air and settled on the ground, strangling any shoots of grass or flowers that tried to grow there. Wriggling along the canyon wall, behind the huts, was a now sluggish creek, dirty yellow and laden with the slag of the mine and the refuse of the camp. Alongside the creek the children played, barefoot, ragged, and often hungry.

Each mining camp was a feudal dominion, with the company acting as lord and master. Every camp had a marshal, a law enforcement officer paid by the company. The "laws" were the company's rules. Curfews were imposed, "suspicious" strangers were not allowed to visit the homes, the company store had a monopoly on goods sold in the camp. The doctor was a company doctor, the schoolteachers hired by the company.

In the early dawn, cages carried the men down into the blackness of the mine. There was usually a main tunnel, with dozens of branch tunnels leading into the "rooms," held up by timbers, where the miners hacked away at the face of the coal seam with hand picks and their helpers shoveled the coal into waiting railroad cars. The loaded cars were drawn along their tracks by mules to the main shaft, where they were lifted to the surface, and then to the top of the tipple, and then the coal showered down through the sorting screens into flatcars.

Since the average coal seam was about three feet high, the miners would often work on their knees or on their sides, never able to straighten up. The ventilation system was a crude affair that depended on the manipulation of tunnel doors by "trapper boys"—often thirteen or fourteen years old—who were being initiated into the work. [. . .]

From the very beginnings of the coal mine industry in Colorado, there was conflict between workers and management: an unsuccessful strike in 1876 (the very year Colorado was admitted to the Union), a successful strike in 1884 against a wage reduction. But the workday was still ten hours long, and in 1894 a strike for the eight-hour day failed.

The United Mine Workers of America was formed in 1890, "to unite in one organization, regardless of creed, color, or nationality, all workmen . . . employed in and around coal mines." The first United Mine Workers local in Colorado was formed in 1900, and three years later there was an eleven-month strike, broken by strikebreakers and the National Guard. Some of those strikebreakers became the strikers of 1913.

The top leadership of the U.M.W. was often criticized by more militant elements of the labor movement as being too conservative. And while it was the United Mine Workers who led the strike in 1913–14, members of two other organizations were on the scene and had varying degrees of influence over the miners. These were the I.W.W. (Industrial Workers of the World) and the Socialist Party, which had locals in Trinidad and other Colorado cities. [. . .]

Meanwhile, organizing was going on at a rapid rate. Miners from all the coal canyons in southern Colorado were being signed up as union members. Secret meetings were held in churches, at picnics, in abandoned workings hidden in the mountains. At hundreds of meetings, delegates were elected to represent the coal camps at the Trinidad convention.

At the same time, the mine operators were not idle. The Baldwin-Felts Agency began importing hundreds of men from the saloons and barrel-houses of Denver, and from points outside the state, to help break the impending strike. In Huerfano County, by the first of September, 326 men had been deputized by Sheriff Jeff Farr, all armed and paid by the coal companies.

On Monday, September 15, 1913, there was a parade of miners through the streets of Trinidad, and then the largest labor convention in Colorado history began its sessions. Two hundred and eighty delegates, representing every mine in Colorado as well as some in New Mexico and Utah, sat in the great opera house and sweated in the late summer heat. [. . .]

A set of demands was adopted: recognition of the union was key, followed by the eight-hour day, wage increases, pay for "dead work" (laying tracks, shoring up the roof, etc.), elected checkweighmen, free choice of stores, boarding houses, and doctors, and the abolition of the guard system.

The operators claimed that the miners earned $20 a week, but the Colorado Bureau of Labor Statistics put their average take-home pay at $1.68 a day.

Perhaps what aroused the miners to rebellion more than anything was the refusal of the mine operators to spend money to ensure the safety of the men as they worked hundreds of feet below the surface. There had been deadly explosions in the southern Colorado mines again and again. There were two primary causes for mine disasters: rotten timbers holding up the roofs of the caverns where the miners dug their coal, and the accumulation of gas and dust in dry conditions under which the gas ignited easily. [. . .]

By the time the labor convention took place in Trinidad on September 15, 1913, the grievances had accumulated. When Mother Jones dramatically appeared to address the delegates, they were ready to be aroused.

Mary Jones, whom the miners came to call Mother, was born Mary Harris in Ireland, where as a child she had seen British troops march through the streets with the heads of Irishmen stuck on their bayonets, and where her grandfather had been hanged during the fight for Irish freedom. Her family had emigrated to Canada, and Mary, then in her twenties, moved to Michigan and then to Memphis, working as a dressmaker and a schoolteacher. At thirty-one, she married an ironworker named George Jones, and they had four children.

In 1867, a yellow fever epidemic struck Memphis. All of Mary Jones's children and her husband died. At the age of thirty-seven she left for Chicago, where she worked as a seamstress, later recalling, "Often while sewing for the lords and barons who lived in magnificent houses on the Lake Shore Drive, I would look out of the plate glass windows and see the poor, shivering wretches, jobless and hungry, walking alongside the frozen lake front."

She began attending meetings of the Knights of Labor, then the only national union that admitted women, and in the 1890s began organizing for the United Mine Workers. In 1903, with 100,000 miners on strike in Pennsylvania, including 16,000 children under age sixteen, she led a group of children on a twenty-two-day march to New York to confront President Theodore Roosevelt at his Oyster Bay home. [. . .]

Mother Jones was scathing in her denunciation of politicians, like the congressmen who passed legislation on behalf of the railroads but did nothing for working people. "I asked a man in prison once how he happened to get there. He had stolen a pair of shoes. I told him if he had stolen a railroad he could be a United States Senator." She was equally scornful of union leaders who compromised with employers, like United Mine Workers president John Mitchell. In her autobiography she wrote, "Mr. Mitchell died a rich man, distrusted by the working people whom he once served."

When the Colorado strike began, Mother Jones had just come from the coalfields of West Virginia. "Medieval West Virginia!" she called it later. "With its tent colonies on the bleak hills! With its grim men and women! When I get to the other side, I shall tell God Almighty about West Virginia!"

She stood on the platform in Trinidad that September of 1913 in a prim black dress embroidered with white lace, wisps of silvery hair curling around her forehead, a black bonnet on her head. She was five feet tall and weighed a hundred pounds. She addressed the delegates: "The question that arises today in the nation is an industrial oligarchy. . . . What would the coal in these mines and in these hills be worth unless you put your strength and muscle in to bring [it out]?" [. . .] "You have . . . created more wealth than they in a thousand years of the Roman Republic, and yet you have not any. . . . When I get Colorado, Kansas and Alabama organized, I will tell God Almighty to take me to my rest. But not until then!"

The convention voted unanimously to strike on September 23, and both sides intensified their preparations. The coal operators, under the leadership of Colorado Fuel & Iron, met at Colorado Springs, deciding to stand together and resist the union's demands.

With evictions of miners from the mining camps quickly under way, the U.M.W. leased land just outside the bounds of company property and ordered tents. Funds were made available by the union to meet the needs of the strikers.

On the day of the walkout 11,000 miners, about 90 percent of the workforce, gathered up their belongings and left their homes in the camps. As they did so, rain began to fall, turning to sleet and snow, but it did not stop the procession of pushcarts and mule wagons, piled high with furniture and personal possessions and tiny children. Wheels sank through the ice into the mud, but they moved on. A reporter for the *Denver Express* called it "an exodus of woe, of a people leaving known fears for new terrors, a hopeless people seeking new hope, a people born to suffering going forth to new suffering." [. . .]

Ludlow was the largest miners' colony, set up at a railroad depot eighteen miles north of Trinidad on a direct line to Walsenburg, at the edge of Colorado Fuel & Iron property. Near the Ludlow depot there were a Greek bakery, a few saloons, a post office, a few stores. There were four hundred tents here, for a thousand people, over a quarter of whom were children. In the course of the strike, twenty-one babies were born in these tents.

At Ludlow a wooden stage was built for meetings, and a large tent was set up for use as a school and as a kind of community center. Committees were elected to arrange for sanitation and entertainment. Miners' colonies were also set up at Aguilar, Forbes, Sopris, Segundo, and Walsenburg.

[. . .] Violence between strikers and company men began almost immediately, and it can't be said with certainty which side committed the first act. Throughout the months of the strike, acts of violence by one side were met with retaliation from the other. But surely it was not an even match. Miners with rifles were arrayed against not only the machine guns of the Baldwin-Felts operatives but also the power of the state and its enforcers of "law and order." By the end of the strike, most of those dead and injured were miners and their families. [. . .]

The newly established U.S. Department of Labor tried to mediate between the U.M.W. and the mining operators, but the manager of Colorado Fuel & Iron, L.M. Bowers, distrusted the mediator, and wrote to Rockefeller that the companies would stand firm against the union until "our bones were bleached as white as chalk in these Rocky Mountains." Rockefeller replied that he agreed with this position. "Whatever the outcome we will stand by you to the end."

The Baldwin-Felts Agency constructed a special auto with a Gatling gun mounted on top, which became known as the Death Special. This auto, its sides armored, roamed the countryside with several agents carrying rifles in the front seat. On October 17, the Death Special attacked the tent colony at Forbes, killing one man and wounding two. A ten-year-old boy was left with nine bullets in his leg. In his book *Buried Unsung*, Zeese Papanikolas writes, "If there is anything that can account for the unconditional hatred the strikers would later show for the guards, for the panic that would sweep through those tents in waves throughout the rest of the strike, it is Forbes."

Meanwhile, hundreds of strikebreakers came into the area in a steady stream. They were deputized and paid $3.50 a day plus expenses. Wholesale arrests began. The sight of strikebreakers coming into the canyons aroused the strikers to fury. When they were intercepted, they were manhandled, once by a crowd of miners' wives and children. Buildings at the Primrose mine were dynamited. A gun battle took place between seventeen mounted mine guards and a group of strikers near the Ludlow colony. The operators told Governor Ammons that they had been attacked by "forty Greek and Montenegrin sharpshooters from the Balkan war." [. . .]

By the end of October there had been at least four battles between strikers and guards, and at least nine men had been killed. On October 28,

Governor Ammons declared martial law. He also issued an order for-bidding the import of strikebreakers from outside the state, but this was largely ignored. [. . .]

On October 29, 1913, Governor Ammons ordered General John Chase, of the Colorado National Guard, to move his troops into the strike area. Chase was a Denver ophthalmologist, a gentleman farmer, and a church organist, but when he put on his National Guard uni-form he saw himself in noble battle with socialists and anarchists. He had missed serving in the Spanish American War and had dreams of military grandeur. The pressures on the governor to call out the Guard are spelled out in a letter from L.M. Bowers to Rockefeller's New York office: "You will be interested to know that we have been able to secure the cooperation of all the bankers of the city, who have had three or four interviews with our little cowboy governor, agree-ing to back the State and lend it all funds necessary to maintain the militia and afford ample protection so our miners could return to work."

Bowers's letter reveals a fundamental truth about labor struggles in American history—that powerful corporations have almost always found useful allies in the government and the press: "Besides the bankers, the chamber of commerce, the real estate exchange, together with a great many of the best business men, have been urging the governor to take steps to drive these vicious agitators out of the state. Another mighty power has been rounded up on behalf of the operators by the getting together of fourteen of the editors of the most important newspapers in the state."

The Colorado National Guard, under General Chase's command, consisted of two cavalry troops, two incomplete infantry regiments, one detachment of field artillery, a hospital corps, and a signal corps. The Guard had 14 horses at first, but bought 279 more; the mine owners paid for the keep of the horses. Six autos were used, two paid for by the operators. The enlisted personnel, according to an official report of the Adjutant-General's Office of Colorado, were mostly "small property-owners, clerks, professional men, farmers." There were about a thou-sand soldiers under Chase's command, although two thousand persons were on duty in the strike zone at various times.

The miners, having faced in the first five weeks of the strike what they considered a reign of terror at the hands of the private guards, now looked forward to the National Guard to "restore order." They did not know that the governor was sending these troops under pressure from the mine operators. [. . .]

In the month of December 1913, Colorado experienced the worst snow seen in thirty years—forty-two inches fell on Denver. Colorado Fuel & Iron officials thought the storms might compel the miners to leave the tents for "the comfortable houses and employment at the mines," as they put it in one of their memos. But they did not understand the miners. And it was this lack of comprehension, and their frustration at the miners' refusal to surrender even under horrendous conditions, that led the mine operators to escalate their attempts to break the strike. The governor became their instrument.

Early in December, Governor Ammons rescinded his original order forbidding strikebreakers to come in from outside the state. It had been ignored in any event, but now that it had been withdrawn the National Guard openly protected the strikebreakers, escorting them to the mines.

The railroad junction of Ludlow became a battleground. Black men from the South and recent immigrants from the Balkans were brought in. Often they were not told that a strike was on. The trains carrying them into the district often had the blinds drawn, the doors locked. As they got off the train they were jeered by people from the Ludlow tent colony—men, women, children—who were lined up at the depot. When found alone, strikebreakers were often beaten.

There were other kinds of encounters. Three black strikebreakers were captured, given food in the Ludlow colony, then released. Another day, strikers intercepted several Greeks at the Walsenburg depot, took them to the house of a miner in Walsenburg, made them a meal, and convinced them to support the union. [. . .]

Through all of this, the National Guard had its hands full trying to keep Mother Jones out of the strike area. General Chase had said, "She will be jailed immediately if she comes to Trinidad. I am not going to give her a chance to make any more speeches here. She is dangerous because she inflames the minds of the strikers."

On January 4, 1914, Mother Jones set out from Denver "to help my boys." She was then eighty-three years old. Arriving in Trinidad, she was immediately arrested and put on a train back to Denver. General Chase declared that if she returned to the strike zone she would be held incommunicado. She responded defiantly that she would return "when

Colorado is made part of the United States." Speaking in Denver to union people she said, "I serve notice on the governor that this state doesn't belong to him—it belongs to the nation and I own a share of stock in it. Ammons or Chase either one can shoot me, but I will talk from the grave." [. . .]

Mother Jones was held incommunicado for ten weeks, with six soldiers guarding her day and night. She spoke later of having friendly conversations with some of them. Finally she was put on a train for Denver, guarded by a National Guard colonel. [. . .]

With the spring approaching, the mine operators began to listen to the incessant complaints of Governor Ammons. The state was heavily in debt to the bankers. Funds were running out for maintaining the National Guard. The payroll alone was $30,000 a month, and critics pointed to the disproportionate number of officers in the guard—397 officers to 695 privates. As the state grew less and less able to pay salaries, the regular enlisted militia began to drop out. Taking the places of many of these men, wearing the same uniforms, were the mine guards of Colorado Fuel & Iron, still drawing pay from the company.

In early April of 1914, without warning, Governor Ammons recalled the bulk of the Colorado National Guard. Only thirty-five men in Company B, mostly former mine guards, were left. On April 18, a hundred deputies in the pay of Colorado Fuel & Iron were formed into Troop A of the National Guard and sent to join Company B. The designated spot: a rocky ridge overlooking the thousand men, women, and children who lived in the tent colony at Ludlow.

The two officers selected to take charge were Major Pat Hamrock, a local saloon keeper, and a man well known to the residents of Ludlow, Lieutenant Karl Linderfelt. Linderfelt's men in Troop A, according to a report to the governor by Major Boughton, were "superintendents, foremen, the clerical force, physicians, storekeepers, mine guards, and other residents of the coal camps." [. . .]

On Monday morning, April 20, the Ludlow colonists were still sleeping in their tents when the quiet of dawn was shaken by a violent explosion. Rushing from their tents, the strikers could see columns of black smoke rising slowly to the sky from the hill where the militia were stationed. Major Hamrock had exploded two dynamite bombs as a signal.

For a little while the countryside was unbearably still and tense. Then, at exactly 9:00 A.M., the dull clatter of a machine gun began and the first bullets ripped through the canvas of the tents. The clatter became a deafening roar as more machine guns went into action. One of the people who died was Frank Snyder. He was ten years old. His father told about it afterward: "The boy Frank was sitting on the floor . . . and he was in the act of stooping to kiss or caress his sister. . . . I was standing near the front door of my tent and I heard the impact of the bullet striking the boy's head and the crack . . . as it exploded inside of his brain."

Mingling with the gunfire were the wild cries of women as they ran from tent to tent, hugging children to their breasts, seeking shelter. Some managed to run off into the hills and hide in nearby ranch houses. Others crawled into the dark pits and caves which had been dug under a few of the tents.

Meanwhile, men were dashing away from the encampment to draw off the fire. They flung themselves into deep arroyos—dried-up stream-beds. Now the high-powered rifles of the militiamen joined in and poured a hail of explosive bullets into the tents and into the arroyos. This continued all through the morning and into the afternoon, while men, women, and children huddled wherever they had found shelter, without food or water. At 4:30 P.M. a train from Trinidad brought more guards— and more machine guns.

Eyewitness Frank Didano reported, "The firing of the machine guns was awful. They fired thousands and thousands of shots. There were very few guns in the tent colony. Not over fifty, including shotguns. Women and children were afraid to crawl out of the shallow pits under the tents. Several men were killed trying to get to them. The soldiers and mine guards tried to kill everybody; anything they saw move, even a dog, they shot at." [. . .]

That afternoon, the man the miners loved, Lou Tikas, was in the big tent, caring for women and children and aiding the wounded, when a telephone, its wires amazingly intact, started ringing. It was Lieutenant Linderfelt, up on the hill. He wanted to see Tikas—it was urgent. Tikas refused, hung up. The phone rang insistently—again and again. Tikas reconsidered. Perhaps he could stop the murder. He answered the phone. He would come.

Carrying a white flag, Tikas met Linderfelt on the hill. The lieutenant was surrounded by militiamen. The two talked. Suddenly Linderfelt, his face contorted with rage, raised his rifle and brought the stock down with all his strength on Tikas's skull. The rifle broke in two as the strike leader fell to the ground.

Godfrey Irwin, a young electrical engineer visiting Colorado with a friend, accidentally witnessed the scene from a nearby cliff. He later described the next few moments for the *New York World*: "Tikas fell face downward. As he lay there, we saw the militiamen fall back. Then they aimed their rifles and fired into the unconscious man's body. It was the first murder I had ever seen." [. . .]

While bullets whistled through the flaming canvas, people fled in panic from their tents and from the caves beneath. A dispatch to the *New York Times* read,

> A seven-year-old girl dashed from under a blazing tent and heard the scream of bullets about her ears. Insane from fright, she ran into a tent again and fell into the hole with the remainder of her family to die with them. The child is said to have been a daughter of Charles Costa, a union leader at Aguilar, who perished with his wife and another child. . . .
>
> James Fyler, financial secretary of the Trinidad local . . . died with a bullet in his forehead as he was attempting to rescue his wife from the flames. . . . Mrs. Marcelina Pedragon, her skirt ablaze, carried her youngest child from the flames, leaving two others behind.

[. . .] The tents became crackling torches, and for hours the countryside was aglow with a ghastly light while men, women, and children roamed like animals in the hills, seeking their loved ones. At 8:30 P.M. the militia "captured" the smoldering pile of ashes that now was Ludlow.

It was on the following day, April 21, that the bodies of the women and children were found in the pit beneath the tent.

The *New York Times* headline read, "WOMEN AND CHILDREN ROASTED IN PITS OF TENT COLONY AS FLAMES DESTROY IT. MINERS STORE OF AMMUNITION AND DYNAMITE EXPLODED, SCATTERING DEATH AND RUIN." It was clear that the tent colony had been set aflame by the National Guard, but the paper was claiming, as has so often happened, that it was the victims who were responsible for the disaster. [. . .]

Now a thousand miners turned from the coffins of the dead, took up their guns, and set out together for the back country. They were joined by union miners from a dozen neighboring camps, who left wives and children behind and swarmed over the hills, carrying arms and ammunition. They swept across the coal country, from Dalagua to Rouse, leaving in their wake the ashes of burned tipples, the rubble of dynamited mines, and the corpses of strikebreakers and militiamen.

Now, with the miners taking up arms against the militia, the *New York Times* editorialized, "With the deadliest weapons of civilization in the hands of savage-minded men, there can be no telling to what lengths the war in Colorado will go unless it is quelled by force. The President should turn his attention from Mexico long enough to take stern measures in Colorado." [. . .]

On April 22, a "Call to Arms" went out from Denver, addressed to "the Unionists of Colorado." The letter was signed by John Lawson, John McLennon, Ed Doyle, and several other U.M.W. officials, as well as Ernest Mills, secretary-treasurer of the Western Federation of Miners. It read,

> Organize the men in your community in companies of volunteers to protect the workers of Colorado against the murder and cremation of men, women, and children by armed assassins in the employ of coal corporations, serving under the guise of state militiamen. . . .
>
> The state is furnishing no protection to us and we must protect ourselves, our wives and children, from these murderous assassins. We seek no quarrel with the state and we expect to break no law. We intend to exercise our lawful right as citizens to defend our homes and our constitutional rights.

Not until April 23 did the militia allow all the bodies to be removed from the Ludlow ruins. [. . .]

The Trinidad Red Cross issued a statement that twenty-six bodies of strikers had been found at Ludlow. There were conflicting reports as to how many had been killed.

Three hundred armed strikers marched from Fremont County tent colonies to aid the embattled miners of southern Colorado. Four train crews of the Colorado and Southern Railroad refused to take soldiers and ammunition from Trinidad to Ludlow. This action touched off talk of a general strike by the Brotherhood of Locomotive Engineers and Trainmen and the Colorado State Federation of Labor.

From coast to coast, people responded to the appeal of the Colorado miners. Hundreds of mass meetings were held. Thousands of dollars were sent for arms and ammunition. Conservative unions as far away as Philadelphia took action.

While various groups called for federal intervention to restore law and order, Rockefeller sent a telegram to Congress saying that mining company officials were the "only ones competent to deal with the questions." A telegram to President Wilson from twenty "independent" coal operators in Colorado declared that "we heartily endorse" the Colorado Fuel & Iron position. Meanwhile, John P. White, president of the United Mine Workers, maintained that the strike was a just one. [. . .]

On April 27, 1914, headlines in the *Times* read, "WILSON TO SEND FEDERAL TROOPS TO COLORADO. AMMONS CALLED TRAITOR. GREAT MASS MEETING OF DENVER CITIZENS DENOUNCE HIM AND LIEUTENANT GOVERNOR FITZGERALD. ASSAIL ROCKEFELLER JR. MEN AND WOMEN WEEP AS BLANCHE BATES' HUSBAND READS RESOLUTION. STRIKERS CAPTURE CHANDLER AFTER TWO DAY BATTLE." The press reported that there was great difficulty getting federal troops because all nearby military posts had been stripped to provide a patrol along the Mexican border.

At the Denver meeting, a crowd of five thousand men and women stood in the pouring rain on the lawn in front of the capital. George Creel, former police commissioner of Denver, read the resolution, asking that Major Hamrock, Lieutenant Linderfelt, and other National Guard officers be tried for murder, and that the state seize the mines and operate them. They branded the governor and lieutenant governor of Colorado as "traitors to the people and accessories to the murder of babies at Ludlow."

While that meeting was in progress, the Denver Cigar Makers Union voted to send five hundred armed men to Ludlow and Trinidad in the morning. The women of the Denver United Garment Workers Union announced that four hundred of their members had volunteered as nurses to aid the Colorado strikers.

Governor Ammons acted. He appointed a special board of officers, consisting of Major Edward J. Boughton and two infantry captains, to report on the massacre. The Boughton Report concluded that the National Guard was friendly to the strikers, except for Company B, headed by Linderfelt. The report blamed Linderfelt for being "tactless." Upon the withdrawal of the National Guard troops from the field, one unit had to remain behind, it stated, and Company B had been selected "because, although hated by the strikers, it was feared and respected by them."

"The tent colony population is almost wholly foreign and without conception of our government," said the report. "A large percentage are unassimilable aliens to whom liberty means license. . . . Rabid agitators had assured these people that when the soldiers left they were at liberty to take for their own, and by force of arms, the coal mines of their former employers. . . . They prepared for battle." [. . .]

The left wing of the American labor movement made its contrasting sentiments very clear. Eugene Debs wrote in the *International Socialist Review*, "Like the shot at Lexington on April 20 in another year, the shots fired at Ludlow were heard around the world. . . . It is more historic than Lexington and . . . will prove, as we believe, the signal for the American industrial revolution." Another article by Debs called for a Gunmen Defense Fund, with "the latest high power rifles, the same ones used by the corporation gunmen, and 500 rounds of cartridges. In addition to this, every district should purchase and equip and man enough Gatling and machine guns to match the equipment of Rockefeller's private army of assassins. This suggestion is made advisedly, and I hold myself responsible for every word of it." Mother Jones told a House of Representatives committee, "The laboring man is tired of working to build up millions so that millionaires' wives may wear diamonds." [. . .]

On April 29 President Wilson proclaimed, "Whereas it is provided by the Constitution of the United States (that the U.S. shall protect states, upon application against domestic violence) . . . now, therefore, I warn all persons . . . to disperse and retire peaceably to their respective abodes on or before the 30th day of April, instant."

Secretary of War Garrison asked all parties to surrender their arms. The commander of the federal troops prohibited the import of strike-breakers from other states, prohibited picketing, and protected scabs.

Finally, the fighting ended. [. . .]

Today, on an isolated patch of desert in southern Colorado, in the shadow of the black hills, stands a monument erected by the United Mine Workers on the spot where the death pit of the Ludlow Massacre existed. The monument lists the names of the individuals found in the pit and declares its dedication "to those who gave their lives for freedom at Ludlow."

Cedelina Costa	Eulala Valdez
Lucy Costa	Rudolph Valdez
Carlo Costa	Frank Petrucci
Onafrio Costa	Joe Petrucci
Parria Valdez	Lucy Petrucci
Elvira Valdez	Cloriva Pedragon
Mary Valdez	

The strike in Colorado, like so many struggles of people through the ages, has often been seen as a defeat for the workers. Certainly it was, at the time. But for those who came to know of the event—mostly outside the classroom—in the decades since the Ludlow Massacre, the story has been educational and inspiring.

We learn something about the symbiotic relationship between giant corporations and government. We learn about the selective control of violence, where the authorities deal one way with the violence of workers and another way with the violence of police and militia. We learn about the role of the mainstream press. At the same time, we are inspired by those ordinary men and women who persist, with extraordinary courage, in their resistance to overwhelming power. It is a story that continues in our time.

THE NEW ABOLITIONISTS

from *SNCC: The New Abolitionists* (1964)

One of Howard's earliest books, *SNCC: The New Abolitionists*, examined the origin and evolution of the Student Nonviolent Coordinating
Committee, a radical organization comprised mostly of young people,
some of them from northern colleges, working in the black freedom
struggle in the Deep South. He called these "youngsters" the "most
serious social force in the nation today," and his perception of them was
clearly influenced by his proximity: Howard himself had become actively involved in civil rights work during his time as a young professor
of history at Spelman College, Atlanta's renowned college for black
women, where he taught such notable students as Marian Wright (now
Edelman), head of the Children's Defense Fund, and Alice Walker, the
Pulitzer Prize–winning writer. Comparing these young activists—
women and men, black and white—to the abolitionists of the ante-
bellum era, Howard described the members of SNCC as "more a
movement than an organization, for no bureaucratized structure can
contain their spirit, no printed program capture the fierce and elusive
quality of their thinking. And while they have no famous leaders, very
little money, no inner access to the seats of national authority, they are
clearly the front line of the Negro assault on the moral comfort of white
America." In this opening chapter, Howard describes SNCC's structure (grassroots), strategy (nonviolent direct action), and rank-and-file
(interracial, but mostly comprised of southern blacks), and links its
origins to the student sit-ins that swept the country in the early 1960s.
Driven more by idealism than ideology, SNCC embodied a new spirit

of youthful impatience—what Dr. King would call a "marvelous new militancy"—that radicalized an older generation of black leaders, announced a new generation of activists, and shook the nation to its moral core. Howard's book was the first account of this revolutionary moment and movement.

———

FOR THE FIRST TIME in our history a major social movement, shaking the nation to its bones, is being led by youngsters. This is not to deny the inspirational leadership of a handful of adults (Martin Luther King and James Farmer), the organizational direction by veterans in the struggle (Roy Wilkins and A. Philip Randolph), or the participation of hundreds of thousands of older people in the current Negro revolt. But that revolt, a long time marching out of the American past, its way suddenly lit up by the Supreme Court decision, and beginning to rumble in earnest when thousands of people took to the streets of Montgomery in the bus boycott, first flared into a national excitement with the sit-ins by college students that started the decade of the 1960s.

And since then, those same youngsters, hardened by countless jailings and beatings, now out of school and living in ramshackle headquarters all over the Deep South, have been striking the sparks, again and again, for that fire of change spreading through the South and searing the whole country.

These young rebels call themselves the Student Nonviolent Coordinating Committee, but they are more a movement than an organization, for no bureaucratized structure can contain their spirit, no printed program capture the fierce and elusive quality of their thinking. And while they have no famous leaders, very little money, no inner access to the seats of national authority, they are clearly the front line of the Negro assault on the moral comfort of white America.

To be with them, walking a picket line in the rain in Hattiesburg, Mississippi, or sleeping on a cot in a cramped "office" in Greenville, Mississippi; to watch them walk out of the stone jailhouse in Albany, Georgia; to see them jabbed by electric prod poles and flung into paddy wagons in Selma, Alabama, or link arms and sing at the close of a church meeting in the Delta—is to feel the presence of greatness. It is a greatness that comes from their relationship to history, and it does not diminish when they are discovered to be human: to make mistakes or feel fear, to act with envy, or hostility or even violence.

All Americans owe them a debt for—if nothing else—releasing the idealism locked so long inside a nation that has not recently tasted the drama of a social upheaval. And for making us look on the young people of the country with a new respect. Theirs was the silent generation until they spoke, the complacent generation until they marched and sang, the money-seeking generation until they renounced comfort and security to fight for justice in the dank and dangerous hamlets of the Black Belt.

Princeton philosopher Walter Kaufmann, writing in *The Faith of a Heretic*, called the young people born during World War II the "uncommitted generation." He said: "What distinguishes them is that they are not committed to any cause." But this was written in 1960. And in that year, out of that same generation which Kaufmann described, there emerged the first rebels of the decade. They came out of unexpected places: they were mostly black and therefore unseen until they suddenly became the most visible people in America; they came out of Greensboro, North Carolina, and Nashville, Tennessee, and Rock Hill, South Carolina, and Atlanta, Georgia. And they were committed. To the point of jail, which is a large commitment. And to the point of death, which hovers always near a heretic in a police state and which turns to stare a Deep South Negro directly in the face at that moment when he utters that word so long taboo for Negroes in America, "*No.*"

How do you measure commitment? Is it the willingness to take a day out of life and sacrifice it to history, to plunge for one morning or one afternoon into the unknown, to engage in one solitary act of defiance against all the arrayed power of established society? Then tens of thousands of young people, mostly black, some white, have committed themselves these past four years, by the simple act of joining a demonstration. Is commitment more than that—the willingness to wrench yourself out of your environment and begin anew, almost alone, in a social jungle which the most powerful forces in the nation have not dared to penetrate? Then the number is reduced to sixteen: those sixteen college youngsters who, in the fall of 1961, decided to drop everything—school and family and approved ambition—and move into the Deep South to become the first guerrilla fighters of the Student Nonviolent Coordinating Committee.

By early 1964, the number was up to 150. In the most heated days of abolitionism before the Civil War, there were never that many dedicated people who turned their backs on ordinary pursuits and gave their lives wholly to the movement. There were William Lloyd Garrison and

Wendell Phillips and Theodore Weld and Frederick Douglass and Sojourner Truth and a handful of others, and there were hundreds of part-time abolitionists and thousands of followers. But for 150 youngsters today to turn on their pasts, to decide to live and work twenty-four hours a day in the most dangerous region of the United States, is cause for wonder. And wherever they have come from—the Negro colleges of the South, the Ivy League universities of the North, the small and medium colleges all over the country—they have left ripples of astonishment behind. This college generation as a whole is not committed, by any means. But it has been shaken.

These 150—who next year will be 250 or more, because the excitement grows daily on the college campuses—are the new abolitionists. It is not fanciful to invest them with a name that has the ring of history; we are always shy about recognizing the historic worth of events when they take place before our eyes, about recognizing heroes when they are still flesh and blood and not yet transfixed in marble. But there is no doubt about it: we have in this country today a movement which will take its place alongside that of the abolitionists, the Populists, the Progressives—and may outdo them all.

Their youth makes us hesitant to recognize their depth. But the great social upsurge of postwar America is the Negro revolt, and this revolt has gotten its most powerful impetus from young people, who gave it a new turn in 1960 and today, as anonymous as infantrymen everywhere, form the first rank in a nonviolent but ferocious war against the old order.

It would be easy to romanticize them, but they are too young, too vulnerable, too humanly frail to fit the stereotype of heroes. They don't match the storybook martyrs who face death with silent stoicism; the young fellows sometimes cry out when they are beaten; the girls may weep when abused in prison. Most often, however, they sing. This was true of the farmer and labor movements in this country, and of all the wars; but there has never been a singing movement like this one. Perhaps it is because most of them were brought up on the gospel songs and hymns of the Negro church in the South, perhaps also because they are young, probably most of all because what they are doing inspires song. They have created a new gospel music out of the old, made up of songs adapted or written in jail or on the picket line. Every battle station in the Deep South now has its Freedom Chorus, and the mass meetings there end with everyone standing, led by the youngsters of SNCC, linking arms, and singing "We Shall Overcome."

The mood of these young people, which they convey to everyone around them in the midst of poverty, violence, terror, and centuries of bitter memories, is joy, confidence, the vision of victory: "We'll walk hand in hand . . . we are not afraid. . . ." Occasionally there is sadness, as in "I Been 'Buked and I Been Scorned." But most often there is an exuberant defiance: "Ain't Gonna Let Chief Pritchett Turn Me Round. . . ." They are happy warriors, a refreshing contrast to the revolutionaries of old. They smile and wave while being taken off in paddy wagons; they laugh and sing behind bars.

Yet they are the most serious social force in the nation today. They are not playing; it is no casual act of defiance, no irresponsible whim of adolescence, when young people of sixteen or twenty or twenty-five turn away from school, job, family, all the tokens of success in modern America, to take up new lives, hungry and hunted, in the hinterland of the Deep South. Jim Forman was a teacher in Chicago before he joined the SNCC, and an aspiring novelist; Bob Moses was a graduate of Harvard, teaching in New York; Charles Sherrod was a divinity school graduate in Virginia; Mendy Samstein, a graduate of Brandeis University, was on the faculty of a Negro college, working for his Ph.D. in history at the University of Chicago. Others found it easier—and harder—for they came right out of the Black Belt and, even though they tasted college, they had nowhere then to go but back towards danger and freedom: John Lewis, Sam Block, Willie Peacock, Lafayette Surney, MacArthur Cotton, Lawrence Guyot and too many more to name.

In his study *Young Man Luther*, the psychologist Erik Erikson ponders the "identity crisis" which young people face. "It occurs in that period of the life cycle when each youth must forge for himself some central perspective and direction, some working unity, out of the effective remnants of his childhood and the hopes of his anticipated adulthood; he must detect some meaningful resemblance between what he has come to see in himself and what his sharpened awareness tells him others judge and expect him to be." It would be hard to imagine a more startling contrast than that between the young Negro as the old South saw him (or rather half-saw him, blurred and not quite human) and the vision of himself he suddenly perceived in the glare of the 1960s.

The entire nation, caught suddenly in the intersection of two images where it always thought there was only one, has begun slowly to refocus its own vision. So that what started as an identity crisis for Negroes turned out to be an identity crisis for the nation. And we are still resolving it. It is one of the conditions of effective psychotherapy that the patient must begin to see himself as he really is, and the United States, now forced by the young Negro to see itself through *his* eyes (an ironic reversal, for the Negro was always compelled to see himself through the eyes of the white man), is coming closer to a realistic appraisal of its national personality.

All young people, in their late teens or early twenties, face this "identity crisis" which Erik Erikson describes. As Erikson points out: "Some young individuals will succumb to this crisis in all manner of neurotic, psychotic, or delinquent behavior; others will resolve it through participation in ideological movements passionately concerned with religion or politics, nature or art." We have seen the delinquent responses, or simply the responses of non-commitment, on the part of millions of young people of this generation who have not been able to find their way. Young Negroes were among these, were perhaps even the most delinquent, the most crisis-ridden of all. But today, by the handful, or the hundreds, or perhaps the thousands, they are making their way through this crisis with a firm grip on themselves, aided immeasurably by the fact that they are anchored to a great social movement.

We ought to note, however, that this "participation in ideological movements" today has a different quality than that of earlier American student movements—the radical movements of the thirties, for instance. The young people in the Student Nonviolent Coordinating Committee have not become followers of any dogma, have not pledged themselves to any rigid ideological system. Unswerving as they are in moving towards certain basic goals, they wheel freely in their thinking about society and how it needs to be changed. Erikson writes of a very few young people who, making their way through their identity crisis, "eventually come to contribute an original bit to an emerging style of life; the very danger which they have sensed has forced them to mobilize capacities to see and say, to dream and plan, to design and construct, in new ways." And this is true of those in the SNCC. They are radical, but not dogmatic; thoughtful, but not ideological. Their thinking is undisciplined; it is fresh, and it is new.

One must listen to Jane Stembridge speaking, a white girl from Virginia, part of that little band of black and white students who organized SNCC out of the turmoil of the 1960 sit-ins:

> . . . finally it all boils down to human relationships. It has nothing to do finally with governments. It is the question of whether we . . . whether *I* shall go on living in isolation or whether there

shall be a we. The student movement is not a cause . . . it is a col-
lision between this one person and that one person. It is a *I am
going to sit beside you* . . . Love alone is radical. Political statements are not; programs are not; even going to jail is not. . . .

These new abolitionists are different from the earlier ones. The movement of the 1830s and 1840s was led by white New Englanders, bom-
barding the South and the nation with words. The present movement is
planted firmly in the deepest furrows of the Deep South, and it consists
mostly of Negroes who make their pleas to the nation more by physical acts of sacrifice than by verbal declamation. Their task is made easier by modern mass communication, for the nation, indeed the whole
world, can *see* them, on the television screen or in newspaper photos—
marching, praying, singing, *demonstrating* their message. The white
people of America, to whom Negroes were always a dark, amorphous
mass, are forced to see them for the first time sharply etched as individuals, their features—both physical and moral—stark, clear, and
troubling.

But in one important way these young people are very much like the
abolitionists of old: they have a healthy disrespect for respectability;
they are not ashamed of being agitators and trouble-makers; they see
it as the essence of democracy. In defense of William Lloyd Garrison,
against the accusation that he was too harsh, a friend replied that the
nation was in a sleep so deep "nothing but a rude and almost ruffian-
like shake could rouse her." The same deliberate harshness lies behind
the activities of James Forman, John Lewis, Bob Moses, and other
leaders of SNCC. What Samuel May once said of Garrison and slavery might be said today of each of these people and segregation:
"He will shake our nation to its center, but he will shake slavery out
of it."

When SNCC leader Gloria Richardson in Cambridge, Maryland,
refused, under a rain of criticism, to subject the issue of segregation to
popular vote, one was reminded of the words of Wendell Phillips, ex-
plaining the apparent strange behavior of the abolitionists: "The reformer
is careless of numbers, disregards popularity, and deals only with ideas,
conscience, and common sense. . . . He neither expects, nor is overanx-
ious for immediate success." Phillips contrasted the reformer with the
politician, who "dwells in an everlasting now. . . ." In a similar mood,
poet James Russell Lowell wrote: "The Reformer must expect comparative isolation, and he must be strong enough to bear it."

Yet the staff member of the Student Nonviolent Coordinating Committee can never be isolated as was the New England abolitionist of the 1830s, who was far from slave territory, and surrounded by whites unconcerned for the slave. The SNCC youngster is in the midst of his people, surrounded by them, protected by them. To be cut off, by harsh criticism of his "extremism," from Northern white intellectuals or from those in national political power is a minor blow, cushioned by a popularity based on the poor and the powerless, but perhaps even more comforting because of that.

Oddly enough—or perhaps naturally enough—the student movement has left the campuses where it began in those sit-ins of early 1960. The sit-in leaders have either graduated from or left college, and the fact that they call themselves the *Student* Nonviolent Coordinating Committee is primarily a reflection of their backgrounds, their youth, and perhaps their hope to return one day and bring a new dynamism to college education. Some go back to college after a year or two with the movement; others find a less formal but more genuine intellectual satisfaction in the movement. All live in a state of tension: there is the recognition that academic life is too far removed from the social struggle, alongside the frustration that exists for any intellectually aroused youngster separated from books and concentrated learning. At the same time, having exchanged college attire and the tree-lined campus for overalls and the dusty back roads of the rural South, they are getting the kind of education that no one else in the nation is getting.

There is another striking contrast to Garrison and Phillips, Lewis Tappan and Theodore Weld: these young people are not middle-class reformers who became somehow concerned about others. They come themselves from the ranks of the victims, not just because they are mostly Negroes, but because for the most part their fathers are janitors and laborers, their mothers maids and factory workers. [. . .]

These are young radicals; the word "revolution" occurs again and again in their speech. Yet they have no party, no ideology, no creed. They have no clear idea of a blueprint for a future society. But they do know clearly that the values of present American society—and this goes beyond racism to class distinction, to commercialism, to profit-seeking, to the setting of religious or national barriers against human contact—are not for them.

They are prepared to use revolutionary means against the old order. They believe in civil disobedience. They are reluctant to rely completely on the niceties of negotiation and conciliation, distrustful of those who hold political and economic power. They have a tremendous respect for the potency of the demonstration, an eagerness to move out of the political maze of normal parliamentary procedure and to confront policymakers directly with a power beyond orthodox politics—the power of people in the streets and on the picket line.

They are nonviolent in that they suffer beatings with folded arms and will not strike back. There have been one or two rare exceptions of discipline being broken, yet this must be laid against hundreds of instances of astounding self-control in the face of unspeakable brutality.

Next to the phrase "nonviolence," however, what you hear most often among SNCC workers is "direct action." They believe, without inflicting violence, and while opening themselves to attack, in confronting a community boldly with the sounds and sights of protest. When it is argued that this will inevitably bring trouble, even violence, the answer is likely to be that given by James Bevel, who in his activity with the Southern Christian Leadership Conference works closely with SNCC in Alabama and Mississippi: "Maybe the Devil has got to come out of these people before we will have peace. . . ."

They have no closed vision of the ideal community. They are fed up with what has been; they are open to anything new and are willing to start from scratch. Erik Erikson talks about young rebels with a "rock-bottom" attitude, who "want to be reborn in identity and to have another chance at becoming once-born, but this time on their own terms." Nineteen-year-old SNCC veteran Cordell Reagan, brown-skinned, slender, explains himself this way:

> It's not hard to interpret what our parents mean by a better world. You know, go to school, son, and get a good education. And what do you do with this? You get a degree, you move out into some little community housing project, you get married, five kids and two cars, and you don't care what's happening. . . . So I think when we talk about growing up in a better world, a new world, we mean changing the world to a different place.

Is it any wonder that Cordell Reagan and so many other SNCC workers have been put in jail again and again by Deep South sheriffs for "contributing to the delinquency of minors"?

A young white student, explaining why he wanted to join SNCC, wrote about his newfound view of life:

I have never felt so intense, alive, such a sense of well-being, which is not to be confused with the illusion of "happiness" equated to "having fun." I have chosen to be outside of society after having been very much inside. I intend to fight that society which lied to and smothered me for so long, and continues to do so to vast numbers of people. . . . My plans are unstructured in regards to anything but the immediate future. I believe in freedom, and must take the jump; I must take the chance of action.

The nation has suddenly become aware that the initiative today is in the hands of these 150 young people who have moved into the Deep South to transform it. Everyone waits on their next action: the local police, the state officials, the national government, the mass media of the country, Negroes and whites sitting at their radios and television sets across the land. Meanwhile, these people are living, hour by hour, the very ideals which this country has often thought about, but not yet managed to practice: they are courageous, though afraid; they live and work together in a brotherhood of black and white. Southerner and Northerner, Jew and Christian and agnostic, the likes of which this country has not yet seen. They are creating new definitions of success, of happiness, of democracy.

It is just possible that the momentum created by their enormous energy—now directed against racial separation—may surge, before it can be contained, against other barriers which keep people apart in the world: poverty, and nationalism, and all tyranny over the minds and bodies of men. If so, the United States may truly be on the verge of a revolution—nonviolent, but sweeping in its consequences—and led by those who, perhaps, are most dependable in a revolution: the young.

CARTER-REAGAN-BUSH:
THE BIPARTISAN CONSENSUS

from *A People's History of the United States: 1492–Present*
(revised edition, 2000)

Howard published several revised editions of *A People's History*, which allowed him to extend his radical analysis of American history to include the Reagan era, the presidencies of George H.W. Bush and Bill Clinton, the contested 2000 election, and the "war on terror." Though these additional chapters focus more attention on the moral failings of modern leaders, they nonetheless demonstrate how the decisions of those in power affect the livelihoods of ordinary people. In this chapter, Howard characterizes the last quarter of the twentieth century as one of "capitalistic encouragement of enormous fortunes alongside desperate poverty, a nationalistic acceptance of war and preparations for war. Governmental power swung from Republicans to Democrats and back again, but neither party showed itself capable of going beyond that vision." This "bipartisan consensus"—wherein the "populism" of Jimmy Carter, Ronald Reagan, and Bill Clinton belied a more aggressive commitment to deregulating the economy, cutting welfare, and expanding the military—resulted in a vast "distance between politics and the people." Here, Howard sets out to shatter the pervasive myths of "prosperity" and "peace" to show how Republicans and Democrats alike presided over the creation of a society at once more greedy, arrogant, and unequal than at any other time in modern American history.

———

HALFWAY THROUGH THE TWENTIETH CENTURY, the historian Richard Hofstadter, in his book *The American Political Tradition*, examined our important national leaders, from Jefferson and Jackson to Herbert Hoover and the two Roosevelts—Republicans and Democrats, liberals and conservatives. Hofstadter concluded that "the range of vision embraced by the primary contestants in the major parties has always been bounded by the horizons of property and enterprise. . . . They have accepted the economic virtues of capitalist culture as necessary qualities of man. . . . That culture has been intensely nationalistic. . . ."

Coming to the end of the century, observing its last twenty-five years, we have seen exactly that limited vision Hofstadter talked about—a capitalistic encouragement of enormous fortunes alongside desperate poverty, a nationalistic acceptance of war and preparations for war. Governmental power swung from Republicans to Democrats and back again, but neither party showed itself capable of going beyond that vision.

After the disastrous war in Vietnam came the scandals of Watergate. There was a deepening economic insecurity for much of the population, along with environmental deterioration, and a growing culture of violence and family disarray. Clearly, such fundamental problems could not be solved without bold changes in the social and economic structure. But no major party candidates proposed such changes. The "American political tradition" held fast.

In recognition of this, perhaps only vaguely conscious of this, voters stayed away from the polls in large numbers, or voted without enthusiasm. More and more they declared, if only by nonparticipation, their alienation from the political system. In 1960, 63 percent of those eligible to vote voted in the presidential election. By 1976, this figure had dropped to 53 percent. In a CBS News and *New York Times* survey, over half of the respondents said that public officials didn't care about people like them. A typical response came from a plumber: "The President of the United States isn't going to solve our problems. The problems are too big."

There was a troubling incongruity in the society. Electoral politics dominated the press and television screens, and the doings of presidents, members of Congress, Supreme Court justices, and other officials were treated as if they constituted the history of the country. Yet there was something artificial in all this, something pumped up, a straining to persuade a skeptical public that this was all, that they must rest their hopes for the future in Washington politicians, none of whom were inspiring because it seemed that behind the bombast, the rhetoric, the promises, their major concern was their own political power.

The distance between politics and the people was reflected clearly in the culture. In what was supposed to be the best of the media, uncontrolled by corporate interest—that is, in *public* television, the public was largely invisible. On the leading political forum on public television, the nightly "MacNeil-Lehrer Report," the public was uninvited, except as viewer of an endless parade of Congressmen, Senators, government bureaucrats, experts of various kinds.

On commercial radio, the usual narrow band of consensus, excluding fundamental criticism, was especially apparent. In the mid-1980s, with Ronald Reagan as President, the "fairness doctrine" of the Federal Communications Commission, requiring air time for dissenting views, was eliminated. By the 1990s, "talk radio" had perhaps 20 million listeners, treated to daily tirades from right-wing talk-show "hosts," with left-wing guests uninvited.

A citizenry disillusioned with politics and with what pretended to be intelligent discussions of politics turned its attention (or had its attention turned) to entertainment, to gossip, to ten thousand schemes for self-help. Those at its margins became violent, finding scapegoats within one's group (as with poor-black on poor-black violence), or against other races, immigrants, demonized foreigners, welfare mothers, minor criminals (standing in for untouchable major criminals).

There were other citizens, those who tried to hold on to ideas and ideals still remembered from the sixties and early seventies, not just by recollecting but by acting. Indeed, all across the country there was a part of the public unmentioned in the media, ignored by political leaders— energetically active in thousands of local groups around the country. These organized groups were campaigning for environmental protection or women's rights or decent health care (including anguished concern about the horrors of AIDS) or housing for the homeless, or against military spending.

This activism was unlike that of the sixties, when the surge of protest against race segregation and war became an overwhelming national force. It struggled uphill, against callous political leaders, trying to reach fellow Americans most of whom saw little hope in either the politics of voting or the politics of protest.

The presidency of Jimmy Carter, covering the years 1977 to 1980, seemed an attempt by one part of the Establishment, that represented in the Democratic party, to recapture a disillusioned citizenry. But Carter, despite a few gestures toward black people and the poor, despite talk of "human rights" abroad, remained within the historic political boundaries of the American system, protecting corporate wealth and power, maintaining a huge military machine that drained the national wealth, allying the United States with right-wing tyrannies abroad.

Carter seemed to be the choice of that international group of powerful influence-wielders—the Trilateral Commission. Two founding members of the commission, according to the *Far Eastern Economic Review*—David Rockefeller and Zbigniew Brzezinski—thought Carter was the right person for the presidential election of 1976 given that "the Watergate-plagued Republican Party was a sure loser. . . ."

Carter's job as President, from the point of view of the Establishment, was to halt the rushing disappointment of the American people with the government, with the economic system, with disastrous military ventures abroad. In his campaign, he tried to speak to the disillusioned and angry. His strongest appeal was to blacks, whose rebellion in the late sixties was the most frightening challenge to authority since the labor and unemployed upsurges in the thirties.

His appeal was "populist"—that is, he appealed to various elements of American society who saw themselves beleaguered by the powerful and wealthy. Although he himself was a millionaire peanut grower, he presented himself as an ordinary American farmer. Although he had been a supporter of the Vietnam war until its end, he presented himself as a sympathizer with those who had been against the war, and he appealed to many of the young rebels of the sixties by his promise to cut the military budget.

In a much-publicized speech to lawyers, Carter spoke out against the use of the law to protect the rich. He appointed a black woman, Patricia Harris, as Secretary of Housing and Urban Development, and a black civil rights veteran, Andrew Young, as ambassador to the United Nations. He gave the job of heading the domestic youth service corps to a young former antiwar activist, Sam Brown.

His most crucial appointments, however, were in keeping with the Trilateral Commission report of Harvard political scientist Samuel Huntington, which said that, whatever groups voted for a president, once elected "what counts then is his ability to mobilize support from the leaders of key institutions." Brzezinski, a traditional cold war intellectual, became Carter's National Security Adviser. His Secretary of Defense, Harold Brown, had, during the Vietnam war, according to the *Pentagon Papers*, "envisaged the elimination of virtually all the constraints under which the bombing then operated." His Secretary of Energy, James Schlesinger, as Secretary of Defense under Nixon, was described by a member of the Washington press corps as showing "an almost missionary drive in seeking to reverse a downward trend in the defense budget." Schlesinger was also a strong proponent of nuclear energy.

His other cabinet appointees had strong corporate connections. A financial writer wrote, not long after Carter's election: "So far, Mr. Carter's actions, commentary, and particularly his Cabinet appointments, have been highly reassuring to the business community." Veteran Washington correspondent Tom Wicker wrote: "The available evidence is that Mr. Carter so far is opting for Wall Street's confidence."

Carter did initiate more sophisticated policies toward governments that oppressed their own people. He used United Nations Ambassador Andrew Young to build up goodwill for the United States among the black African nations, and urged that South Africa liberalize its policies toward blacks. A peaceful settlement in South Africa was necessary for strategic reasons; South Africa was used for radar tracking systems. Also, it had important U.S. corporate investments and was a critical source of needed raw materials (diamonds, especially). Therefore, what the United States needed was a stable government in South Africa; the continued oppression of blacks might create civil war.

The same approach was used in other countries—combining practical strategic needs with the advancement of civil rights. But because the chief motivation was practicality, not humanity, there was a tendency toward token changes—as in Chile's release of a few political prisoners. When Congressman Herman Badillo introduced in Congress a proposal that required the U.S. representatives to the World Bank and other international financial institutions to vote against loans to countries that systematically violated essential rights, by the use of torture or imprisonment without trial, Carter sent a personal letter to every Congressman urging the defeat of this amendment. It won a voice vote in the House, but lost in the Senate.

Under Carter, the United States continued to support, all over the world, regimes that engaged in imprisonment of dissenters, torture, and mass murder: in the Philippines, in Iran, in Nicaragua, and in Indonesia, where the inhabitants of East Timor were being annihilated in a campaign bordering on genocide.

The *New Republic* magazine, presumably on the liberal side of the Establishment, commented approvingly on the Carter policies: ". . . American foreign policy in the next four years will essentially extend the philosophies developed . . . in the Nixon-Ford years. This is not at all a negative prospect. . . . There should be continuity. It is part of history. . . ."

Carter had presented himself as a friend of the movement against the war, but when Nixon mined Haiphong harbor and resumed bombing of

North Vietnam in the spring of 1973, Carter urged that "we give President Nixon our backing and support—whether or not we agree with specific decisions." Once elected, Carter declined to give aid to Vietnam for reconstruction, despite the fact that the land had been devastated by American bombing. Asked about this at a press conference, Carter replied that there was no special obligation on the United States to do this because "the destruction was mutual."

Considering that the United States had crossed half the globe with an enormous fleet of bombers and 2 million soldiers, and after eight years left a tiny nation with over a million dead and its land in ruins, this was an astounding statement.

One Establishment intention, perhaps, was that future generations see the war not as it appeared in the Defense Department's own *Pentagon Papers*—as a ruthless attack on civilian populations for strategic military and economic interests—but as an unfortunate error. Noam Chomsky, one of the leading antiwar intellectuals during the Vietnam period, looked in mid-1978 at how the history of the war was being presented in the major media and wrote that they were "destroying the historical record and supplanting it with a more comfortable story . . . reducing 'lessons' of the war to the socially neutral categories of error, ignorance, and cost." [. . .]

In 1979, while the poor were taking cuts, the salary of the chairman of Exxon Oil was being raised to $830,000 a year and that of the chairman of Mobil Oil to over a million dollars a year. That year, while Exxon's net income rose 56 percent to more than $4 billion, three thousand small independent gasoline stations went out of business.

Carter made some efforts to hold onto social programs, but this was undermined by his very large military budgets. Presumably, this was to guard against the Soviet Union, but when the Soviet Union invaded Afghanistan in 1979, Carter could take only symbolic actions, like reinstituting the draft, or calling for a boycott of the 1980 Moscow Olympics.

On the other hand, American weaponry was used to support dictatorial regimes battling left-wing rebels abroad. A report by the Carter administration to Congress in 1977 was blunt, saying that "a number of countries with deplorable records of human rights observance are also countries where we have important security and foreign policy interests."

Thus, Carter asked Congress in the spring of 1980 for $5.7 million in credits for the military junta fighting off a peasant rebellion in El Salvador. In the Philippines, after the 1978 National Assembly elections,

President Ferdinand Marcos imprisoned ten of the twenty-one losing opposition candidates; many prisoners were tortured, many civilians were killed. Still, Carter urged Congress to give Marcos $300 million in military aid for the next five years.

In Nicaragua, the United States had helped maintain the Somoza dictatorship for decades. Misreading the basic weakness of that regime, and the popularity of the revolution against it, the Carter administration continued its support for Somoza until close to the regime's fall in 1979.

In Iran, toward the end of 1978, the long years of resentment against the Shah's dictatorship culminated in mass demonstrations. On September 8, 1978, hundreds of demonstrators were massacred by the Shah's troops. The next day, according to a UPI dispatch from Teheran, Carter affirmed his support for the Shah:

> Troops opened fire on demonstrators against the Shah for the third straight day yesterday and President Jimmy Carter telephoned the royal palace to express support for Shah Mohammad Reza Pahlevi, who faced the worst crisis of his 37-year reign. Nine members of parliament walked out on a speech by Iran's new premier, shouting that his hands were "stained with blood" in the crackdown on conservative Moslems and other protesters.

On December 13, 1978, Nicholas Gage reported for the *New York Times:*

> The staff of the United States Embassy here has been bolstered by dozens of specialists flown in to back an effort to help the Shah against a growing challenge to his rule according to embassy sources. . . . The new arrivals, according to the embassy sources, include a number of Central Intelligence Agency specialists on Iran, in addition to diplomats and military personnel.

In early 1979, as the crisis in Iran was intensifying, the former chief analyst on Iran for the CIA told *New York Times* reporter Seymour Hersh that "he and his colleagues knew of the tortures of Iranian dissenters by Savak, the Iranian secret police set up during the late 1950s by the Shah with help from the CIA." Furthermore, he told Hersh that a senior CIA official was involved in instructing officials in Savak on torture techniques.

It was a popular, massive revolution, and the Shah fled. The Carter administration later accepted him into the country, presumably for medical treatment, and the anti-American feelings of the revolutionaries reached a high point. On November 4, 1979, the U.S. embassy in Teheran was taken over by student militants who, demanding that the Shah be returned to Iran for punishment, held fifty-two embassy employees hostage.

For the next fourteen months, with the hostages still held in the embassy compound, that issue took the forefront of foreign news in the United States and aroused powerful nationalist feelings. When Carter ordered the Immigration and Naturalization Service to start deportation proceedings against Iranian students who lacked valid visas, the *New York Times* gave cautious but clear approval. Politicians and the press played into a general hysteria. An Iranian American girl who was slated to give a high school commencement address was removed from the program. The bumper sticker "Bomb Iran" appeared on autos all over the country.

It was a rare journalist bold enough to point out, as Alan Richman of the Boston *Globe* did when the fifty-two hostages were released alive and apparently well, that there was a certain lack of proportion in American reactions to this and other violations of human rights: "There were 52 of them, a number easy to comprehend. It wasn't like 15,000 innocent people permanently disappearing in Argentina. . . . They [the American hostages] spoke our language. There were 3000 people summarily shot in Guatemala last year who did not."

The hostages were still in captivity when Jimmy Carter faced Ronald Reagan in the election of 1980. That fact, and the economic distress felt by many, were largely responsible for Carter's defeat.

Reagan's victory, followed eight years later by the election of George Bush, meant that another part of the Establishment, lacking even the faint liberalism of the Carter presidency, would be in charge. The policies would be more crass—cutting benefits to poor people, lowering taxes for the wealthy, increasing the military budget, filling the federal court system with conservative judges, actively working to destroy revolutionary movements in the Caribbean.

The dozen years of the Reagan-Bush presidency transformed the federal judiciary, never more than moderately liberal, into a predominantly conservative institution. By the fall of 1991, Reagan and Bush had filled more than half of the 837 federal judgeships, and appointed enough right-wing justices to transform the Supreme Court.

In the seventies, with liberal justices William Brennan and Thurgood Marshall in the lead, the Court had declared death penalties unconstitutional, had supported (in *Roe v. Wade*) the right of women to choose abortions, and had interpreted the civil rights law as permitting special attention to blacks and women to make up for past discrimination (affirmative action).

William Rehnquist, first named to the Supreme Court by Richard Nixon, was made Chief Justice by Ronald Reagan. In the Reagan-Bush years, the Rehnquist Court made a series of decisions that weakened *Roe v. Wade*, brought back the death penalty, reduced the rights of detainees against police powers, prevented doctors in federally supported family planning clinics from giving women information on abortions, and said that poor people could be forced to pay for public education (education was not "a fundamental right").

Justices William Brennan and Thurgood Marshall were the last of the Court's liberals. Old and ill, though reluctant to give up the fight, they retired. The final act to create a conservative Supreme Court was President Bush's nomination to replace Marshall. He chose a black conservative, Clarence Thomas. Despite dramatic testimony from a former colleague, a young black law professor named Anita Hill, that Thomas had sexually harassed her, Thomas was approved by the Senate and now the Supreme Court moved even more decisively to the right.

With conservative federal judges, with pro-business appointments to the National Labor Relations Board, judicial decisions and board findings weakened a labor movement already troubled by a decline in manufacturing. Workers who went out on strike found themselves with no legal protection. One of the first acts of the Reagan administration was to dismiss from their jobs, en masse, striking air traffic controllers. It was a warning to future strikers, and a sign of the weakness of a labor movement which in the thirties and forties had been a powerful force.

Corporate America became the greatest beneficiary of the Reagan-Bush years. In the sixties and seventies an important environmental movement had grown in the nation, horrified at the poisoning of the air, the seas and rivers, and the deaths of thousands each year as a result of work conditions. After a mine explosion in West Virginia killed seventy-eight miners in November 1968 there had been angry protest in the mine district, and Congress passed the Coal Mine Health and Safety Act of 1969. Nixon's Secretary of Labor spoke of "a new national passion, passion for environmental improvement."

The following year, yielding to strong demands from the labor movement and consumer groups, but also seeing it as an opportunity to win the support of working-class voters, President Nixon had signed the Occupational Safety and Health Act of 1970. This was an important piece of legislation, establishing a universal right to a safe and healthy workplace, and creating an enforcement machinery. Reflecting on this years later, Herbert Stein, who had been the chairman of Nixon's Council of Economic Advisers, lamented that "the juggernaut of environmental regulation proved not to be controllable by the Nixon administration."

While President Jimmy Carter came into office praising the OSHA program, he was also eager to please the business community. The woman he appointed to head OSHA, Eula Bingham, fought for strong enforcement of the act, and was occasionally successful. But as the American economy showed signs of trouble, with oil prices, inflation, and unemployment rising, Carter seemed more and more concerned about the difficulties the act created for business. He became an advocate of removing regulations on corporations and giving them more leeway, even if this was hurtful to labor and to consumers. Environmental regulation became more and more a victim of "cost-benefit" analysis, in which regulations protecting the health and safety of the public became secondary to how costly this would be for business.

Under Reagan and Bush this concern for "the economy," which was a shorthand term for corporate profit, dominated any concern for workers or consumers. President Reagan proposed to replace tough enforcement of environmental laws by a "voluntary" approach, leaving it to businesses to decide for themselves what they would do. He appointed as head of OSHA a businessman who was hostile to OSHA's aims. One of his first acts was to order the destruction of 100,000 government booklets pointing out the dangers of cotton dust to textile workers.

Political scientist William Grover (*The President as Prisoner*), evaluating environmental policy under Carter and Reagan as part of his penetrating "structural critique" of both presidents, concluded:

> OSHA appears caught in a cycle of liberal presidents—who want to retain some health and safety regulatory programs, but who also need economic growth for political survival—and conservative presidents, who focus almost exclusively on the growth side of the equation. Such a cycle will always tend to subordinate the need for safe and healthful workplaces to . . . ensuring that commitment to OSHA will only be as strong as the priorities of business will allow.

George Bush presented himself as the "environmental president," and pointed with pride to his signing of the Clean Air Act of 1990. But two years after that act was passed, it was seriously weakened by a new rule of the Environmental Protection Agency that allowed manufacturers to increase by 245 tons a year hazardous pollutants in the atmosphere.

Furthermore, little money was allocated for enforcement. Contaminated drinking water had caused over 100,000 illnesses between 1971 and 1985, according to an EPA report. But in Bush's first year in office, while the EPA received 80,000 complaints of contaminated drinking water, only one in a hundred was investigated. And in 1991 and 1992, according to a private environmental group, the Natural Resources Defense Council, there were some 250,000 violations of the Safe Water Drinking Act (which had been passed during the Nixon administration).

Shortly after Bush took office, a government scientist prepared testimony for a Congressional committee on the dangerous effects of industrial uses of coal and other fossil fuels in contributing to "global warming," a depletion of the earth's protective ozone layer. The White House changed the testimony, over the scientist's objections, to minimize the danger (*Boston Globe*, October 29, 1990). Again, business worries about regulation seemed to override the safety of the public.

The ecological crisis in the world had become so obviously serious that Pope John Paul II felt the need to rebuke the wealthy classes of the industrialized nations for creating that crisis: "Today, the dramatic threat of ecological breakdown is teaching us the extent to which greed and selfishness, both individual and collective, are contrary to the order of creation."

At international conferences to deal with the perils of global warming, the European Community and Japan proposed specific levels and timetables for carbon dioxide emissions, in which the United States was the leading culprit. But, as the *New York Times* reported in the summer of 1991, "the Bush Administration fears that . . . it would hurt the nation's economy in the short term for no demonstrable long-term climatic benefit." Scientific opinion was quite clear on the long-term benefit, but this was not as important as "the economy"—that is, the needs of corporations.

Evidence became stronger by the late eighties that renewable energy sources (water, wind, sunlight) could produce more usable energy than nuclear plants, which were dangerous and expensive, and produced radioactive wastes that could not be safely disposed of. Yet the Reagan and Bush administrations made deep cuts (under Reagan, a 90 percent cut) in research into renewable energy possibilities.

In June 1992 more than a hundred countries participated in the Earth Summit environmental conference in Brazil. Statistics showed that the armed forces of the world were responsible for two-thirds of the gases that depleted the ozone layer. But when it was suggested that the Earth Summit consider the effects of the military on environmental degradation, the United States delegation objected and the suggestion was defeated.

Indeed, the preservation of a huge military establishment and the retention of profit levels of oil corporations appeared to be twin objectives of the Reagan-Bush administrations. Shortly after Ronald Reagan took office, twenty-three oil industry executives contributed $270,000 to redecorate the White House living quarters. According to the Associated Press:

> The solicitation drive . . . came four weeks after the President decontrolled oil prices, a decision worth $2 billion to the oil industry . . . Jack Hodges of Oklahoma City, owner of Core Oil and Gas Company, said: "The top man of this country ought to live in one of the top places. Mr. Reagan has helped the energy business."

While he built up the military (allocations of over a trillion dollars in his first four years in office), Reagan tried to pay for this with cuts in benefits for the poor. There would be $140 billion of cuts in social programs through 1984 and an increase of $181 billion for "defense" in the same period. He also proposed tax cuts of $190 billion (most of this going to the wealthy).

Despite the tax cuts and the military appropriations, Reagan insisted he would still balance the budget because the tax cuts would so stimulate the economy as to generate new revenue. Nobel Prize–winning economist Wassily Leontief remarked dryly: "This is not likely to happen. In fact, I personally guarantee that it will not happen."

Indeed, Department of Commerce figures showed that periods of lowered corporate taxes (1973–1975, 1979–1982) did not at all show higher capital investment, but a steep drop. The sharpest rise of capital investment (1975–1979) took place when corporate taxes were slightly higher than they had been the preceding five years.

The human consequences of Reagan's budget cuts went deep. For instance, Social Security disability benefits were terminated for 350,000 people. A man injured in an oil field accident was forced to go back to work, the federal government overruling both the company doctor and a state supervisor who testified that he was too disabled to work. The man died, and federal officials said, "We have a P.R. problem." A war hero of Vietnam, Roy Benavidez, who had been presented with the Congressional Medal of Honor by Reagan, was told by Social Security officials that the shrapnel pieces in his heart, arms, and leg did not prevent him from working. Appearing before a Congressional committee, he denounced Reagan.

Unemployment grew in the Reagan years. In the year 1982, 30 million people were unemployed all or part of the year. One result was that over 16 million Americans lost medical insurance, which was often tied to holding a job. In Michigan, where the unemployment rate was the highest in the country, the infant death rate began to rise in 1981.

New requirements eliminated free school lunches for more than one million poor children, who depended on the meal for as much as half of their daily nutrition. Millions of children entered the ranks of the officially declared "poor" and soon a quarter of the nation's children— twelve million—were living in poverty. In parts of Detroit, one-third of the children were dying before their first birthday, and the *New York Times* commented: "Given what's happening to the hungry in America, this Administration has cause only for shame."

Welfare became an object of attack: aid to single mothers with children through the AFDC (Aid to Families with Dependent Children) program, food stamps, health care for the poor through Medicaid. For most people on welfare (the benefits differed from state to state) this meant $500 to $700 a month in aid, leaving them well below the poverty level of about $900 a month. Black children were four times as likely as white children to grow up on welfare.

Early in the Reagan administration, responding to the argument that government aid was not needed, that private enterprise would take care of poverty, a mother wrote to her local newspaper:

> I am on Aid to Families with Dependent Children, and both my children are in school. . . . I have graduated from college with distinction, 128th in a class of over 1000, with a B.A. in English and sociology. I have experience in library work, child care, social work and counseling.
>
> I have been to the CETA office. They have nothing for me. . . . I also go every week to the library to scour the newspaper Help Wanted ads. I have kept a copy of every cover letter that I have

sent out with my resume; the stack is inches thick. I have applied for jobs paying as little as $8000 a year. I work part-time in a library for $3.50 an hour, welfare reduces my allotment to compensate. . . .

It appears we have employment offices that can't employ, governments that can't govern and an economic system that can't produce jobs for people ready to work. . . .

Last week I sold my bed to pay for the insurance on my car, which, in the absence of mass transportation, I need to go job hunting. I sleep on a piece of rubber foam somebody gave me.

So this is the great American dream my parents came to this country for: Work hard, get a good education, follow the rules, and you will be rich. I don't want to be rich. I just want to be able to feed my children and live with some semblance of dignity. . . .

Democrats often joined Republicans in denouncing welfare programs. Presumably, this was done to gain political support from a middle-class public that believed they were paying taxes to support teenage mothers and people they thought too lazy to work. Much of the public did not know, and were not informed by either political leaders or the media, that welfare took a tiny part of the taxes, and military spending took a huge chunk of it. Yet, the public's attitude on welfare was different from that of the two major parties. It seemed that the constant attacks on welfare by politicians, reported endlessly in the press and on television, did not succeed in eradicating a fundamental generosity felt by most Americans.

A *New York Times*/CBS News poll conducted in early 1992 showed that public opinion on welfare changed depending on how the question was worded. If the word "welfare" was used, 44 percent of those questioned said too much was being spent on welfare (while 50 percent said either that the right amount was being spent, or that too little was being spent. But when the question was about "assistance to the poor," only 13 percent thought too much was being spent, and 64 percent thought too little was being spent.

This suggested that both parties were trying to manufacture an anti-human-needs mood by constant derogatory use of the word "welfare," and then to claim they were acting in response to public opinion. The Democrats as well as the Republicans had strong connections to wealthy corporations. Kevin Phillips, a Republican analyst of national politics, wrote in 1990 that the Democratic Party was "history's second-most enthusiastic capitalist party." [. . .]

The press was especially timid and obsequious during the Reagan years, as Mark Hertsgaard documents in his book *On Bended Knee*. When journalist Raymond Bonner continued to report on the atrocities in El Salvador, and on the U.S. role, the *New York Times* removed him from his assignment. Back in 1981 Bonner had reported on the massacre of hundreds of civilians in the town of El Mozote, by a battalion of soldiers trained by the United States. The Reagan administration scoffed at the account, but in 1992, a team of forensic anthropologists began unearthing skeletons from the site of the massacre, most of them children; the following year a UN commission confirmed the story of the massacre at El Mozote.

The Reagan administration, which did not appear at all offended by military juntas governing in Latin America (Guatemala, El Salvador, Chile) if they were "friendly" to the United States, became very upset when a tyranny was hostile, as was the government of Muammar Khadafi in Libya. In 1986, when unknown terrorists bombed a discotheque in West Berlin, killing a U.S. serviceman, the White House immediately decided to retaliate. Khadafi was probably responsible for various acts of terrorism over the years, but there was no real evidence that in this case he was to blame.

Reagan was determined to make a point. Planes were sent over the capital city of Tripoli with specific instructions to aim at Khadafi's house. The bombs fell on a crowded city; perhaps a hundred people were killed, it was estimated by foreign diplomats in Tripoli. Khadafi was not injured, but an adopted daughter of his was killed.

Professor Stephen Shalom, analyzing this incident, writes (*Imperial Alibis*): "If terrorism is defined as politically motivated violence perpetrated against non-combatant targets, then one of the most serious incidents of international terrorism of the year was precisely this U.S. raid on Libya."

Early in the presidency of George Bush, there came the most dramatic developments on the international scene since the end of World War II. In the year 1989, with a dynamic new leader, Mikhail Gorbachev, at the head of the Soviet Union, the long suppressed dissatisfaction with "dictatorships of the proletariat" which had turned out to be dictatorships *over* the proletariat erupted all through the Soviet bloc.

There were mass demonstrations in the Soviet Union and in the countries of Eastern Europe which had been long dominated by the Soviet Union. East Germany agreed to unite with West Germany, and the wall separating East Berlin from West Berlin, long a symbol of the tight control of its citizens by East Germany, was dismantled in the presence of wildly exultant citizens of both Germanies. In Czechoslovakia, a new non-Communist government came into being, headed by a playwright and former imprisoned dissident named Vaclav Havel. In Poland, Bulgaria, Hungary, a new leadership emerged, promising freedom and democracy. And remarkably, all this took place without civil war, in response to overwhelming popular demand.

In the United States, the Republican party claimed that the hard-line policies of Reagan and the increase in military expenditures had brought down the Soviet Union. But the change had begun much earlier, after the death of Stalin in 1953, and especially with the leadership of Nikita Khrushchev. A remarkably open discussion had been initiated.

But the continued hard line of the United States became an obstacle to further liberalization, according to former ambassador to the Soviet Union George Kennan, who wrote that "the general effect of cold war extremism was to delay rather than hasten the great change that overtook the Soviet Union by the end of the 1980s." While the press and politicians in the United States exulted over the collapse of the Soviet Union, Kennan pointed out that, not only did American policies delay this collapse, but these cold war policies were carried on at a frightful cost to the American people:

> We paid with forty years of enormous and otherwise unnecessary military expenditures. We paid through the cultivation of nuclear weaponry to the point where the vast and useless nuclear arsenal had become (and remains today) a danger to the very environment of the planet. . . .

The sudden collapse of the Soviet Union left the political leadership of the United States unprepared. Military interventions had been undertaken in Korea and Vietnam with enormous loss of life, also in Cuba and the Dominican Republic, and huge amounts of military aid had been given all over the world—in Europe, Africa, Latin America, the Middle East, Asia—on the supposition that this was necessary to deal with a Communist menace emanating from the Soviet Union. Several trillion dollars had been taken from American citizens in the form of taxes to maintain a huge nuclear and nonnuclear arsenal and military bases all over the world—all primarily justified by the "Soviet threat."

Here then was an opportunity for the United States to reconstruct its foreign policy, and to free hundreds of billions of dollars a year from the budget to be used for constructive, healthy projects.

But this did not happen. Along with the exultation "We have won the cold war" came a kind of panic: "What can we do to maintain our military establishment?"

It became clearer now, although it had been suspected, that United States foreign policy was not simply based on the existence of the Soviet Union, but was motivated by fear of revolution in various parts of the world. The radical social critic Noam Chomsky had long maintained that "the appeal to security was largely fraudulent, the Cold War framework having been employed as a device to justify the suppression of independent nationalism—whether in Europe, Japan, or the Third World" (*World Orders Old and New*).

The fear of "independent nationalism" was that this would jeopardize powerful American economic interests. Revolutions in Nicaragua or Cuba or El Salvador or Chile were threats to United Fruit, Anaconda Copper, International Telephone and Telegraph, and others. Thus, foreign interventions presented to the public as "in the national interest" were really undertaken for special interests, for which the American people were asked to sacrifice their sons and their tax dollars.

The CIA now had to prove it was still needed. The *New York Times* (February 4, 1992) declared that "in a world where the postwar enemy has ceased to exist, the C.I.A. and its handful of sister agencies, with their billion-dollar satellites and mountains of classified documents, must somehow remain relevant in the minds of Americans."

The military budget remained huge. The cold war budget of $300 billion was reduced by 7 percent to $280 billion. The Chairman of the Joint Chiefs of Staff, Colin Powell, said: "I want to scare the hell out of the rest of the world. I don't say that in a bellicose way."

As if to prove that the gigantic military establishment was still necessary, the Bush administration, in its four-year term, launched two wars: a "small" one against Panama and a massive one against Iraq.

Coming into office in 1989, George Bush was embarrassed by the new defiant posture of Panama's dictator, General Manuel Noriega. Noriega's regime was corrupt, brutal, authoritarian, but President Reagan and Vice-President Bush had overlooked this because Noriega was useful to the United States. He cooperated with the CIA in many ways, such as offering Panama as a base for contra operations against the Sandinista government of Nicaragua and meeting with Colonel Oliver North to discuss sabotage targets in Nicaragua. When he was director of the CIA in 1976–1977, Bush had protected Noriega.

But by 1987 Noriega's usefulness was over, his activities in the drug trade were in the open, and he became a convenient target for an administration which wanted to prove that the United States, apparently unable to destroy the Castro regime or the Sandinistas or the revolutionary movement in El Salvador, was still a power in the Caribbean.

Claiming that it wanted to bring Noriega to trial as a drug trafficker (he had been indicted in Florida on that charge) and also that it needed to protect U.S. citizens (a military man and his wife had been threatened by Panamanian soldiers), the United States invaded Panama in December 1989, with 26,000 troops.

It was a quick victory. Noriega was captured and brought to Florida to stand trial (where he was subsequently found guilty and sent to prison). But in the invasion, neighborhoods in Panama City were bombarded and hundreds, perhaps thousands of civilians were killed. It was estimated that 14,000 were homeless. Writer Mark Hertsgaard noted that even if the official Pentagon figure of several hundred civilian casualties was correct, this meant that in Panama the U.S. had killed as many people as did the Chinese government in its notorious attack on student demonstrators at Tiananmen Square in Beijing six months earlier. A new president friendly to the United States was installed in Panama, but poverty and unemployment remained, and in 1992 the *New York Times* reported that the invasion and removal of Noriega "failed to stanch the flow of illicit narcotics through Panama."

The United States, however, succeeded in one of its aims, to reestablish its strong influence over Panama. The *Times* reported: "The President [of Panama] and his key aides and the American Ambassador, Deane Hinton, have breakfast together once a week in a meeting that many Panamanians view as the place where important decisions are taken."

Liberal Democrats (John Kerry and Ted Kennedy of Massachusetts, and many others) declared their support of the military action. The Democrats were being true to their historic role as supporters of military intervention, anxious to show that foreign policy was bipartisan. They seemed determined to show they were as tough (or as ruthless) as the Republicans.

But the Panama operation was on too small a scale to accomplish what both the Reagan and Bush administrations badly wanted: to overcome the American public's abhorrence, since Vietnam, of foreign military interventions.

Two years later, the Gulf War against Iraq presented such an opportunity. Iraq, under the brutal dictatorship of Saddam Hussein, had taken over its small but oil-rich neighbor, Kuwait, in August 1990.

George Bush needed something at this point to boost his popularity among American voters. The *Washington Post* (October 16, 1990) had a front-page story headline: "Poll Shows Plunge in Public Confidence: Bush's Rating Plummets." The *Post* reported (October 28): "Some observers in his own party worry that the president will be forced to initiate combat to prevent further erosion of his support at home."

On October 30, a secret decision was made for war against Iraq. The United Nations had responded to the invasion of Kuwait by establishing sanctions against Iraq. Witness after witness testified before Congressional committees in the fall of 1990 that the sanctions were having an effect and should continue. Secret CIA testimony to the Senate affirmed that Iraq's imports and exports had been reduced by more than 90 percent because of the sanctions.

But after the November elections brought gains for the Democrats in Congress, Bush doubled American military forces in the Gulf, to 500,000, creating what was now clearly an offensive force rather than a defensive one. According to Elizabeth Drew, a writer for the *New Yorker*, Bush's aide John Sununu "was telling people that a short successful war would be pure political gold for the President and would guarantee his re-election."

Historian Jon Wiener, analyzing the domestic context of the war decision shortly afterward, wrote that "Bush abandoned sanctions and chose war because his time frame was a political one set by the approaching 1992 presidential elections."

That and the longtime U.S. wish to have a decisive voice in the control of Middle East oil resources were the crucial elements in the decision to go to war against Iraq. Shortly after the war, as representatives of the thirteen oil-producing nations were about to gather in Geneva, the business correspondent of the *New York Times* wrote: "By virtue of its military victory the United States is likely to have more influence in the Organization of Petroleum Exporting Countries than any industrial nation has ever exercised."

But those motives were not presented to the American public. It was told that the United States wanted to liberate Kuwait from Iraqi control. The major media dwelled on this as a reason for war, without noting

that other countries had been invaded without the United States showing such concern (East Timor by Indonesia, Iran by Iraq, Lebanon by
Israel, Mozambique by South Africa; to say nothing of countries invaded
by the United States itself—Grenada, Panama).

The justification for war that seemed most compelling was that Iraq
was on its way to building a nuclear bomb, but the evidence for this was
very weak. Before the crisis over Kuwait, Western intelligence sources
had estimated it would take Iraq three to ten years to build a nuclear
weapon. Even if Iraq could build a bomb in a year or two, which was
the most pessimistic estimate, it had no delivery system to send it anywhere. Besides, Israel already had nuclear weapons. And the United
States had perhaps 30,000 of them. The Bush administration was trying
hard to develop a paranoia in the nation about an Iraqi bomb which did
not yet exist.

Bush seemed determined to go to war. There had been several chances
to negotiate an Iraqi withdrawal from Kuwait right after the invasion,
including an Iraqi proposal reported on August 29 by *Newsday* correspondent Knut Royce. But there was no response from the United States.
When Secretary of State James Baker went to Geneva to meet with
Iraqi foreign minister Tariq Aziz, the instruction from Bush was "no
negotiations."

Despite months of exhortation from Washington about the dangers
of Saddam Hussein, surveys showed that less than half of the public
favored military action.

In January 1991, Bush, apparently feeling the need for support, asked
Congress to give him the authority to make war. This was not a *declaration* of war, as called for by the Constitution; but since Korea and Vietnam, that provision of the Constitution seemed dead, and even the
"strict constructionists" on the Supreme Court who prided themselves
on taking the words of the Constitution literally and seriously would
not intervene.

The debate in Congress was lively. (At one point, a Senate speech
was interrupted by protesters in the balcony shouting "No blood for
oil!" The protesters were hustled out by guards.) It is likely that Bush
was sure of having enough votes, or he would have launched the invasion
without Congressional approval; after all, the precedent for ignoring Congress and the Constitution had been set in Korea, Vietnam, Grenada, and
Panama.

The Senate voted for military action by only a few votes. The House
supported the resolution by a larger majority. However, once Bush

ordered the attack on Iraq, both houses, with just a few dissents, Democrats as well as Republicans, voted to "support the war and support the troops."

It was in mid-January 1991, after Saddam Hussein defied an ultimatum to leave Kuwait, that the U.S. launched its air war against Iraq. It was given the name Desert Storm. The government and the media had conjured up a picture of a formidable military power, but Iraq was far from that. The U.S. Air Force had total control of the air, and could bomb at will.

Not only that, U.S. officials had virtual total control of the airwaves. The American public was overwhelmed with television photos of "smart bombs" and confident statements that laser bombs were being guided with perfect precision to military targets. The major networks presented all of these claims without question or criticism.

This confidence in "smart bombs" sparing civilians may have contributed to a shift in public opinion, from being equally divided on going to war, to perhaps 85 percent support for the invasion. Perhaps more important in winning over public support was that once American military were engaged, it seemed to many people who had previously opposed military action that to criticize it now meant betraying the troops who were there. All over the nation yellow ribbons were displayed as a symbol of support for the forces in Iraq.

In fact, the public was being deceived about how "smart" the bombs being dropped on Iraqi towns were. After talking with former intelligence and Air Force officers, a correspondent for the Boston *Globe* reported that perhaps 40 percent of the laser-guided bombs dropped in Operation Desert Storm missed their targets.

John Lehman, Secretary of the Navy under President Reagan, estimated there had been thousands of civilian casualties. The Pentagon officially had no figure on this. A senior Pentagon official told the *Globe*, "To tell you the truth, we're not really focusing on this question."

A Reuters dispatch from Iraq described the destruction of a seventy-three-room hotel in a town south of Baghdad, and quoted an Egyptian witness: "They hit the hotel, full of families, and then they came back to hit it again." Reuters reported that the air raids on Iraq first used laser-guided bombs, but within a few weeks turned to B-52s, which carried conventional bombs, meaning more indiscriminate bombing.

American reporters were kept from seeing the war close-up, and their dispatches were subject to censorship. Apparently recalling how press reports of civilian casualties had affected public opinion during the Vietnam war, the U.S. government was taking no chances this time.

A *Washington Post* reporter complained about the control of information, writing (January 22, 1991):

> The bombing has involved . . . dozens of high-flying B-52 bombers equipped with huge, unguided munitions. But the Pentagon has not allowed interviews with B-52 pilots, shown videotapes of their actions or answered any questions about the operations of an aircraft that is the most deadly and least accurate in the armada of more than 2000 U.S. and allied planes in the Persian Gulf region. . . .

In mid-February, U.S. planes dropped bombs on an air raid shelter in Baghdad at four in the morning, killing 400 to 500 people. An Associated Press reporter who was one of few allowed to go to the site said: "Most of the recovered bodies were charred and mutilated beyond recognition. Some clearly were children." The Pentagon claimed it was a military target, but the AP reporter on the scene said: "No evidence of any military presence could be seen inside the wreckage." Other reporters who inspected the site agreed.

After the war, fifteen Washington news bureau chiefs complained in a joint statement that the Pentagon exercised "virtual total control . . . over the American press" during the Gulf War.

But while it was happening, leading television news commentators behaved as if they were working for the United States government. For instance, CBS correspondent Dan Rather, perhaps the most widely seen of the TV newsmen, reported from Saudi Arabia on a film showing a laser bomb (this one dropped by British aircraft in support of the American war) hitting a marketplace and killing civilians. Rather's only comment was: "We can be sure that Saddam Hussein will make propaganda of these casualties."

When the Russian government tried to negotiate an end to the war, bringing Iraq out of Kuwait before the ground war could get under way, top CBS correspondent Lesley Stahl asked another reporter: "Isn't this the nightmare scenario? Aren't the Soviets trying to stop us?" (Ed Siegel, TV reporter for the *Boston Globe*, February 23, 1991).

The final stage of the war, barely six weeks after it had begun, was a ground assault which, like the air war, encountered virtually no resistance. With victory certain and the Iraqi army in full flight, U.S. planes kept bombing the retreating soldiers who clogged the highway out of Kuwait City. A reporter called the scene "a blazing hell . . . a gruesome testament. . . . To the east and west across the sand lay the bodies of those fleeing."

A Yale professor of military history, Michael Howard, writing in the *New York Times* (January 28, 1991), quoted the military strategist Clausewitz approvingly: "The fact that a bloody slaughter is a horrifying act must make us take war more seriously, but not provide an excuse for gradually blunting our swords in the name of humanity." Howard went on to say: "In this conflict of wills, the bottom line remains a readiness to kill and be killed. . . ."

The human consequences of the war became shockingly clear after its end, when it was revealed that the bombings of Iraq had caused starvation, disease, and the deaths of tens of thousands of children. A U.N. team visiting Iraq immediately after the war reported that "the recent conflict has wrought near-apocalyptic results upon the infrastructure. . . . Most means of modern life support have been destroyed or rendered tenuous. . . ."

A Harvard medical team reporting in May said that child mortality had risen steeply, and that 55,000 more children died in the first four months of the year (the war lasted from January 15 to February 28) than in a comparable period the year before.

The director of a pediatric hospital in Baghdad told a *New York Times* reporter that on the first night of the bombing campaign the electricity was knocked out: "Mothers grabbed their children out of incubators, took intravenous tubes out of their arms. Others were removed from oxygen tents and they ran to the basement, where there was no heat. I lost more than 40 prematures in the first 12 hours of the bombing."

Although in the course of the war Saddam Hussein had been depicted by U.S. officials and the press as another Hitler, the war ended short of a march into Baghdad, leaving Hussein in power. It seemed that the United States had wanted to weaken him, but not to eliminate him, in order to keep him as a balance against Iran. In the years before the Gulf War, the United States had sold arms to both Iran and Iraq, at different times favoring one or the other as part of the traditional "balance of power" strategy.

Therefore, as the war ended, the United States did not support Iraqi dissidents who wanted to overthrow the regime of Saddam Hussein. A *New York Times* dispatch from Washington, datelined March 26, 1991, reported: "President Bush has decided to let President Saddam Hussein put down rebellions in his country without American intervention rather than risk the splintering of Iraq, according to official statements and private briefings today."

This left the Kurdish minority, which was rebelling against Saddam Hussein, helpless. And anti-Hussein elements among the Iraqi majority were also left hanging. The *Washington Post* reported (May 3, 1991): "Major defections from the Iraqi military were in the offing in March at the height of the Kurdish rebellion, but never materialized because the officers concluded the U.S. would not back the uprising. . . ."

The man who had been Jimmy Carter's National Security Adviser, Zbigniew Brzezinski, a month after the end of the Gulf War, gave a cold assessment of the pluses and minuses of the event. "The benefits are undeniably impressive. First, a blatant act of aggression was rebuffed and punished. . . . Second, U.S military power is henceforth likely to be taken more seriously. . . . Third, the Middle East and Persian Gulf region is now clearly an American sphere of preponderance."

Brzezinski, however, was concerned about "some negative consequences." One of them was that "the very intensity of the air assault on Iraq gives rise to concern that the conduct of the war may come to be seen as evidence that Americans view Arab lives as worthless. . . . And that raises the moral question of the proportionality of response."

His point about Arab lives being seen as "worthless" was underlined by the fact that the war provoked an ugly wave of anti-Arab racism in the United States, with Arab Americans insulted or beaten or threatened with death. There were bumper stickers that said "I don't brake for Iraqis." An Arab American businessman was beaten in Toledo, Ohio.

Brzezinski's measured assessment of the Gulf War could be taken as close to representing the view of the Democratic Party. It went along with the Bush administration. It was pleased with the results. It had some misgivings about civilian casualties. But it did not constitute an opposition.

President George Bush was satisfied. As the war ended, he declared on a radio broadcast: "The specter of Vietnam has been buried forever in the desert sands of the Arabian peninsula."

The Establishment press very much agreed. The two leading news magazines, *Time* and *Newsweek*, had special editions hailing the victory in the war, noting there had been only a few hundred American casualties, without any mention of Iraqi casualties. A *New York Times* editorial (March 30, 1991) said: "America's victory in the Persian Gulf war . . . provided special vindication for the U.S. Army, which brilliantly exploited its firepower and mobility and in the process erased memories of its grievous difficulties in Vietnam."

A black poet in Berkeley, California, June Jordan, had a different view: "I suggest to you it's a hit the same way that crack is, and it doesn't last long."

INTERLUDE: WHO CONTROLS THE PAST CONTROLS THE FUTURE

Interview with David Barsamian, Boulder, Colorado, 1992

from *Failure to Quit: Reflections of an Optimistic Historian*

During the last two decades of his career, Howard was interviewed numerous times by David Barsamian, founder and director of the widely syndicated program *Alternative Radio*. Their conversations covered a broad range of themes related to Howard's life, scholarship, and activism. A gifted, pioneering journalist, Barsamian had an uncanny knack for getting Howard to reflect deeply on the relationship between the personal, intellectual, and political. For his part, Howard enjoyed their conversations very much. "I had a lot of fun with it," he wrote of the following interview, conducted in Boulder, Colorado, in 1992. And you could tell. When David jokingly begins a question about the Columbus quincentennial with "I know you were present at the 1892 celebration of the four-hundredth anniversary of Columbus's voyage," Howard quips, "Of course, I try to be at all these important events. I tried to be there in 1492 but I didn't make it." More seriously, this interview gets its title from George Orwell's famous dictum "Who controls the past controls the future. Who controls the present controls the past." Here, Howard discusses his own history, his rejection of "objectivity" in the writing of history, and the role of media and culture in shaping and manipulating our collective understanding of the past.

———

THIS INTERVIEW TOOK PLACE in Boulder, Colorado in 1992, and David Barsamian and I had a lot of fun with it, which is hard to recapture in a transcript, so readers will have to content themselves with what is left after the tape was scrupulously edited to remove the fun. I met David some years ago when I was invited to speak in Boulder by a remarkable veteran journalist named Sender Garlin, now ninety and brimming with energy. David has been a pioneer in what is mysteriously called "alternative radio," and when I spoke a few years ago to a national conference of several hundred "alternative radio" people, everyone seemed to know him. He drew from me things about my life which I was saving for my own slightly shorter version of *Remembrance of Things Past*.

DAVID BARSAMIAN: *I want to know something about your roots, growing up in the projects on the lower East Side.*

I grew up in the slums of Brooklyn. Not projects. They weren't advanced enough to have projects. I think maybe the first New Deal housing project was in Williamsburg, Brooklyn. But that was too good for us. I grew up in the slums of Brooklyn, a working class family. My parents were European immigrants, factory workers in New York. They met as factory workers. They were Jewish immigrants. My father came from Austria, my mother from Asiatic Russia, Siberia. I remember moving all the time. We were always one step ahead of the landlord. And changing schools all the time. My father struggled, went from job to job, he was unemployed and under WPA. I wanted to get out of the house all the time. Where we lived was never a nice place to be. So I was in the streets a lot. I understand what it's like for kids to live in and prefer the streets. That's how I grew up.

When I got to be college age I went to work in a shipyard and became a shipyard worker for three years. My family needed the money. The East Side came later, after the war. I volunteered for the Air Force and was a bombardier. I got married before I went overseas. After the war my wife and I first lived in Bedford-Stuyvesant in a rat-infested basement. I'm building up my sordid past, trying to evoke tears. We were so happy when we were accepted into the Lillian Wald housing project, a low-income housing project on the East Side of New York. We lived there for seven years while I went to New York University under the GI Bill and to graduate school at Columbia. My wife worked. Our two kids were in nursery school.

DB: *What was the language at home? Did you speak Yiddish?*

Not me. My parents spoke Yiddish to each other, so I understood it. When they spoke to us they spoke English, nicely accented, with a few

Yiddish words thrown in. I never actually used Yiddish, but I still can understand it. Words like "bagel" and "knish."

DB: *I remember you telling me about your father being a waiter for many years. He'd work a bar mitzvah and then there'd be no work, and then he'd do a bat mitzvah.*

He did a lot of Jewish weddings. In fact, when I was about seventeen he introduced me to it. On New Year's Eve they would be short and the waiters would be able to bring their sons in. They called them "juniors." It was an AFL craft union. Everything was hereditary: the leadership of the union, the jobs, etc. I really hated being a waiter, and I felt for my father. They used to call him "Charlie Chaplin" because he walked like Charlie Chaplin. His feet were flat. They said it was the result of all those years of being a waiter. I don't know if that's true or not, but that was the story. He worked very hard. He was a great fan of Roosevelt during the New Deal, he and a lot of other people who didn't have any jobs any more. People were still getting married, but they weren't paying waiters, so my father worked as a ditch digger with the WPA. My mother had been a factory worker before she was married. When she got married she began having kids, and it was my father's job to support the family.

DB: *Was there any kind of intellectual life at home, books, magazines?*

No. There were no books or magazines. The very first book I read I picked up on the street. Ten pages were ripped off, but it didn't matter to me because it was my first book. I was already reading, and this was *Tarzan and the Jewels of Opar.* I'll always remember that. No books at home. However, my parents knew that I liked books and liked to read. The *New York Post* came out with this gift, that if you clipped these coupons and sent in twenty-five cents, they would send you a volume of Dickens. So my parents sent away for the whole set of Dickens, the collected works, twenty volumes. I read every single one. Dickens was my first author. Some of them I didn't understand, like *The Pickwick Papers.* Sometimes I got the humor and sometimes I didn't. I went through them in order. I thought if the *New York Post* sent you the books in order, somehow they must have a reason for it. So first it was *David Copperfield,* then *Oliver Twist,* then *Dombey and Son,* then *Bleak House.*

When I was thirteen my parents bought me a typewriter. They didn't know about typewriters or books, but they knew I was interested in reading and writing, so they paid five dollars for a remade Underwood No. 5, which I had for a very long time.

DB: *I want you to talk about your World War Two bombardier experience. I've heard you discuss it in public lectures, and you write about it. There were two missions in particular that you always mention, one over Pilsen in Czechoslovakia and the other in France in the town of Royan. Why are they so important to you?*

These things weren't important at the time. I was just another member of the Air Force doing my duty, listening to my briefings before going out on the flight and dropping the bombs where I was supposed to, without thinking, where am I dropping them? What am I doing? Who lives here? What's going on here? I flew the last missions of the war. By then we were well into Germany. We were running out of targets, and so we were bombing Eastern Europe. I dropped bombs on Hungary. I remember the raid on Pilsen. A lot of planes went over. I remember reading about the raid after the war. It was described by Churchill in his memoirs as, Well, we bombed Pilsen and there were very few civilian casualties. Then I was in Europe years after that, sometime in the mid-1960s, in Yugoslavia. I ran into a couple from Pilsen. Hesitantly, I told them that I had been in one of the crews that bombed Pilsen. They said, when you finished the streets were full of corpses, hundreds and hundreds of people killed in that raid.

It was only after the war that I began to think about the raids I had been on. The thing about being in the Air Force and dropping bombs from 35,000 feet is that you don't see anybody, human beings, you don't hear screams, see blood, see mangled bodies. I understand very well how atrocities are committed in modern warfare: from a distance. So there I was doing these things.

The raid on Royan was an even more difficult experience for me as I thought about it later. It was just a few months before the end of the war. We thought we weren't going to fly any more missions, because we had already overrun France, taken most of Germany, there was virtually nothing left to bomb, and everybody knew the war was going to be over in a few weeks. We were awakened at one in the morning, the usual waking up time if you're going to fly at six. It's not like in the movies where you leap out of bed into the cockpit, rev up the engines and you're off. Five boring hours of listening to briefings, getting your equipment, putting on your electrically heated suit, going to the bombardiers' briefing, the officers' briefing, going to eat and deciding whether you eat square eggs or round eggs. That means powdered eggs or real eggs. If you were going on a bombing mission you got real eggs—as many as you wanted. They briefed us and told us we were going to bomb this little town on the Atlantic coast near Bordeaux, a town called Royan. They showed it to us on the map. Nobody asked why. You don't ask questions at briefings. To this day I feel ashamed that it didn't even occur to me to ask, Why are we doing this when the war is almost over? Why are we bombing this little French town when France is all ours? There were a few thousand German soldiers holed up near this town, waiting for the war to end, not doing anything, not bothering anybody. But we were going to destroy them.

So twelve hundred heavy bombers were sent over. I didn't know how many bombers were sent. All I knew was my squadron of twelve bombers were going over. I could see other squadrons. It wasn't until later, when I did research into it after the war, that I realized that it was twelve hundred heavy bombers going over against two or three thousand German soldiers. But they told us in the briefing, You're going to carry a different type of bomb in the bomb bay. Not the usual demolition bomb. You're going to carry canisters, long cylinders of jellied gasoline. It didn't mean anything to us, except we knew jellied gasoline would ignite. It was napalm.

It was only after the war that I began to think about that raid and did some research and visited Royan. I went into the ruins of the library, now rebuilt, and read what they had written about it. I wrote an essay about that bombing. It epitomized the stupidity of modern warfare and how the momentum of military machines carries armies on to do the most atrocious things that any rational person sitting down for five minutes and thinking about it would stop immediately.

So we destroyed the town, the German soldiers, the French also who were there. In one of my essays I coupled it with the bombing of Hiroshima as two bombings that at the time, I am ashamed to say, I welcomed. With Royan it wasn't that I welcomed it, I was just doing it. With Hiroshima I welcomed it because it meant that the war would end and I wouldn't have to go to the Pacific and fly any more bombing missions.

DB: *Some years after that, in the mid-1960s, you visited Hiroshima. You had intended to make certain remarks at a gathering of survivors. You weren't able to make those remarks.*

It was a terrible moment. A few Americans were visiting Hiroshima every August, an international gathering to commemorate the dropping of the bomb. We were taken to visit a house of survivors, where people who had survived Hiroshima gathered and socialized with one another. They brought this little international group, a few Americans, a Frenchman, a Russian. The Japanese, the survivors, were sitting on the floor. We were expected to get up and say something to them as visitors from other countries. The Russian woman spoke about what the Russians had suffered in the war and how she could commiserate with the Japanese. As I planned to get up and speak, I thought, I don't know what I can say. But I have to be honest. I have to say I was a bombardier, even though I didn't bomb Japan. I bombed people, innocent people, civilians, just as in Hiroshima. So I got up to speak and looked out at the people sitting there. Suddenly something happened to my eyesight, my brain. I saw this blur of people who were blind, with missing arms, missing legs, people whose skin was covered with sores. This was real. That's what these people looked like. I looked out at them and I couldn't speak. In all the speaking I've ever done, nothing like that has ever happened to me. It was impossible. I just stood there. My voice choked up. That was it.

DB: *I'd like to focus now on something else. What about the notion of history as a commodity, something that can be bought and sold? Do you accept that?*

I once wrote an essay called "History as Private Enterprise." What I meant was that I thought so much history was written without a social conscience behind it. Or if there was a social conscience somewhere in the historian, it was put aside for the writing of history, because writing history was done as a professional duty. It was done to get something published, to get a job at a university, to get tenure, to get a promotion, to build up one's prestige. It was printed by publishers in books that would sell and make a profit. The profit motive, which has so distorted our whole economic and social system by making profit the key to what is produced and therefore leaving important things unproduced and stupid things produced and leaving some people rich and some people poor. That same profit system had extended to that world, which as an innocent young student I thought was a world separated from the world of commerce and business. But the world of the university, of publishing, of history, of scholarship is not at all separated from the profit-seeking world. The historian doesn't think of it consciously this way. But there is the fact of economic security that operates in every profession. The professional writer and historian is perhaps conscious, perhaps semiconscious, or perhaps it has already been absorbed into the bloodstream, is thinking about economic security and therefore about playing it safe. So we get a lot of safe history.

DB: *You're fond of quoting Orwell's dictum "Who controls the past controls the future. Who controls the present controls the past."*

Orwell is one of my favorite writers in general. When I came across that I knew I had to use it. We writers are real thieves. We see something good and use it, and then if we're nice we say where we got it. Sometimes we don't. What the Orwell quote means to me is a very important observation that if you can control history, what people know about history, if you can decide what's in people's history and what's left out, you can order their thinking. You can order their values. You can in effect organize their brains by controlling their knowledge. The people who can do that, who can control the past, are the people who control the present. The people who would dominate the media, who publish the textbooks, who decide in our culture what are the dominant ideas, what gets told and what doesn't.

DB: *Who are they? Who are the guardians of the past? Can you make some general comments about their class background, race?*

They are mostly guys, mostly well off, mostly white. Sometimes this is talked about as the history of rich, white men. There's a history which is done by rich white men. Not that historians are rich. But the people who publish the textbooks are, the people who control the media, the people who decide what historians to invite on the networks at special moments when they want to call on a historian. The people who dominate the big media networks, they're rich. Not only are the controllers of our information rich and white and male, but they then ask that history concentrate on those who are rich and white and male. That is why the point of view of black people has not been a very important one in the telling of our history. The point of view of women certainly has not been. The point of view of working people is something that has not been given its due in the histories that we have mostly been given in our culture.

DB: *You've made the astounding comment that objectivity and scholarship in the media and elsewhere is not only "harmful and misleading, it's not desirable."*

I've said two things about it. One, that it's not possible. Two, it's not desirable. It's not possible because all history is a selection out of an infinite number of facts. As soon as you begin to select, you select according to what you think is important. Therefore it is already not objective. It's already biased in the direction of whatever you, as the selector of this information, think people should know. So it's really not possible.

Some people claim to be objective. The worst thing is to claim to be objective. Of course you can't be. Historians should say what their values are, what they care about, what their background is, and let you know what is important to them so that young people and everybody who reads history are warned in advance that they should never count on any one source, but should go to many sources. So it's not possible to be objective, and it's not desirable if it were possible. We should have history that does reflect points of view and values, in other words, history that is not objective. We should have history that enhances human values, humane values, values of brotherhood, sisterhood, peace, justice, and equality. The closest I can get to it is the values enunciated in the Declaration of Independence. Equality, the right of all people to have life, liberty, and the pursuit of happiness. Those are values that historians should actively promulgate in writing history. In doing that they needn't distort or omit important things. But it does mean if they have those values in mind, that they will emphasize those things in history which will bring up a new generation of people who read history books and who will care about treating other people equally, about doing away with war, about justice in every form.

DB: *How do you filter those biases, or can you even filter them?*

As I've said, yes, I have my biases, my leanings. So if I'm writing or speaking about Columbus, I will try not to hide or omit the fact that Columbus did a remarkable thing in crossing the ocean and venturing out into uncharted waters. It took physical courage and navigational skill. It was a remarkable event. I have to say that so that I don't omit what people see as the positive side of Columbus. But then I have to go on to say the other things about Columbus which are much more important than his navigational skill, than the fact that he was a religious man. His treatment of the human beings that he found in this hemisphere. The enslavement, the torture, the murder, the dehumanization of these people. That is the important thing.

There's an interesting way in which you can frame a sentence which will show what you emphasize and which will have two very different results. Here's what I mean. Take Columbus as an example. You can frame it, and this was the way the Harvard historian Samuel Eliot Morison in effect framed it in his biography of Columbus: Columbus committed genocide, but he was a wonderful sailor. He did a remarkable and extraordinary thing in finding these islands in the Western Hemisphere. Where's the emphasis there? He committed genocide, but . . . he's a good sailor. I say, He was a good sailor, but he treated people with the most horrible cruelty and committed genocide. Those are two different ways of saying the same facts. Depending on which side of the "but" you're on, you show your bias. I believe that it's good for us to put our biases in the direction of a humane view of history.

DB: *I know you were present at the 1892 celebration of the four-hundredth anniversary of Columbus's voyage. . . .*

Of course, I try to be at all these important events. I tried to be there in 1492 but I didn't make it.

DB: *In terms of 1992, were you surprised at the level of protest, indignation, and general criticism of Columbus?*

I was delightfully surprised. I did expect more protest this year than there ever has been, because I knew, just from going around the country speaking and from reactions to my book [*A People's History of the United States*], which has sold a couple of hundred thousand copies. It starts off with Columbus, so anybody who has read my book is going to have a different view of Columbus, I hope. I knew that there had been more literature in the last few years. Hans Koning's wonderful book, which appeared before mine, *Columbus: His Enterprise*, to give one example. I was aware that Native American groups around the country were planning protests.

So I knew that things would happen, but I really wasn't prepared for the number of things that have happened and the extent of protest that there has been. It has been very satisfying. What's interesting about it, much as people like me and you rail against the media, they don't have total control. It is possible for us, and this is a very heartwarming thing and it should be encouraging, even though we don't control the major media and major publishing organizations, by sheer word of mouth, a little radio broadcast, community newspapers, speaking here and there, Noam Chomsky speaking seventeen times a day in a hundred cities, it's possible by doing these things to actually change the culture in a very important way. When the *New York Times* had a story saying that this year the Columbus quincentennial is marked by protests, it became clear that the challenge was noticed. In Denver they called off a parade because of the protest that they expected. This has happened in a number of other places. Berkeley changed Columbus Day to Indigenous Peoples Day.

DB: *So in this doom and gloom atmosphere that the left loves to wash itself in at times there are glimpses of light?*

Traveling around the country I am encouraged by what I see. Not just about Columbus, but that as soon as you give people information that they didn't have before, they are ready to accept it. When I went around the country speaking about Columbus, I was worried that suddenly, as I started telling about these atrocities that Columbus committed, people in the audience would start yelling and shouting and throwing things at me, threatening my life. That hasn't happened at all. Maybe the worst that happened is that one Italian American said to me in a low voice, plaintively, "What are Italians going to do? Who are we going to celebrate?" I said, "Joe DiMaggio, Arturo Toscanini, Pavarotti, Fiorello LaGuardia, a whole bunch of wonderful Italians that we can celebrate."

It's been very encouraging. I believe that all over this country there are people who really want change. I don't mean the miniscule change that Clinton represents. I suppose a miniscule change is better than no change that we've been having. But there are people around this country who want much more change than the parties are offering.

DB: *Are you encouraged also by the development of new media, community radio stations, cable TV, Z, Common Courage Press, South End Press and the Open Magazine pamphlet series?*

Oh, yes.

DB: *Is there anything in American history that parallels this burst of independent media in the last ten or fifteen years?*

There have been periods in American history when pamphlets and newspapers have had an important effect in arousing and organizing a movement. In the period leading up to the Revolutionary War there was a lot of pamphleteering that was not under the control of the colonial governors. In the time of the antislavery movement, the abolitionists, the antislavery people spread literature all over the country. So much so that Andrew Jackson ordered the Postmaster General to bar abolitionist literature from the Southern states. That's Andrew Jackson, our great hero. We've had labor newspapers, the populist movement put out an enormous number of pamphlets.

But in this era of television and radio, where they soon became dominated by these monstrous, fabulously wealthy networks crowding critical voices off the air, it's been very refreshing just in the past few years to see these new media. I could see this in the Gulf War. I was invited to a gathering of several hundred community broadcasters in Boston. I didn't know so many existed. During the Gulf War they were about the only place where you could hear critical voices, Noam Chomsky and other people who would give you an analysis of the war in a critical way. You weren't getting that on public television, certainly not on the major media. Now there are satellite dishes. It's amazing that people in the progressive movement are able to use these satellite dishes to beam broadcasts all over. Wherever I go there are community newspapers. That's what we have to depend on, and we should make the most of it.

DB: *In the popular culture, ideology and propaganda are attributes of our adversaries. It's not something that we have here in our democracy. How do you persuade people in your talks and writings that in fact there is a good deal of propaganda and a great amount of ideology right here in the United States?*

The best way I can persuade them that what we get mostly from the media and the textbooks and the histories is ideological, biased not in the humanist direction but towards wealth and power, expansion, militarism, and conquest, is to give them examples from history and to show how the government has manipulated our information. You can go back to the Spanish-American War and talk about how the history textbooks all said that the reason we got into that war was that popular opinion demanded it. Therefore the president went along. There were no public opinion polls then, no mass rallies on behalf of going into Cuba. By public opinion they meant a few powerful newspapers. So when I get to the Vietnam War I talk about how the government manipulated the information, not only the general public, but the newspapers, Congress, how they fabricated incidents in the Gulf of Tonkin in the summer of 1964 to give Lyndon Johnson an excuse to go before Congress and get them to pass a resolution giving him carte blanche to start the war full-scale. I talk about the history books and how they omit what the United States has done in Latin America, and how when they get to the Spanish-American War they will talk about what we did in Cuba but not much about what we did in the Philippines: The war in Cuba lasted three months, while the war in the Philippines lasted for years. A big, bloody, Vietnam-type war. So I try to give historical examples to show how that ideology manifests itself.

DB: *Speaking of the Vietnam War, it seems it never ends, never will end. You saw examples of that in the 1992 presidential campaign, about draft status, who fought and who didn't. And the ongoing MIA/POW issue. Why is that? Why does it persist?*

The administrations, the powers that be, the people who got us into the Vietnam War and kept us in it, didn't like the way it ended. They're trying to change the ending, to rewrite history. They're saying, the reason we lost is because of the media, the antiwar movement. Or we fought with one hand behind our back. We dropped seven million tons of bombs, twice as much as we dropped in World War II, and that was "one hand tied behind our back." Incredible. They were very unhappy not just that we lost the war, but that people became aware of what happened in the war, became aware of the carnage. The My Lai massacre. The destruction of the Vietnamese countryside. The deaths of a million people in Vietnam and of 55,000 Americans. They worry that those events made the American people leery of military intervention. All the surveys taken after the Vietnam War in the late 1970s showed that the American people did not want military intervention anywhere in the world, for any reason. The establishment has been trying desperately—the military-industrial-political establishment—to change that view and to try to get the American people to accept military intervention as once more the basic American policy. Grenada was a probe, Panama another, the war in the Middle East a bigger one.

DB: *They were all short and fast.*

Exactly. They learned a number of things from Vietnam. If you're going to have a war, do it quickly. Don't give the public a chance to know what's happening. Control the information, so the war will be over before anybody really knows the truth about what happened. Here it is now, a year or two years later, and only now we're finding out that the Bush administration was arming Saddam Hussein right up to just before the war. So keep the war short. And try to have very few casualties, and don't mention the casualties on the other side. Then you can call it a "costless war." Even if 100,000 Iraqis die, even if tens of thousands of children die in Iraq, they don't count as people. So you can say it was an easy war.

DB: *You're fond also of quoting Chomsky and Edward Herman in* Manufacturing Consent. *They observe that it's hard to make a case about the manipulation of the media when they find that they're so willing to go along.*

I like that quote because so many people fall in with the media when the media say the government is controlling the information. They say, we want desperately to tell the truth to the public. But of course they don't. In the Iraqi war they showed themselves to be such weak, pathetic, absolutely obsequious yea-sayers to the briefers in Washington. They kept putting generals and ex–Joint Chiefs of Staff personnel on the air, military experts, to make us all exult in the smart bombs that were being dropped. The media did not use anybody who would give any historical background, or who would criticize the war on the air.

DB: *One of your intellectual favorites is Alan Dershowitz. In a recent column he was writing about the atrocities in the Balkans and decrying the use of the Nazi analogy. He says it is "overused and automatically invoked and as a result nearly bereft of cognitive content." What do you think of that?*

Analogies have to be used carefully. They can be misused, and sometimes they are not used as analogies but as identities, and if you say something is like something, people will say, Oh, you're saying it *is* that. It is possible to overuse the Nazi analogy until it loses its force. I was speaking to a group of high school students in Boston the other day. One of them asked, Who was worse, Hitler or Columbus? There's a nice analogy. They are two different situations, two different forms of genocide. In fact, in that situation it was not an exaggeration. In terms of the numbers of people who died, the Hitler killing was smaller than the number of people who died in the genocide not committed directly by Columbus, but as a result of the work of the *conquistadores*, Columbus, and the others, when they got through with the Caribbean and Latin America. Perhaps fifty million people or more died, the indigenous population, as a result of enslavement, overwork, direct execution, disease, a much higher toll even than the genocide of Hitler.

I think it's all right to invoke analogies, so long as you invoke them carefully and make clear what the differences are and the similarities.

DB: *In addition to wiping out the indigenous population, the Europeans had to initiate the slave trade and bring over the Africans to work the land.*

When the Indians were gone as workers, that's when the slave trade began, and another genocide took place, tens of millions of black slaves brought over, dying by the millions on the way and then dying in great numbers when they got here.

DB: *In that same Dershowitz column, he talks about the uniqueness of the Jewish Holocaust in terms of genocide, that it stands by itself. Would you accept that?*

It depends on what you mean by "unique." Every genocide obviously stands by itself in that every genocide has its own peculiar historical characteristics. But I think it is wrong, and we should understand that, to take any one genocide and concentrate on it to the neglect of others and act as if there has only been one great genocide in the world and nobody should bring up any other because it's a poor analogy. The greatest gift the Jews could give to the world is not to remember Hitler's genocide for exactly what it was, that is, the genocide of Jews, but to take what that horrible experience was for Jews and then to apply it to all the other things that are going on in the world, where huge numbers of people are dying for no reason at all. Apply it to the starvation in Somalia and the way people are treated by the advanced industrial countries in the Third World, where huge numbers of people die in wars or for economic reasons. I think in that sense what happened in the Holocaust is not unique. It should not be left alone. It should be applied everywhere it can, because that is past. The other genocides are present and future.

DB: *Let's talk a little about Hollywood and history. Michael Parenti, in a book entitled* Make-Believe Media, *suggests that in an increasingly non-literate society, film has the "last frame," the last chapter of history. I'd like you to connect that with a discussion about Oliver Stone's docudrama* JFK. *He has said, "The American people deserve to have their history back." What about the assumption that history was once ours and is now lost?*

Of course, it was never ours. History has always belonged to the people who controlled whatever present there was. They control history. So it's not a matter of taking it back. Very often people will say, Let us restore America to what it once was. To what? Slavery? Let us restore the good old days? The good old days lie ahead. Film is tremendously important. I don't know whether it's the last frame. I'm even dubious about whether films, as powerful as they are at the moment that they capture you, have the lasting effect that literature and writing have. I don't know this for sure. We have fewer and fewer people reading books. Are the statistics on that clear? I know everybody says this. I know that students are not reading books the way they used to. I know there are millions of people in this country who read books, and obviously many more millions who don't read books. In that sense it's true. They are watching videos, watching television, and going to the movies. People who are not reached by books have only videos, movies, and television. Then they become especially important. I agree with the importance of the visual media. I love the movies. I'm very happy when I see a movie made that I think does something to advance people's social consciousness. I have a special place in my heart for movies that have something important to say.

When I saw Oliver Stone's movie *Salvador* I thought it was a very powerful statement about the brutal American policy supporting the dictatorship and the death squads of El Salvador. When I saw *Born on the Fourth of July*, I thought, This is great. He's bringing the antiwar movement before millions of people and showing that there's no conflict between soldiers in Vietnam and the antiwar movement. Soldiers came back from Vietnam and joined the antiwar movement, as Ron Kovic did.

When I saw *JFK* I did not have the same feeling. I thought he was contradicting what he was doing in *Born on the Fourth of July*, where he was saying, We had an antiwar movement in this country. If the war came to an end, it was in good part because people like Ron Kovic and Vietnam veterans and all the other people who protested against the war showed us what a social movement was like. But in *JFK* he is telling us that the key to ending the war was the president of the United States. If Kennedy had lived he would have ended the war. That viewpoint perpetuates an elitist notion in history which I've been struggling against. I think that Oliver Stone in his better films is also struggling against it, the idea that history is made from the top, and if we want change to come about we must depend on our presidents, on the Supreme Court, on Congress. If history shows anything, to me, it shows that we cannot depend on those people on top to make the necessary changes towards justice and peace. It's social movements we must depend on to do that.

Part 2

THE POLITICS OF HISTORY

WHAT IS RADICAL HISTORY?

from *The Politics of History* (1970)

Howard Zinn is the most well-known and bestselling radical historian in American history. He believed deeply in the power of history to illuminate social problems and inspire people to social action, and he devoted his career to producing works that would do just that. In this essay, Howard calls for a "value-laden historiography," advancing "the idea of writing history in such a way as to extend human sensibilities." Here, he offers not so much a defense of radical history as a clarion call for more of it. Citing the emergence of Black Studies programs in the late 1960s as the modern catalyst for a more radical interpretation of the past, Howard outlines five ways that this approach to history can "untie our minds, our bodies, our disposition to move": by sharpening our understanding of social problems and forging greater empathy for human suffering; by showing that the pretentions of government are neither neutral nor usually benevolent; by exposing those ideologies that seek merely to preserve the status quo; by highlighting past moments or movements where social change has been possible; and by offering sober lessons about why such moments or movements sometimes falter or fail. Eschewing "objectivity" as the central aspiration of historians, Howard begins this essay with one of his signature assertions—"the historian cannot choose to be neutral; he writes on a moving train"—one that would eventually become the title of his acclaimed 1994 memoir, *You Can't Be Neutral on a Moving Train*. For Howard, history "is not a well-ordered city (despite the neat stacks of the library), but a jungle. . . . The only thing I am really sure of is that we who plunge into the jungle need to think about what we are doing, because there *is* somewhere we want to go." Howard Zinn was always a man on the move, and this essay describes the engine that powered his career.

————

HISTORICAL WRITING ALWAYS has some effect on us. It may reinforce our passivity; it may activate us. In any case, the historian cannot choose to be neutral; he writes on a moving train.

Sometimes, what he tells may change a person's life. In May 1968 I heard a Catholic priest, on trial in Milwaukee for burning the records of a draft board, tell (I am paraphrasing) how he came to that act:

> I was trained in Rome. I was quite conservative, never broke a rule in seminary. Then I read a book by Gordon Zahn, called *German Catholics and Hitler's Wars*. It told how the Catholic Church carried on its normal activities while Hitler carried on his. It told how SS men went to mass, then went out to round up Jews. That book changed my life. I decided the church must never behave again as it did in the past; and that I must not.

This is unusually clear. In most cases, where people turn in new directions, the causes are so complex, so subtle, that they are impossible to trace. Nevertheless, we all are aware of how, in one degree or another, things we read or heard changed our view of the world, or how we must behave. We know there have been many people who themselves did not experience evil, but who became persuaded that it existed, and that they must oppose it. What makes us human is our capacity to reach with our mind beyond our immediate sensory capacities, to feel in some degree what others feel totally, and then perhaps to act on such feelings.

I start, therefore, from the idea of writing history in such a way as to extend human sensibilities, not out of this book into other books, but into the going conflict over how people shall live, and whether they shall live.

I am urging value-laden historiography. For those who still rebel at this—despite my argument that this does not determine answers, only questions; despite my plea that aesthetic work, done for pleasure, should always have its place; despite my insistence that our work is value-laden whether we choose or not—let me point to one area of American education where my idea has been accepted. I am speaking of "Black Studies," which, starting about 1969, began to be adopted with great speed in the nation's universities.

These multiplying Black Studies programs do not pretend to just introduce another subject for academic inquiry. They have the specific intention of so affecting the consciousness of black and white people in this country as to diminish for both groups the pervasive American belief in black inferiority.

This deliberate attempt to foster racial equality should be joined, I am suggesting, by similar efforts for national and class equality. This will probably come, as the Black Studies programs, not by a gradual acceptance of the appropriate arguments, but by a crisis so dangerous as to *demand* quick changes in attitude. Scholarly exhortation is, therefore, not likely to initiate a new emphasis in historical writing, but perhaps it can support and ease it.

What kind of awareness moves people in humanistic directions, and how can historical writing create such awareness, such movement? I can think of five ways in which history can be useful. That is only a rough beginning. I don't want to lay down formulas. There will be useful histories written that do not fit into preconceived categories. I want only to sharpen the focus for myself and others who would rather have their writing guided by human aspiration than by professional habit.

1. *We can intensify, expand, sharpen our perception of how bad things are, for the victims of the world.* This becomes less and less a philanthropic act as all of us, regardless of race, geography, or class, become potential victims of a burned, irradiated planet. But even our own victimization is separated from us by time and the fragility of our imagination, as that of others is separated from us because most of us are white, prosperous, and within the walls of a country so over-armed it is much more likely to be an aggressor than a victim.

History can try to overcome both kinds of separation. The fascinating progression of a past historical event can have greater effect on us than some cool, logical discourse on the dangerous possibilities of present trends—if only for one reason, because we learn the end of that story. True, there is a chill in the contemplation of nuclear war, but it is still a contemplation whose most horrible possibilities we cannot bring ourselves to accept. It is a portent that for full effect needs buttressing by another story whose conclusion is known. Surely, in this nuclear age our concern over the proliferation of H-bombs is powerfully magnified as we read Barbara Tuchman's account of the coming of the First World War:[1]

> War pressed against every frontier. Suddenly dismayed, govern-
> ments struggled and twisted to fend it off. It was no use. Agents at

frontiers were reporting every cavalry patrol as a deployment to beat the mobilization gun. General staffs, goaded by their relentless timetables, were pounding the table for the signal to move lest their opponents gain an hour's head start. Appalled upon the brink, the chiefs of state who would be ultimately responsible for their country's fate attempted to back away but the pull of military schedules dragged them forward.

There it is, *us*. In another time, of course. But unmistakably us.

Other kinds of separation, from the deprived and harried people of the world—the black, the poor, the prisoners—are sometimes easier to overcome across time than across space: hence the value of historical recollection. Both the *Autobiography of Malcolm X* and the *Autobiography of Frederick Douglass* are history, one more recent than the other. Both assault our complacency. So do the photos on television of blacks burning buildings in the ghetto today, but the autobiographies do something special: they let us look closely, carefully, personally behind the impersonality of those blacks on the screen. They invade our homes, as the blacks in the ghetto have not yet done; and our minds, which we tend to harden against the demands of *now*. They tell us, in some small degree, what it is like to be black, in a way that all the liberal clichés about the downtrodden Negro could never match. And thus they insist that we act; they explain why blacks are acting. They prepare us, if not to initiate, to respond.

Slavery is over, but its degradation now takes other forms, at the bottom of which is the unspoken belief that the black person is not quite a human being. The recollection of what slavery is like, what slaves are like, helps to attack that belief. Take the letter Frederick Douglass wrote his former master in 1848, on the tenth anniversary of his flight to freedom:[2]

> I have selected this day to address you because it is the anniversary of my emancipation. . . . Just ten years ago this beautiful September morning yon bright sun beheld me a slave—a poor, degraded chattel—trembling at the sound of your voice, lamenting that I was a man . . .
>
> When yet but a child about six years old I imbibed the determination to run away. The very first mental effort that I now remember on my part, was an attempt to solve the mystery, Why am I a slave. . . . When I saw a slave driver whip a slave woman . . . and heard her piteous cries, I went away into the corner of the fence, wept and pondered over the mystery. . . . I resolved that I would someday run away.

> The morality of the act, I dispose as follows: I am myself; you
> are yourself; we are two distinct persons. What you are, I am. I
> am not by nature bound to you nor you to me. . . . In leaving you
> I took nothing but what belonged to me . . .

Why do we need to reach into the past, into the days of slavery? Isn't
the experience of Malcolm X, in our own time enough? I see two values in going back. One is that dealing with the past, our guard is down,
because we start off thinking it is over and we have nothing to fear by
taking it all in. We turn out to be wrong, because its immediacy strikes
us, affects us before we know it; when we have recognized this, it is too
late—we have been moved. Another reason is that time adds depth and
intensity to a problem which otherwise might seem a passing one, sus-
ceptible to being brushed away. To know that long continuity, across the
centuries, of the degradation that stalked both Frederick Douglass and
Malcolm X (between whose lives stretched that of W.E.B. Du Bois,
recorded in *The Souls of Black Folk* and *Dusk of Dawn*) is to reveal how
infuriatingly long has been this black ordeal in white America. If nothing else, it would make us understand in that black mood of today what
we might otherwise see as impatience, and what history tells us is over-
long endurance.

Can history also sharpen our perception of that poverty hidden from
sight by the foliage of the suburbs? The poor, like the black, become
invisible in a society blinded by the glitter of its own luxury. True, we can
be forcefully reminded that they exist, as we were in the United States in
the 1960s when our sensibilities had been sharpened by the civil rights
revolt, and our tolerance of government frayed by the Vietnamese war.
At such a time, books like Michael Harrington's *The Other America* jabbed
at us, without going back into the past, just supplying a periscope so
that we could see around the corner, and demanding that we look.

Where history can help is by showing us how other people similarly
situated, in other times, were blind to how their neighbors were living,
in the same city. Suppose that, amidst the "prosperity" of the 1950s, we
had read about the 1920s, another era of affluence. Looking hard, we
might find the report of Senator Burton Wheeler of Montana, investigating conditions in Pennsylvania during the coal strike of 1928:[3]

> All day long I have listened to heartrending stories of women
> evicted from their homes by the coal companies. I heard pitiful
> pleas of little children crying for bread. I stood aghast as I heard

most amazing stories from men brutally beaten by private policemen. It has been a shocking and nerve-racking experience.

Would this not suggest to us that perhaps in our time too a veil is drawn
over the lives of many Americans, that the sounds of prosperity drown
out all else, and the voices of the well-off dominate history?

In our time, as in the past, we construct "history" on the basis of accounts left by the most articulate, the most privileged members of
society. The result is a distorted picture of how people live, an underes-
timation of poverty, a failure to portray vividly the situations of those
in distress. If, in the past, we can manage to find the voice of the under-
dog, this may lead us to look for the lost pleas of our own era. True, we
could accomplish this directly for the present without going back. But
sometimes the disclosure of what is hidden in the past prompts us, particularly when there is no immediate prod, to look more penetratingly
into contemporary society. (In my own experience, reading in the
papers of Fiorello LaGuardia the letters from the East Harlem poor in
the twenties, made me take a second look at the presumed good times
of the fifties.)

Is the picture of society given by its victims a true one? There is no
one true picture of any historical situation, no one objective description. This search for a nonexistent objectivity has led us, ironically, into
a particularly retrogressive subjectivity, that of the bystander. Society
has varying and conflicting interests; what is called objectivity is the
disguise of one of these interests—that of neutrality. But neutrality is a
fiction in an unneutral world. There are victims, there are executioners,
and there are bystanders. In the dynamism of our time, when heads roll
into the basket every hour, what is "true" varies according to what happens to your own head—and the "objectivity" of the bystander calls for
inaction while other heads fall. In Camus's *The Plague*, Dr. Rieux says:
"All I maintain is that on this earth there are pestilences, and there are
victims, and it's up to us, so far as possible, not to join forces with the
pestilences." Not to act is to join forces with the spreading plague.

What is the "truth" about the situation of the black man in the
United States in 1968? Statistics can be put together which show that his
position has improved. Statistics can be put together which show that
his situation is as bad as it always was. Both sets of statistics are "true."*

---

*See Vivian Henderson, *The Economic Status of Negroes*, Southern Regional Council,
1963. One sentence in the *Report of the National Advisory Commission on Civil Disorders*,

But the first leads to a satisfaction with the present rate of change; the second leads to a desire for quickening the rate of change. The closest we can come to that elusive "objectivity" is to report accurately *all* of the subjectivities in a situation. But we emphasize one or another of those subjective views in any case. I suggest we depart from our customary position as privileged observers. Unless we wrench free from being what we like to call "objective," we are closer psychologically, whether we like to admit it or not, to the executioner than to the victim.

There is no need to hide the data which show that some Negroes are climbing the traditional American ladder faster than before, that the ladder is more crowded than before. But there is a need—coming from the determination to represent those still wanting the necessities of existence (food, shelter, dignity, freedom)—to emphasize the lives of those who cannot even get near the ladder. The latest report of the Census Bureau is as "true," in some abstract sense, as the reports of Malcolm X and Eldridge Cleaver on their lives. But the radical historian will, without hiding the former (there are already many interests at work to tell us that, anyway) emphasize those facts we are most likely to ignore—and these are the facts as seen by the victims.

Thus, a history of slavery drawn from the narratives of fugitive slaves is especially important. It cannot monopolize the historiography in any case, because the histories we already have are those from the standpoint of the slaveholder (Ulrich Phillip's account, based on plantation diaries, for instance), or from the standpoint of the cool observer (the liberal historian, chastising slavery but without the passion appropriate to a call for action). A slave-oriented history simply fills out the picture in such a way as to pull us out of lethargy.

The same is true in telling the story of the American Revolution from the standpoint of the sailor rather than the merchant,[4] and for telling the story of the Mexican War from the standpoint of the Mexicans. The point is not to omit the viewpoint of the privileged (that dominates the field anyway), but to remind us forcibly that there is always a tendency, now as then, to see history from the top. Perhaps a history of the Opium War seen through Chinese eyes would suggest to Americans that the Vietnamese war might also be seen through Vietnamese eyes.*

Bantam, 1968, p. 13, reveals the complexity: "Although there have been gains in Negro income nationally, and a decline in the number of Negroes below the 'poverty level,' the condition of Negroes in the central city remains in a state of crisis."

*See the letter of Commissioner Lin to Queen Victoria in Teng, Ssu-yü, and Fairbank, John K., *China's Response to the West*, Harvard University, 1954, p. 24.

2. *We can expose the pretensions of governments to either neutrality or beneficence.* If the first requisite for activating people is to sharpen their awareness of what is wrong, the second is to disabuse them of the confidence that they can depend on governments to rectify what is wrong.

Again, I start from the premise that there are terrible wrongs all about us, too many for us to rest content even if not everyone is being wronged. Governments of the world have not been disposed to change things very much. Indeed, they have often been the perpetrators of these wrongs. To drive this point at us strongly pushes us to act ourselves.

Does this mean I am not being "objective" about the role of governments? Let us take a look at the historical role of the United States on the race question. For instance, what did the various American governments do for the black person in America right after the Civil War? Let's be "objective," in the sense of telling *all* the facts that answer this question. Therefore we should take proper note of the Thirteenth, Fourteenth, Fifteenth Amendments, the Freedman's Bureau, the stationing of armed forces in the South, the passage of civil rights laws in 1866, 1870, 1871, and 1875. But we should also record the court decisions emasculating the Fourteenth Amendment, the betrayal of the Negro in the 1877 Hayes-Tilden agreement, the nonenforcement of the civil rights acts. Ultimately, even if we told all, our emphasis in the end would be subjective—it would depend on who we are and what we want. A present concern, that citizens need to act themselves, suggests we emphasize the unreliability of government in securing equal rights for black people.

Another question: to what extent can we rely on our government to equitably distribute the wealth of the country? We could take proper account of the laws passed in this century which seemed directed at economic justice: the railroad regulation acts of the Progressive era, the creation of the graduated income tax in the Wilson administration, the suits against trusts initiated in the Theodore Roosevelt and Taft administrations. But a *present* recognition of the fact that the allocation of wealth to the upper and lower fifths of the population has not fundamentally changed in this century would suggest that all that legislation has only managed to maintain the status quo. To change this, we would need to emphasize what has not so far been emphasized, the persistent failure of government to alter the continuing inequities of the American economic system.

Historians' assessments of the New Deal illustrate this problem. We can all be "objective" by including in any description of the New Deal both its wealth of reform legislation and its inadequacies in eradicating poverty and unemployment in America. But there is always an emphasis, subtle or gross, which we bring to bear on this picture. One kind of emphasis adds to a feeling of satisfaction in how America has been able to deal with economic crisis. Another stimulates us to do more ourselves, in the light of the past failure at dealing with the fundamental irrationality by which our nation's resources are distributed. The needs of the present suggest that the second kind of historical presentation is preferable.*

Thus, it is worth putting in their proper little place the vaunted liberal reforms of the Wilson administration. For instance, in a situation like the Ludlow Massacre of 1914, Wilson called out the federal troops not when the striking miners of Colorado were being machine-gunned by the Baldwin-Felts detectives or their homes burned by the National Guard, but when they began to arm and retaliate on a large scale. To take another case, it is useful to know that social security measures were proposed in 1935 beyond those supported by FDR, but that he pushed more moderate proposals. In the light of our belated recognition that social security payments are now and have always been pitifully inadequate, how we view FDR's social security program may or may not reinforce our determination to change things.

A radical history, then, would expose the limitations of governmental reform, the connections of government to wealth and privilege, the tendencies of governments toward war and xenophobia, the play of money and power behind the presumed neutrality of law. It would illustrate the role of government in maintaining things as they are, whether by force, or deception, or by a skillful combination of both—whether by deliberate plan or by the concatenation of thousands of individuals playing roles according to the expectations around them.

Such motivating facts are available in the wealth of data about present governments. What historical material can do is to add the depth that time imparts to an idea. What one sees in the present may be

---

*This should not be confused with "the search for culpability," as Jerald S. Auerbach puts it, criticizing the New Left critics of the New Deal. The point is not to denounce the New Deal of FDR, nor to praise it; that kind of historical evaluation is useless, as I suggest in my discussion of responsibility in Chapter 17 of this book. Auerbach, in "New Deal, Old Deal, or Raw Deal:Some Thoughts on New Left Historiography," *Journal of Southern History*, February 1969, mistakes the intention of those who (like myself in *New Deal Thought*, Bobbs-Merrill, 1966, or like Paul Conkin, in *The New Deal*, Thomas Crowell, 1967) stress the inadequacies of the Roosevelt reforms. Our aim is not castigation of past politics, but stimulation of present citizens.

attributable to a passing phenomenon; if the same situation appears at various points in history, it becomes not a transitory event, but a long-range condition, not an aberration, but a structural deformity requiring serious attention.

For instance, we would see more clearly the limitations of government investigating committees set up to deal with deep-rooted social problems if we knew the history of such committees. Take Kenneth Clark's blunt testimony to the National Advisory Commission on Civil Disorders, which was set up after the urban outbreaks of 1967. Pointing to a similar investigation set up after the 1919 riot in Chicago, he said:[5]

> I read that report . . . of the 1919 riot in Chicago, and it is as if I were reading the report of the investigating committee on the Harlem riot of '35, the report of the investigating committee on the Harlem riot of '43, the report of the McCone Commission on the Watts riot. I must again in candor say to you members of this Commission—it is a kind of Alice in Wonderland—with the same moving picture, reshown over and over again, the same analysis, the same recommendations, and the same inaction.

3. *We can expose the ideology that pervades our culture—using "ideology" in Mannheim's sense: rationale for the going order.* There is the open sanctification of racism, of war, of economic inequality. There is also the more subtle supportive tissue of half-truths ("We are not like the imperialist powers of the nineteenth century"); noble myths ("We were born free"); pretenses ("Education is the disinterested pursuit of knowledge"); the mystification of rhetoric ("freedom and justice for all"); the confusion of ideals and reality (The Declaration of Independence and its call for revolution, in our verbal tradition; the Smith Act and its prohibition of calls for revolution, on our lawbooks); the use of symbols to obscure reality ("Remember the *Maine*," vis-à-vis rotten beef for the troops); the innocence of the double standard (deploring the violence of John Brown; hailing the violence of Ulysses Grant); the concealment of ironies (using the Fourteenth Amendment to help corporations instead of Negroes).

The more widespread is education in a society, the more mystification is required to conceal what is wrong; church, school, and the written word work together for that concealment. This is not the work of a conspiracy; the privileged of society are as much victims of the going mythology as the teachers, priests, and journalists who spread it. All simply do what comes naturally, and what comes naturally is to say what has always been said, to believe what has always been believed.

History has a special ability to reveal the ludicrousness of those beliefs which glue us all to the social frame of our fathers. It also can reinforce that frame with great power, and has done so most of the time. Our problem is to turn the power of history—which can work both ways—to the job of demystification. I recall the words of the iconoclast sociologist E. Franklin Frazier to Negro college students one evening in Atlanta, Georgia: "All your life, white folks have bamboozled you, preachers have bamboozled you, teachers have bamboozled you; I am here to debamboozle you."

Recalling the rhetoric of the past, and measuring it against the actual past, may enable us to see through our current bamboozlement, where the reality is still unfolding, and the discrepancies still not apparent. To read Albert Beveridge's noble plea in the Senate January 9, 1900, urging acquisition of the Philippines with "thanksgiving to Almighty God that He has marked us as His chosen people, henceforth to lead in the regeneration of the world," and then to read of our butchery of the Filipino rebels who wanted independence, is to prepare us better for speeches about our "world responsibility" today. That recollection might make us properly suspicious of Arthur Schlesinger's attempt to set a "historical framework" for Vietnam comprised of "two traditional and entirely honorable strands in American thinking," one of which "is the concept that the United States has a saving mission in the world."[6] In the light of the history of idea and fact in American expansionism, that strand is not quite honorable. The Vietnam disaster was not, as Schlesinger says, "a final and tragic misapplication" of those strands, a wandering from a rather benign historical tradition, but another twining of the deadly strands around a protesting foreign people.

To take another example where the history of ideas is suggestive for today: we might clarify for ourselves the puzzling question of how to account for American expansion into the Pacific in the post–World War II period when the actual material interests there do not seem to warrant such concern. Marilyn B. Young, in her study of the Open Door period, indicates how the mystique of being "a world power" carried the United States into strong action despite "the lack of commercial and financial interest." Thus, "The Open Door passed into the small body of sacred American doctrine and an assumption of America's 'vital stake' in China was made and never relinquished."[7] Her book documents the buildup of this notion of the "vital stake," in a way that might make us more loath to accept unquestioningly the claims of American leaders defending incursions into Asian countries today.

For Americans caught up in the contemporary glorification of efficiency and success, without thought of ends, it might be liberating to read simultaneously *All Quiet on the Western Front* (for the fetid reality of World War I) and Randolph Bourne's comment on the American intellectuals of 1917:[8]

> They have, in short, no clear philosophy of life except that of intelligent service, the admirable adaptation of means to ends. They are vague as to what kind of a society they want or what kind of society America needs, but they are equipped with all the administrative attitudes and talents necessary to attain it. . . . It is now becoming plain that unless you start with the vividest kind of poetic vision, your instrumentalism is likely to land you just where it has landed this younger intelligentsia which is so happily and busily engaged in the national enterprise of war.

4. *We can recapture those few moments in the past which show the possibility of a better way of life than that which has dominated the earth thus far.* To move men to act it is not enough to enhance their sense of what is wrong, to show that the men in power are untrustworthy, to reveal that our very way of thinking is limited, distorted, corrupted. One must also show that something else is possible, that changes can take place. Otherwise, people retreat into privacy, cynicism, despair, or even collaboration with the mighty.

History cannot provide confirmation that something better is inevitable; but it can uncover evidence that it is conceivable. It can point to moments when human beings cooperated with one another (the organization of the underground railroad by black and white, the French Resistance to Hitler, the anarchist achievements in Catalonia during the Spanish Civil War). It can find times when governments were capable of a bit of genuine concern (the creation of the Tennessee Valley Authority, the free medical care in socialist countries, the equal-wages principle of the Paris Commune). It can disclose men and women acting as heroes rather than culprits or fools (the story of Thoreau or Wendell Phillips or Eugene Debs, or Martin Luther King or Rosa Luxemburg). It can remind us that apparently powerless groups have won against overwhelming odds (the abolitionists and the Thirteenth Amendment, the CIO and the sit-down strikes, the Vietminh and the Algerians against the French).

Historical evidence has special functions. It lends weight and depth to evidence which, if culled only from contemporary life, might seem frail. And, by portraying the movements of men over time, it shows the possibility of change. Even if the actual change has been so small as to leave us still desperate today, we need, to spur us on, the faith that change is possible. Thus, while taking proper note of how much remains to be done, it is important to compare the consciousness of white Americans about black people in the 1930s and in the 1960s to see how a period of creative conflict can change people's minds and behavior. Also, while noting how much remains to be done in China, it is important to see with what incredible speed the Chinese Communists have been able to mobilize seven hundred million people against famine and disease. We need to know, in the face of terrifying power behind the accusing shouts against us who rebel, that we are not mad; that men in the past, whom we know, in the perspective of time, to have been great, felt as we do. At moments when we are tempted to go along with the general condemnation of revolution, we need to refresh ourselves with Thomas Jefferson and Tom Paine. At times when we are about to surrender to the glorification of law, Thoreau and Tolstoi can revive our conviction that justice supersedes law.

That is why, for instance, Staughton Lynd's book, *Intellectual Origins of American Radicalism*, is useful history. It recalls an eighteenth-century Anglo-American tradition declaring:[9]

> . . . that the proper foundation for government is a universal law of right and wrong self-evident to the intuitive common sense of every man; that freedom is a power of personal self-direction which no man can delegate to another; that the purpose of society is not the protection of property but fulfillment of the needs of living human beings; that good citizens have the right and duty, not only to overthrow incurable oppressive governments, but before that point is reached to break particular oppressive laws; and that we owe our ultimate allegiance, not to this or that nation, but to the whole family of man.

In a time when that tradition has been befogged by cries on all sides for "law and order" and "patriotism" (a word playing on the ambiguity between concern for one's government and concern for one's fellows) we need to remind ourselves of the *depth* of the humanistic, revolutionary impulse. The reach across the centuries conveys that depth.

By the criteria I have been discussing, a recollection of that tradition is radical history. It is therefore worth looking briefly at why Lynd's book has been criticized harshly by another radical, Eugene Genovese, who is a historian interested in American slavery.[10]

Genovese is troubled that *Intellectual Origins of American Radicalism* is "plainly meant to serve political ends." If he only were criticizing "the assumption that myth-making and falsifying in historical writing can be of political use" (for instance, the history written by so-called Marxists in the Stalinist mode) then he would be right. But Genovese seems to mean something else, for Lynd is certainly telling us the straight truth about the ideas of those early Anglo-American thinkers. He says a historical work should not deal with the past in terms of "moral standards abstracted from any time and place."

Specifically, Genovese does not like the way Lynd uses the ideas of the Declaration of Independence as a kind of "moral absolutism" transcending time, connecting radicals of the eighteenth century with those of the twentieth, while failing to discuss "the role of class or the historical setting of the debates among radicals." He is critical of the fact that "Lynd never discusses the relation of these ideas to the social groups that hold them" and claims Lynd "denies the importance of the social context in which ideas occur," rather seeing the great moral truths as "self-evident and absolute." This means to Genovese that Lynd "thereby denies the usefulness of history except for purposes of moral exhortation." He says Lynd leaves out "the working class, the socialist movements" and the "counter-tendencies and opposing views of the Left," thus making the book "a travesty of history."

It is a powerful and important criticism. But I believe Genovese is wrong—not in his description of what Lynd does, but in his estimate of its worth. His plea not to discuss the past by moral standards "abstracted from time and place" is inviting because we (especially we professional historians) are attached to the anchor of historical particularity, and do not want some ethereal, utopian standard of judgment. But to abstract from time and place is not to remove completely from time and place; it is rather to remove enough of the historical detail so that common ground can be found between two or more historical periods—or more specifically, between another period and our own. (It is, indeed, only carrying further what we must of necessity do even when we are discussing *the* moral standard of any one time and place, or *the* view of any one social movement—because all are unique on the most concrete level.) To study the past in the light of what Genovese calls "moral absolutism" is really to study the past *relative* to ideals which move us in the present but which are broad enough to have moved other people in other times in history.

The lure of "time and place" is the lure of the professional historian interested in "my period" or "my topic," These particularities of time and place can be enormously useful, depending on the question that is asked. But if the question being asked is (as for Lynd): What support can we find in the past for values that seem worthwhile today?—a good deal of circumstantial evidence is not especially relevant. Only if *no* present question is asked, does all the particular detail, the rich, complex, endless detail of a period become important, without discrimination. And that, I would argue, is a much more abstract kind of history, because it is abstracted from a specific present concern. That, I would claim, is a surrender to the absolute of professional historiography: Tell as much as you can.

Similarly, the demand for "the role of class" in treating the natural-right ideas of Locke, Paine, and others, would be very important if the question being asked was: how do class backgrounds and ideas interact on one another (to better understand the weaknesses of both ideological and Utopian thinking today). But for Staughton Lynd's special purpose, another emphasis was required. When one focuses on history with certain questions, much is left out. But this is true even when there is a lack of focus.

Similar to the professional dogma requiring "time and place" is a dogma among Marxist intellectuals requiring "the role of class" as if this were the touchstone for radical history. Even if one replaced (as Genovese is anxious to do) the economic determinism of a crude Marxism with "a sophisticated class analysis of historical change," discussing class "as a complex mixture of material interests, ideologies, and psychological attitudes," this may or may not move people forward toward change today. That—the total effect of history on the social setting today—is the criterion for a truly radical history, and not some abstract, absolute standard of methodology to which Marxists as well as others can get obsessively attached.

For instance, Genovese agrees that one of the great moral truths Lynd discusses—the use of conscience against authority as the ultimate test for political morality—was a revolutionary force in the past. But for Genovese this is a historical fact about a particular period, whereas: "Lynd seeks to graft them on to a socialist revolution, the content of which he never discusses. He merely asserts that they form the kernel of revolutionary socialist thought, although no socialist movement has ever won power with such an ideology. . . ." This is precisely the reason for asserting a moral value shared by certain eighteenth-century thinkers (and, on a certain level, by Marx and Engels): that socialist movements thus far have *not* paid sufficient attention to the right of conscience against *all* states. To be truly radical is to maintain a set of transcendental beliefs (yes, absolutes) by which to judge and thus to transform any particular social system.

In sum, while there is a value to specific analysis of particular historical situations, there is another kind of value to the unearthing of ideals which cross historical periods and give strength to beliefs needing reinforcement today. The trouble is, even Marxist historians have not paid sufficient attention to the Marxian admonition in his *Theses on Feuerbach*: "The dispute over the reality or nonreality of thinking which is isolated from practice is a purely scholastic question." Any dispute over a "true" history cannot be resolved in theory; the real question is, which of the several possible "true" histories (on that elementary level of factual truth) is *true*, not to some dogmatic notion about what a radical interpretation should contain, but to the practical needs for social change in our day? If the "political ends" Genovese warns against and Lynd espouses are not the narrow interests of a nation or party or ideology, but those humanistic values we have not yet attained, it is desirable that history should serve political ends.

5. *We can show how good social movements can go wrong, how leaders can betray their followers, how rebels can become bureaucrats, how ideals can become frozen and reified.* This is needed as a corrective to the blind faith that revolutionaries often develop in their movements, leaders, theories, so that future actors for social change can avoid the traps of the past. To use Karl Mannheim's distinction, while *ideology* is the tendency of those in power to falsify, *utopianism* is the tendency of those out of power to distort. History can show us the manifestations of the latter as well as the former.

History should put us on guard against the tendency of revolutionaries to devour their followers along with their professed principles. We need to remind ourselves of the failure of the American revolutionaries to eliminate slavery, despite the pretensions of the Declaration of Independence, and the failure of the new republic to deal justly with the Whiskey Rebels in Pennsylvania despite the fact a revolution had been fought against unjust taxes. Similarly, we need to recall the cry of protest against the French Revolution, in its moment of triumph, by Jacques

Roux and the poor of Gravillers, protesting against profiteering, or by Jean Varlet, declaring: "Despotism has passed from the palace of the kings to the circle of a committee."* Revolutionaries, without dimming their enthusiasm for change, should read Khrushchev's speech to the Twentieth Party Congress in 1956, with its account of the paranoid cruelties of Stalin.

The point is not to turn us away from social movements but into *critical* participants in them, by showing us how easy it is for rebels to depart from their own claims. For instance, it might make us aware of our own tendencies—enlightened though we are—to be paternal to the aggrieved to read the speech of the black abolitionist Theodore S. Wright, at the 1837 Utica convention of the New York Anti-Slavery Society. Wright criticized "the spirit of the slaver" among white Abolitionists. Or we might read the reply of Henry Highland Garnet in 1843 to the white Abolitionist lady who rebuked him for his militancy:[11]

> You say I have received "bad counsel." You are not the only person who has told your humble servant that his humble productions have been produced by the "counsel" of some Anglo-Saxon. I have expected no more from ignorant slaveholders and their apologists, but I really looked for better things from Mrs. Maria W. Chapman, antislavery poetess and editor pro tem of the Boston *Liberator* . . .

The history of radical movements can make us watchful for narcissistic arrogance, the blind idolization of leaders, the substitution of dogma for a careful look at the environment, the lure of compromise when leaders of a movement hobnob too frequently with those in power. For anyone joyful over the election of socialists to office in a capitalist state, the recounting by Robert Michels of the history of the German Social Democratic Party is enlightening. Michels shows how parliamentary power can be corrupting, because radicals elected to office become separated from the rank and file of their own movement, and are invested with a prestige which makes it more difficult to criticize their actions.[12]

> During the discussions in the Reichstag concerning the miners' strike in the basin of the Ruhr (1905), the deputy Hue spoke of the

*For a marvelous historical document of this aspect of the French Revolution, see Scott, ed., *The Defense of Gracchus Babeuf Before the High Court of Vendôme*, University of Massachusetts Press, 1967.

maximum program of the party as "utopian," and in the socialist press there was manifested no single symptom of revolt. On the first occasion on which the party departed from its principle of unconditional opposition to all military expenditure, contenting itself with simple abstention when the first credit of 1,500,000 marks was voted for the war against the Hereros, this remarkable innovation, which in every other socialist party would have un-questionably evoked a storm from one section of the members . . . aroused among the German socialists no more than a few dis-persed and timid protests.

Such searching histories of radical movements can deter the tendency to make absolutes of those instruments—party, leaders, platforms—which should be constantly subject to examination.

That revolutionaries themselves are burdened by tradition, and cannot completely break from thinking in old ways, was seen by Marx in the re-markable passage opening *The Eighteenth Brumaire of Louis Bonaparte*:

Men make their own history, but they do not make it just as they please; they do not make it under circumstances chosen by them-selves, but under circumstances directly found, given and trans-mitted from the past. The tradition of all the dead generations weighs like a nightmare on the brain of the living. And just when they seem engaged in revolutionizing themselves and things, in creating something entirely new, precisely in such epochs of rev-olutionary crisis they anxiously conjure up the spirits of the past to their service and borrow from them names, battle slogans and costumes in order to present the new scene of world history in this time-honored disguise and this borrowed language . . .

How to use the past to change the world, and yet not be encumbered by it—both skills can be sharpened by a judicious culling of past experi-ence. But the delicate balance between them cannot come from historical data alone—only from a clearly focused vision of the human ends which history should serve.

History is not inevitably useful. It can bind us or free us. It can de-stroy compassion by showing us the world through the eyes of the com-fortable ("the slaves are happy, just listen to them"—leading to "the poor are content, just look at them"). It can oppress any resolve to act by mountains of trivia, by diverting us into intellectual games, by preten-tious "interpretations" which spur contemplation rather than action, by limiting our vision to an endless story of disaster and thus promoting cynical withdrawal, by befogging us with the encyclopedic eclecticism of the standard textbook.

But history can untie our minds, our bodies, our disposition to move—to engage life rather than contemplating it as an outsider. It can do this by widening our view to include the silent voices of the past, so that we look behind the silence of the present. It can illustrate the foolishness of depending on others to solve the problems of the world—whether the state, the church, or other self-proclaimed benefactors. It can reveal how ideas are stuffed into us by the powers of our time, and so lead us to stretch our minds beyond what is given. It can inspire us by recalling those few moments in the past when men did behave like human beings, to prove it is *possible*. And it can sharpen our critical faculties so that even while we act, we think about the dangers created by our own desperation.

These criteria I have discussed are not conclusive. They are a rough guide. I assume that history is not a well-ordered city (despite the neat stacks of the library) but a jungle. I would be foolish to claim my guidance is infallible. The only thing I am really sure of is that we who plunge into the jungle need to think about what we are doing, because there *is* somewhere we want to go.

Notes

1. Barbara Tuchman, *The Guns of August*, Macmillan, 1962, p. 72.
2. Herbert Aptheker, *A Documentary History of the Negro People*, Citadel, 1951, p. 2.
3. New York *Daily News*, February 6, 1928.
4. Jesse Lemisch, "The American Revolution from the Bottom Up," Barton Bernstein, ed., *Towards a New Past*, Pantheon, 1968.
5. *Report of the National Advisory Commission on Civil Disorders*, Bantam, 1968, p. 483.
6. Richard Pfeffer, ed., *No More Vietnams*, Harper & Row, 1968, pp. 7, 8.
7. Marilyn Young, *The Rhetoric of Empire*, Harvard University, 1968, p. 231.
8. "Twilight of Idols," *The Seven Arts*, October 1917, reprinted in Randolph S. Bourne, *War and the Intellectuals*, Harper (Torchbook edition), 1964, p. 60.
9. Staughton Lynd, *Intellectual Origins of American Radicalism*, Pantheon, 1968, p. vi.
10. *New York Review of Books*, September 26, 1968.
11. Herbert Aptheker, *A Documentary History of the Negro People*, Citadel, 1951.
12. Robert Michels, *Political Parties*, Free Press (Collier edition), 1962, p. 154.

"MY NAME IS FREEDOM": ALBANY, GEORGIA AND SELMA, ALABAMA

from *You Can't Be Neutral on a Moving Train: A Personal History of Our Times* (1994)

As described in these early chapters of his memoir, Howard's first academic job at Spelman College coincided with the emergence and expansion of the black freedom struggle. From his new home in Atlanta,
Howard traveled to various parts of the South—Albany, Georgia,
Jackson, Mississippi, and Selma, Alabama—both to document and
participate in the Civil Rights Movement. In 1962, he was hired by the
Southern Regional Council, a liberal research group, to write a report
about the arrest and abuse of civil rights activists in Albany, Georgia,
who had staged a series of protests against Jim Crow segregation, including the famous "Freedom Rides," where black and white activists had
been beaten and imprisoned for trying to integrate interstate bus lines and
other forms of public transportation. The following year, Howard became an adviser to the Student Nonviolent Coordinating Committee
(SNCC), under whose auspices he traveled throughout the South to in-
vestigate the repression of civil rights activists by local law enforcement
and government officials. Taken together, these experiences—teaching
at a historically black women's college and participating in the bur-
geoning black freedom movement—awakened in Howard a new "spirit
of defiance," a more radical commitment to racial and economic justice,
and a strong belief that ordinary people could rise up and defeat extraordinary prejudice. Of the Albany protestors, in chapter 4, he writes:
"What black men, women, children did in Albany at the time was
heroic. They overcame a century of passivity, and they did it without
the help of the national government. They learned that despite the
Constitution, despite the promises, despite the political rhetoric of the

government, whatever they accomplished in the future would have to come from them." At the end of chapter 5, Howard recalls meeting his friend Whitney Young, head of the National Urban League, at the airport immediately following the 1965 Voting Rights March from Selma to Montgomery. "The woman who came to wait on our table looked us over," Howard writes. "She was not happy. I saw that on her apron she wore a huge button with the one word that had become the defiant slogan of the segregationist: NEVER! But something had changed in Alabama, because she brought us coffee. Obviously, although the marchers' song was not quite true ('Freedom's coming and it won't be long'), the claim on her button was now certainly false." As these excerpts demonstrate, *You Can't Be Neutral on a Moving Train* is the powerful firsthand account of a man who both wrote and made history.

"My Name Is Freedom": Albany, Georgia

One day in the summer of 1962, as a thirty-nine-year-old professor of history who had begun to wander out of the classroom to see some history, I walked into the office of Sheriff Cull Campbell of Daugherty County, in the city of Albany, a city surrounded by the cotton and pecan land of southwest Georgia.

I was visiting Sheriff Campbell as part of an assignment I had undertaken for the Southern Regional Council, a liberal research group in Atlanta. In the winter of 1961 and the spring and summer of 1962, the black population of Albany, surprising itself and the world, rose up in rebellion against racial segregation. I was asked to look into the turmoil in Albany and write a report.

I wanted to talk with the sheriff because of something that had recently happened in his jurisdiction. A white civil rights worker named Bill Hansen, jailed with sixteen other people for praying in front of City Hall and refusing to move, had been put into a cell with a white prisoner who was given meaningful instructions: "This is one of those guys who came down here to straighten us out." As Hansen sat on the cell floor reading a newspaper he was attacked and beaten into unconsciousness, his jaw broken, his lip split, a number of ribs broken.

That same afternoon, a young lawyer, C.B. King, a native of Albany and the first black attorney in the history of the city, went into Sheriff Campbell's office to ask about what had happened to Bill Hansen. The sheriff was clearly infuriated by the sight of a black man, indeed a hometown "boy" who had grown up, gone to law school, and now appeared in suit and tie like any white lawyer, asking about a client.

He said, "Nigger, haven't I told you to wait outside?" He then pulled a walking stick out of a basket and brought it down with all his force on King's head. The attorney staggered from the office, blood streaming down his face and onto his clothes, and made his way across the street to police chief Pritchett, who called for medical aid.

Sheriff Campbell, inviting me into his office a few weeks after that happened, turned and said, "You're not with the goddam niggers, are you?" I chose not to answer, but asked him about what happened to King. He stared at me. "Yeah, I knocked hell out of the son-of-a-bitch, and I'll do it again. I wanted to let him know . . . I'm a white man and he's a damn nigger."

As I listened to the sheriff I saw the basket of walking sticks near his desk. On it was a sign saying they were made by the blind and sold for fifty cents. I had a quick macabre vision of a black man in the county home for the blind making the cane that was used to beat C.B. King.

I walked across the street to Chief Pritchett's office. Pritchett had been hailed in newspapers all over the country for maintaining "order" in Albany. A reporter for the New York *Herald Tribune* said Pritchett "brought to Albany a standard of professional achievement that would be difficult to emulate in a situation so made to order for violence."

Pritchett earned this praise from the establishment press by simply putting into prison ("nonviolently," as he boasted) every man, woman, and child in the city of Albany who tried to exercise their constitutional rights of free speech and assembly. He and Sheriff Campbell were the classic bad cop–good cop team: Campbell would beat someone bloody and Pritchett would call for an ambulance.

I asked Pritchett why he did not arrest Sheriff Campbell, who was clearly guilty of assault. He smiled and said nothing. His secretary walked in. "Your next appointment is here." Pritchett stood up and shook my hand. I started to leave. His next appointment walked in: it was Dr. Martin Luther King. We greeted one another (we had met a number of times in Atlanta) and I left just as Pritchett—the good cop—shook hands cordially with King.

Back in my Albany motel room, starting to put together my report, I thought about all that had happened in the eight months since December of 1961:

Pritchett's arrest of SNCC workers who took the train to Albany from Atlanta and on arrival sat in the "white" waiting room. SNCC, the Student Nonviolent Coordinating Committee, was the newly formed organization composed mostly of young black college students who had been in the sit-ins all over the South the year before and now had decided to challenge racial segregation in the toughest, most violent regions of the country: Georgia, Alabama, Mississippi.

The arrest of four hundred black high school and college students who marched and sang downtown to protest the arrest of those SNCC "Freedom Riders."

The arrest of seventy more Albany blacks who knelt and prayed at City Hall.

The arrest of three hundred more who marched to City Hall; and two hundred and fifty more (this time including the recently arrived Martin Luther King Jr.) who marched, singing, through downtown.

The arrest of even more people for sitting at lunch counters and refusing to leave until they were served.

Pritchett told reporters, "We can't tolerate the NAACP or the SNCC or any other nigger organization to take over this town with mass demonstrations."

In my report for the Southern Regional Council, I was searching for a central focus. Here, in concentrated form, was the racism, the brutality, of the segregated South. Just one instance: Mrs. Slater King (C.B. King's sister-in-law), with her three children and in her sixth month of pregnancy, tried to bring food to someone in jail. She was kicked and knocked to the ground by a deputy sheriff. She lost consciousness. Months later she lost her baby.

A question kept nagging at me: Where was the government of the United States in all this?

I taught courses in constitutional law, but that expertise was not necessary for a person to see that the First Amendment and Fourteenth Amendment rights in the United States Constitution were being violated in Albany again and again—freedom of speech, freedom of assembly, the equal protection of the law—I could count at least thirty such violations. Yet the president—sworn to uphold the Constitution—and all the agencies of the United States government at his disposal were nowhere to be seen. Was Albany, Georgia, was all of the South, outside the jurisdiction of the United States? Had the Confederacy really won the Civil War and morally, effectively seceded?

I knew that a post–Civil War law passed to enforce the Fourteenth Amendment made it a federal crime for any official to violate any citizen's constitutional rights. In the nation's capital a liberal Democratic administration had recently taken office. John F. Kennedy was president; Robert F. Kennedy was attorney general, head of the Justice

Department, and therefore in charge of enforcing federal law. But this was not being done in Albany, Georgia.

My report to the Southern Regional Council became a front-page story in the *New York Times*. In it, I pointed to the failure of the national government in protecting constitutional rights. *I. F. Stone's Weekly* carried excerpts, and *The Nation* published an article of mine on the Albany events, entitled, "Kennedy, the Reluctant Emancipator."

Martin Luther King Jr. was asked by the press if he agreed with the report. He said he did, pointing to racism in the FBI. This comment apparently enraged J. Edgar Hoover, the self-appointed "white knight" of patriotism, the anti-crime and anti-Communist "hero" of America, who was not accustomed to criticism. The press contributed to Hoover's fury by playing up the criticism of the FBI, but confined itself to that issue, while my report went beyond the FBI to the Justice Department and the White House. It was an example of a common phenomenon in American journalism (perhaps in social criticism in general), the shallow focusing on agents or on individuals, thus concealing what a deeper analysis would reveal—the failure of the government itself, indeed, of the political system.

At the great March on Washington of 1963, the chairman of the Student Nonviolent Coordinating Committee, John Lewis, speaking to the same enormous crowd that heard Martin Luther King's "I Have a Dream," was prepared to ask the right question: "Which side is the federal government on?" That sentence was eliminated from his speech by organizers of the march to avoid offending the Kennedy administration, but Lewis and his fellow SNCC workers had experienced, again and again, the strange passivity of the national government in the face of Southern violence—strange, considering how often this same government had been willing to intervene *outside* the country, often with overwhelming force.

John Lewis and SNCC had reason to be angry. John had been beaten bloody by a white mob in Montgomery as a Freedom Rider in the spring of 1961. The federal government had trusted the notoriously racist Alabama police to protect the riders, but done nothing itself except to have FBI agents take notes. Instead of insisting that blacks and whites had a right to ride the buses together, the Kennedy administration called for a "cooling-off period," a moratorium on Freedom Rides.

When the movement people insisted on continuing the rides into Mississippi, Attorney General Kennedy made a deal with the governor of Mississippi: the Freedom Riders would not be beaten, but they would be arrested. Some three hundred were, by the end of that summer, and spent hard time in Mississippi jails because the government of the United States did not see fit to protect their rights.

The Freedom Rides pushed the Justice Department into getting the Interstate Commerce Commission to issue regulations barring racial segregation on trains and in terminals, effective November 1, 1961. It was that order that SNCC people decided to test in the train terminal of Albany, Georgia. They were arrested and notified the Department of Justice, which, by its silence, then failed the test.

SNCC (known to its friends as "Snick") had been formed in the spring of 1960, when veterans of the recent sit-ins got together in Raleigh, North Carolina. Inspiring and overseeing its beginning was the extraordinary Ella Baker, veteran of struggles in Harlem and elsewhere. When Albany blacks turned out in the streets by the hundreds to protest the arrests of the Albany Freedom Riders, and were arrested themselves, Ella Baker was there. Months later, when SNCC asked me to join their executive committee as one of their two "adult advisers," along with Miss Baker (that's how movement people referred to her), I felt honored.

When I first arrived in Albany in December of 1961, hundreds of people were coming out of jail. Many of them had been fired by their white employers, and they gathered in the Shiloh Baptist Church for help. Ella Baker sat in a corner of the church, pen and paper in hand. She was a middle-aged, handsome woman with the resonant voice of a stage actress, who moved silently through the protest movements in the South, doing the things the famous men didn't have time to do. Now, hour after hour, she sat there as people lined up before her, patiently taking down names, addresses, occupations, immediate money needs.

I spoke to those sitting on a bench waiting to see Miss Baker. They described their prison experiences. One woman said, "We were eighty-eight in one room with twenty steel bunks and no mattresses. Sheriff took us to Camilla. On the bus he told us, 'We don't have no singin', no prayin', and no handclappin' here.' " A young married woman who was a student at Albany State College said, "I didn't expect to go to jail for kneeling and praying at City Hall."

The people I encountered in Albany in those days made me think of what stored-up courage and self-sacrifice one finds in so many people who never make the headlines but represent millions.

I think of Ola Mae Quarterman, eighteen years old, who took a front seat on a city bus and refused to move. She said, in language that was apparently new to the black-white culture of Albany, "I paid my damn twenty cents and I can sit where I want." She was arrested for "obscenity."

I think of Charles Sherrod. He was a SNCC "field secretary" and one of those young people who went into the toughest towns in the deep South to set up Freedom Houses and help local folk organize to change their lives. Sherrod was a Freedom Rider, jailed in Mississippi. Now he and Cordell Reagon, another SNCC fellow, went into Albany to see what they could do. (Yes, they were "outside agitators"—what great social movement ever did without such people?) Sherrod told me, "I remembered walking dusty roads for weeks without food. I remembered staying up all night for two and three nights in succession writing and cutting stencils and mimeographing and wondering, How long?" Sherrod was one of those just out of jail when I arrived in Albany. When he told the sheriff, "We may be in jail, but we're still human beings," the sheriff hit him in the face. (Twenty-five years later the sheriff was gone, but Sherrod was still in Albany, organizing farming cooperatives.)

I think of Lenore Taitt, one of the eight Freedom Riders into Albany whose arrest had sparked all the demonstrations. She was one of my students at Spelman—a delightful young woman, far from the sober agitator of myth—a happy Freedom Rider of unquenchable spirit. I walked downtown to the county jail, a small stone building surrounded by a barbed wire fence, and asked to see her. Can't be done, said the deputy sheriff on duty. "You can holler through the fence like everyone else does." I shouted Lenore's name at a thick steel mesh window, impossible to see through, and then I heard Lenore's voice, incredibly hoarse. She explained that she'd lost it yelling all night to get help for a woman in her cell who was sick.

I think of Bob Zellner, one of the few white field secretaries in SNCC, from the Gulf coast of Alabama, who was arrested with Lenore Taitt and the other Freedom Riders. I was with the crowd waiting to greet them when they all came out of jail, but as Bob emerged with them, the sheriff grabbed him. "We've got another charge against *you*." Bob flashed his indomitable grin and waved to his friends as he was taken away.

Bob told me later that he'd had two books with him in jail. One was Henry Miller's *Tropic of Cancer*, which the sheriff glanced at and let him keep; the other was Lillian Smith's novel about a black man and a white woman, and the sheriff took it away, saying, "This is *obscene*."

And there was Stokely Carmichael, whom I first met in Albany on a steamy-hot night, sitting on the steps outside a church where a meeting was going on, a small group of neighborhood kids gathered around him.

He gave the impression he would stride cool and smiling through hell, philosophizing all the way. He had left Howard University to join the Freedom Rides and was jailed on arrival in Jackson, Mississippi, making his way past a mob of howling, cursing people who threw lighted cigarettes at him. In Parchman State Prison he drove his captors crazy with his defiance, and they were relieved when after forty-nine days he was out. Now he was in Albany for SNCC.

And Bernice Johnson, who organized the Albany Freedom Singers and was expelled from Albany State College for her determined involvement in the movement. I helped her get into Spelman College, but both the college and its famous glee club were too narrow to contain her spirit and her voice. She sat in our living room one day to tell us this, and then sang, with that magnificent deep voice. (Later, she would get a Ph.D. in history, but that does not begin to suggest her power. She would become an indefatigable curator of oral history at the Smithsonian, inspire countless audiences, and sing at Carnegie Hall and all over the country with her group Sweet Honey in the Rock.)

There was the Albany youngster who was in the line of black people being booked at the City Hall after a protest parade.

"How old are you?" Chief Pritchett asked.

"Nine."

"What is your name?" asked the chief.

The boy answered. "Freedom. Freedom."

The chief said, "Go home, Freedom."

It has often been said, by journalists, by scholars, that Albany, Georgia, was a defeat for the movement, because there was no immediate victory over racial segregation in the city. That always seemed to me a superficial assessment, a mistake often made in evaluating protest movements. Social movements may have many "defeats"—failing to achieve objectives in the short run—but in the course of the struggle the strength of the old order begins to erode, the minds of people begin to change; the protesters are momentarily defeated but not crushed, and have been lifted, heartened, by their ability to fight back. The boy may have been sent home by Chief Pritchett, but he was a different boy than he had been a month before. Albany was changed forever by the tumultuous events of 1961 and 1962, however much things *looked* the same when the situation quieted down.

The white population could not possibly be unaffected by those events—some whites perhaps more stubborn in their defense of segregation, but others beginning to think in different ways. And the black population was certainly transformed, having risen up in mass action for the first time, feeling its power, knowing that if the old order could be shaken, it could be toppled.

Indeed, in 1976, fifteen years after he arrived and was arrested, Charles Sherrod was elected to the Albany city commission. He responded to the pessimists, "Some people talk about failure. Where's the failure? Are we not integrated in every facet? Did we stop at any time? Did any injunction stop us? Did any white man stop us? Did any black man stop us? Nothing stopped us in Albany, Georgia. We showed the world."

What black men, women, children did in Albany at that time was heroic. They overcame a century of passivity, and they did it without the help of the national government. They learned that despite the Constitution, despite the promises, despite the political rhetoric of the government, whatever they accomplished in the future would have to come from them.

One day I drove out of Albany, from dirt road onto dirt road, deep into Lee County to talk to James Mays, a teacher and a farmer. The night before, thirty bullets had been fired into his house, crashing into the walls and barely missing the sleeping children inside.

He knew there was no point in making a call to the Department of Justice. Many, many calls had been made. When dawn came he lettered a sign of protest and stood with it, alone, on the main road to the county seat. It was clear that although he was a citizen of a nation whose power stretched around the globe and into space, that power was absent for him. He and his people were on their own.

For an aggrieved group to learn that it must rely on itself, even if the learning is accompanied by bitter losses in the immediate sense, is to strengthen itself for future struggles. The spirit of defiance that appeared in Albany in that time of turmoil was to outlast the momentary "defeat" that the press and the pundits lamented so myopically.

That spirit is epitomized by eighteen-year-old Ola Mae Quarterman: "I paid my damn twenty cents and I'll sit where I please."

Selma, Alabama

I traveled to Selma, Alabama, in October 1963 as an adviser to SNCC, to observe its voter registration campaign there, which had been accompanied by a number of acts of intimidation and violence. The town was the seat of Dallas County, whose population was 57 percent black, with 1 percent of those registered to vote. (Sixty-four percent of whites were registered.)

The 1 percent figure was understandable when you looked at the registration process. You didn't register, you applied to register. There was a long questionnaire, then an oral examination, with different questions for blacks and whites. A typical question for blacks: "Summarize the Constitution of the United States." (The county registrar was undoubtedly an expert on the Constitution.) Later, a postcard saying if you passed or failed.

Selma was a slave market before the Civil War, a lynching town at the turn of the century, and by the 1960s still a place where any young black person growing up there had to say to himself or herself, as a Selma-born black attorney living in Tennessee told me, "I must get out of this town."

Not long before I arrived, thirty-two schoolteachers who had tried to register to vote had been fired, and John Lewis had been arrested for leading a picket line at the county courthouse. (Only one of his many arrests and brutal beatings. In the 1980s, he would be elected to the U.S. Congress from Georgia.) Worth Long, another SNCC man, was arrested and beaten by a deputy sheriff in the county jail. A nineteen-year-old girl was knocked off a stool in a store and prodded with an electric pole

as she lay on the floor unconscious. Bernard Lafayette, a SNCC field or-
ganizer whose job was to try to register black voters, was clubbed as he
stopped on the street to help a white man who said his car needed a push.

My experience in Albany had made me especially conscious of the
federal role in keeping the institutions of racism going. A systematic
failure to enforce civil rights law had marked every national administration since 1877, whether Democrat or Republican, liberal or conservative. Racism was not southern policy, it was national policy. Selma
was an *American* city.

Still, there was something unreal about Selma. It was as if a Hollywood producer had reconstructed a pre–Civil War Southern town—
decaying buildings, muddy streets, little cafés, and a mule drawing a
wagonload of cotton down the street. In the midst of that, startlingly, the
huge red brick Hotel Albert, modeled after a medieval Venetian palace.

In every such Southern town I visited there seemed to be one black
family that was the rock-like center of any freedom movement. In
Selma it was the family of Mrs. Amelia Boynton. In her home I spoke to
three young local fellows. "Do you know any white man in Selma—
just one even—who is sympathetic with your cause?" They thought
there might be one Jewish storekeeper who was secretly sympathetic,
but knew only one white man who openly helped the movement. This
was a thirty-seven-year-old Catholic priest, Father Maurice Ouillet, in
charge of the St. Edmonds Mission in Selma, who had received abusive
phone calls and warnings he might be killed.

SNCC had declared October 7 as Freedom Day. The idea was to
bring hundreds of people to register to vote, hoping that their numbers
would decrease fear. And there was much to fear. John Lewis and seven
others were still in jail. Sheriff Jim Clark, huge and bullying, had deputized a force that was armed and on the prowl. To build up courage,
people gathered in churches night after night before Freedom Day. The
churches were packed as people listened to speeches, prayed, sang.

Two nights before Freedom Day, I went to a crowded church meeting to hear Dick Gregory, who had just arrived in Selma; his wife Lillian had been arrested while demonstrating there. Armed deputies ringed
the church outside. Three white police officers sat in the audience taking
notes, and Gregory was determined to speak about them and to them in
a manner unheard of in Selma—to show that it was possible to speak to
white people insubordinately.

I traveled in those days with a cheap tape recorder. (I had written to
my alma mater, Columbia University, which had an oral history project,

suggesting that they take time off from interviewing ex-generals and ex–secretaries of state and send someone south to record the history being made every day by obscure people. One of the nation's richest universities wrote back saying something like, "An excellent idea. We don't really have the resources.") I recorded Gregory's performance with my little machine.

He spoke for two hours, lashing out at white Southern society with passion and with his extraordinary wit. Never in the history of this area had a black man stood like this on a public platform ridiculing and denouncing white officials to their faces. The crowd loved it and applauded wildly again and again. He spoke of the irony of whites' maltreatment of black people, whose labor they depended on for their lives. He said he wished that the whole Negro race would disappear overnight—"They would go crazy looking for us!" The crowd roared and applauded.

Then Gregory lowered his voice, suddenly serious. "But it looks like we got to do it the hard way, and stay down here, and educate them."

After him, Jim Forman spoke. He was the executive director of SNCC, working in the Atlanta office, but moving onto the firing line again and again with an awesome quiet bravery. He was Chicago born, but grew up in Mississippi, spent four years in the Air Force, was a college graduate. Now he set about organizing the people in the church for Freedom Day. "All right, let's go through the phone book. . . . You take a baloney sandwich and a glass of cool water and go down there and stay all day." He pointed to the big sign up on the platform: DO YOU WANT TO BE FREE? He paused. "Who'll take the letter *A*?"

The evening ended with the Selma Freedom Chorus, including some small children, some teenagers, and a boy at the piano—the most beautiful singing I had heard since the mass meetings in Albany. (That is something impossible to convey in words—the singing, the everpresent singing—in churches, at staff meetings, everywhere, raising the emotional level, giving people courage, almost always ending with everyone, knowing one another or not, holding hands.)

Then everyone went home, through the doors out into the street, where two cars with white men had been sitting all evening in the darkness outside the church.

Some of us waited that night at Mrs. Boynton's for James Baldwin to arrive. He was flying into Birmingham to be driven by SNCC people to Selma, coming to observe Freedom Day. While waiting, we sat around in the kitchen and talked. Jim Forman expertly scrambled eggs in a frying pan with one hand, gesturing with the other to make a point.

Baldwin arrived after midnight, his brother David with him. We all sat in the living room and waited for him to say something. He smiled broadly. "You fellows talk. I'm new here. I'm trying to find out what's happening."

I made notes on Freedom Day, almost minute by minute, starting at 9:30 in the morning, standing on the street near the Dallas County courthouse as the line of black people grew into the hundreds. The editor of the local newspaper told me that the application process was slow. I calculated that at the rate it was going it would take ten years for blacks to catch up to whites in percentage of registered voters.

By 11:00 A.M. there were two hundred and fifty people in the line, which extended the full length of the block, around the corner, and halfway down that street. Standing guard over these people—including elderly men and women, young mothers carrying babies in their arms—were helmeted men with clubs and guns, members of Sheriff Jim Clark's posse. The sheriff was there, a six-footer with a big belly, on his green helmet the confederate flag and a gold medallion with an eagle, a gold star on his shirt, epaulets on his shoulders, gun at his hip.

Directly across the street from the county courthouse in Selma was the federal building. On the first floor of that building was the office of the FBI, its windows looking out at the county courthouse. Standing on the street, witnessing everything that happened that day, were four FBI agents and two lawyers from the Justice Department, one white, one black.

By 11:40 A.M. no one could find a black person who had come out of the courthouse who had actually gone through the registration procedure. I was standing with Jim Forman and another SNCC man when Sheriff Clark came over. "All right, clear out of here. You're blocking the sidewalk."

A man with sound equipment spoke to James Baldwin, whose eyes looked enormous, fiery. Baldwin waved toward the line of helmeted troopers. "The federal government is not doing what it is supposed to do."

It was almost noon, the sun was beating down, and Forman was musing about the problem of getting water to the people on line, who had been standing there almost three hours. I looked across the street to the federal building. There on the steps were two SNCC fellows holding signs that faced the registration line. One of them, in overalls and fedora, had a sign saying, "REGISTER TO VOTE."

I moved across the street to get a better look. As I did so, Sheriff Clark and three helmeted deputies came walking fast across the street. They went past the two Justice Department attorneys and two FBI men, up the steps of the building, and grabbed the two SNCC men. Clark called out, "You're under arrest for unlawful assembly." The deputies pulled the two down the steps and pushed them into a police car. A third man at the side entrance to the building, also holding a voter registration sign, was also arrested.

There could hardly be a more clear-cut violation of the 1957 Civil Rights Act, which prohibits interference with the right to vote—to say nothing of the First Amendment's right to free speech. And this had taken place on the steps of the U.S. government's building, before the eyes of government men. I turned to the Justice Department man near me. "Is that a *federal* building?" I asked with some anger. "Yes," he said, and turned away. The police car with the three SNCC men sped off.

Jim Forman told me that the night before he had wired the Justice Department for federal marshals, sure there would be trouble. The Justice Department had not replied.

Word came that the registrars had stopped registering for the lunch period. People stayed on the line and Forman began planning how to get food to them. A caravan of state troopers had arrived at the courthouse. Their autos were lined up along the curb from one end of the street to the other, searchlights mounted on top. Forty troopers, with blue helmets, clubs, and guns, stationed themselves alongside the registration line. In charge of the troopers was Colonel Al Lingo, the veteran bully of Birmingham. Some of his men were holding electric cattle prods.

At 1:55 P.M. (people had now been on line five hours), Jim Forman and Mrs. Boynton walked over to talk to Sheriff Clark.

Forman said, "Sheriff, we'd like to give these people some food."

Clark replied, "They will not be molested in any way."

Forman said, "We don't want to molest them. We want to give them food and to talk to them about registration."

Now Clark began shouting. "If you do, you'll be arrested! They will not be molested in any way and that includes talking to them."

Forman and Mrs. Boynton went back across the street, to the alley alongside the federal building, where a shopping cart with sandwiches and a keg of water was set up. Newsmen were called over. Forman told them about his wire to the Justice Department and their silence. Mrs. Boynton said, "We're determined to reach these people on line with food."

At 2:00 P.M. I looked up at the windows of the county courthouse and saw the faces of county employees jammed up against the glass.

I spoke to the senior Justice Department attorney. "Is there any reason why a representative of the Justice Department can't go over and talk to the state troopers and say these people are entitled to food and water?"

He seemed agitated by the question. There was a long pause. Then he said, "I won't do it." He paused again. "I believe they do have the right to receive food and water. But I won't do it. It's no use. Washington won't stand by me."

Two SNCC field secretaries stood before the shopping cart and filled their arms with food. One of them was Avery Williams, Alabama born; another was Chico Neblett from Carbondale, Illinois. Both had left college to work for SNCC.

Chico gave his wallet to Forman—a final small acceptance of going to jail. He said to Avery, "Let's go, man."

They walked down to the corner and crossed (SNCC people took care not to jaywalk in the South) with all eyes on the street focused on them. A group of us—photographers, newsmen, others—crossed the street at the same time. It was 2:20 P.M.

As Chico and Avery came close to the line, a bulky trooper with cigar and blue helmet (he had been identified to us as Major Smelley) barked at them (Am I being unfair? Is there a kinder verb?). "Move on!" They kept going toward the line of registrants.

The major called out, "Get 'em!" The next thing I saw was Chico Neblett on the ground, troopers all around him. I heard him cry out and saw his body jump convulsively again and again. They were jabbing him and Avery with their cattle prods. Then they lifted them by their arms and legs and threw them into the green arrest truck that stood at the curb.

Now the troopers and deputies turned on the group of us who had followed all this, pushing and shoving us to prevent pictures being taken. There was a young reporter for the *Montgomery Advertiser* with a camera. They smashed it with a billy club, pinned him against a parked truck, and ripped his shirt, and then a deputy backhanded him across the mouth. This was a military operation and national security demanded secrecy.

The green arrest truck pulled away. Chico and Avery waved. The Justice Department attorney took the name of the photographer who had been hit. James Baldwin and I went into the FBI office to talk to the chief. Baldwin was angry, upset. I asked, "Why didn't you arrest Sheriff Clark and the others for violating federal law?" (After my Albany experience I could cite the law, Section 242, Title 18 of the U.S. Code: "Whoever, under color of any law . . . or custom, willfully subjects . . . any inhabitant . . . to the deprivation of any rights . . . secured or protected by the Constitution . . . shall be fined . . . or imprisoned.")

The FBI chief looked at us. "We don't have the right to make arrests in these circumstances." It was an absurd statement. Section 3052, Title 18 of the U.S. Administrative Code gives FBI agents the power to make arrests without warrants "for any offense against the United States committed in their presence." The FBI makes arrests in kidnappings, bank robberies, drug cases, espionage cases. But not in civil rights cases? Then not only were black people second-class citizens, but civil rights law was second-class law.

Four of us sat on the steps of the federal building and talked: James Baldwin, myself, the senior attorney from the Justice Department, and a young black attorney from Detroit who had come to observe Freedom Day. The Detroit attorney said, "Those cops could have massacred all those three hundred Negroes on line, and still nothing would have been done." The Justice man was defensive. He asked Baldwin what he was working on now. Answer: a play. What was the title? "Blues for Mister Charlie," Baldwin replied.

At 4:30 P.M. the county courthouse closed its doors. The line was breaking up. The Detroit attorney watched men and women walk slowly away. His voice trembled. "Those people should be given medals." We made our way back to SNCC headquarters.

(Years later, I was in the House of Representatives office building in Washington. Near the elevator I ran into the lawyer from Detroit. "What are you doing here?" he asked. "The Vietnam War," I answered. "What about you?" He smiled. "I've just been elected to Congress." This was John Conyers, who in the years to come would be one of the stalwarts for justice and against war, as a member of the Congressional Black Caucus.)

A mass meeting was called for 8:00 P.M. at a church. At five minutes of eight the church was packed, every seat taken, people standing along the walls. Father Ouillet and another Catholic priest sat in the audience.

A chandelier hung way up in the domed ceiling, a circle of twenty-five bare lightbulbs glowing. A seventy-three-year-old man, a veteran of World War I, told me, "Nothing like this ever happened to Selma. Nothing—until SNCC came here."

Jim Forman told the crowd, "We ought to be happy today, because we did something great." There was bitterness that unarmed black people of Dallas County had to defend the Constitution themselves, against Jim Clark and his posse, with no help from the United States government. But there was exultation that three hundred and fifty of them had stood on line from morning to evening, without food or water, in full view of the armed men who ruled Dallas County, and had not flinched.

The young people in the chorus were up front, singing. "Oh, that light of fre-ee-dom, I'm gonna let it shine!"

James Baldwin stood at the rostrum, his eyes burning into the crowd. "The sheriff and his deputies . . . were created by the good white people on the hill—and in Washington—and they've created a monster they can't control. . . . It's not an act of God. It is deliberately done, deliberately created by the American Republic."

The meeting closed as always, with everyone linking arms and singing "We Shall Overcome," youngsters and old people and young women holding their babies, the SNCC people and the Catholic priests. Over on the other side of the church I saw the young black Justice Department attorney, his arms crossed like everyone else, singing.

I wrote up a short account of Freedom Day for the *New Republic*, which they headed, "Registration in Alabama: Negroes Are Dragged off Federal Property as the FBI Looks On." The Justice Department was not happy with my piece. The chief of its Civil Rights Division, Burke Marshall, wrote a long letter to the *New Republic*, saying that "litigation" was the proper remedy for what happened in Selma and that the Justice Department had two voting rights suits pending in Selma. He said there could be "no summary action." (Marshall chose to ignore, as the FBI chief had done, the arrest powers of FBI agents, which could be invoked "for any offense" committed in their presence.)

A year or so later, Marshall wrote a small book in which he elaborated his defense of federal inaction in such cases as Selma. He talked about the "federal system," with its division of powers between nation and states. It was an astounding argument, as if the Fourteenth Amendment had not permanently altered that division, giving the federal government enormous power to act when local officials failed to protect constitutional rights. Section 333, Title 10 of the U.S. Code made this power clear.

I received in the mail one day a copy of the *University of Chicago Law Review*, and in it was a review of Marshall's book. It was a devastating critique of his reasoning by a law professor named Richard Wasserstrom. I was startled—and pleased. Richard Wasserstrom was the Justice Department lawyer I had met in Selma that day. I learned that he had quit the department after the Selma events, become a dean at Tuskegee Institute in Alabama, and was now a professor of law and philosophy at the University of California. Around the same time, I heard that the black Justice Department attorney I had met in Selma and who joined in singing "We Shall Overcome" had also left the department.

That was not my last experience in Selma. In early 1965, Selma became a national scandal, and an international embarrassment for the Johnson administration. Demonstrations against racial segregation were met with mass arrests, the clubbing to death of a white Unitarian Universalist minister named James Reeb, the shooting of a black man, Jimmie Lee Jackson, and the bloody beating of blacks trying to march across a bridge out of Selma toward the state capital of Montgomery.

Finally, Johnson asked Congress to pass a strong voting rights act, and ordered a federalized Alabama National Guard to protect the planned civil rights walk from Selma to Montgomery. It would be a fifty-mile trek, a triumphant march after all the beatings, all the bloodshed.

I was writing an article for the hundredth-anniversary issue of *The Nation*, based on the idea of revisiting the South a century after the end of the Civil War, and so I traveled to Lynchburg, Virginia, John's Island, South Carolina, and Vicksburg, Mississippi. Then I joined the Selma to Montgomery march for its final eighteen miles to the Alabama capital.

Arriving the night before, I found the marchers settling down just off the main highway. It had rained hard that day, and the field chosen to serve as our camp for the night was a bed of pure mud so deep your shoes went into it up to the ankles.

We were given plastic sheets and sleeping bags. I lay down in the darkness, listened to the hum of portable generators, and watched as people coming off the main highway were checked by two husky "security" men, young Episcopalian priests with turned-around collars who carried walkie-talkies.

The plastic sheet under me was soaked in mud and slime, but the inside of the sleeping bag was dry. Two hundred feet away, in a great arc around the field, were fires lit by soldiers on guard through the night. It was hard to believe—the movement was finally getting the federal protection it had asked for.

I awoke just before dawn, with a half-moon pushing through the clouds. The soldiers' fires at the perimeter were low now, but still burning. Nearby, sleepers were beginning to awaken.

A line formed for hot oatmeal, hard-boiled eggs, coffee. Then everyone gathered to resume the march. A black girl washed her bare feet, then her sneakers, in a stream alongside the road. Near her was a minister, his coat streaked with mud. A black woman without shoes had her feet wrapped in plastic. Andy Young was calling over the main transmitter to Montgomery. "Get us some shoes. We need forty pairs of shoes, all sizes, for women and kids. They've been walking barefoot the past twenty-four hours."

At exactly 7:00 A.M., an Army helicopter fluttered overhead and the march began, down to the main highway and on to Montgomery, with Martin Luther King and Andy Young and some SNCC people in the lead. On both sides of the march, as far forward and back as you could see, there were soldiers.

I was walking next to Eric Weinberger, a legendary pacifist, a veteran of torture in Southern jails, of beatings and cattle prods, who once fasted thirty-one days in jail. As Eric and I walked along, he pointed to the soldiers guarding the march. "Do you agree with that?" he asked.

"Yes, I'm glad they're there," I said. I understood his point. He was holding steady to pacifist-anarchist principle: do not use the instruments of the state, even on your behalf; do not use coercion, even against violent racists. But I was not an absolutist on the use of the state if, under popular pressure, it became a force for good. We agreed to disagree.

With the sun shining beautifully overhead, the marchers sang. "Free*dom*! Free*dom*! Freedom's coming and it won't be long." Of course it would be long, but did that matter if people were on the move, knowing they were shortening the distance however long it was?

It was seventeen miles to the edge of Montgomery, the original straggling line of three hundred thickening by the hour as thousands joined, whites and blacks who had come from all over the country. There was sunshine most of the way, then three or four bursts of drenching rain. On the porch of a cabin set way back from the road, eight tiny black children stood in a line and waved, an old hobby horse in the front yard.

A red-faced portly Irishman, newly arrived from Dublin, wearing a trench coat, held the hand of a little black boy who walked barefoot next to him. A Greyhound bus rode past with black kids on the way to school. They leaned out the window, shouting, "Freedom!" A one-legged young white man on crutches, a black skullcap over his red hair, marched along quickly with the rest.

A group of white workingmen along the road watched silently. As we reached the outskirts of Montgomery, students poured out of a black high school, lined the streets, and waved and sang as the marchers went by. A jet plane zoomed close overhead and everyone stretched arms to the sky, shouting, "FREEDOM! FREEDOM!"

Once in the city, I left the march. I knew there would be a wonderful gathering at the capitol and a huge crowd, which King and others would address, but I wanted to get home. I made my way to the airport, and ran into Whitney Young, my old Atlanta University colleague, now head of the National Urban League. He was coming off a plane to join the celebration.

Whitney and I went into the airport cafeteria and sat down at a table to have a cup of coffee. We weren't sure if that would work. And we must have looked odd together, not just because of the difference in race, but because Whitney, tall and handsome as always, was in a dark suit, white shirt, and tie, and I was quite bedraggled, unshaven, my clothes still splattered with mud from the march.

The woman who came to wait on our table looked us over. She was not happy. I saw that on her apron she wore a huge button with the one word that had become the defiant slogan of the segregationists: NEVER! But something had changed in Alabama, because she brought us our coffee. Obviously, although the marchers' song was not quite true ("Freedom's coming and it won't be long"), the claim on the button was now certainly false.

THE POLITICS OF HISTORY IN THE ERA OF THE COLD WAR: REPRESSION AND RESISTANCE

from *The Cold War and the University: Toward an Intellectual History of the Postwar Years* (1997)

Howard believed that politics shaped the writing of history and that history too often served the interests of those in power. This was perhaps never more the case than during the Cold War era, when the "practice of history" experienced a profound tension "between a spurious objectivity disguising conservatism and an openly declared commitment to social change." In this essay, part of an earlier New Press collection on the impact of Cold War ideology on American intellectual life, Howard explores the influence of two competing currents of postwar America on the historical profession: 1950s McCarthyism and the various dissident rebellions of the 1960s. Writing as a participant-historian, Howard positions his own intellectual autobiography within the larger transformations in the academy during the second half of the twentieth century. He pays particular attention to the way "national loyalties" (especially during wartime) distort historical sensibility, citing, among others, the "patriotic fervor by distinguished scholars" during World War II as well as the work of "consensus" historians like Arthur Schlesinger Jr. and other "servants to national power" who became apologists for some of the worst excesses of Cold War ideology and brinkmanship. In addition, Howard chronicles the political silencing and professional purging of Marxist historians during this period, especially Philip Foner, Herbert Aptheker, Jesse Lemisch, and his friend and former Spelman colleague Staughton Lynd, whose rise and fall serves as a chilling reminder of the academy's tendency toward political and intellectual repression. The final part of the essay charts the emergence of a new generation of historical "revisionists," shaped by the radical politics of the 1960s and 1970s, who produced an impressive body of historical scholarship focused on the lives and contributions of ordinary people—women and workers, gays and lesbians, African Americans and other people of color. These "new histories" (including Howard's most celebrated work, *A People's History of the United States*) appealed to "a whole new generation of people—teachers, students, others in the general population—who were hungry for a history less celebratory, more critical, more conscious of the victimization as well as the resistance of ordinary people." In the post–Cold War era, this new body of scholarship has played an indispensable role, transforming the historical "consensus" and keeping the nation honest about its complicated, often checkered past.

———

THE ACADEMY IS "NO IVORY TOWER," to borrow the title of Ellen Schrecker's fine study of McCarthyism and the universities. The practice of history, therefore, has been affected by the various currents of postwar America, by McCarthyism in the 1950s, and the rise of "radical history" in the 1960s. During the decades that followed, there was a persistent conflict—in politics, between repression and resistance; in the historical profession, between a spurious objectivity disguising conservatism and an openly declared commitment to social change.

What I hope to do in this essay is to describe that conflict, as I experienced it, as observer and participant, in the fifty-year postwar period through which I have lived. During World War II, I was a shipyard worker who enlisted in the Army Air Corps and became a bombardier flying missions over Europe. After the war, I worked as a ditchdigger, waiter, city employee, and brewery worker. In 1949, with my tuition paid by the G.I. Bill of Rights, I began formally to study history, then to teach and write as a professional historian. All through those years, whether outside the academy or in it, I was involved in political activity, from organizing shipyard workers to participating in the civil rights and antiwar movements.

At the time I enlisted in the air force, I had read a smattering of works in history: Charles Beard's *The Rise of American Civilization*, the journalist George Seldes's account of Mussolini's rise to power (*Sawdust Caesar*), and enough on German Naziism to make me yearn to fight in "the good war."[1]

The political nature of history was at that time a concept foreign to me. I did not learn until much later that historians often have their work distorted by national loyalties. This is always most evident in wartime, when historians are invited to enlist their professional talents for the goal of military victory.

When the United States declared war on Germany in 1917, some of the nation's leading historians (Frederick Jackson Turner, J. Franklin Jameson among them) gathered in Washington to discuss "what History men can do for their country now." One of the things they did was to produce over 33 million copies of pamphlets distributed by various government agencies. In a study of historical propaganda during "the great war," George T. Blakey concludes that many historians "succumbed to the pressures of national bias and placed war aims above scholarly restraint."[2]

The same writer says that later historians were sobered by that experience. But, as Peter Novick shows in his extraordinary study of the claim to historical objectivity,[3] World War II brought another burst of patriotic fervor by distinguished scholars.

Harvard University's Samuel Eliot Morison, in an essay written during the war, affirmed his traditional commitment "to explain the event exactly as it happened." Yet, in the same essay, Morison criticized those historians who had expressed disillusionment with World War I. He said that they made the World War II generation of youth "spiritually unprepared for the war they had to fight. . . . Historians . . . are the ones who should have pointed out that war does accomplish something, that war is better than servitude."[4]

On the opposite side of the World War II controversy was Charles Beard, who bitterly denounced Roosevelt for bringing the nation, through deception and manipulation, he asserted, into the war. Beard was more forthright than Morison in acknowledging the inevitably political nature of historical writing. In his prewar presidential address to the American Historical Association (AHA), Beard quoted the philosopher Benedetto Croce that history is "contemporary thought about the past," and stressed that history involves the selection and arrangement of facts. The historian, he said, "helps to make history, petty or grand."[5]

It was only after the war that I began to think about the political character of the history I read with total acceptance as a teenager. It was the troubled state of the postwar world that made it more and more impossible for me to separate the study of history from the conflicts, different ones, that were under way.

I had been an enthusiastic bombardier, but, returning home, the promises of a different postwar world were soon emptied of meaning.

Fascism was defeated in Germany and Italy but was displaced to other areas of the world. The imperial powers of the West, despite the pledge of self-determination in the Atlantic Charter, were waging war in Malaya, Africa, Indochina, the Philippines to hold onto their old colonies. Militarism, so hateful as embodied in the Fascist states, was rising again, now on a nuclear scale, with the start of the Cold War between the United States and the Soviet Union.

As I began my formal study of history in 1949 at New York University, and soon at Columbia University, while living with my wife and two children in a low-income housing project in Manhattan, and loading trucks in a warehouse on the four-to-midnight shift, I was very much aware of the new old climate of ferocious anti-Communism. The political and ideological clashes in the world were coming home.

That very year, 1949, my wife, six months pregnant, our two-year-old daughter Myla, and I traveled in our antiquated 1932 Buick to Peekskill, New York, to attend an outdoor Paul Robeson concert. Robeson was, for so many radicals, old and young, a cultural and political hero. The concert was being held in defiance of threats by right-wing veterans groups in the Hudson Valley to prevent the concert from taking place, as they had done successfully not long before. But we assumed, naively, that because of the earlier publicity, and the huge crowd now going to Peekskill in a picnic atmosphere, that it would be safe. We were wrong. Robeson sang. Pete Seeger sang. But as they did, a boisterous mob gathered on the periphery of the concert ground, and as the audience moved out on the one dirt road, the mob attacked vehicles and individuals with rocks and sticks while the police stood by without interfering. My wife and daughter crouched down in the front seat. A fusillade of rocks smashed every window in the car. I felt more fear, mingled with anger, than I felt flying bombing missions through German flak. A rock smashed the head of a young woman who was riding with us, fracturing her skull.

Various events in the world were creating a climate of fear and hysteria in the United States: the Soviet occupation of Eastern Europe, the victory of Communism in China, the explosion by the Soviet Union of its first atomic bomb, the start of war in Korea. At home, there were the trials of communists and suspected communists, whether for "perjury," as in the case of Alger Hiss, or for "conspiracy to teach and advocate the overthrow of the government by force and violence," as with the leaders of the American Communist Party.

Walking out of our "project" apartment one evening in 1950, I came upon a tumultuous scene in a nearby building. Men and women, bleeding from face and head, were staggering down the street. They had just attended a Quaker meeting protesting U.S. involvement in the Korean War, and had been attacked by superpatriots.

Another time, walking home to our project apartment with a bag of groceries, I was stopped by two men in trenchcoats (they knew how to dress, having watched many movies) who flashed their FBI credentials and asked if I would talk to them about communists I knew. I refused. The next day, in an impulsive move that I have regretted ever since, my wife and I gathered the box of letters we had written to one another during the war, in which we had sometimes mentioned friends in the Communist movement. We walked out into the hall and threw them down the incinerator chute in the hall. They were historical documents, it is fair to say, and became victims of the Cold War.

The intensity of the conflict between the two postwar superpowers was soon matched by the unabashed partisanship of some of the most eminent American historians. Peter Novick writes:

> It was the community of diplomatic historians who contributed most wholeheartedly and directly to the support and defense of the American cause in the Cold War. These scholars' principal contribution was providing a version of recent history which would justify current policy, linking America's struggles with the Axis and with the Soviet Union as successive stages in one continuous and unavoidable struggle against expansionist totalitarians.[6]

National policy defined historical tasks for some leading historians. After Winston Churchill's "Iron Curtain" speech in 1946, came the promulgation of the Truman Doctrine of March 1947, offering military and economic aid to Greece and Turkey to protect their governments from Communist insurgency. That same month, Truman's Executive Order #9835 established loyalty-security criteria for all federal employees, with even "sympathetic association" with Communists a ground for dismissal.

In the early 1950s, William L. Langer and S. Everett Gleason wrote a two-volume history of American entry into World War II, to chronicle, as they put it, "the tortured emergence of the United States of America as leader of the forces of light in a world struggle which even today has scarcely abated." Although they were given access to privileged government documents, they claimed that no government official "has made the slightest effort to influence our views."[7] However, the connection between these two scholars and the government was not a subtle one. Langer was director of research of the Central Intelligence Agency, and Gleason was deputy executive secretary of the National Security Council.

Perhaps the most widely used college textbook in the history of U.S. foreign policy, *A Diplomatic History of the American People*, by Thomas Bailey, concluded: "Not all Americans . . . are prepared to recognize that their very way of life is jeopardized by the communist menace. Many are grumbling over defense expenditures, not realizing that to Moscow the most eloquent language is that of force."[8] The 1949 presidential address to the AHA, by Conyers Read, declared: "Total war, whether it be hot or cold, enlists everyone and calls upon everyone to assume his part . . . [W]e can never be altogether free agents, even with our tongue and our pen."[9]

The presidential address of diplomatic historian Samuel Flagg Bemis to the AHA in 1961 was equally blunt:

> Too much self-study, too much self-criticism is weakening to a people. . . . A great people's culture. . . . begins to decay when it commences to examine itself. . . . [W]e have been losing sight of our national purpose . . . our military preparedness held back by insidious strikes for less work and more pay. . . . How can our lazy social dalliance and crooning softness compare with the stern discipline and tyrannical compulsion of subject peoples that strengthen the aggressive sinews of our malignant antagonist.[10]

The Cold War against the Soviet Union was seen as a continuity of the war against fascism, of democracy against totalitarianism. But I think it is fair to say that these historians, during the rise of Fascism in Europe, had not lent their scholarship with such fervor to the antifascist struggle. The "other" totalitarianism occupied them much more strenuously—matching the record of the Western powers, who were loath to confront fascism until it began to challenge their imperial standing in the world.

As I took courses in "Western Civilization," it did not occur to me that this very choice as a basic university curriculum came out of a nationalist bias that fitted the requirements of the Cold War. In 1945,

Harvard's General Education Committee issued a report (*The Reforming of General Education*), which was described by Daniel Bell as reinforcing "the principles of a free society . . . the definition of democracy in a world of totalitarianism . . . the need to provide a 'common learning' for all Americans as a foundation of national unity."[11]

The phenomenon of McCarthyism—a frenzied searching for communists, defined broadly enough to include any strong critic of American society or of U.S. foreign policy—went far beyond the work of Senator Joseph McCarthy of Wisconsin. But McCarthy carried the Communist hunt to the point of hysteria. He burst upon the national scene early in 1950, when he created a sensation by announcing that he possessed lists of communists high up in the U.S. government. It turned out that his "lists" were spurious.

Nevertheless, in a series of hearings before the Senate Committee on Government Operations, specifically, its Subcommittee on Investigations, both of which he chaired, he attacked as Communist-influenced not only the State Department but the Voice of America and the Government Printing Office.

The crusade against communists spread, and historians suspected of Communist connections were among its victims. At hearings in 1952 of the Senate Committee on Internal Security, headed by Senator Pat McCarran of Nevada, historian M.I. Finley was named by two witnesses as having organized a Communist study group while a graduate student at Columbia University in the 1930s. Called before the committee, he denied membership in the Communist Party, but refused to answer questions about people he knew.

Now at Rutgers University, Finley was considered an outstanding teacher and scholar, and a university committee, after its own investigation, concluded that both Finley and another faculty member who had refused to answer questions by the McCarran Committee (Simon Heimlich, a mathematician) were within their constitutional rights in their responses to the committee.

The Rutgers University Board of Trustees, however, decided, in a unanimous vote, to fire the two men. One of the trustees referred to the faculty report: "What the Committee has done is to treat this whole thing as an abstract situation in which the niceties of the law . . . are given preeminence. It seems to me that we lost sight of the fact that we are at war with Communism." Another trustee pointed out that with 60 percent of its budget coming from the state, the university "cannot offend public opinion."[12]

Indeed, the statement on public opinion was accurate. The congressional investigations, the muted response of the American press, the increasingly heated atmosphere of the Cold War, were reflected in American public opinion. Whereas, in 1946, a Gallup Poll found that 44 percent of respondents favored making it a crime to join the Communist Party, by 1949, the figure was 68 percent. By 1954, a survey conducted by social scientist Samuel Stouffer of Harvard found that 52 percent of those polled were in favor of imprisoning all communists.[13]

Although some historians defied the congressional committees and lost their jobs (Finley left the country and went on to a distinguished career in England, being knighted by the Crown), others cooperated with the inquisition. Historian Daniel Boorstin testified before the House Committee on Un-American Activities in 1953 that he had briefly been a Communist Party member in the late 1930s, but now said that no communist should be allowed to teach in an American university. He agreed that the committee "had not in any way impinged on [his] academic freedom."[14]

Boorstin, asked by the committee to show how he had expressed his opposition to Communism, said: "First, in the form of an affirmative participation in religious activities, because I think religion is a bulwark against Communism. . . . The second form of my opposition has been an attempt to discover and explain to students in my teaching and in my writing the unique virtues of American democracy."[15]

McCarthy, at the height of his public notoriety, puffed up with success, overreached himself. While investigating what he claimed were communist influences in the U.S. Army itself, McCarthy attacked the widely respected General George Marshall. Soon after, his credibility declined rapidly, his support disappeared, and finally in 1954 the U.S. Senate voted to "condemn" him.

The senator had gone so far as to become embarrassing to the Establishment, but the crusade against communists continued in other forms, and historians suspected of communist connections were among its victims. Presidents and chancellors of the leading universities in the country rushed to declare their opposition to Communism. In 1953, their organization, the Association of American Universities (AAU), declared that membership in the Communist Party "extinguishes the right to a university position."[16] The heads of Harvard, Yale, Columbia, Princeton, MIT, Chicago, Caltech, and thirty other institutions subscribed to that statement. The effect of the anticommunist inquisitions on the work of historians went far beyond the dismissal of suspected radicals. And went beyond the work of McCarthy himself. Ellen Schrecker notes "the political reticence that blanketed the nation's colleges and universities." She writes:

> Marxism and its practitioners were marginalized, if not completely banished from the academy. Open criticism of the political status quo disappeared. . . . [T]he full extent to which American scholars censored themselves is hard to gauge. There is no sure way to measure the books that were not written, the courses that were not taught, and the research that was never undertaken.[17]

In the very year Daniel Boorstin was testifying before Congress, I was finishing my graduate course work at Columbia and choosing a topic for my doctoral dissertation. When I suggested to a senior member of the Columbia history faculty, himself a distinguished defender of civil liberties, that I might write something in that field, he cautioned me to try another area. Civil liberties were too controversial and might make it more difficult for me to get my degree.

But was this caution the result of the specific phenomenon of 1950s McCarthyism, or was it part of the ongoing situation in the United States—before and after McCarthyism—of "books that were not written . . . courses that were not taught . . . research that was never undertaken." Has there not been a persistent conservatism in American culture, including the practice of history, which is challenged significantly only in times of social protest—the 1930s, the 1960s?

Richard Hofstadter wrote his book *The American Political Tradition* before the Cold War atmosphere took hold. In it he characterized the boundaries of American political leadership: "property and enterprise . . . the economic virtues of capitalist culture," a culture which he described as "intensely nationalistic."[18] Those boundaries have also marked the limits of respectable historical scholarship throughout our national history, before and after the specific phenomenon of McCarthyism.

When Charles Beard stepped firmly outside those boundaries with the publication in 1913 of his groundbreaking *An Economic Interpretation of the Constitution*, the *New York Times* went to the trouble of writing an editorial denouncing his book. When, in the 1930s, a history text by Harold Rugg, which showed a degree of consciousness about class, became widely used, the National Association of Manufacturers launched an attack on Rugg's work. They succeeded in pushing his work out of the schools, thus sending a cautionary warning to writers and publishers of historical texts in the 1940s.[19]

As for Marxist historians, they were certainly beyond the pale, even before the McCarthy period. Thus, the pioneering historical work of Herbert Aptheker and Philip Foner could only be accepted by houses on the margin of the publishing industry. Aptheker's classic *A Documentary History of the Negro People in the United States*, a collection immensely valuable, indeed indispensable to anyone doing research in African American history, was published by the small Citadel Press. Foner's multivolume *A History of the Labor Movement in the United States*, an extremely useful resource for anyone doing work in labor history, was published by the left-wing International Publishers.

Both of those works could have been done by non-Marxists, in the sense that they did not represent "Marxist" interpretations of American history, but it seems that Marxist historians were simply more conscious than others about the importance of the history of black people and of working people. It is a revealing commentary on American society that mainstream historians paid so little attention to African American history. Judging from the titles of approximately 450 articles in the *American Historical Review* from 1945 to 1968, only five dealt with African American themes.

To find extensive work on African American history, one had to go to the venerable *Journal of Negro History* and other publications stimulated by the Association for the Study of Life and History, which was founded by Carter Woodson in 1915, shortly after the formation of the NAACP. A small body of published books by black historians did exist: Woodson, John Hope Franklin's *From Slavery to Freedom*, W.E.B. Du Bois's *Black Reconstruction*, and Rayford Logan's *The Betrayal of the Negro: From Rutherford B. Hayes to Woodrow Wilson*.

What was available to me, a young aspiring historian, entering the profession at the outset of the Cold War, in the early 1950s? No overview of American history written from a radical point of view. No critical history of American foreign policy—not until the end of the decade would William Appleman Williams publish the book which would initiate an era of "revisionist" history, *The Tragedy of American Diplomacy*.

It was a time when high praise was given to historians like Arthur Schlesinger Jr., whose book, *The Age of Jackson*, won a Pulitzer prize. Colorfully written, it presented Jackson as a hero of the democratic tradition, a forerunner of Franklin D. Roosevelt. But, even after a war that should have made scholars more sensitive to issues of racial hatred, Schlesinger's book, emphasizing Jackson as an opponent of national banking interests, overlooked him as a racist, a slaveholder, a mutilator and killer of Indians. (I must say that I was oblivious to those omissions myself at that time, and read Schlesinger with enjoyment and admiration.)

Mainstream history of the 1950s has often been described as "consensus" history—in which conflicts in American society are seen as muted, kept within a narrow band, not subject to the violent upheavals found in societies where class lines are drawn more sharply. The so-called consensus historians agreed on this as a description of the American past, but disagreed on the merits of this consensus.

Daniel Boorstin reveled in this consensus, this continuity, considered it "the genius of American politics" (in a series of lectures at the University of Chicago in 1952, and a book of that title published in 1955). Daniel Bell, in his book *The End of Ideology*, also welcomes this lack of conflict, both ideological and actual, as a sign of the maturing of American society.

On the other hand, Richard Hofstadter was critical of the ideologies—capitalism, nationalism—that bound the political leadership of the country in that consensus. Louis Hartz, while tracing the lack of class conflict to the absence of feudalism in the origin of the American colonies, clearly was unhappy with the narrow boundaries within which American discourse was kept.[20]

While doing my graduate work at Columbia, I found the boundaries that both Hofstadter and Hartz described—in my courses, in the literature offered to me. I did find liberal scholars: Henry Steele Commager, teaching constitutional history, David Donald, Mississippi-born but clearly an admirer of the abolitionists. Their work fit well within the liberal tradition.

On the conservative side of the consensus was their colleague, Allan Nevins, a prolific writer, who, while writing his eight-volume history of the Civil War, found time also to write a spirited defense of the Rockefellers and the other wealthy entrepreneurs of the Gilded Age. His work could be seen as a rejoinder to the critical studies of the "Progressive" era and the 1930s: Matthew Josephson's *The Robber Barons* and Gustavus Myers's 1907 classic *A History of the Great American Fortunes*.

Josephson, in a reissue of his book in 1962, referred to historians like Nevins as "revisionists" who "have proposed rewriting parts of America's history so that the image of the old-school capitalists should be retouched and restored, like rare pieces of antique furniture." (Later, the term "revisionist" would be applied to writers who carried on in the Josephson tradition of historical muckraking.)

To follow my interests in history, I found that I had to go outside the reading lists of my courses, outside the traditional curriculum. So I read Matthew Josephson and Gustavus Myers. And I began to read extensively in the history of the labor movement in the United States. As an undergraduate at NYU in 1951, I could not find any course in labor history, but managed to do an independent course of study, which led me to Foner's work and other books on working-class history.

I was especially attracted to a book by Samuel Yellen (not a historian but an English teacher), *American Labor Struggles*, which told of events, dramatic and violent, that I had not encountered (except, occasionally, in the briefest of mentions) in any of my American history classes. I read for the first time of the great railroad uprisings of 1877, of the Haymarket affair of 1886, the Lawrence textile strike of 1912. I was fascinated especially by the story of the Colorado Coal Strike of 1913–14.

That event was absent from the courses in American history at Columbia, and I decided to make it the subject of my master's thesis. The excitement of the 1930s' labor struggles was now gone, and the labor movement was in decline. With the Taft-Hartley law in effect, trade unions themselves began hunting down Communists in their leadership, adapting themselves to the Cold War atmosphere of the time. But I found sympathetic mentors in one of the grand old men of the Columbia faculty, Harry Carman, and his teaching assistant, James Shenton.

To dig into the details of the Colorado Coal Strike was to affirm and strengthen whatever radical criticism I had of American society. It was class struggle, American-style, as intense and violent as anything depicted in Émile Zola's novel of French miners—*Germinal*. It showed the ties between the Rockefeller corporate interests and the political leaders of Colorado, the use of the courts and soldiers to burn and kill (culminating in the Ludlow Massacre of April 1914), the role of the presumably "objective" press in serving the interests of the wealthy, and the role of a liberal federal government (the Wilson administration) in cooperating with the mine owners. It was also inspiring, in showing how miners and their families, apparently without resources, could resist the most powerful corporation in America.

For my doctoral thesis, I once more had to look outside the liberal-conservative consensus for a subject. I found it in Fiorello LaGuardia, who, before he joined the consensus as mayor of New York, was a radical congressman from East Harlem in the 1920s. This was presumed to be the "Jazz Age," an age of prosperity (a description never challenged in my courses in American history). But LaGuardia angrily denied this. He spoke up in Congress for the poor people of his district, as well as for striking miners in Pennsylvania and debt-ridden farmers of the Midwest. He declared:

> I am not at all shocked by being called a radical. Something is radically wrong when a condition exists that permits the manipulation of prices, the creation of monopolies on food to the extent of driving the farmer off his farm by foreclosures and having thousands of underfed and ill-nourished children in the public schools of our cities.[21]

Virtually alone, LaGuardia challenged the dispatch of U.S. Marines to Nicaragua in 1927, which Secretary of State Frank Kellogg said was necessary to prevent a communist takeover of Nicaragua and to save American lives. LaGuardia said there was no proof of communist activity in Nicaragua and added: "The protection of American life and property in Nicaragua does not require the formidable naval and marine forces operating there now. Give me fifty New York cops and I can guarantee full protection."[22]

I was reading these words of LaGuardia just after the United States, in 1954, charging that the government in Guatemala, elected in one of the few free elections in the history of that country, was Communist controlled (it had taken over the lands of the United Fruit Corporation), set in motion an invasion to overthrow that government.

In the 1950s, there was no organized activity by historians (or by other scholars) and extremely few individual protests took place against the military actions of the United States. These interventions were against Third World countries, always on the grounds of "stopping Communism." The United States intervention in Korea had cost over a million Korean lives. In 1953, the same year the Korean War ended, the U.S. government organized the overthrow of the nationalist leader Mossadegh in Iran. The French were trying to reconquer their old colony in Indochina, and the United States was supplying most of the military supplies for that war. In 1958, President Eisenhower sent 14,000 marines into Lebanon to protect the government there against a rebellion.

The silence of the academy in regard to Cold War foreign policy in the 1950s was matched by its passive acceptance of the Cold War's equivalent on the domestic scene: the firings, the blacklistings, the attacks on unions, the FBI harassments—all justified as part of the fight against Communism. As Ellen Schrecker concludes, after her careful study of McCarthyism in the universities:

> Professors and administrators overrode the civil liberties of their colleagues and employees in the service of such supposedly higher values as institutional loyalty and national security. . . . The extraordinary facility with which the academic establishment accommodated itself to the demands of the state may well be the most significant aspect of the academy's response to McCarthyism.[23]

For some historians, subservience to the state, as it pursued foreign military interventions and domestic Communist-hunting, went beyond silence to complicity. The election of John F. Kennedy to the presidency in 1960 brought into the White House as advisers a number of important scholars: political scientist-historian McGeorge Bundy of Harvard, economist Eugene Rostow of MIT, and historian Arthur Schlesinger Jr. of Harvard.

In the presence of cold war policies he thought unwise, Schlesinger would remain silent, as when President Kennedy made the decision to go ahead with the covert invasion of the Bay of Pigs in Cuba. In his book *A Thousand Days*, Schlesinger tells how he did write a private memo to the president expressing his opposition to the invasion. However: "In the months after the Bay of Pigs I bitterly reproached myself for having kept so silent during those crucial discussions in the Cabinet Room." He attributed his silence to "the circumstances of the discussion." As he put it:

> It is one thing for a Special Assistant to talk frankly in private to a President at his request and another for a college professor, fresh to the government, to interpose his unassisted judgment in open meeting against that of such august figures as the Secretaries of State and Defense and the joint Chiefs of Staff, each speaking with the full weight of his institution behind him.[24]

Schlesinger's opposition to the Cuban invasion was not based on a moral objection to a military intervention aimed at overthrowing a popular revolutionary government. The popularity of the Castro revolution was important to Schlesinger only because it meant that the invasion would be protracted. "If we could achieve it by a swift surgical stroke I would be for it." Further, "a course of bullying intervention would destroy the new image of the United States" and "might recklessly expend one of our greatest national assets—John F. Kennedy himself."[25]

Schlesinger's reasoning was well within the traditional bipartisan consensus on foreign policy, where objections to a particular tactic might be made, not on fundamental issues of right and wrong, not on something as basic as the principle of self-determination, but on grounds of "will it work?" and "what effect will it have on our image?"

In his book, Schlesinger did not reveal all the contents of his memo to Kennedy. But in an article in *The Nation* in 1977, another historian, Ronald Radosh, disclosed more information about Schlesinger's role in the Bay of Pigs invasion. It seems that in order to protect "one of our greatest national assets—John F. Kennedy himself," Schlesinger suggested that: "When lies must be told they should be told by subordinate officials."[26] (In the Reagan-era scandals of Iran-Contragate, this tactic of "plausible denial" became notorious.)

Deception would be necessary, Schlesinger said, because "a great many people simply do not at this moment see that Cuba presents so grave and compelling a threat to our national security as to justify a course of action which much of the world will interpret as calculated aggression against a small nation."[27]

He went on to include in his memo sample questions and lying answers, if the issue of invasion should come up in a press conference:

Q. Mr. President, is CIA involved in this effort?
A. I can assure you that the United States has no intention of using force to overthrow the Castro regime.[28]

Four days before the invasion, President Kennedy told a press conference: "There will not be, under any conditions, any intervention in Cuba by U.S. armed forces."[29]

Schlesinger and the other scholars who played roles as servants to national power were following the prescription of the nineteenth-century historian Leopold von Ranke, who is considered the apostle of "objective" history because of statements such as "The strict presentation of the facts . . . is undoubtedly the supreme law." But, at another time, von Ranke wrote: "For history is not simply an academic subject: the knowledge of the history of mankind . . . should above all benefit our own nation, without which our work could not have been accomplished."[30]

Few historians, of course, were in the position of a Schlesinger or a Bundy, who could possibly exert some influence on national policy. Most of us could expect, at the most, to have some influence on our students, both by what we did and by how we played our roles as citizens in the world outside the classroom.

Granted that the circumstances were difficult, as they always are, in a situation where one's job is within someone else's power to grant or to withhold, still, there is the possibility of choice. And the choice is between teaching and acting according to our most deeply felt values, whether or not it meets approval from those with power over us—or being dishonest with ourselves, censoring ourselves, in order to be safe.

For me, from the start of my teaching career, I resisted self-censorship. I do not attribute this to any special bravery but to the circumstances of my life. The fact that I entered the academic world late—after three years in a shipyard, my experience as a wartime bombardier, my various jobs—gave a strength and confidence to my political views. I knew that, unless it were simply defined as *honesty*, "objectivity" was neither possible nor desirable.

I thought that history might play some role in bringing about a better world, but not as a buttress to any particular party, nation, or ideology. I decided that, in the inevitable selection of material that goes with teaching and writing history, I would choose issues and present information designed to raise questions about war and peace, racial discrimination, and economic inequality. And I could not imagine that I would confine my life to the classroom and the library, that I would stand aside during the important conflicts of our time.

For teachers and scholars in any time, this is a prescription for trouble. And in the atmosphere of the Cold War, college administrators were more nervous than usual about the possibility that some faculty member would come under public political scrutiny.

The fact that my first teaching job was in a southern black college for women probably diminished the risk. I did not deliberately seek out a position in a Negro college, but when the job was offered to me, I was happy to accept. It did not occur to me that Negro colleges, being out of the main line of vision in American education, could be a kind of refuge for unorthodox teachers, but this was often the case.

As I became involved in the developing civil rights movement in Atlanta—the sit-ins, the demonstrations, the picketing, the boycotts—I was asked to join the executive committee of the newly formed Student Nonviolent Coordinating Committee (SNCC), which was born out of the sit-in movement. Along with Ella Baker, a black woman who had been on the staff of Martin Luther King and the Southern Christian Leadership Conference, I was considered an "adult adviser" to SNCC.

I became a kind of historian-participant in the movement, writing articles for *Harper's Magazine, The Nation,* the *New Republic,* and other publications, in the midst of teaching and working with SNCC. I did not know that the FBI was monitoring my activities at Spelman. But in the mid-1970s I succeeded, through the Freedom of Information Act, in getting at least part of my FBI file—hundreds of pages of FBI memos, news clippings, and assorted documents.

In a memo from FBI agent M.A. Jones to "Mr. DeLoach" (a top official of the FBI), Jones wrote: "In connection with an article entitled 'Don't Call Students Communists' by captioned individual which appeared in the 10-24-65 issue of the 'Boston Globe', the Director has inquired as to what do we have in files on Zinn." Jones then went through my military and educational record. And: "While with Spelman College he was quite active in racial matters and information we have received indicates that he continues to be involved in various civil rights matters. He is currently on the Security Index of our Boston Office."

In 1961 and 1962, I was asked by the Southern Regional Council, an Atlanta research group, to make a report on the demonstrations and mass arrests in Albany, Georgia, a small city 150 miles south of Atlanta. I interviewed black people just out of jail, as well as leaders of the Albany movement, and SNCC people who had set up a "Freedom House" in Albany at the start of the demonstrations there. I also talked with the police chief of the city and the sheriff of Daugherty County, of which Albany was the seat.

My report, "Albany, Georgia: A Study in Federal Responsibility," declared very bluntly that the U.S. government was failing to enforce the Constitution in Albany. The constitutional rights of black people and civil rights statutes dating back to the Civil War were being violated again and again by local law enforcement officials while the president, the Department of Justice, and the FBI looked the other way. My report was a front-page story in the *New York Times,* and was also quoted in *I.F. Stone's Weekly.*

When the press asked Martin Luther King Jr. if he agreed with my criticism of the FBI, he made a strong statement about racism in the

FBI. This clearly infuriated J. Edgar Hoover. The FBI had opened a file on King in New York in September 1958 when King was approached outside a New York church by the black Communist leader Benjamin Davis.[31] In the report on me requested by Hoover, agent M.A. Jones said: "Zinn has written many articles criticizing the Director and the FBI in the past, some of which have appeared in 'The Nation.'"

As I observed and participated in civil rights activity in the Deep South—in Atlanta; in Selma, Alabama; in Hattiesburg, Mississippi—I continued to criticize the federal government for its failure to protect black people from violations of their civil rights by local officials. I also spoke out on other issues, including U.S. foreign policy. The FBI memo commented on my actions while teaching at Spelman College:

> Zinn's continued demonstration of procommunist and anti-U.S. sympathies appears to stem from his activities at Spelman College . . . which involved such activities as: organizing a seminar in Atlanta, Georgia, on 'American Policy Toward Cuba' at which one of the speakers denounced U.S. policy toward Cuba; calling for a demonstration in front of the White House in February, 1962 by students from all over the United States demanding the end of the nuclear testing.

The report on me concluded:

> Subject's activities make this a close case as to whether he belongs on the Reserve Index or the Security Index. [People on the Security Index were to be arrested and placed in camps whenever the president decided that national security required invoking the Emergency Detention Program passed by Congress in 1950.] He can, however, be included on the Security Index under the criterion [that] facts have been developed which clearly and unmistakably depict the subject as a dangerous individual who might commit acts inimical to the national defense and public safety of the United States in time of emergency. . . . Security Index cards are being forwarded to the Boston Office.

Clearly, a historian who decided to participate in history was even more dangerous to the government and its agencies of surveillance than one who wrote about it, however unorthodox that writing might be.

In 1963, after seven years at Spelman College, during which the president became more and more nervous about my political activity, he finally fired me for "insubordination." Was the problem my support of Spelman students in their rebellion against the authoritarianism of the administration? Or was it my activities in the Atlanta community in the civil rights movement, and in protests against U.S. foreign policy? I knew I was being insubordinate, both to the college administration and to the government. And I thought that there might have been outside influences at work—perhaps the conservative white businesspeople on the board of trustees, perhaps the FBI, or both.

My closest colleague at Spelman College was a friend and fellow historian, Staughton Lynd. He also participated in various activities of the civil rights movement (he was director of the Freedom Schools in the Mississippi Summer Project in 1964). We walked the same picket line in Atlanta to protest U.S. policy toward Cuba, participated in the same forum against the House Committee on Un-American Activities, and watched with concern the growth of nuclear arsenals on both sides, in a race which we believed was initiated by the United States, the dramatic symbol being the bombings of Hiroshima and Nagasaki.

The trajectory of Staughton Lynd, from brilliant student at Harvard and Columbia, prize-winning historian, teacher at Spelman, professor at Yale, to disappearance from the historical profession, tells much about the effect of the Cold War on the academy.

After I was fired from Spelman, and about the time I was offered a post at Boston University, Staughton resigned his job at Spelman and was immediately hired by Yale University. In 1965, as the U.S. war in Vietnam sharply escalated, he joined Tom Hayden of Students for a Democratic Society (SDS) and Herbert Aptheker, a historian and communist, in a trip to enemy territory—North Vietnam. Shortly after that, he was dropped from the Yale faculty.

One would think that Lynd, on the basis of his academic record, would be sought after by colleges and universities. But when he applied for a position at Chicago State College, he was turned down because of his "public activities." Seeking a job at the University of Chicago, he was rejected because he showed "bad judgment" in commenting on the experience of radical historian Jesse Lemisch. Lemisch had been fired after one term by the University of Chicago, told by his department chair: "Your convictions interfered with your scholarship."[32]

Staughton Lynd was unable to get a teaching job in the Chicago area. Convinced now that he was being blacklisted, he left the historical profession, enrolled at the University of Chicago Law School, and subsequently became a labor lawyer.

It was not surprising that Lynd's trip to North Vietnam made him persona non grata to the academy. The war in Vietnam epitomized the anticommunism of the Cold War years. But it was also a turning point.

In the civil rights struggles of the early 1960s, the attempts of J. Edgar Hoover and others to paint the various movements as influenced by communism (former President Harry Truman said he was sure the sit-in movement was inspired by communists) had to confront the growing acceptance of these movements by mainstream America. Martin Luther King Jr. and SNCC had such overwhelming support in the black community, and more and more in the white community, that the Communist accusations did not work. Indeed, Hoover was reduced to lascivious spying in a desperate effort to find a basis for discrediting King.

The very fact that the war in Vietnam was justified as a war to "stop Communism," that the Cold War against Communism became inextricably tied to the conflict in Vietnam, meant that as the war itself became discredited, the American public became more and more skeptical when the government invoked "a communist threat" to justify military action.

But that was a ten-year process, from 1965, when the public accepted the government's rationale for the large-scale dispatch of U.S. troops to Vietnam, to 1975, when all the surveys showed an enormous public disillusionment with the nation's political leaders. During that period, historians, like the rest of the country, struggled with their consciences and with one another over the issue of U.S. involvement in the war. But also, they battled about the proper role of historians, in the classroom, in their writing, and in the society at large.

My antiwar activity, which began in the spring of 1965 when I spoke at an early protest meeting on the Boston Common along with Herbert Marcuse, took me in the summer of 1966 to Japan. An organization of Japanese intellectuals called Beheiren, which opposed the American war in Vietnam, invited me and a fellow veteran of SNCC, an African American named Ralph Featherstone, to do a whirlwind speaking tour of thirteen Japanese cities in fourteen days.

When we returned to Tokyo after our tour, I arranged a meeting with the American ambassador to Japan, Edwin Reischauer. I had known Reischauer when I was a Fellow in East Asian Studies at Harvard and he was teaching Japanese history there. I had attended a celebratory dinner for him at Joyce Chen's famous Chinese restaurant in Cambridge when he was appointed ambassador by President Kennedy.

Our meeting in Tokyo, however, was a clash of historians with opposing views on the Vietnam War. I recalled to Reischauer his 1954 book, *Wanted: An Asian Policy*, in which he wrote that a policy based largely on stopping communism was "a dangerous oversimplification of our Asian problem."[33] But now, he was defending U.S. policy in Vietnam in the traditional manner of ambassadors, who, whatever their personal views, think it their obligation to go along with their administration. Perhaps, also, those personal views change in the awesome atmosphere of an embassy.

At the very time that Featherstone and I were in Japan, Noam Chomsky was giving a talk at Harvard, which later became reprinted in the *New York Review of Books* as "The Responsibility of Intellectuals." "It is the responsibility of intellectuals," Chomsky wrote, "to speak truth and to expose lies."[34]

But, he said, there were intellectuals who had a different view. He quoted the German philosopher and supporter of the Nazis, Martin Heidiegger, who said in 1933 that "truth is the revelation of that which makes a people certain, clear, and strong in its action and knowledge." And he pointed to Arthur Schlesinger's admitted lies at the time of the Bay of Pigs invasion, and to his complimenting the *New York Times* for suppressing information on the planned invasion of Cuba.

Chomsky wrote: "it is significant that such events provoke so little response in the intellectual community—no feeling, for example, that there is something strange in the offer of a major chair in humanities to a historian who feels it to be his duty to persuade the world that an American-sponsored invasion of a nearby country is nothing of the sort."[35]

Schlesinger had characterized U.S. policies in Vietnam in 1954 as "part of our general program of international goodwill." Chomsky commented: "Unless intended as irony, this remark shows either a colossal cynicism or an inability, on a scale that defies comment, to comprehend elementary phenomena of contemporary history."[36]

Chomsky pointed to statements made by other intellectual supporters of the Vietnam War, advisers to President Kennedy, as examples of flagrant historical distortion: Walter Rostow had written: "Throughout the 19th century, in good conscience, Americans could devote themselves to the extension of both their principles and their power on this continent"; and McGeorge Bundy wrote that "American democracy has no enduring taste for imperialism."[37]

In 1967, Beacon Press published my book *Vietnam: The Logic of Withdrawal*, which quickly went through eight printings. Although books had been published that were critical of the war, mine was the first to call for an immediate withdrawal from Indochina.

Around that time, the Department of Political Science at Boston University was voting on whether or not to give me tenure. They were supposed to have made the decision in 1965 and 1966, but clearly opposition existed in the department by a few senior members who criticized my very public activity against the Vietnam War. However, in the spring of 1967, it finally came to a vote. Again, there was opposition, again because of my stands on the war, but I had published more than anyone in the department and had excellent student evaluations of my classes. I was narrowly approved.

It was hard to say how many academics in the United States were denied tenure, refused appointments, or in other ways punished for speaking out against the war. Or how many remained silent in order to save their academic careers. I was lucky to have barely made it. But my involvement in the antiwar movement continued to put my job in jeopardy.

When, in 1968, I traveled to North Vietnam with the poet-priest Daniel Berrigan to receive three American pilots freed by the Vietnamese, there was grumbling at the administrative level. In 1972, when I made another trip to North Vietnam, the Dean of the College of Liberal Arts suggested that I was in violation of my contract for missing classes, although I had arranged for all of my classes to be covered by colleagues for the ten days that I was gone.

And when, in 1972, I denounced the new president of Boston University, John Silber, for inviting the U.S. Marines to campus to recruit for the war, and then calling the police to arrest protesters, I became a target for punishment for the rest of my teaching years at Boston University. My salary was kept low; I was denied teaching assistants (though 400 students signed up for my course each semester); I was turned down for a leave when I was invited to teach for a semester at the University of Paris. And when I refused to cross the university secretaries' picket line during a strike, I and a few other faculty were threatened with dismissal, then saved by an outpouring of protest.

None of this was life-threatening, and I was not willing to trade my freedom of speech and action for the tiny emoluments of the profession. But it made me wonder how many other faculty, around the country, were enduring some kind of pressure because of their stands against the war.

The risk of speaking out is always present in the academy, where jobs and prestige depend on the approval of administrators, businessmen-trustees, and politicians. But there are times when faculty are more impelled to take the risks. The Vietnam era was one of those times, because the war struck powerfully at the consciences of many scholars. And as the whole country turned, year by year, against the war, faculty felt more secure about criticizing government policy.

That security had not existed in the 1950s, when there was no domestic movement able to mount a critique of American military policy abroad, whether the intervention in Korea, the subversion of governments in Iran and Guatemala, or the enormous buildup of nuclear weapons. The resurgence of militarism after 1950 created a convenient atmosphere for weakening the labor movement in the way that foreign "threats" have been historically used to preempt challenges to corporate power.

However, the movement for civil rights of the early 1960s encouraged protest and grassroots organization, and paved the way for the antiwar movement. The struggle against racial segregation emboldened some historians, as well as other academics, to break from the stifling atmosphere of the 1950s, in their actions as citizens, in their professional organizations, and in their scholarship. Martin Duberman of Princeton, who had written some distinguished works in American history, turned his talents to the stage, and wrote a documentary drama, *In White America*, which was both troubling and inspiring as it traced the history of racism in the United States from early slavery up to the 1950s.

After the escalation of the war in Vietnam, historians, as did scholars in other fields (notably Noam Chomsky, who had made his reputation in linguistic philosophy), spoke at teach-ins, walked picket lines, joined demonstrations against the war. I became one of a crew of academics who traveled the country speaking against the war wherever we were invited.

In October of 1967, along with Noam Chomsky and others, I spoke at a meeting of thousands on the Boston Common—duly noted by the FBI in the file that I received from them. After that meeting, there was a long procession to the Arlington Street Church, where the historic church candelabra was lit and young men filed up to hold their draft cards in the flames. Harvard graduate student Michael Ferber spoke eloquently about the war. Soon he and four others (Dr. Benjamin Spock, Rev. William Sloane Coffin, writers Mitchell Goodman and Marcus Raskin) would be indicted for conspiring to induce young men to defy conscription.

Early in 1968, I traveled to Hanoi with Daniel Berrigan to bring back to Laos three American fliers who had been shot down over Vietnam, imprisoned, and were now being released by the North Vietnamese. Later that year, I made a trip to Paris with several other academics—historians Marilyn Young, George Kahin, Jonathan Mirsky, and economist Douglas Dowd—to meet with the North Vietnamese peace delegation in Paris.

The fall of 1969 saw the antiwar movement at its height, as several million people around the country gathered in towns and cities, many of them places that had never had an antiwar gathering, to protest the war. That was Moratorium Day. On the Boston Common, 100,000 people gathered. I was among many speakers that day, with the main speaker Senator George McGovern.

It is impossible to say how many of the tens of thousands of people arrested for protesting the war were historians. I was arrested five times, and I suppose my record is suggestive of the kinds of actions that took place in that time.

1970: About a hundred of us arrested for blocking buses carrying inductees at the Boston Army Base.

1971: I was one of thousands arrested in Washington in early May during several days of blocking streets and protesting the war. A few days later, I was arrested again, this time in Boston, picked out of a crowd of thousands who were encircling the Federal building.

1972: The "B.U. 62" were faculty and students arrested in the Student Union Lounge after we had occupied a dean's office to protest campus police brutality against antiwar demonstrators. Two teachers of English and one visiting writer were there. I was the lone historian.

Several hundred of us—academics, writers, people in the arts—in an action organized by psychologist Robert J. Lifton, were arrested for sitting in the corridor of the Capitol in Washington to protest President Nixon's continuation of the war.

A number of times in the 1960s and 1970s I was called upon to testify in the trials of antiwar protesters. Here I found a way of practicing my trade as a historian in an unusual way, to "teach" juries about American history in practical situations where more than a step up the academic ladder was at stake. I often testified as an "expert witness" on the history of civil disobedience in the United States. In 1973, in the trial of Daniel Ellsberg and Anthony Russo for distributing the "top secret" documents, which came to be known as the Pentagon Papers, I spoke to the jury for hours about the history of the Vietnam War.

A few historians threw the weight of their training on the other side. They became "court historians": Arthur Schlesinger Jr. for President Kennedy; John Roche for Lyndon Johnson. But historians by the thousands around the country participated in one way or another in the antiwar movement. And for the first time, the war became an issue at an annual meeting of the AHA in December of 1969. At that meeting, a group of historians formed a radical history caucus and decided to introduce an antiwar resolution at the business meeting of the association.

No such turnout for a business meeting of the AHA had ever taken place. A large auditorium was packed to the rafters because word had gotten out about the Radical Caucus and about the determination of the old guard of the AHA to block the caucus's plans. The resolution was introduced—it was I who was chosen to present it—calling for the withdrawal of the United States from the war. A heated debate took place and the old guard pulled a trump card: two historians associated with the left—Stuart Hughes and Eugene Genovese—spoke against the resolution on the ground that it would "politicize" the AHA, which was established for professional advancement, not political controversy.

A brief and almost comical jockeying for the microphone ensued between me and historian John Fairbank, the dean of China scholars in the United States, with whom I had always had a friendly relationship. Fairbank wrote to me later: "They voted you down because they did not believe the Vietnam War had affected their rights, opportunities, and procedures as historians. . . . The AHA exists for professional purposes only."

My rejoinder (we had an exchange of "open letters" printed in the AHA Newsletter, June 1970) was as follows:

> Let us assume the war does not affect us "as historians"; . . . It only affects us "as citizens." Well, when *do* you assemble with other citizens to speak out on the crucial issues of our time? . . . What can democracy possibly mean if not that people assembled whenever and wherever they can, for whatever reason, may express their preferences on the important issues of the day? If they may not, democracy is a fraud, because it means that the political leaders have effectively isolated the citizenry by taking up their

time in various jobs, while the leaders make the policies, and the citizens, in 99% of their life, remain silent.

C. Vann Woodward, a widely respected historian of the South, was in the chair as president of the AHA. Although he had done important pioneering scholarly work in moving away from the old racist histories, he was clearly troubled by the introduction of the Vietnam issue into the proceedings of the association.

The resolution that did get the approval of the organization shows both the broad antiwar sentiment among historians and the limits they saw to involvement in the issue. It was presented immediately after the defeat of the radical caucus resolution, and called also for the withdrawal of the United States from the war, but based this on the fact that the historical profession was being hurt by so much of the national wealth going into the war.

This belief that historians should not be concerned with what was happening in the world, except as it affected their professional lives, was even stronger in the early stages of the American war in Vietnam. At an International Congress of Historical Sciences (ICHS) held in Vienna, Austria, in the fall of 1965, with 140 historians from the United States among the 2,400 delegates, the editor of the *American Historical Review*, Boyd Shafer, reported to the AHA:

> One attempt . . . to introduce current political views (on Vietnam) failed. The Bureau . . . firmly opposed the introduction of any current political question and . . . the secretary-general, Michel Francois, delivered a strong admonition against such attempts, saying that ICHS had been and could only be devoted to scientific historical studies.[38]

Nevertheless, in the 1960s, affected undoubtedly by the powerful currents of the civil rights and antiwar movements, historians began to write a new kind of American history, which came to be known as "revisionist history." It repudiated the idea of "scientific historical studies" (one must recall that it was Stalinism in the Soviet Union that insisted on the Marxist interpretation of history as a "science"), called into question traditional interpretations, and explored areas of the American past that had been largely ignored in the orthodox accounts.

Forerunners of this new history, went back to the early part of century, and Charles Beard's *An Economic Interpretation of the Constitution of the United States*, when dared to depart from the traditional deification of the founding fathers. James Harvey Robinson, around the same time in *The New History*, prefigured the 1960s' call for "relevance" when he wrote: "The present has hitherto been the willing victim of the past; the time has now come when it should turn on the past and exploit it in the interest of advance."[39]

These were lone voices, not part of a larger movement in the profession. This was true also of a few historians in the 1950s such as Carl Becker, who wrote:

> Our libraries are filled with this stored-up knowledge of the past; and never before has there been at the disposal of society so much reliable knowledge of human experience. What influence has all this expert research had upon the social life of our time? . . . Very little surely, if anything.[40]

Philosophers who were interested in history were also divided on this issue. Alfred North Whitehead wrote: "The understanding which we want is an understanding of an insistent present. The only use of a knowledge of the past is to equip us for the present." Arthur O. Lovejoy, representing the more dominant view, wrote that the aims of the historian must not be confused with those of the "social reformer." The job of the historian, he declared is "to know whether . . . certain events or sequence of events, happened at certain past times, and what . . . the characters of those events were."[41]

The 1960s saw a movement away from the orthodoxy of "objectivity," indeed saw it as a cover for acceptance of the injustices that existed in the nation. As the status quo was being challenged in many different areas of American life, similar challenges began to appear in the realm of ideas.

The seminal work breaking from the traditional benign interpretations of American foreign policy was William Appleman Williams's *The Tragedy of American Diplomacy*, which he published in 1959, where he declared boldly that American relations with other countries "denies and subverts American ideas and ideals." He saw American policy as one of expansionism, which came out of the needs of capitalism. The worldview of the United States was that "freedom and prosperity depend upon the continued expansion of its economic and ideological system through the policy of the open door."[42]

As the foreign policies of the Cold War came more and more under criticism—the subversion of governments undesirable to the United States, the support of right-wing dictatorships around the globe, the frightening growth of nuclear weapons and the arms race with the Soviet Union—Williams's view became the basis for a new school of "revisionist" historians. A new publication of the 1960s, *Studies on the Left*, became an outlet for them.

The ranks of the new radical scholars in diplomatic history grew through the 1960s and in the decades that followed. Between Marilyn Young's 1968 book *The Rhetoric of Empire*, and her 1991 book *The Vietnam Wars*, dozens of historians began to look critically at the record of American diplomacy. Indeed, it was a tribute to their influence that Princeton University Press in 1973 published a strong critique of the W.A. Williams school (Robert Maddox, *The New Left and the Origins of the Cold War*).

As the various movements of the 1960s and 1970s influenced millions of Americans, new histories challenged orthodox treatments of every aspect of the American past. Alfred Young fathered a new school of historical interpretations of the American Revolution, emphasizing the role of farmers, working people, women, black people. Traditional accounts of slavery had been superficial and even apologetic. Now the "political economy of slavery" was analyzed by Eugene Genovese in *Roll Jordan Roll*, and the remarkable culture kept alive in the slave communities was chronicled by Lawrence Levine in *Black Culture and Black Consciousness*.

Du Bois's classic, *Black Reconstruction*, was now joined by new accounts. C. Vann Woodward's *Reunion and Reaction* traced the economic motives of the northern republican establishment in bringing black Reconstruction to a halt in 1977. Black and white historians (John Hope Franklin, Eric Foner) now replaced the old racist accounts of the Reconstruction period with powerful and comprehensive histories. Vincent Harding, a historian who had been in the civil rights movement in the South, began a multivolume history of the black experience.

Whole shelves of books on the history of women began to appear in the bookstores, written by a new generation of women historians. Eleanor Flexner's *A Century of Struggle* showed how women, throughout American history, resisted their treatment as inferiors and demanded equal rights. Gerda Lerner put together the writings and speeches of black women and white women in her anthologies *Black Women in White*

America and *The Female Experience*. Roslyn Baxandall, Linda Gordon, and Susan Reverby edited two editions of *America's Working Women*.

A respectful new attention began to be paid to the history of the indigenous peoples of North America, both by white historians and Indian scholars. Gary Nash's *Red, White, and Black* was an important account of the relations between the races in early America. In *The Invasion of America*, Franklin Jameson unhesitatingly described the ruthlessness with which American settlers took over Indian land and went about the destruction of Indian tribal life. In the 1980s and 1990s, Indian scholars (Donald Grinde, Ward Churchill) began more and more to reclaim the cultural history of their people.

When, in the late 1970s, I set out to write *A People's History of the United States*, I had the work of the new histories to draw upon. In the next fifteen years, the book went through at least twenty-five printings, and sold over 400,000 copies. What was clear was that the movements of the 1960s and 1970s had created a whole new generation of people—teachers, students, others in the general population—who were hungry for a history less celebratory, more critical, more conscious of the victimization as well as the resistance of ordinary people.

How powerfully the new history had gained ground in the profession could be ascertained by noting that some of its practitioners, far being marginalized, now had a certain prominence, and even became presidents of the Organization of American Historians in the 1980s and 1990s, starting with William Appleman Williams himself, and then Eric Foner and Blanche Wiesen Cook. The AHA had moved from its conservatism enough to ask Foner to edit a volume of essays, *The New American History*. The Association had come some distance since 1968, when Barton Bernstein's anthology, *Towards a New Past*, was clearly at the margin of the profession.

Published in 1990, Foner's volume began by saying: "In the course of the past twenty years, American history has been remade."[43] It devoted much of its space to "Major Themes," the choice of which reflected the new sensibility. Essays appeared by Alice Kessler-Harris and Linda Gordon, who had done distinguished work in social history and women's history. Essays in African American history and labor history also appeared, as well as one by Walter LaFeber, a diplomatic historian in the tradition of William Appleman Williams.

The new history was arousing heated reactions from defenders of both the old order in foreign and domestic policy and the old order in historiography. Conservative politicians joined conservative historians in denouncing "the revisionists." Senate Republican leader Robert Dole told a cheering audience of American Legionnaires that the purpose of the new approaches to history was "to denigrate America."

One conservative historian, Gertrude Himmelfarb, writing in the *Times Literary Supplement*, associated the new history with "postmodernism," and accused it of denying "any objective truth about the past," and of promoting "history at the pleasure of the historian." She invoked the traditional aim of historical writing as reconstructing the past as it "actually was."

This was a theme echoed again and again in the criticism of the new history. But Peter Novick, in *That Noble Dream*, had demonstrated the hypocrisy of historians who called for "objectivity," and then revealed their own strong point of view. Does not the very selection of subject matter, the decision about what is important in history, make objectivity a myth?

Himmelfarb, in that same essay, shows what she thinks is important when she expresses delight at a student's excitement in discovering that Andrew Jackson's first message to Congress was written by the historian George Bancroft. And then declares her annoyance at the emphasis in the new history on "race-class-gender."

Lynne Cheney, former head of the National Endowment for the Humanities during a Republican administration, said: "The new history is disdainful of facts, as if there are no such things as facts, only interpretation."[44] But in the same statement, she said that too much emphasis was placed on criticism of the established power structure. Would she have complained about "interpretation" if that interpretation defended the power structure?

In Dickens's *Hard Times*, his caricature of a pedant, Mr. Gradgrind, admonishes a young teacher: "Now what I want is Facts. Teach these boys and girls nothing but facts. Facts alone are wanted in life. . . . Stick to facts, sir." But behind every fact presented to a reader or a listener is a judgment—the judgment that *this* fact is important. And so to Himmelfarb the discovery of George Bancroft's authorship is important, but the new historians see importance in information about blacks, women, working people, whom they (we) see as neglected in the orthodox histories.

The shattering of the Soviet Union, the disappearance of "the Soviet threat," did not bring an end to the Cold War as waged by the United States, both in the world and within American society. Expansionist policies in the world, and the marginalization of opposition at home, antedated the existence of the Soviet Union and continued after its demise. However, with the social movements of recent decades, that opposition became less marginal, and the writing of history, while not replacing traditional history, became a force to be recognized.

This was evident in a number of ways. For instance, the traditional story of Columbus as hero, presented for generation after generation to schoolchildren, as well as in higher education, and reproduced in the national culture, was challenged for the first time in the 1980s and 1990s. The opening chapter of my *People's History*, drawing on the ancient accounts by the Spanish priest Bartolome de las Casas, saw Columbus, driven by a ruthless quest for gold, and bringing about the annihilation of the Indian population of Hispaniola, as a forerunner of modern imperialism.

By the time of the quincentennial celebrations of 1992, because of the pioneering work of middle-school teacher Bill Bigelow and others, teachers all over the country were beginning to teach the Columbus story in a different, and undoubtedly troubling, way. Demonstrations took place in various parts of the country against celebrations of Columbus. A parade in Denver had to be called off because of the protests. Children's books now appeared with a new version of the Columbus story.

In the early 1990s, a group of historians drew up a set of "National Standards" for the teaching of history, with the emphases of the new history. These were distributed to 20,000 school districts around the country, and drew the ire of conservative historians and politicians. The U.S. Senate passed 99–1 a resolution denouncing it, calling for a more patriotic treatment of history and a greater admiration for "western civilization."

The year 1995, with celebrations everywhere commemorating the end of World War II, saw the controversy over the bombing of Hiroshima, which had begun right after the war, reach its height. The trajectory of that controversy through the postwar period is indicative of what was happening during that time in the field of history.

In 1962, while a fellow in East Asian Studies at Harvard (the fellowships were part of an energetic effort by American foundations, after the victory of the Communists in China, to pay more scholarly attention to Asia), I became interested in the Hiroshima-Nagasaki bombings. Part of my interest came from my own experience as a bombardier in the European theater in World War II, when I had participated in the totally senseless napalm bombing of a French village (Is there such a thing as a bombing that is only partially senseless?) just before the end of the war.

I wrote an essay for the *Columbia University Forum* called "A Mess of Death and Documents," in which I concluded that there was no justification, moral or military, for dropping the atomic bombs on Hiroshima and Nagasaki. I based my argument on the official report of the U.S. Strategic Bombing Survey, the interviews with Japanese leaders conducted by Robert Butow in his book, *Japan's Decision to Surrender*, the narrative of the Swiss writer Robert Jungk, *Brighter Than a Thousand Suns*, and Herbert Feis (who had access to State Department documents), *Japan Subdued*.

A few years later (1965), Gar Alperovitz published his groundbreaking book *Atomic Diplomacy*, which was based on extensive research into the diaries of important political leaders involved in the decision to drop the bombs (Henry Stimson, James Byrnes, James Forrestal). Alperovitz argued that the decision, certainly not necessary to win the war, was a political move, aimed at the Soviet Union.

In the decades that followed, more of the new historians did research that corroborated Alperovitz's conclusions. Barton Bernstein collected documents and wrote for the *Bulletin of Atomic Scientists*, using new data from the papers of government officials. Martin Sherwin's *A World Destroyed*, based on extensive research into government archives and presidential papers, underlined Alperovitz's thesis: "Believing that the bomb should be used if it was ready before the Japanese surrendered, Truman, Stimson, and Byrnes reasoned that such a clear demonstration of its extraordinary power would induce the Soviets to exchange territorial objectives for the neutralization of this devastating weapon."[45]

In 1995, I wrote an essay, which became part of the *Open Magazine Pamphlet Series*, called "Hiroshima: Breaking the Silence," in which I made use of much of the scholarly work that had been done on the subject, in which I raised, more sharply than I had in my earlier essay, the moral issue. I urged that we "reject the belief that the lives of others are worth less than the lives of Americans."[46]

The same year, Gar Alperovitz, having struggled for years and finally succeeding in getting thousands of classified government documents released to him under the Freedom of Information Act, published his massive work, *The Decision to Use the Atomic Bomb*. It was a powerful argument against deception and silence, and received much more attention than the book he had written thirty years before.

What was important was that now the argument against the use of the atomic bombs was no longer on the margin of the culture. It was in the forefront. There was still great resistance among the American public to accepting that the United States was wrong in that decision. The memory of Pearl Harbor, the continued ignorance about the readiness of the Japanese to surrender whether or not the bomb was used, contributed to that resistance. But, as Alperovitz pointed out: "A poll taken in 1991 [*New York Times*, December 8, 1991] at the time of the fiftieth anniversary of Pearl Harbor reported that roughly half of those surveyed felt that both sides should apologize for the respective acts which marked the beginning and the end of World War."[47]

The intensity of the antagonism toward the new history was itself a measure of how much had changed over the long course of the Cold War. Back in 1961, in his presidential address to the AHA, Samuel Flagg Bemis had declared that "Too much . . . self-criticism is weakening to a people."[48] But thirty-odd years later, there was a new generation of historians, many of whom agreed with John Dower, who said: "We accuse the Japanese of sanitizing their history, but we're doing the same thing, . . . anyone who's critical is called an America-hater. Is that what America stands for—unquestioning, blind, patriotic nationalism?"[49]

In 1995, the U.S. Congress was dominated by Republican and Democratic conservatives. The president was a centrist Democrat who seemed inclined to compromise again and again with the conservative agenda. And yet, out of the movements of the 1960s and 1970s, even in the midst of military interventions, there had developed in the nation something that conservatives spoke of with apprehension as "a permanent adversarial culture."[50]

In that adversarial culture, the new history had come to play an important part.

Notes

1. *Sawdust Caesar* (New York: Harper, 1935).
2. George T. Blakey, *Historians on the Homefront: American Propagandists for the Great War* (Univ. Press of Kentucky, 1970).
3. Peter Novick, *That Noble Dream* (Cambridge, UK: Cambridge Univ. Press, 1988).
4. Novick, *Dream* "Faith of a Historian."
5. "History as an Act of Faith," *American Historical Review* (1934).
6. Novick, *Dream*.
7. Ibid.
8. (New York: Appleton-Century-Crofts, 1950).
9. Novick, *Dream*.
10. Ibid.
11. Ibid.
12. Ellen Schrecker, *No Ivory Tower: McCarthyism and the Universities* (New York: Oxford Univ. Press, 1986).

13. David Caute, *The Great Fear* (New York: Simon & Schuster, 1978).

14. Novick, *Dream*.

15. Ibid.

16. Schrecker, *Tower*

17. Ibid.

18. (New York: Knopf, 1948).

19. James Loewen, *Lies My Teacher Told Me* (New York: The New Press, 1995).

20. See Hartz, *The Liberal Tradition in America* (New York: Harcourt Brace, 1955).

21. Congressional Record, May 23, 1924.

22. LaGuardia Papers, Municipal Archives, New York, January 13, 1927.

23. Schrecker, *Tower*.

24. Arthur Schlesinger Jr., *A Thousand Days* (Boston: Houghton Mifflin, 1965).

25. Ibid.

26. Ronald Radosh, "Historian in the Service of Power," *Nation*, August 6,1977.

27. Ibid.

28. Ibid.

29. Victor Bernstein and Jesse Gordon, "The Press and the Bay of Pigs," Columbia University Forum, Fall 1967.

30. Fritz Stern, *The Varieties of History* (New York: Meridian, 1956).

31. See David J. Garrow, *The F.B.I. and Martin Luther King, Jr.* (New York: Penguin, 1983).

32. Jesse Lemisch, *On Active Service in War and Peace* (Chicago: New Hogtown Press, 1975).

33. Edwin Reischauer, *Wanted: An Asian Policy* (New York: Alfred Knopf, 1955).

34. Reprinted in Noam Chomsky, *American Power and the New Mandarins* (New York: Pantheon, 1969).

35. Ibid.

36. Ibid.

37. Ibid.

38. Newsletter of the American Historical Association, 1966.

39. (New York: Macmillian, 1912).

40. Carl Becher, "What Are the Historical Facts?" *The Western Political Quarterly*, September 1955.

41. Alfred North Whitehead, *The Aims of Education* (New York: Mentor, 1956).

42. Williams, *Tragedy* (New York: Dell, 1962).

43. Eric Foner, *The New American History* (Philadelphia Temple Univ. Press, 1990).

44. TK

45. (New York: Vintage, 1977).

46. (Westfield, NJ: Open Magazine Pamphlets, 1995).

47. Gar Alperovitz et al., *The Decision to Use the Atomic Bomb* (New York: Knopf, 1995).

48. Novick, *Dream*.

49. John Dower, Quoted in Boston *Globe*, July 25, 1995.

50. Adam Garfinkle, *Telltale Hearts*, (New York: St. Martin's Press, 1995).

A YELLOW RUBBER CHICKEN: BATTLES AT BOSTON UNIVERSITY

from *You Can't Be Neutral on a Moving Train: A Personal History of Our Times* (1994)

Howard was always a troublemaker, perhaps never more so than at the two academic institutions, Spelman College and Boston University, where he earned his bread as an immensely popular if controversial teacher and scholar. After being dismissed from Spelman in 1963 for "insubordination" because of his civil rights activism, Howard moved to Boston and was hired a year later by B.U.'s political science department. The timing was hardly ideal for a young professor awaiting tenure review, and, to be sure, Howard was no ordinary junior faculty member. He would eventually receive tenure in 1967, though the decision was delayed several years on account of his ongoing involvement in the Civil Rights Movement and his outspoken opposition to the Vietnam War. The penultimate chapter of Howard's memoir begins with his arrival in Boston: "From the start, my teaching was infused with my own history. I would try to be fair to other points of view, but I wanted more than 'objectivity'; I wanted my students to leave my classes not just better informed, but more prepared to relinquish the safety of silence, more prepared to speak up, to act against injustice wherever they saw it. This, of course, was a recipe for trouble." The rest of the chapter details his "battles at Boston University," especially during the long and controversial tenure of John Silber, a man of short stature, vast ego, and mean spirit who presided over the university for more than thirty years. The two men "clashed almost immediately," and had several high-profile confrontations, including one episode where Silber lied to members of the faculty, claiming that Howard had once tried to burn down the president's office. In a rare expression of regret, Silber later apologized publicly to Howard at a faculty meeting. Still, Silber's academic "reign of terror"—which included crackdowns on union organizing and free speech, routine gender discrimination, anti-gay purges, shady fund-raising activities, and ideological warfare against liberal and leftist faculty—inspired in Howard and many of his courageous fellow colleagues a renewed determination to fight back in an attempt "to honor the idea that a university should provide a free and humane atmosphere for humane learning."

———

FROM THE START, my teaching was infused with my own history. I would try to be fair to other points of view, but I wanted more than "objectivity"; I wanted students to leave my classes not just better informed, but more prepared to relinquish the safety of silence, more prepared to speak up, to act against injustice wherever they saw it. This, of course, was a recipe for trouble.

Boston University's Department of Political Science, knowing I was no longer at Spelman (I was in Boston, writing two books on the South and the movement) offered me a job, to start in the fall of 1964. I accepted. They did not seem to be interested in the circumstances of my leaving Spelman. They had heard me give a lecture at B.U. several years earlier, they knew I had written a book which was given a prize by the American Historical Association (*LaGuardia in Congress*), and articles on the South for *Harper's*, the *Nation*, and the *New Republic*. So I seemed to them a likely prospect.

But the beginning of my teaching at Boston University coincided almost exactly with the steep escalation of the United States' war in Vietnam, after the hazy incident in the Gulf of Tonkin. I became involved immediately in the protests against the war: rallies, teach-ins, demonstrations, articles—one of these, for the *Nation*, arguing the case for withdrawal from Vietnam.

When I was hired, I was promised tenure after a year, which is a fairly strong guarantee of lifetime employment. But following that first year I was still without a tenure contract. A secretarial error, I was told. Another year passed (in which my antiwar activity increased) and another excuse was given.

Finally, in early 1967, the Department of Political Science held a meeting to vote on my tenure. There were a few professors opposed, saying flatly that my actions against the war were embarrassing to the university. On the other hand, student evaluations of my teaching were enthusiastic, and my fifth book was being published that spring. The department voted for tenure.

Approval came soon from the dean and the president. (This was four years before John Silber became president of the university.) All that remained was a vote of the Board of Trustees.

That spring of 1967, some students came to my office saying that the trustees were going to have their annual meeting, to coincide with a Founders Day dinner, and that the guest speaker would be Dean Rusk, secretary of state, in a splendid affair at the Sheraton Boston Hotel. Rusk was one of the strategists of the Vietnam War, and the students were going to organize a demonstration in front of the hotel. They wanted me to be one of the speakers.

I hesitated as I thought of my tenure decision in the hands of the trustees. But I could hardly say no—hadn't I always maintained that risking your job is a price you pay if you want to be a free person? I must confess that my courage was not absolute; I envisioned that I would be one of many speakers and perhaps not be noticed.

When the evening of the big event came, I made my way to the Sheraton Boston and joined several hundred demonstrators circling in front of the hotel. Soon one of the organizers came to escort me to the microphone, which was set up near the hotel entrance. I looked around. "Where are the other speakers?" I asked. He looked puzzled. "There are no other speakers."

And so I held forth to the crowd assembled in front of the hotel, talking about the war and why the United States did not belong in Vietnam. As I spoke, limousines drew up, one by one, and tuxedoed guests, including Dean Rusk, the trustees, and others, stepped out, stopped for a moment to take in the scene, and went into the hotel.

A few days later I received a letter from the Office of the President. As I opened it, I thought of that other letter of 1963 from the office of another president. But this one said, "Dear Professor Zinn, I am happy to inform you that you have been awarded tenure by a meeting of the Board of Trustees on the afternoon of . . ." So the trustees had voted me tenure in the afternoon, then arrived in the evening for the Founders Day dinner to find their newly tenured faculty member denouncing their honored guest.

Without that lucky winning of tenure, John Silber's arrival as president of Boston University would have ended my job. He had been a professor of philosophy and a dean at the University of Texas. He was fast talking and fast thinking and two philosophers on the B.U.

presidential search committee had recommended him on the basis of what I believe is a common fallacy among intellectuals, that to say someone is "bright," even "brilliant," as was said of Silber, is equivalent to saying someone is *good.*

Silber and I clashed almost immediately. What seemed to infuriate him was that I dared to criticize him publicly and unsparingly. (Yes, as the president of Spelman had said, I was insubordinate.)

One of the first things President Silber did upon taking office was to invite the U.S. Marines to the university to recruit students for the Marine Corps. This was in the spring of 1972, with the war in Vietnam still going on. Antiwar students organized a demonstration, sitting on the steps of the building where the recruiters were ensconced. It was nonviolent, but obstructive, no doubt, making it not impossible but difficult for students to meet with the recruiter.

I was not in that demonstration, but home in bed with a bad viral infection. Someone phoned me with the news: Silber had called the police, and was there on the scene with a bullhorn, acting like a general in a military operation as the police moved in, using police dogs and clubs, to arrest the demonstrators.

The next day, the official administration newspaper carried the headline "Disruptive Students Must Be Taught Respect for Law, Says Dr. Silber."

Still in bed, I wrote an article about the incident for a Boston newspaper, and it was widely reprinted on campus. I wanted to engage Silber on the history of the U.S. Marines, the philosophy of civil disobedience, and the concept of an "open university," a principle he claimed he was upholding by inviting the Marines to recruit.

"It is true," I wrote, "that one crucial function of the schools is training people to take the jobs that society has to offer. . . . But the much more important function of organized education is to teach the new generation that rule without which the leaders could not possibly carry on wars, ravage the country's wealth, keep down rebels and dissenters— the rule of obedience to legal authority. And no one can do that more skillfully, more convincingly than the professional intellectual. A philosopher turned university president is best of all. If his arguments don't work on the students—who sometimes prefer to look at the world around them than to read Kant—then he can call in the police, and after that momentary interruption (the billy club serving as exclamation point to the rational argument) the discussion can continue, in a more subdued atmosphere."

In what seemed to me a peculiar interpretation, Silber pointed to the example of Martin Luther King Jr. in arguing that students should give themselves up to arrest for what they had done. This led me to write: "How odd that a man whose own behavior that day more closely resembled that of Birmingham's Bull Connor—replete with police dogs, hidden photographers, and club-wielding police—should invoke the name of Martin Luther King, who would have been there on the steps with the students."

Silber declared his educational philosophy in 1976 on the op-ed page of the *New York Times*. He wrote: "As Jefferson recognized, there is a natural aristocracy among men. The grounds of this are virtue and talent. . . . Democracy freed from a counterfeit and ultimately destructive egalitarianism provides a society in which the wisest, the best, and the most dedicated assume positions of leadership. . . . As long as intelligence is better than stupidity, knowledge than ignorance, and virtue than vice, no university can be run except on an elitist basis." On another occasion, Silber said, "The more democratic a university is, the lousier it is."

His supreme confidence in his own intelligence, knowledge, and virtue led him to be arrogant with faculty, contemptuous of students, and to behave more and more like a petty dictator in running the university.

When his five-year contract expired in 1976, there was a campus-wide movement involving students, faculty, and deans, urging that he not be kept on. The faculty voted overwhelmingly that he should not be rehired, and fifteen of the sixteen deans concurred.

The decision, however, rested with the Board of Trustees. When a committee of the trustees recommended that his contract should not be renewed, Silber, ever the fighter, insisted on appearing before the board, and persuaded them to keep him on. After that close call, he set about to ensure his position. The deans who had called for his departure did not stay long. One by one they disappeared. A new chairman of the Board of Trustees took over—Arthur Metcalf, an industrialist and militarist (he wrote a column for a right-wing journal on military strategy) and a close friend of Silber's. (Soon after, Silber acquired stock in Metcalf's corporation, which he later sold for over a million dollars.)

After twenty years in the presidency, Silber pointed to how much money he had added to the university's endowment, and this was true, although it was also true that he had added a comparable amount to the university's debt. He was proud of the fact that he brought some distinguished people to the faculty. Indeed he did, but it was also a fact that many fine teachers left Boston University because they could not stand the atmosphere created by his administration.

His claim was that he had turned a mediocre institution into a "world-class university." To many of us, this was a bit like Mussolini trampling on civil liberties while boasting that he had made Italy into an important power, had brought order, had made the trains run on time.

Shortly after the trustees renewed his contract in 1976, Silber established censorship of student publications, requiring them to have faculty advisers who would have approval over what was printed. I was an adviser to one student newspaper, *The Exposure*, whose bold criticism of the administration undoubtedly led to the censorship policy. When I refused to act as censor the paper was denied funds to operate, and when student organizations voted to allocate money for it, the administration blocked the funding.

In 1978, the radical attorney William Kunstler was invited to speak at the B.U. Law School. In the course of his remarks he made a joking and unflattering remark about President Silber. The executive director of the Boston University radio station, who had planned to air the speech, was ordered to delete the remark from the tape. He refused, and, as he told me later, an administration official took him outside the building and presented him with a choice: resign or be fired. He resigned.

The Civil Liberties Union of Massachusetts, in its report of 1979, said it had "never, in memory, received such a large and sustained volume of complaints about a single . . . institution" as about Boston University, and that its investigation had led it to believe "that B.U. has violated fundamental principles of civil liberties and academic freedom."

Faculty members who did not have tenure became fearful of voicing criticism of the president. Those who spoke out, even if faculty committees on four different levels voted for them, faced the loss of their jobs. Silber had absolute power to overrule all faculty decisions on tenure, and used it.

Boston University, under Silber, became notorious throughout academia. University police, sometimes overtly, sometimes surreptitiously, took photos of students and faculty who participated in demonstrations. I remember one such picket line, with faculty and students walking peacefully outside the building where the trustees were meeting, carrying signs against apartheid in South Africa. A university security guard, with a dean standing nearby, put his camera right up to our faces, one by one, to take his photos.

A student who distributed leaflets in the hall outside another trustees' meeting was suspended for a semester. Another student, who distributed leaflets outside the stadium where a commencement was taking place, was ordered to leave or be arrested.

A graduating honors student about to go to law school, Maureen Judge, being interviewed for a university brochure, was asked to name "my two most inspiring and enjoyable professors." She named me as one of them, and then was told the interview would not be published unless she deleted my name. She refused.

One day a student named Yosef Abramowitz, active in Zionist affairs and also in the campaign to get B.U. to divest itself of its South African stocks, came to my office to tell me a disturbing story. He had hung a sign from his dormitory window with one word on it: "Divest." University workers were ordered to remove the sign. Twice more he put it up, twice more it was removed. He received a letter from the administration: he would be evicted from his room if he insisted on replacing the sign.

From my office, we called the Civil Liberties Union. They contacted a young lawyer in the area to ask if he would handle the case—it was an opportunity to test a new Massachusetts law on civil rights. The lawyer responded, "I'll be happy to take the case. I just graduated from the B.U. Law School."

I went to court to listen. The university's lawyer insisted that the word "divest" was not the problem. The issue was an aesthetic one: the sign, he said, disturbed the beauty of the neighborhood. To anyone who knew that neighborhood, or the architecture of Boston University, this was a hilarious statement.

Abramowitz's lawyer put on the witness stand student after student who testified about the things they had hung from their windows (for one, a yellow rubber chicken) without any complaint from the administration.

The judge made his decision: B.U. must stop interfering with Abramowitz's right of free speech.

As word spread about the strange events at Boston University, journalists trying to uncover what was going on reported again and again that faculty members were afraid to go on public record as being critical of the administration. A reporter for the *New York Times Magazine* wrote, "Most of the people—B.U. students and faculty, former faculty, former trustees—interviewed for this article, even those with nothing critical to say, wished to remain anonymous for fear of reprisals."

Meanwhile, Silber was raising his own salary in huge jumps, so that soon, at $275,000 a year, he made more than the presidents of Harvard,

Yale, Princeton, or M.I.T. Furthermore, he was getting special deals from the Board of Trustees: real estate sold to him at below the market price for his use as rental property, loans at little or no interest, a generous bonus package on top of his salary. As university president he had become a millionaire, not a customary thing in the academic world.

When questioned about the money spent to lavishly furnish his rent-free house, Silber would respond, "Do you want your president to live in a pup tent on the Charles River?"

His employees, on the other hand, had difficulty getting raises in their wages or their benefits. In self-defense they organized into unions: the faculty, the secretaries and staff, the librarians. And in 1979, with various grievances not met, all of these groups, at different times, went out on strike. For the faculty, the provocation was the university reneging on a contract at first agreed to by its negotiating committee.

I was one of the co-chairs of the strike committee of the faculty union (officially called, in the cautious language of college professors, the Postponement Committee). My job was to organize the picket lines at the entrance to every university building, to establish a rotation system among the hundreds of picketers. The faculty was admirable in its tenacity, showing up day after day, from early morning to evening, to walk the picket lines.

Some students complained about the canceled classes, but many came to our support. The normal functioning of the university became impossible. The College of Liberal Arts and a number of other schools were virtually closed down.

After nine days of picketing, endless meetings, strategy sessions, the university gave in. But Silber hated to acknowledge defeat. In a telegram sent to the trustees just before the settlement, he urged that in no way should it be conceded that it was the strike which brought about the university's acceptance of the contract with the union.

In the meantime, however, the secretaries had gone out on strike, too, and we all walked the picket lines together, a rare event in the academic world. Some of us in the faculty union tried to get our colleagues to refuse to go back to work until the administration agreed to a contract with the secretaries, but we failed to persuade. Our contract was signed, and teachers returned to their classes, with the secretaries still walking the picket line.

A number of us refused to cross those picket lines and held our classes out of doors. I met my class of about two hundred students on Commonwealth Avenue, one of the main Boston thoroughfares, in front of the building where we normally met. I rented a loudspeaker system and explained to the class why we were not going inside. We had a lively discussion about the reasons for the strike and how it connected with the subject of our course, "Law and Justice in America."

In the midst of our sidewalk class, the dean of the College of Liberal Arts showed up and handed me a circular from the administration: faculty were expected to meet their classes in their regular places or be considered in violation of their contracts.

A few days later, five faculty who had refused to cross the picket lines were charged with violation of the union contract, which prohibited "sympathy strikes." The article under which we were charged contained a provision which could lead to our being fired, though we all had tenure. In addition to me, there was my friend and colleague in the political science department, Murray Levin, one of the most popular lecturers in the university; Fritz Ringer, a distinguished historian; Andrew Dibner, a much-respected member of the psychology department; and Caryl Rivers, a nationally known columnist and novelist who taught journalism.

Ours soon became "the case of the B.U. Five." We had the help of the faculty union attorney and several outside lawyers. A Nobel Prize laureate at M.I.T., Dr. Salvadore Luria, organized a defense committee and circulated support petitions to faculty members all over the country. A group of academics in France sent a letter of protest to the Silber administration. The *Boston Globe* and other newspapers wrote editorials accusing the university of violating academic freedom.

A group of distinguished women writers—Grace Paley, Marilyn French, Marge Piercy, Denise Levertov—did readings for an overflow audience at the Arlington Street Church, to raise money for our defense.

The noise around the case must have become too much for John Silber. He backed down. The charges against us were dropped.

Faculty with tenure cannot easily be fired, but they can be punished for dissidence in other ways. When Murray Levin and I were recommended for raises by our department, Silber overturned them, year after year. One of the leaders of the union, Freda Rebelsky, an award-winning teacher and nationally known psychologist, was punished in the same way. Arnold Offner, a historian who had won an award for distinguished teaching, was denied a raise because a right-wing faculty member, a friend of Silber's, objected to something he said in class about American foreign policy.

Silber vetoed raises for me again and again. But our faculty contract had a procedure for appeal to an arbitration committee. In the early

1980s, when Silber once again overruled a department recommendation, the arbitration group went over the evidence (that year, my book *A People's History of the United States* was nominated for an American Book Award) and gave me my raise.

What seemed to anger Silber most was that every semester four hundred or more students would sign up for my lecture course: in the fall, "Law and Justice in America," in the spring, "Introduction to Political Theory." He refused to allot money for a teaching assistant, although classes with a hundred students would routinely have one or two assistants. He let it be known that I could get a teaching assistant if I limited enrollment in my classes to sixty students.

He knew that my classes discussed the most controversial social issues: freedom of expression, the race question, military intervention abroad, economic justice, socialism, capitalism, anarchism. On these issues, Silber and I had very different views. He was an admirer of the military, and apparently believed in supporting any government, whatever its record on human rights, so long as it was anti-Communist. (El Salvador's, for instance, even while that government was collaborating with death squads and terrorism.) He was extremely intolerant of homosexuality and not very enthusiastic about heterosexuality (he instituted a rule forbidding overnight guests of the opposite sex in dorms).

Speaking to a gathering of university presidents on the West Coast, Silber talked darkly about those teachers who "poison the well of academe." His two chief examples: Noam Chomsky and Howard Zinn.

In the fall of 1979, after all the strikes, the faculty began circulating a petition to request the trustees to dismiss Silber. A special assembly of the university faculty was called to vote on the issue. The day before that assembly I was sitting in my office with a student when a colleague who taught in the School of Education walked in. He said that he had just come from a faculty meeting at his school, where Silber had appealed to the faculty to vote down the petition for his removal. The backers of this petition, Silber said, were longtime troublemakers. Even before he'd became president, he said, Howard Zinn had tried to set fire to the president's office.

"You're not serious," I said.

"Oh, yes. He accused you of arson. We all sat there, bewildered. Do you have any idea what he was talking about?"

"No."

The student sitting in the office was interested. She was a graduate student in journalism. She said she would look into this.

Next morning the *Boston Globe* carried a story, prominently displayed, with photos of both Silber and me, and a headline: "Silber Accuses Zinn of Arson." The byline was that of the student who had been in my office. She verified that Silber had made such a statement to the School of Education, but also wrote that she had checked with the fire department. Indeed, there once had been a fire reported in the president's office, before Silber's time, but there was never any indication of whether it was accidental or deliberate and no one had ever been accused.

I began to get phone calls from lawyer friends. This is, they said, a textbook case of defamation, of libel. A terrific opportunity to sue Silber for all he's worth (now a fortune). I wouldn't hear of it. I was not going to get involved in a lawsuit—whatever the prize—that would then dominate my life for years.

That afternoon the faculty assembled for its special meeting. Silber presided. Since the main business was the petition calling for his removal, some thought he would turn the chair over to someone else. But Silber was not one to do that. It was said of Theodore Roosevelt that he had such an ego he wanted to preside over his own funeral; Silber was going to take charge of this meeting.

The hall filled and filled—clearly the largest turnout of faculty anyone could remember. Then Silber took the microphone: "Before the meeting officially begins, I want to apologize to Professor Howard Zinn." There was a buzz of astonishment—no one could imagine Silber ever apologizing to anyone for anything. What I suspected was that his lawyer friends had advised him to do so to minimize what might be a costly and losing lawsuit for defamation of character.

The hall became very quiet as Silber gave his explanation. When he became president he'd been shown slides of the history of activism at B.U. One of them showed an occupation of the president's office, in protest against police brutality on campus, and it showed me as part of the sit-in. Another slide showed a fire at the president's office. They were two separate events, but, Silber explained, he "conflated the two incidents."

The meeting began. Silber's supporters, mostly administrators and department heads, spoke to oppose the resolution. In defense of Silber, one department head rose to quote an American president speaking of a Caribbean dictator: "He may be a son-of-a-bitch. But he's *our* son-of-a-bitch."

Silber's faculty opponents rose to give evidence of financial mismanagement, of how Silber had preempted all important decisions, disregarded faculty opinion, inhibited freedom of expression, abused the rights of employees, and created conditions which blighted teaching and learning.

The vote was taken. It was 457–215 in favor of calling on the trustees to oust Silber. By now, Silber and Metcalf had tight control of the board. The trustees rejected the faculty resolution.

Not long after this, a woman in the English department named Julia Prewitt Brown came up for tenure. She was hopeful; she had written a much-praised book on novelist Jane Austen. However, she also had picketed in front of Silber's office during the strike. Her department voted for her unanimously. Two more faculty committees voted for her unanimously. When Silber's provost then turned her down for tenure, an outside committee of three scholars was called in. They voted in her favor. That added up to forty-two of her peers urging that she get tenure. But John Silber said no.

Julia Brown was a fighter. As she told me, at one time her father had been an amateur boxer back in St. Louis, and she'd been a fight fan from the time she was a girl. She admired fighters (Sugar Ray Leonard was one) who fought to the end, against whatever odds. She would not be bullied. She was the mother of three young children, but she would take all her money, sell her condominium in Boston, hire a lawyer, and sue Silber and B.U.

Her lawyer was Dahlia Rudavsky, also a young mother, who had been an attorney for the faculty union during and after the strike. Rudavsky drew up a double charge: political discrimination and sexual discrimination.

There was a history of Silber mistreating women faculty. Women were much less likely to get tenure than men, and women whose political views Silber disliked were especially vulnerable. Two women in the philosophy department, each exceptional in her own way, both voted tenure by their departments, were turned down by Silber, as was a woman in the sociology department who had been a strong supporter of the strike. Tenure for a woman in the economics department, a white South African who was outspoken in her disagreements with Silber about South Africa, was approved by her department, then vetoed by the president's office.

Much of the evidence in the trial centered on the importance of Julia Brown's book on Jane Austen. Silber expressed disdain for Jane Austen as a "lightweight" among novelists, but in the trial admitted he had not read Julia Brown's book. He did not deny that he had called the English department "a damned matriarchy."

The jury quickly came to a conclusion. Boston University and John Silber were guilty of sex discrimination. Julia Brown was awarded $200,000. The judge, in an extraordinary decision (courts customarily stay out of tenure disputes), ordered B.U. to grant her tenure. It had taken six years of persistence on her part, but in the end, like her hero Sugar Ray Leonard outlasting Marvin Hagler for the middleweight championship, she won.

For so many of us who worked at Boston University, it was often discouraging to see how a tyrannical president could hold on to power for so long. But the administration, though it had its admirers, never won the affection of the campus community. And it never succeeded in beating down those students and faculty who were determined to speak their minds, to honor the idea that a university should provide a free and humane atmosphere for humane learning.

INTERLUDE: HOW SOCIAL CHANGE HAPPENS

Interview with David Barsamian, Boulder, Colorado, 1996

from *The Future of History: Interviews with David Barsamian*

This interview with David Barsamian, published in *The Future of History*, was conducted on December 16, 1996. Typically, it touches upon a broad range of topics—the power of Langston Hughes's poetry, the radicalizing influence of the black freedom struggle, the culture of conformity in academia—within the broader context of understanding the dynamics of social change. Howard also describes the origins and evolution of his legendary friendship with MIT professor Noam Chomsky. He says: "Like rock and roll groups. I was the warm-up. I had lots of emotional statements surrounding several facts. Noam would come on with one vaguely emotional statement and 7,000 facts. It seemed to me a good combination." For nearly half a century, Chomsky and Zinn were the radical deans of American public intellectual life, in large part because they allowed themselves, in Howard's words, to "be encouraged by historical examples of social change, by how surprising changes take place suddenly, when you least expect it, not because of a miracle from on high, but because people have labored patiently for a long time." We could do worse than follow their example.

––––––

DAVID BARSAMIAN: *I was just looking at a book of poetry of Langston Hughes. You had an opportunity to meet while you were at Spelman College in Atlanta. Do you remember that?*

Do I remember that? I'm the one who told you about that! I could have pretended to your audience that you just know all these things.

But I told you that I met Langston Hughes, because I tell everybody I've met important people, whether I've met them or not. I actually did meet Langston Hughes. Not a serious meeting. It's not like when you and I sit down together and have cappuccino at the Cafe Algiers in Cambridge. This wasn't like that at all. I was teaching at Spelman. They invited him down to the Atlanta University Center. I was dispatched to pick him up at the airport, which I think I've told you is my claim to being a revolutionary. I pick people up at the airport. Sometimes even bring them back to the airport. So I picked him up at the airport and spent a little time with him, a great guy. I love his poetry. Class-conscious, simple, clear, strong. I quote it whenever I can.

DB: *He was an ally of the anti-fascist forces in Spain as well. He went to Spain.*

That's right. There are pictures of him speaking in Spain. He suffered because of his left-wing connections. They put a lot of pressure on him and so he had a hard time. I think at one point in his life he relented and tried to move away from that to protect himself. He was vulnerable in many ways. His personal life made him vulnerable.

DB: *Because he was gay?*

Exactly, because he was gay. It's bad enough in our time, but in that time to be gay, forget it.

DB: *You've used "Ballad of the Landlord."*

"Ballad of the Landlord" is one of my favorite poems because it's so ferociously class-conscious. Maybe you'd like to read it. Do you know that this is the poem that got Jonathan Kozol fired from his job here in Boston? I guess that's what attracted me to the poem. I said, Any poem that can get anybody fired is worth paying attention to.

DB: *Jonathan Kozol, a National Book Award winner and noted educator, was fired for reading the poem?*

Yes, he got fired. College professors can be fired for what they do, but it's always done very indirectly because universities are supposed to be places of free inquiry. But elementary schools and middle schools and high schools make no pretense. They are totalitarian places, and they don't make any claim to anything else. After all, they say, these are very young minds. We mustn't expose them to class conflict. We mustn't make them think that the country is run by the rich. We mustn't give them the idea that you should oppose your landlord and fight eviction, which is what happens in this poem.

DB: *Do you want to read it?*

I'll tell you what. Let's both read it. We'll have a duet. You read one and I'll read the other.

DB: *"Ballad of the Landlord," by Langston Hughes.*

Landlord, landlord, my roof has sprung a leak.
Don't you 'member I told you about it way last week?

Landlord, landlord, these steps is broken down.
When you come up yourself it's a wonder you don't fall down.

Ten bucks you say I owe you?
Ten bucks you say is due?
That's ten bucks more'n I'll pay you
Till you fix this house up new.

What? You're gonna get eviction orders?
You're gonna to cut off my heat?
You're gonna to take my furniture
And throw it in the street?

Um-huh! You talking high and mighty.
Talk on till you get through.
You ain't gonna to be able to say a word
If I land my fist on you.

Police! Police! come and get this man!
He's trying to ruin the government
And overturn the land!

Copper's whistle! patrol bell! arrest
Precinct station.

Iron cell.
Headlines in press:

MAN THREATENS LANDLORD
TENANT HELD. NO BAIL.
JUDGE GIVES NEGRO
90 DAYS IN COUNTY JAIL.

What an incendiary poem. It's a poem about civil disobedience. Challenging a law, but so obviously you being right and them being wrong. So you don't want young kids to hear that. So if a teacher reads that to young kids, or has them read it, he's got to go. So Jonathan Kozol went. But he had his revenge. He wrote this book (*Death at an Early Age*) which brought this to the attention of an awful lot of people.

DB: *His subsequent books on education,* Savage Inequalities *and* Amazing Grace, *are very powerful works.*

He's a wonderfully eloquent and passionate person about poverty and inequality and racism. That connection between him and Langston Hughes was a good one.

DB: *Perhaps Langston Hughes's most famous poem is "Raisin In the Sun. A Dream Deferred." Why don't you read that?*

I think I quote that. I shouldn't say that, "I *think* I quote that." We always say that in modesty. I *know* I quote that in *A People's History of the United States* when I start talking about the movement of the 1960s and how much led up to it in black poetry and literature. Some of the people know that title "Raisin In the Sun" because there's this famous play by Lorraine Hansberry and Sidney Poitier starred in this famous movie and on television and all that, but not a lot of people know that it came from Langston Hughes.

What happens to a dream deferred?

Does it dry up
like a raisin in the sun?
Or fester like a sore—
And then run?

Does it stink like rotten meat?
Or crust and sugar over—
like a syrupy sweet?

Maybe it just sags like a heavy load.
Or does it explode?

His language is so simple but so powerful. That image of all of that pent-up explosion. Richard Wright sort of did the same thing. Richard Wright always talked about that pent-up anger in the black population. In *Black Boy*, in which he talks about growing up in the South and what he went through and the humiliation and looking around him and seeing all the black people are toeing the line out of necessity, out of self-protection, but thinking, Something's going to happen here.

DB: *Speaking of something that's going to happen here, Hughes asks, What happens to a dream deferred? Does it explode if that dream is not realized? In late October in Boulder you said that, "We can't go on with the present polarization of wealth and poverty."*

I don't know how long we can go on, but I know we can't go on indefinitely. That growing gap between wealth and poverty is a recipe for trouble, for disaster, for conflict, for explosion. Here's the Dow Jones average going up, up, up and there are the lives of people in the city. The Dow Jones average in the last fifteen years has gone up 400%. In the same period, the wages of working people, of 80% of the population, have gone down 15%. 400% up, 15% down. Now the richest 1% of the population owning 43%, 44% of the wealth. Up from the usual maybe 28%, 30%, 32%, which is bad enough and which has been a constant throughout American history. In fact it's been so constant that when they did studies of the tax rolls in Boston in the seventeenth and eighteenth centuries, they concluded that 1% of the population owned 33% of the wealth. If you look at the statistics all through American history, you see that figure, a little more, a little less, around the same. Now it's even worse and worse. So something's got to give.

DB: *Given that enormous growth in income and wealth, the inequality, if you were a member, let's say, of the ruling class, I know you're not, that's why I say if—*

How do you know I'm not?

DB: *You're just a historian, retired, professor emeritus. But let's say if you were, wouldn't this trend toward increasing polarization give you cause for concern? Because for you to keep your power and privilege you need stability. You don't need unrest and upheaval.*

That's true. But there's always this conflict within the ruling class. The people who know this from a long-term point of view say, Hey, we'd better do something about it. That's why you see people up there in the ruling class, that's your phrase, "ruling class." I would never use a class-conscious phrase like that. But you used it, so I can use it. The ruling class. There have always been some members of the ruling class who wanted reforms, who wanted to ease things, who worried about a future explosion. These are the people who supported Roosevelt. They were members of the ruling class who supported Roosevelt and the New Deal reforms because they knew that they couldn't let things go on the way they were, with the turmoil of the 1930s, that there was a revolution brewing. So there have always been people like that. I think of Felix Rohatyn, who's this big banker. He says, Let's not go on like this. This polarization of wealth is going too far. But on the other hand, there are all those other greedy ones. They want it now. They think of the short term. OK, maybe there'll be rebellion against my grandchildren. It shows how their family values operate. They don't care if the rebellion takes place against their grandchildren. But now I'm going to haul in as much as I can. And that's what they're doing.

DB: *I'm saving the easy questions as we proceed into the interview. How does social change happen?*

Thanks. I can deal with that in thirty seconds. You think I know? We know how it has happened, and we can sort of extrapolate from that, not that you can extrapolate mathematically, but you can sort of get suggestions from that. You see change happening when there has been an accumulation of grievance until it reaches a boiling point. Then something happens. When I say, look at historical situations and try to extrapolate from that, what happens in the South in the 1950s and 1960s? It's not that suddenly black people were put back into slavery. It's not as if there was some precipitating thing that suddenly pushed them back. They were, as the Southern white ruling class was eager to say, making progress. It was glacial progress, extremely slow. But they were making progress. But it's not the absolute amount of progress that's made that counts. It's the amount of progress made against what the ideal should be in the minds of the people who are aggrieved. And the ideal in the minds of the black people was, We have to be equal. We have to be treated as equals. The progress that was being made in the South was so far from that. The recognition of that gap between what should be and what is, which existed for a long time but waited for a moment when a spark would be lit. The thing about sparks being lit is that you never know what spark is going to ignite and really result in a conflagration. After all, before the Montgomery bus boycott there had been other boycotts. Before the sit-ins of the 1960s, there had been between 1955 and 1960 sit-ins in sixteen different cities which nobody paid any attention to and which did not ignite a movement. But then in Greensboro, on February 1, 1960, these four college kids go in, sit in, and everything goes haywire. Then things are never the same. You never know, and this is I think an encouragement to people who do things, not knowing whether they will result in anything, and you do things again and again and nothing happens, that you have to do things, do things, do things, you have to light that match, light that match, light that match, not knowing how often it's going to sputter and go out and at what point it's going to take hold, at what point other people, seeing what happens, are going to be encouraged, provoked to do the same. That's what happened in the civil rights movement and that's what happens in other movements. Things take a long time. It requires patience, but not a passive patience, the patience of activism.

When I was in South Africa in 1982, I was invited there to give a lecture to the University of Capetown. At the time, apartheid defined the country, Mandela was in Robben Island, the African National Congress was outlawed, people were being banned. We know about books being banned, there, it was people who were banned. They couldn't speak. They couldn't go here or there. The secret police everywhere. Just before I arrived at the University of Capetown the secret police of South Africa had just broken into the offices of the student newspaper at the university and made off with all of their stuff. It was the kind of thing that happened all the time. The atmosphere was an atmosphere of terror. You would think perhaps, only seeing that, nothing is going to happen here, like you would think in the South in the early 1950s. You don't see any sign of a civil rights revolution in the South in the early 1950s. But having come from that experience in the South, I became aware, just talking to people, going to meetings, going to a huge rally outside of Johannesburg, where everybody did everything illegal, where they sang the anthem of the African National Congress, raised the flags of the African National Congress, where banned people spoke. I suddenly was aware that underneath the surface of total control things were simmering, things were going on. I didn't know when it would break through, but we saw it break through not long ago. Suddenly Mandela comes out of Robben Island and becomes president of the new South Africa. We should be encouraged. We shouldn't be discouraged. We should be encouraged by historical examples of social change, by how surprising changes take place suddenly, when you least expect it, not because of a miracle from on high, but because people have labored patiently for a long time.

DB: *Do you think it's important to rethink the way we think about time? Everyone's in a hurry. Well, this change you're suggesting, Professor, I'm a very busy guy. I've got about fifteen minutes.*

It's true. We have to rethink the whole question of time. We have to get used to the idea that the great society—I'm sorry to use that phrase. All those phrases were OK: the Great Society, the New Frontier, the New Deal. They weren't realized. We have to get accustomed to the idea that it may not come in our lifetime. We will see changes in our lifetime. Who knows what we will see? Think of Mandela, in prison for decades. Think of people in the South living in humiliation for a hundred years, waiting. I'm not saying it will take a hundred years or it will take decades. I don't know how long it will take for important changes to take place. You never know. But when people get discouraged because they do something and nothing happens, they should really understand that the only way things will happen is if people get over the notion that they must see immediate success. If they get over that notion and persist, then they will see things happen before they even realize it.

DB: *Was your job at Spelman College in Atlanta the first job you got when you got out of the university?*

I call it my first "real" teaching job. I had a number of unreal teaching jobs. By unreal I mean I was teaching part-time at Upsala College in New Jersey.

DB: *Now bankrupt, incidentally.*

Because I taught there?

DB: *This just happened. Literally, colleges are now going bankrupt.*

I said patience. It took a while after I was there to reap the fruits of my being there and go bankrupt. I wouldn't be surprised if every other place that I've touched goes bankrupt. I have written articles for a number of magazines. Those magazines are now defunct. I'm warning you about what will happen to Alternative Radio after this interview. You never know.

DB: *I'll take my chances.*

I taught at Upsala College. How do you know about all these defunct places? Do you have a list? Anyway, I did teach there part-time. Maybe it's defunct because it was very Lutheran. So strict. It was like being back in the time of Luther, back in the sixteenth century. But in any case, I had a part-time job there and a part-time job at Brooklyn College. But Spelman College was my first full-time teaching job. I immediately catapulted from graduate student at Columbia University to chair—I want you to take full cognizance of that—of a department. Four persons in the department. Like being head waiter in a two-waiter restaurant. Not just history. Four persons included everything: history, political science, sociology, philosophy. Four people doing all of that. We were renaissance people.

DB: *What year was that?*

That was in 1956 when my wife Roz and my two kids Myla and Jeff—mind if I mention their names? I want to give them air time—all trundled into our old Chevy, went down.

DB: *I assume it was in terms of your socialization a rather radicalizing experience for you. I presume you lived in a black neighborhood near the college.*

Actually, the first year we were there—we were there a total of seven—we lived in a white, working-class neighborhood on the edge of Atlanta, which was an interesting experience in itself. We weren't far from Stone Mountain, which is a Ku Klux Klan gathering place. We were living in this first house we'd ever lived in. We had always lived in the slums in New York or in low-income housing projects. Here we were in a little house like the other little houses on this block of working-class white people. One of the first things that happened when we were there is we hear all this noise. We go outside. There was a main street about a block from our house. There was a parade of people with white hoods, KKK, marching to Stone Mountain.

We spent a year there. It was sort of inconvenient traveling back and forth. We moved to the Spelman College campus, which was surrounded by a black community. We lived essentially in the black community for the next six years. You say radicalizing experience? I guess so. Of course I like to think that I was a radical even before I came to Spelman College. But we all like to pretend that we were radical at the age of three, right? You might say I had been radicalized by working in the shipyards, but maybe a little more radicalized by being in a war. But probably that time at Spelman College was the most intense experience of learning in my life. I think it's fair to say that. Talk about social change, I could see social change happening all around me and then writing about it, observing it, participating in it, seeing my Spelman College students so controlled in that old guard atmosphere of the old South in which students, especially young black women, were being trained to take their obedient places in the segregated society. Trained to pour tea and wear white gloves and march into and out of chapel and really to be kept inside this kind of nunnery. Then suddenly to see them break out of this when they look at television and watch the sit-ins taking place in Greensboro and Rock Hill, South Carolina, and Nashville and to see them gathering. Julian Bond across the street at Morehouse College meeting with Lonnie King, the football captain at Morehouse College, gathering people from Spelman and getting together and planning the first sit-ins in the spring of 1960 in Atlanta. My students literally leaping over that stone wall that surrounded the Spelman campus and doing what they weren't supposed to do. Seeing this remarkable change in them, this growth of courage and getting arrested, going to jail. Marian Wright Edelman, my student at Spelman, going to jail. A photo of her appearing in the newspapers the next day showing this very studious Spelman student behind bars reading a book which she had brought along with her so she wouldn't miss her class or homework. Seeing the South change in that time, seeing white Southerners change, seeing white Southerners get used to the idea that the South is going to change and accepting it.

DB: *What I meant by radicalizing you, I was thinking in terms of being a witness to an oppressive mechanism, segregation, U.S.-style apartheid, Jim Crow, and then watching the resistance to it grow.*

Anybody who was in any way in the U.S. socially conscious knew vaguely that there was racial segregation. But to be right there and to witness it in action, to talk to my students about their early lives, about the first time they realized that they were black and being considered different and treated differently. To participate in sit-ins and to see the atmosphere around us in Rich's Department Store suddenly change from friendly to hostile when four of us, two black and two white, my wife and I and two black students from Spelman, sit down in this lunch counter at Rich's. Suddenly it's as if a bomb had been dropped or plague had been visited on it. The people gathering around us and shouting and cursing. Getting an inkling, being white people, just an inkling, of what it is to be black and be subject all your life to the thought that if you step one foot out of line you'll be surrounded by people who are threatening you. That's a learning experience. Learning comes in layers. There's something you think you know? You don't know it until you see it very up close, penetrating you. So it was a learning experience.

I learned a lot about teaching, too. I learned that the most important thing about teaching is not what you do in the classroom but what you do outside of the classroom and what you do to bring the lessons of books and the writings of thinkers and the facts of history, what you do to make a connection between that and the world outside. To go outside the classroom yourself, to bring your students outside the classroom, or to have them bring you outside the classroom, because very often they do it first and you say, I can't hang back. I'm their teacher. I have to be there with them. And to learn that the best kind of teaching is the one that makes this connection between social action and book learning.

DB: *Why do you think so many of your colleagues, and I think this is a fair statement to make, really want to just busy themselves with their scholarship and turning out papers and attending conferences? I'm not saying that doesn't have any value. But when it comes to "out there," to being engaged with what's happening in the streets, in society, they don't feel it's appropriate.*

There's a powerful drive in our society for safety and security. And everybody is vulnerable because we all are part of a hierarchy of power in which unless we're at the very, very top, unless we're billionaires, or the president of the U.S., or the boss, and very few of us are bosses, we are somewhere on some lower rung in the hierarchy of power, where somebody has power over us, somebody has the power to fire us, to withhold a raise, to punish us in some way. Here in this rich country, so prideful of the economic system, the most prominent, the most clear-cut thing you can say about this great economic success is that everybody is insecure. Everybody is nervous. Even if you're doing well, you're nervous. Something will happen to you. In fact, the people who are doing fairly well, the middle class, are more nervous than the people at the bottom, who know what to expect and have smaller expectations. There's this nervousness, this insecurity, and this economic fear of saying the wrong thing, doing the wrong thing, stepping out of line. The academic world has its own special culture of conformity and being professional. All the professions have the cult of professionalism, even in your profession, radio broadcasters. Being professional means not being committed.

DB: *Not having an agenda.*

Right. There are people who might call you unprofessional, because sometimes I suspect you have an agenda. Sometimes I suspect you care about what's going on in the world. Sometimes I suspect that the people you interview are the people whose ideas you want to broadcast. You're not supposed to do that. It's unprofessional. It's unprofessional to be a teacher who goes out on picket lines, or who even invites students out on picket lines. It's unprofessional to be a teacher who says to students, Look, instead of giving you a final exam, your assignment for the semester is to go out into the community and work with some organization that you believe in and then do a report on that instead of taking a final exam of multiple choice questions asking you who was President during the Mexican War. So that's unprofessional. And you will stand out. You will stick out if the stuff you write is not written for scholarly journals but is written for everybody to read, because certainly, the stuff written for scholarly journals is not written for everybody to read. It's deliberately written in such a way that not everybody can read it. Very few people can read it. So if you write stuff that the ordinary person can read, you're suspect. They'll say you're not a scholar, you're a journalist. Or you're not a scholar, you're a propagandist, because you have a point of view. They don't have a point of view. Scholarly articles don't have a point of view. Of course, they really do. They have an agenda.

But they don't say it. They may not even know they have an agenda. The agenda is obedience. The agenda is silence. The agenda is safety. The agenda is, Don't rock the boat.

DB: *One of the criticisms of* Alternative Radio *that I hear from program directors around the country is that it's "not objective." It's not balanced. These are terms of abuse in order to actually limit the possibility of people actually hearing dissenting voices such as yours.*

This business of "balance" is very funny. What is balance? The *MacNeil/Lehrer NewsHour* is balanced, right? They have people on the far right balanced by people on the not-so-far right balanced by people in the middle balanced by one person two degrees to the left of the middle. That's balanced. If you said to MacNeil/Lehrer, Why don't you have Noam Chomsky on as a regular commentator to balance all the Assistant Secretaries of State and the Secretaries of Defense and the Congressmen, just one person to balance hundreds of others? They would say, No, that's not what we mean by balance.

The fact is, things are already unbalanced. The pretense is that things are balanced and you want to keep them that way. But of course they're already so far out of balance, we would have to put an enormous amount of left-wing weight onto the scales in order even to make the scales move slightly towards balance.

DB: *You just mentioned that MIT professor Noam Chomsky. When did you first meet Chomsky?*

I first met Noam—do you mind if I call him Noam? I call you David.

DB: *Very familiar.*

Very familiar. Unprofessional. I first met Noam, I had moved not long before to Boston from the South. It was the summer of 1965. I had vaguely heard of him from somebody who talked about him as a linguist. I knew there was a guy named Chomsky at MIT and that he was brilliant in the field of linguistics. That's all I knew about him. I didn't know that he had any interest in politics. This is a funny thing to say. If somebody said today about Noam Chomsky, Oh, I didn't know that he was interested in politics, well! And then, something was happening. I moved out of the South but I was still in touch with things in the region. A lot of people were being arrested in Jackson, Mississippi, black people, SNCC people, and being held in the big compound because there were too many of them to fit into the jails. It was decided to send a delegation of people from the Boston area down to take a look at things and make a report. Bob Zellner, one of the original SNCC people, one of the few white people in SNCC, a white Southerner from Alabama, a fantastic person, organized this and asked me to come. I said OK. I found myself on a plane going south sitting next to a guy who introduced himself as Noam Chomsky. A very immodest statement, don't you think, for him to say, I'm Noam Chomsky? So we talked all the way down. Then we talked while we were there and we talked on the way back. We became friends. I became aware of the fact that he was a guy who wasn't just interested in linguistics—although he had a slight interest in linguistics—but he was very, very deeply concerned about what was going on in the country and the world and it occurred to me, talking to him, that he was very smart. So from then on, and then of course with the Vietnam War escalating just about that time, the two of us found ourselves on the same platform again and again at the same rallies. So we got to know one another.

DB: *You've said that you were often the opening act for Chomsky.*

Like rock and roll groups. I was the warm-up. I had a lot of emotional statements surrounding several facts. Noam would come on with one vaguely emotional statement and 7,000 facts. It seemed to me a good combination.

DB: *As you know, he's not a flamboyant, charismatic speaker. He would be the first to acknowledge that. What accounts for the enormous crowds that he attracts, not just in the U.S. but all around the world?*

You say, Not just in the U.S. He attracts bigger crowds in Canada and in Europe and now lately in Latin America. I just talked to him today. He just returned from Latin America. Everywhere he goes there are huge crowds. Everywhere I go to speak, five hundred people show up. They inform me quietly, Noam Chomsky was here two weeks ago. Two thousand people came to hear him. Is this a message they're trying to give me? I'm inadequate? The reason so many people turn out to hear him is one, they've heard about him. I guess he's famous. It's interesting that he should be famous, because all the organs of power in the U.S. are trying their best not to make him famous, to shut him up, not to publish him, not to pay attention to him, not to put him on national radio or TV. But his message has been so powerful and so outrageously true and so backed up by information and so very often ahead of everybody else. Look, he was the first one in this country to talk about East Timor. Now the East Timor rebels get the Nobel Prize. As I go around the country, wherever I go Noam has already spoken or is about to speak there. Plus he speaks at a lot of places where I don't speak. I have run into so many people all over who say that they went to hear him speak and it had an amazing effect on them, as you say, without him being flamboyant. Just the power of what he says, the information that piles up, so devastating and so obviously true, and with such documentation. It amounts to a powerful indictment of our society, of our economic system, of our political system, of the hypocrisy, of the failure of the press to report what is going on in the world. To me it's a very encouraging thing that wherever Noam speaks huge crowds turn out. It shows me that there is an enormous population in this country that is hungry for information that they don't get in the major media.

Another encouraging thing to me is the alternate radio and alternate media. I can't tell you how many people have said to me, I know you think I'm buttering you up, yes, I guess I am buttering you up. Call it margarine, it's the New Age. People say to me, Hey, I heard the talk you gave. And they mention some radio station somewhere that I never heard of and apparently you have this satellite that's floating around. You bounce a talk by Noam Chomsky or by me or by Barbara Ehrenreich off these satellites and they go out to radio stations. You notice how technologically astute I am in my accurate description of exactly how this thing works? It bounces off the satellite, goes to these radio stations and then into people's homes? Isn't that how it works exactly?

DB: *So despite what the pundits are telling us about the population being passive and quiescent, you think there's an audience there for dissidence?*

Absolutely. I talk very often to captive audiences. Not prisoners, I mean people who turn out to hear me talk, and I imagine this is even more true of the larger crowds that turn out to hear Noam. These are not the radicals of the community. Five hundred people come to hear me in Duluth, Minnesota. There are not five hundred radicals in Duluth, Minnesota, who have come to hear me tell them what they already know. I don't know why they're there. Maybe there's not a lot to do in Duluth that night. That seems like an insult to Duluth. There are a few things to do. Who knows why? What I'm trying to say is they're not people who are already aficionados of the left and of radical messages. They come maybe out of curiosity. Their interest has been piqued by an article in the newspaper or whatever and they come to hear me. Then I deliver what I believe is a radical message: this is what's wrong with our economic system. It's fundamental. This is what's wrong with our political system. It's fundamental. We need to redistribute the wealth in this country. We need to use it in a rational way. We need to take this enormous arms budget and not just cut it slightly but dismantle it because we have to make up our minds we're not going to go to war anymore. We're not going to militarily intervene anymore. If we're not going to go to war anymore, then we have $250 billion. Then we don't have to worry about Medicare, Social Security, child care, universal health care, education. We can have a better society. I say things which if you mentioned them to MacNeil/Lehrer they would say, That's a little too much for our listeners. It's not too much. I think this is what Noam does too. You tell people what makes common sense, it makes common sense that if you're a very, very rich country nobody in the country should be hungry. Nobody should be homeless. Nobody should be without health care. The richest country in the world. Nobody should be without these things. We have the resources but they're being wasted or given somewhere to somebody. It's common sense. So there are people all over this country, millions of people, who would listen to such a message and say, yes, yes, yes. The problem is to organize these people into a movement.

DB: *Mike Moore, the celebrated film director of* Roger and Me *and of* TV Nation *very effectively uses humor to convey political ideas, as do Molly Ivins and Jim Hightower and yourself. Do you feel that humor is a way to maybe hook a larger audience and to make left, progressive ideas more attractive?*

I don't like to think of it that way. I don't go home and say, I think we've got to reach people, so I'll try to get humorous. Rather, it's a way of having a little fun with the world in a world that is not giving us a lot of fun, that's giving us tragedy, pictures of hungry people and pictures of war. Maybe it's something I learned from being in the South and being in the black community, to see how much humor there was among people who you might say have no right to laugh. There's nothing to laugh about, and these people are laughing and having fun. Or people in the army, people at war. They've got to have humor. They've got to have fun. They need to laugh. We've got to have fun even while we're dealing with serious things. We've got to represent in the present what we want in the future. I suppose that's why we do that. It's not a planned conspiracy.

DB: *Have you noticed any changes in your profession, history? I hesitate to use the term "revisionist," because it smacks of the Soviet era. But along the lines of* A People's History, *your book, there's James Loewen's book* Lies My Teacher Told Me. *Have there been some changes in this area?*

No question there have been changes. Obviously not enough to say, The teaching of history has changed. But obviously enough changes to alarm the right wing in this country, to alarm the American Legion, to alarm senators, to alarm Lynne Cheney, Robert Dole, William Bennett, Gertrude Himmelfarb, and to alarm all these people who are holding on to the old history. They're alarmed because there have been changes. The story of Columbus has changed now, not in the majority of schools around the country, but in thousands. This is alarming. What? Young kids are going to begin to think of Columbus as not just an adventurer, but as a predator, a kidnapper, an enslaver, a torturer, a bad person and think maybe that conquest and expansion are not good things and that the search for gold is not something to be welcomed? Kids, be happy! Gold has been found! No, greed is no good. And maybe, let's take a look at the Indian societies that Columbus came upon. How did they live? How did they treat one another? Columbus stories that are told in the schools don't usually include stories of how the Indians were living on this continent.

Somebody sent me a letter reminding me of the work of William Brandon. He has done research for decades about Indians and their communities on this hemisphere before Columbus came and after. His research was in the French archives because he works in France. The reports came back from the French missionaries, the Jesuits, on how the Indians live. It's an amazing story and one that would make anybody question capitalism, greed, competition, disparate wealth, hierarchy. To start to hint about that, telling a new kind of Columbus story, a new kind of Native American story, is subversive of the way things are. Also, the Reconstruction period is being told in a new way. Eric Foner's book *Reconstruction* is marvelous. It's a very different treatment of Reconstruction and the books on Reconstruction that existed when I was going to graduate school in the 1950s, where incidentally they did not put on my reading list W.E.B. Du Bois's *Black Reconstruction*, which you might say is an earlier version of Eric Foner's book, at least a vital predecessor to it. So a lot of history teaching has changed. Not enough yet. We need to do a lot more. But just enough to frighten the keepers of the old.

DB: *We had an opportunity in late October to visit the new maximum security prison in Florence, Colorado. It was a rather extraordinary trip.*

Don't deny the fact that you drove the getaway car. Also the get-there car. I didn't have a car at my disposal, I was speaking in Boulder, and I had this old friend of mine in prison, in this maximum maximum, they call it "ad max" security federal prison in southern Colorado. It was good that we had a lot of fun on the way, because when we got there it was no fun. Grim. Frightening. Something out of some fantasy of totalitarianism. New. Technologically admirable. But holding these prisoners in such a tight grip. The man that I visited I've known for twenty-five years, and he is actually an extraordinary human being. There are some extraordinary human beings behind bars. Sure, there are mad killers and rapists. There are those. But there are also extraordinary people behind bars who shouldn't be there. He is one of them. I could not shake hands with him when I visited. We were separated by this glass wall. We had to talk through these phones. So there's no contact. It's called a no-contact visit. Yet, although there is no contact, there's all this between us, before he comes out to see me he is strip-searched by the guards. After he sees me he is strip-searched again by the guards. That's humiliating, taking all his clothes off, inspecting all the cavities of his body. Assuming that I, Houdini-like, have managed to slip things through the glass to him which will enable him to escape from there. It was a nightmare. What was amazing was that not everybody commits suicide in a situation like that, that somebody like my friend Jimmy Barrett, and I think it's because of his social consciousness, has the strength to withstand that. You talk about patience. Jimmy says: Patience. Things will change. I will get out of here and things will be different.

DB: *I was wondering also about the larger societal message that a building like that sends. I was sitting in the lobby while you were inside talking to your friend. What do I see? An incredible building costing a lot of money, with tiled inlaid floors, high ceilings, huge glass windows, smiling photos of Clinton and Janet Reno and the prison warden and assistant warden. You see in the back "Florence ADX. First in Security." While I was sitting there waiting for you I had a very mischievous thought that I'd like to connect the words "in" and "security" together. What struck me was that about the same time that we were there the* New York Times, *a well-known source of radical information, reported that kids in the New York City public school system, the largest one in the country, were meeting in gymnasiums, cafeterias, and locker rooms because of overcrowding. That contrast was startling.*

I remember you pointing that out to me on our way back, which was not as fun-filled as our way there. Those ironies, those contrasts, are such as to make one think very, very hard about our society. To think that there are more young black people in prison than in college, or to think that the state of California spends more money on prisons than on schools. Or to think that it costs more to house one person in a prison than to send one person to Harvard, room and board, tuition and everything. Maybe we should have a prisoner exchange, Harvard students and prisoners, just for a little while, and see what happens.

Part 3

PROTEST NATION

BUNKER HILL: BEGINNINGS

from *Postwar America: 1945–1971* (1973)

In this wide-ranging essay, Howard invokes the symbolic location of
Bunker Hill—site of the first major battle of the American Revolution,
and nearly two centuries later the site of an antiwar protest led by Vietnam veterans—to discuss the emergence and evolution of social protest movements in the decades after World War II. Americans were
generally slow to express dissent in the decade following the ghastly
bombings of Hiroshima and Nagasaki, especially during the anti-
Communist purges of the McCarthy era. And yet, Howard writes,
"something remarkable did begin to develop in those . . . postwar years,
especially in the United States. A broad, heterogeneous movement
started to take form. Disorganized, troubled, unsure of itself, vague
about its vision of the good society, puzzled about the means of building that society, the movement, nevertheless, was alive and in motion
as the seventies began." The turning point, he argues, was the 1955
Montgomery Bus Boycott, which set in motion a relentless series of challenges to white racism and Jim Crow segregation that included economic boycotts, student sit-ins, Freedom Rides, Mississippi Freedom
Summer, voting rights marches, and Black Power. Inspired by the black
freedom struggle, other movements soon emerged alongside it, including the student movement, the women's liberation movement, and the
peace movement, which played a central role in ending the war in Vietnam. All of this amounted to a wholesale confrontation with American
liberalism, "a tradition in which racial [or other forms of] equality was
either promised in words or granted on paper, but without the needed
radical changes in the society's economic and political institutions,

without the necessary changes in the value structure of the culture." Near the end of the essay, Howard sketches the "rough outlines of some future world" beckoned by these protest movements—one where the nation-state would be obsolete; where resources would be taken away from both private corporations and centralized socialist states and used to promote the broad public good; where political democracy would extend beyond the two-party system; where the circulation of ideas would be completely free; where prisons would be abolished; and where authoritarianism and hierarchy in any form, public or private, would be eradicated. Of course, the realization of this world would be no easy task. As Howard concludes, it would involve a "long revolutionary process of struggle and example. The process would have to be long enough, intense enough, to change the thinking of people, to act out, as far as possible, the future society." Nonetheless, the postwar era witnessed the spectacular beginnings of a "long revolutionary process" that continues today.

———

SEVERAL HUNDRED VETERANS of the war, bedraggled, bearded, in remnants of their uniforms, were camping on Bunker Hill, in defiance of local regulations. These were not farmers, fresh from Concord and Lexington, resisting the tyranny of England across the ocean. These were veterans of another war, nearly two centuries later, anxious about the tyranny at home, angry about the brutal use of American power abroad.

They were veterans back from Vietnam who, on May 30, 1971 (Memorial Day weekend), were protesting the continuation of the war in Southeast Asia. But more than that, they were part of a great, loose, tangled movement in postwar America—of men and women, white and black, of all ages and backgrounds—that was trying, against overwhelming odds, to change the institutions, the human relations, the ways of thinking that had marked American society for so long.

The World War II armies of the capitalist and Communist worlds united to destroy the Nazi and Fascist military machines. But they did not destroy the values represented by fascism—racism, nationalism, militarism, bureaucracy, secret police, the violence of war abroad and the repression of freedoms at home, the supremacy of *things* over the individual. In the postwar years, the disparity between the promises and the reality of these societies, both capitalist and socialist, became distressingly clear. Their wealth and power had never been greater—their failure in human terms never more stark.

Yet something remarkable did begin to develop in those same postwar years, especially in the United States. A broad, heterogeneous movement started to take form. Disorganized, troubled, unsure of itself, vague about its vision of the good society, puzzled about the means of building that society, the movement, nevertheless, was alive and in motion as the seventies began.

America has had reform movements and even radical movements in its past, but never anything quite like this one, where in one decade, protests against racism, against war, against domination by males, reverberated one against the other, to produce a widespread feeling that the traditional liberal solutions were not enough. Fundamental changes were needed, it came to be thought, not just in America's political and economic institutions, but in its sexual and personal and work relationships, in the way in which Americans thought about themselves and about one another.

Beyond sheer political questions, more and more evidence began to appear of a fundamental unease deep within the culture of the nation. People began boldly to question the very assumptions they had grown up with and had been taught to believe—that America was a God-given place. Two women of different backgrounds expressed this questioning in their own ways. One was a professional writer, Joan Didion:

> The center was not holding. . . .
>
> It was not a country in open revolution. It was not a country under enemy siege. It was the United States of America in the cold late spring of 1967, and the market was steady and the G.N.P. high and a great many articulate people seemed to have a sense of high social purpose and it might have been a spring of brave hope and national promise, but it was not, and more and more people had the uneasy apprehension that it was not. All that seemed clear was that at some point we had aborted ourselves and butchered the job.

The other was a young mother, whose job was tending a counter in a cheap department store. She felt her own life stunted; she had just experienced the death of an old woman close to her, who had spent her last days in one of those macabre city hospitals, those department stores of death, rotting away, uncared for until the end. One day in 1970, amidst counters piled with shoddy merchandise, in a sea of price tags, she scrawled her feelings on a piece of brown wrapping paper:

> I feel so damn angry Lord, so angry! I hate the thought that fills my mind—that sight before me! It was cruel, the cruelest of all

things I've seen—man is so awful cruel in his damn modern plastic ways. Look! Look! All around—too modern, too plastic!

In the ten years that followed World War II, America was relatively
calm. Neither the Korean War, nor McCarthyism, nor the continued
humiliation of blacks, nor the increasing diversion of the country's
wealth to the nuclear arms race aroused any widespread movement of
opposition. Amidst the general complacency, based on middle-class
prosperity, on lower-class fatalism, on agreement that communism was
the great enemy, and on faith in the two-party system, only a few flur-
ries of dissent were visible.[. . .]

The sixties was an angry decade. The most powerful protest movement
of all was against the war in Vietnam, starting with a handful of Americans in 1964, and involving millions by 1971. The war exposed, as
nothing else had in American history, the great gap between political
rhetoric and national behavior. The war tested the elements of the liberal
creed, and they were found wanting by large numbers of Americans.
The implications of the war reached far beyond foreign policy, into the
fundamental character of American political institutions, American culture, American values.

Antiwar movements had sprung up before in American history—
indeed, in every war, but especially in the Mexican War, the Spanish-
American War, and World War I. Yet never did an antiwar movement
touch so many Americans, never did one take on such intensity, with so
many demonstrations, as did the one against the Vietnam War. National
polls—Gallup and Harris—showed a steady rise in the late sixties in
the number of Americans who wanted the United States to withdraw
from Vietnam, a number that by 1970 reached a majority. In cities where
the issue of American intervention in Vietnam was put on the ballot, a
clear change in opinion was registered from 1967, when, for instance, in
Dearborn, Michigan, 41 percent of the voters called for immediate withdrawal from Vietnam, to 1970, when in several cities on the West Coast
and in Madison, Wisconsin, from half to two-thirds of the voters called
for immediate total withdrawal or withdrawal within the year. At the
same time, the polls also showed that most Americans did not believe
what the government was telling them about the situation in Vietnam.

In part, the dimension of this antiwar movement was due to the special brutality of the Vietnam War—the use of napalm against women
and children, the bombing of villages and hamlets, the forcible removal

of millions of Vietnamese from their homes, the use of chemicals to ruin the forests and soil of Vietnam, the spoliation of an ancient culture by the intrusion of five hundred thousand American troops and one hundred fifty billion American dollars, in defiance of international and national laws and in support of a succession of strong-arm regimes in Saigon. In part, it was due to the astounding disparity between the two adversaries: the world's most powerful nation raining shells and bombs on one of the least powerful, the kind of bullying that had shocked Americans when Germany invaded Czechoslovakia and when Russia invaded Finland.

When, in early 1965, the United States began the sustained and systematic bombing of North Vietnam, on the pretext that the North Vietnamese had attacked two American destroyers in the Gulf of Tonkin, groups of several hundred people gathered in protest here and there throughout the country. On Moratorium Day, four years later, two million Americans across the nation participated in antiwar demonstrations; the size of the outpouring was unprecedented in American history.

It was not surprising that blacks in the United States—fresh from their encounters with the government, disillusioned with the liberal performance as contrasted with the liberal promise—should look with distaste on the Vietnam War. In August 1964, when the Gulf of Tonkin incidents were allegedly taking place, funeral services were being held in Philadelphia, Mississippi, for James Chaney, the black civil-rights worker who, with two young white men, had been murdered by a gang of whites, while the federal government claimed lack of protective jurisdiction. The contrast was stark. LBJ SAYS "SHOOT TO KILL" IN GULF OF TONKIN, read the headline in the Jackson, Mississippi, newspaper; while the United States was ready for aggressive military action ten thousand miles away, it was not ready to defend blacks at home against violence.

In mid-1965, black people in McComb, Mississippi, learning that a classmate had been killed in Vietnam, distributed a leaflet in McComb:

> No Mississippi Negroes should be fighting in Viet Nam for the White man's freedom, until all the Negro People are free in Mississippi.
>
> Negro boys should not honor the draft here in Mississippi. Mothers should encourage their sons not to go. . . .
>
> No one has a right to ask us to risk our lives and kill other Colored People in Santo Domingo and Viet Nam, so that the White American can get richer. We will be looked upon as traitors by all

the Colored People of the world if the Negro people continue to fight and die without a cause.

In early 1966, the Student Nonviolent Coordinating Committee declared that "the United States is pursuing an aggressive policy in violation of international law," and called for withdrawal from Vietnam. That summer, six members of SNCC were arrested for an aggressive invasion of an induction center in Atlanta, and were later convicted and given sentences of several years in jail. When Secretary of Defense Robert McNamara went to Jackson, the issue between civil rights and Vietnam was clearly joined by his own words, as he praised Mississippi Senator John Stennis, one of the country's archsegregationists, as "a man of very genuine greatness, . . . a man of courage and selflessness." White and black students joined in picketing him, after a march downtown "In Memory of the Burned Children of Vietnam."

The words of Eldridge Cleaver were strong, but the mood of the Black Panther leader was not foreign to that found in vast numbers of young blacks. He wrote "To My Black Brothers in Vietnam," reminding them that police had murdered Fred Hampton, the Panther leader in Chicago, in his bed:

> We appeal to you Brothers to come to the aid of your people. Either quit the army, now, or start destroying it from the inside. Anything else is a form of compromise and a form of treason against your own people. Stop killing the Vietnamese people. You need to start killing the racist pigs who are over there with you giving you orders. Kill General Abrams and his staff, all his officers. Sabotage supplies and equipment, or turn them over to the Vietnamese people. Talk to the other Brothers and wake them up.

How widespread and popular black antagonism was to the war, and how greatly the attitude of the black population had changed since World War II, was illustrated by the case of Muhammad Ali (Cassius Clay). He was the hero-successor to Joe Louis, heavyweight champion at the time of World War II. Louis had urged blacks to fight for their country. Now Muhammad Ali set an example for other blacks by refusing to serve in a "white man's war," and took the risk of years in prison for doing so. Martin Luther King, by 1967, was speaking out powerfully against the war in Vietnam. That April, from a pulpit in New York, he declared:

Somehow this madness must cease. We must stop now. I speak as a child of God and brother to the suffering poor of Vietnam. I speak for those whose land is being laid waste, whose homes are being destroyed, whose culture is being subverted. I speak for the poor of America who are paying the double price of smashed hopes at home and death and corruption in Vietnam. I speak as a citizen of the world, for the world as it stands aghast at the path we have taken. I speak as an American to the leaders of my own nation. The great initiative in this war is ours. The initiative to stop it must be ours. . . .

The black protest against the war separated blacks still further from the country and its behavior. They were not ashamed to shun patriotism. Alice Walker, a young black poet from Georgia, put it lightly but firmly in verse:

then there was
the
picture of
the
bleak-eyed
little black
girl
waving the
American
flag
holding it
gingerly
with
the very
tips
of her
fingers.

One of the most sustained and effective forms of antiwar protest was the draft-resistance movement. Most poor whites and blacks stayed out of this movement; they found their own quiet ways of avoiding the draft, or they went into the service, despite a lack of enthusiasm for the war, because it was expected of them, because for many it meant economic and training opportunities that were closed to them in civilian life. White middle-class students formed the core of draft resisters.

As early as May 1964, the slogan "We Won't Go" was heard, and the following year young men who refused to be inducted were put on trial. For the next several years, the public burning of draft cards became a dramatic way of declaring refusal to fight in the war, and the prosecutions multiplied. In October 1967, there were organized draft-card "turn-ins" all over the country; in San Francisco alone, three hundred draft cards were returned. On the eve of the great demonstration of tens of thousands of people at the Pentagon that month, a sack of draft cards was presented to the Justice Department in a gesture of defiance— one of the acts that led to the indictment the following year of Dr. Benjamin Spock, pediatrician and author; Yale chaplain William Sloane Coffin Jr.; author Mitchell Goodman; Marcus Raskin of the Institute for Policy Studies; and Harvard graduate student Michael Ferber for interfering with the Selective Service system.

From mid-1964 to mid-1965, according to Justice Department figures, 380 prosecutions were begun against those who refused to be inducted; by mid-1968, the figure was 3,305. Mass protests were held outside induction centers with many of the demonstrators attacked by police and many arrested. The number of people trying in one way or other to avoid induction was much larger than the number prosecuted. In May 1969, the Oakland induction center, which had jurisdiction over draftees for all of northern California, reported that more than half the young men ordered to report for induction did not show up (2,400 out of 4,400), and that 11 percent of those who did show up refused to serve. A graduate student in history at Boston University wrote on May 1, 1968, to his draft board in Tucson, Arizona:

> I am enclosing the order for me to report for my pre-induction physical exam for the armed forces. I have absolute *no* intention to report for that exam, or for induction, or to aid in any way the American war effort against the people of Vietnam.
>
> I fully realize the consequences of my decision, there will be a trial, and then prison. I regret the suffering this will mean for my family and friends. But even more I realize what the war has meant for the Viet Namese people. It has meant six years of ceaseless and often senseless slaughter, largely of civilians. It has meant continual hunger, fear, unspeakable atrocities, and unimaginable suffering for a people, whose only dreams are for Land, Unification, and Independence. . . .
>
> At the height of the Spanish Civil War, that country's greatest philosopher, Miguel de Unamuno, condemned the Fascist

intervention [of Italy and Germany] (who were also trying to "save" that country from Communism) and declared: "Sometimes to be Silent is to Lie." . . .

Hoping, praying, for a just and early Peace, I am,

Respectfully yours,
Philip D. Supina

Supina was sentenced to four years in prison.

As the war went on, draft resistance grew, and general support for it increased. By February 1968, a poll among Harvard graduate students showed that 40 percent of them would either go to jail or leave the United States if called for induction. A Harris poll among just-graduated seniors revealed a sharp reversal in attitude in just one year: whereas in 1969, 50 percent of those polled said they would not respect persons who refused to go into the armed forces, only 34 percent felt that way in 1970, and many more declared their respect for draft resisters.

By 1970, it was becoming more evident that this horror of a war was very much the product of the "liberal" leaders of national politics. What Carl Oglesby, an SDS leader, had told peace demonstrators in Washington on November 27, 1965, was, five years later, more widely recognized: that the war was not an aberration from normal American liberalism, but was its expression. Oglesby had pointed out:

The original commitment in Vietnam was President Truman's—signer of the first civil-rights act. That commitment was seconded by the moderate liberal, President Eisenhower—who mobilized the National Guard to integrate Central High School in Little Rock—and intensified by President Kennedy, who gave us the Peace Corps, the Alliance for Progress, and the beginning of the anti-poverty program. Think of the men who now engineer that war—those who study the maps, give the commands, push the buttons, and tally the dead: Bundy, McNamara, Rusk, Lodge, Goldberg, the President himself.

They are not moral monsters.

They are all honorable men.

They are all liberals.

But so, I'm sure, are many of us who are here today. To understand the war, then, it seems necessary to take a closer look at this American liberalism. Maybe we are in for some surprises. Maybe we have here two quite different liberalisms: one authentically humanist, the other not so human at all. . . .

Not only did passive support of antiwar activity grow throughout the country, as shown in polls and city referendums, the activism of the handful in 1965 became adopted by all sorts of people to whom overt signs of protest were not familiar. In August of 1965, it was a few hundred protesters who joined David Dellinger, who had formed the National Mobilization Committee to End the War in Vietnam; historian Staughton Lynd; and SNCC leader Robert Moses in Washington to protest the war. Opponents splattered them with red paint as they marched down the Mall to the Capitol. By May 1971, twenty thousand people would come to Washington committed to acts of civil disobedience in trying to stop the war.

As the sixties came to a close, denunciations of the war emanated from all sides. Peace Corps volunteers by the hundreds protested against the war; in Chile, ninety-two volunteers were threatened by the Peace Corps director with punitive action if they did not dissociate themselves from a circular protesting the Vietnam War. Eight hundred former members of the Peace Corps also denounced the war. Poets and writers refused to attend White House functions. Robert Lowell was one, Arthur Miller was another. Miller's telegram to the White House read: "When the guns boom, the arts die." Singer Eartha Kitt scandalized Washington society by her criticism of the war during a White House affair. Teen-agers called to the White House to accept 4-H Club prizes expressed their displeasure with the war. In Hollywood, local artists erected a sixty-foot Tower of Protest on Sunset Boulevard to symbolize opposition to the war.

At the National Book Award ceremonies in New York, fifty authors and publishers walked out on a speech by Vice President Humphrey in a display of anger at his role in the war.

In London, two young Americans gate-crashed the American ambassador's elegant Fourth of July reception, and, calling for attention, proposed a toast: "To all the dead and dying in Vietnam"; they were carried out by guards. In the Pacific, two young American seamen hijacked an American munitions ship to divert its load of bombs from Thailand to Cambodia in protest against the war. (At the time, Cambodia, headed by Prince Norodom Sihanouk, was in sympathy with the Communist cause.) For four days, they took command of the ship and its crew, eating amphetamines to stay awake, until the ship was in Cambodian waters.

Middle-class and professional people who had never engaged in overt protest before began to act. In May 1970, the *New York Times* reported

1000 "ESTABLISHMENT" LAWYERS JOIN WAR PROTEST. The lawyers were on their way to Washington to urge immediate withdrawal from Indochina. Only with the acceleration of public protests did Congress begin to react in any meaningful way against the war; resolutions were introduced in both houses to put a definite date limit for American withdrawal, though as late as June 1971, such resolutions still could not pass.

The crumbling of support for the government was exemplified also in the wave of "defections" by former government officials, who now, out of office, criticized the war they had supported or been silent on while in office: Humphrey, presidential adviser McGeorge Bundy, Professor Roger Hilsman, U.N. Ambassador Arthur Goldberg, Ambassador Edwin Reischauer. The war was unpopular now. There was at least one much more rare phenomenon: that of a person high up in the war bureaucracy who left his job and not only criticized the war, but became an active member of the antiwar movement, to the point of civil disobedience. This was Daniel Ellsberg, a former aide to Secretary of Defense McNamara, who had spent years with the Rand Corporation doing war research for the government, two years in Vietnam with the pacification program. Joining him in his rebellion against the war establishment was a former Rand colleague, Anthony Russo.

In June 1971, defying a possible penalty of many years in jail, Ellsberg turned over to the *New York Times* and other newspapers part of a ten-thousand-page study of the history of American involvement in Vietnam, a study he had worked on while at the Rand Corporation, ordered by the Pentagon, and labeled "Top Secret." Its publication in the *Times* caused a national furor, with the government charging "security violation." What was at stake was no one's security, only the government's embarrassment at having its plans and deceptions disclosed to the public: its planning for military action in mid-1964, while Johnson, campaigning for president, was talking peace; its control over the Saigon government; its opposition to peace negotiations; its use of bombing for psycho-political purposes; its violations of the Geneva Accords; its covert military operations against North Vietnam long before the 1965 escalation.

In the fall of 1967, a new constituency was added to the antiwar movement—Roman Catholic priests and nuns, and Catholic lay men and women. Again, here was evidence that the Vietnam War was causing tumultuous changes in all parts of American society. On October 27, Father Philip Berrigan, veteran of World War II and a Josephite priest, anguished over the killing in Vietnam, joined David Eberhardt, Thomas Lewis, and James Mengel in the invasion of a draft board office in Baltimore. They drenched the board records with blood, waited to be arrested, were tried, and sentenced to prison terms of two to six years.

The following May, Berrigan—out on bail on the Baltimore charges—was joined by his brother Daniel, a Jesuit priest, and seven other priests and lay men and women in the destruction of draft records at Catonsville, Maryland. They became famous as the Catonsville Nine, were tried, convicted, and sentenced to prison. Two of them, Mary Moylan, a former nun, and Daniel Berrigan, refused to surrender and became "fugitives from injustice." After four months in a strange kind of underground, in which he spoke from a church pulpit, gave interviews to reporters, and met with groups of people to discuss the war and civil disobedience, Daniel Berrigan was captured by the FBI. Mary Moylan remained at large.

The war troubled the church. The priests and nuns who resisted shook a whole generation of Catholics, particularly the young, who began to rethink the heritage of Christ, the meaning of patriotism, the message of the Cross, the value of resistance. As Daniel Berrigan put it:

> The madness goes on, it proliferates mightily. Behind a façade of sobriety and temperate action, the worst instincts of man are armed, rewarded, and set loose upon the world. An unthinkable Asian war, once a mere canker on the national body, a scratch on the tegument, undergone heedlessly and borne without a second thought—it has festered and flowered, a wasting fever, a plague, a nightmare rushing into full day and again into night, and on and on for months and years, until only Jeremiah and Kafka could encompass its irrational horror.

At his sentencing in Catonsvilte, Philip Berrigan tried to explain to the court why he and Lewis, while still on bail after Baltimore, had again broken the law:

> As a Christian, I must love and respect all men—loving the good they love, hating the evil they hate. If I know what I am about, the brutalization, squalor and despair of other men, demeans me and threatens me if I do not act against its source. This is perhaps why Tom Lewis and I acted again with our friends. . . .

The Catholic Resistance (sometimes joined by Protestants and Jews) spread, in draft board raids across the country: the Boston Two, the Milwaukee Fourteen, the DC Nine, the Pasadena Three, the Silver Springs Three, the Chicago Fifteen, the Women Against Daddy Warbucks, the New York Eight, the Boston Eight, the East Coast Conspiracy to Save Lives, the Flower City Conspiracy. Some went to jail, some fled; what was called the "ultra-resistance" dramatized the change in a former stronghold of American conservatism—the Catholic Church and its constituents.

Anger against the war thus moved up and down through the layers of American society, across faiths, from class to class, race to race, well-to-do to poor. By 1969 and 1970, this anger also emanated from those involved in the war itself, from the GIs in the armed forces, from the soldiers and sailors in Vietnam, from the young men who had returned from the war as veterans. Whether or not their bodies were still whole, their sensibilities had been changed. Nothing like it had happened in American history: soldiers and veterans of a war turning against that war while it was still going on.

At first, there were individual and sporadic protests. As early as June 1965, Richard Steinke, a West Point graduate in Vietnam, refused to board an aircraft taking him to a remote Vietnamese village where a Special Forces team was operating. "The Vietnamese war," he said, "is not worth a single American life." Steinke was court-martialed and dismissed from the service. The following year, three army privates, ordered to embark for Vietnam, denounced the war as "immoral, illegal, and unjust" and refused to go. They were court-martialed and sent to prison.

In early 1967, an army doctor at Fort Jackson, South Carolina, Captain Howard Levy, refused to teach Green Berets, members of the elite Special Forces; Levy argued that they were "murderers of women and children" and "killers of peasants." He was court-martialed on the ground that he was trying to promote disaffection among enlisted men by his statements on the war. The colonel who presided at the trial ruled out truth as a defense for Levy. "The truth of the statements is not an issue in this case," he said. Levy was convicted and sentenced to prison.

There were others: a black private in Oakland refused to broad a troop plane to Vietnam, although he faced eleven years at hard labor. A navy nurse, Lieutenant Susan Schnall, was court-martialed for marching in a peace demonstration while in uniform and for dropping antiwar leaflets on navy installations from a plane. In Norfolk a sailor opposed to the war refused to train fighter pilots because he believed the Vietnam War was immoral. An army lieutenant was arrested in early 1968 in Washington, D.C., for picketing the White House with a sign that said "120,000 American Casualties—Why?" Two black marines, George Daniels and William Harvey, were given long prison sentences (originally six and ten years each, later reduced) for talking to other black marines against the war.

Desertions from the armed forces mounted as the war went on. Thousands went to Western Europe, and estimates on how many GIs crossed over into Canada ranged from fifty thousand to one hundred thousand. A few deserters made a public demonstration of their act, by openly taking "sanctuary" in a church or other place, where, surrounded by antiwar friends and sympathizers, they waited for capture and court-martial. At Boston University, a thousand students kept a vigil for five days and nights in the chapel surrounding an eighteen-year-old, Ray Kroll, who, when hauled into court on a charge of drunkenness, had been inveigled into the army by the judge. On a Sunday morning, federal agents arrived at the chapel, stomped their way through aisles clogged with students, smashed down doors, and took Kroll away. From the stockade, he sent a poem to the friends he had made in the Marsh Chapel sanctuary:

> *My Dream*
> They told me I got to go off to war
> Just to get rid of the big red sore
> Well they got me all wrong
> Me? I wanna live a happy song
> I wanna live and love
> and hold that peace dove
> Oh you mean ole Turnkey
> Why don'tcha just set me free
> You keep me hanging on
> You really don't love me
> I ain't gonna kill
> It's against my will
> When they gonna let me live in peace
> and all wars come to a cease?

He wrote: "Marji gave me some books with some sayings in them. . . . 'What we have done will not be lost to all Eternity. Everything ripens at its time and becomes fruit at its hour.'"

As the GI antiwar movement grew, it became more organized. Near Fort Jackson some enterprising young men and women set up the first GI coffeehouse, called The UFO, a place where GIs could have coffee and doughnuts and find literature about the war and current affairs. It was a low-key, deliberate attempt to encourage discussion among GIs about the war. The UFO was closed by local harassment and court action, with the coffeehouse declared "a public nuisance." In the meantime, however, many GIs at Fort Jackson had come to know and like it, and the GI coffeehouse idea grew. A half-dozen coffeehouses were opened across the country, and at least two bookstores (to avoid the ruse of closing them for "health" reasons), one near Fort Devens, Massachusetts, and one at the Newport, Rhode Island, naval base.

Underground newspapers sprang up at army and navy bases across the country; by 1970, more than fifty were in operation. Among them: *About Face* in Los Angeles; *Fed Up!* at Tacoma; *Short Times* at Fort Jackson; *Vietnam GI* in Chicago; *Graffiti* in Heidelberg, Germany; *Bragg Briefs* in North Carolina; *Last Harass* at Fort Gordon, Georgia; *Helping Hand* at Mountain Home Air Base, Idaho. They printed antiwar articles, revealed harassment of GIs, gave practical advice on the legal rights of men in the service, told how to resist military domination. In June 1970, twenty-eight commissioned officers of the army, air force, navy, and marine corps, including some veterans of Vietnam, saying they represented about 250 other officers, announced formation of the Concerned Officers Movement to protest the war.

Anger among those in the armed forces against the war was mixed with bitter resentment against the cruelty, the dehumanization of military life. And nowhere was this more true than in Army stockades. In 1968 at the Presidio stockade in California, after a guard had shot to death a disturbed prisoner for walking away from a work detail, twenty-seven prisoners decided to show their outrage by sitting down during a work detail, and singing "We Shall Overcome." They were court-martialed, found guilty of mutiny, and sentenced to terms of up to fourteen years, later reduced after much public attention and protest.

The antiwar dissidence spread to the war front itself. When, on October 16, 1969, the great Moratorium demonstrations were taking place, some GIs in Vietnam wore black armbands to show their support. A news photographer reported that in a platoon on patrol near Da Nang, about half of the men were wearing black armbands. One soldier stationed at Cu Chi wrote to a friend on October 26, 1970, that separate companies had been set up for men refusing to go into the field to fight.

"It is no big thing here anymore to refuse to go." Earlier in 1970, the Saigon correspondent for *Le Monde* had written:

> Indifference, rancor, disgust, hostility: the war less and less pleases the Americans who wage it. In four months, 109 soldiers of the First Cav, America's first air cavalry division, have been charged with refusal to fight. At Saigon, as at Danang, the security services pursue deserters. In most units, more than half the soldiers smoke marijuana. A common sight is the black soldier, with his left fist clenched in defiance of a war he has never considered his own. . . . Yet most of the troops fight well.

More and more, in military units in Vietnam, there were cases of "fragging"—incidents in which servicemen rolled fragmentation bombs under the tents of officers who were ordering them into combat, or against whom they had other grievances. The Pentagon reported 209 fraggings in Vietnam in 1970 alone.

By early 1970, many veterans back from Vietnam joined together in a group called Vietnam Veterans Against the War. In December, 1970, hundreds of them went to Detroit for the "Winter Soldier" investigations; there they testified publicly about atrocities they had participated in or seen in Vietnam, committed by Americans against the Vietnamese. In April 1971, more than a thousand of them went to Washington, D.C., to demonstrate against the war and discard the medals they had won in Vietnam; they passed before a wire fence around the Capitol, threw their medals over the fence, and made impassioned statements about the war. One of them, a former navy lieutenant in the Mekong Delta, John Kerry, testified before the Senate Foreign Relations Committee. He told what GIs had seen in Vietnam: rapes; the random shooting of civilians, prisoners of war, and livestock; torture; the burning and sacking of villages; the forcible relocation of the civilian population. "It seems," Kerry said, "that someone has to die every day so Richard Nixon doesn't have to be the first President to lose a war. How do you ask a man to be the last soldier to die for a mistake?" When Memorial Day came around in 1971, the outburst of GI resentment against the war continued. A thousand American servicemen stationed in Britain announced their opposition to the war in petitions handed into the United States embassy. Circulating among them was an underground military newspaper called *PEACE*—People Emerging Against Corrupt Establishments.

It was on that Memorial Day weekend that several hundred veterans against the war camped out on the green at Lexington, Massachusetts, the cradle of the American revolution. They were joined by three hundred local citizens, and then all were arrested for refusing to leave the green. After getting out of jail, the veterans went to Bunker Hill, spent the night, and held an antiwar rally on the Boston Common the next day. This defection from violence, from war, this rebellion against authority, this suspicion of government, this independence of spirit, came twenty-five years after the passive acceptance by American soldiers in 1945 of the dropping of the atomic bomb on the men, women, and children of Hiroshima and Nagasaki. Something important was happening to the spirit and mind of many people in the United States.

Was a revolution—at least the first stirrings of one—taking place in postwar America? Many with a strong sense of history were dubious. Historians in the fifties, such as Richard Hofstadter and Louis Hartz, stressed the continuity in American politics and values, despite reforms in race and economics and politics and civil liberties. Would not the United States bounce back from the Vietnam War to its ordinary, if somewhat masked, injustices at home, and a quieter imperialism abroad?

And yet, there was something qualitatively different this time. Perhaps it was because Americans had now gone through the New Deal reforms, and knew these were inadequate in dealing with the gross waste and destruction of their resources. Perhaps it was because Americans had passed all those civil rights bills, and found they failed to touch the core of the race problem. Perhaps it was because Americans had defeated McCarthyism and made many procedural changes in the judicial process, and yet realized, particularly the many thousands who had experienced courts and jail, that the whole system was still essentially unjust.

In short, perhaps by the 1960s Americans had exhausted the deceptions of mild reforms at home, and, with Vietnam, had learned enough about foreign policy for many to be dissatisfied with the old excuses for war, for military and economic domination of other parts of the world. Perhaps the nation really had run out of all that time and space it had when other countries were the great imperial powers of the world. Now Americans were right up against a wall on all sides, and they had to tear it down, or climb over it into a new world, because they could no longer get along by meandering within its limits.

It was hard to be sure, in 1971, but there were signs of hopeful changes in America. They appeared first among the black people of the country, who so often in its history have been the key to understanding the level of American humanity or inhumanity. Blacks in the sixties got their civil rights bills and their token payments, but it was exactly as this was happening that they broke out in the greatest black rebellion in the nation's history. They then embarked on a cultural revolution of sorts, to change the *minds* of blacks and whites on the race question, while trying to figure out a way to change the basic relations of wealth and power, beyond laws and tokens.

There were indications that this more fundamental approach to changing American society, early and tentative as it was, was spreading to other problems besides race. Perhaps it was the concentration of so many crucial issues in one decade—race, education, the war—but sharper questions were being asked, a revolt was under way against not just a specific policy, but against ways of thinking, ways of life.

The most personal, most intimate of human relationships began to be examined. It was an attempt to pierce the many layers of artifice piled up by "civilization" and rediscover the root needs of man and woman, to hear again that primeval cry for companionship and freedom. That cry had been stifled by modern technology, by unnecessary things, by false relationships, money, success, status, superiority; all these things had replaced genuine affection. At the pinnacle of American success— unprecedented wealth, power, resources—people suddenly felt a failure at the core. Some were unhappy and distraught, others vaguely, con- fusedly dissatisfied, but almost everywhere in the country, Americans were uneasy about what they were and where they were going.

Parents and children found themselves in a conflict. Some called it "the generation gap," but there had always been a chronological differ- ence; the conflict in the sixties was deeper. It both intensified hostility and speeded up changes in attitude, as crises and conflict tend to do. A woman named Marina Matteuzzi wrote to the *Boston Globe* one day in 1967 about how that conflict had changed her:

> Last week my 20-year-old son left home. He put on some old clothes, beads, a pair of granny sunglasses. He took no bags, little money, told me goodby, he had to go to Frisco to see the beautiful people. He said, "Mama, don't cry." So I didn't cry. I cried the day after. I cried for my dead dreams, to see my only son drop out (as he put it). I wanted him to be a doctor, teacher, something I never had the opportunity of being.

Then she told of a Negro friend, about to be sent to Vietnam, who looked for housing for his wife and two children, and was turned away again and again from one community after another.

I was angry and so was he. This country is like a South Africa underground. They are scared stiff of the Godless Communists, when they themselves are Christians without God.

So today I don't cry for my son dropping out. Let him stay out. I will write to him to ask if among the 300,000 men like him there is room for a 43-year-old hippie woman—me!

Both the parents and the children spoke of "a sick society," but it was the young who rebelled, probably because they had more space and freedom to do so. The young had not yet taken their proper places in the order of things, had less to lose, and were closer not only to their own childhood but to the yearnings of all people.

The dropouts—young people leaving the family, leaving their home towns, leaving their schools—became a mass phenomenon among the youth. They began to gather in urban centers around the country—San Francisco or Cambridge or Manhattan—and in rural enclaves in Vermont and New Mexico. The new folk music and rock music and country music of the postwar period connected them esthetically with one another and with something transcendental in a society they wanted desperately to escape.

Perhaps the degree to which the political disaffection of the thirties had become a much broader cultural phenomenon in the sixties is shown in the difference between the innocuous songs of sentimental love that dominate the popular culture of the thirties, and the more biting, vital, serious lyrics of folk-rock in the sixties. Bob Dylan became a hero because he expressed what so many felt:

Come mothers and fathers throughout the land,
Don't criticize what you can't understand.
Your sons and your daughters are beyond your command,
Your old road is rapidly aging.
Please get out of the new one if you can't lend your hand,
For the times they are a-changing.

Why were the young rebelling? It was hardly because of intellectual political analyses. No, it was more because of images and sounds that poured in on them in this intense period of history and stirred some inner recollection that life was supposed to be different, according to the precepts of the Bible, the Declaration of Independence, or the Communist Manifesto. On television they saw weeping Vietnamese women watching

American soldiers burn down their huts and aim rifles at their children. As teen-agers, they had seen police hose down and club blacks in the streets of Birmingham.

The new mood of freedom, of defiance, caused the young to re-think everything about their lives. They remembered—because it was yesterday—their classrooms, which even an older, cooler observer, af-ter three years of observation and study, found horrifying. Social critic Charles Silberman wrote:

> It is not possible to spend any prolonged period visiting public school classrooms without being appalled by the mutilation visi-ble everywhere—mutilation of spontaneity, of a joy in learning, of pleasure in creating, of sense of self. . . . what grim, joyless places most American schools are, how oppressive and petty are the rules by which they are governed, how intellectually sterile and esthetically barren the atmosphere, what an appalling lack of civility obtains on the part of teachers and principals, what con-tempt they unconsciously display for children as children.

The rebellion of the young was the most visible, the most troubling, but not the only, defection from culture. Older people, too, were moving out of their accustomed lines, and in parts of life so close to the heart of American culture that the move could not be dismissed as ephemeral or superficial. When Catholic nuns and priests moved out of line, when 4-H Club youngsters did the same, when young doctors and lawyers formed communes, then something important was happening. Even su-perstars of the football and baseball worlds began to challenge their coaches and their publics, the Cult of competition, dollars, success. A professional football linebacker, Dave Meggyesy of the Saint Louis Car-dinals, announced he was retiring from the game early in his career, ex-plaining: "It's no accident that the most repressive political regime in our history is ruled by a football freak, President Nixon." Another line-backer, Chip Oliver of the Oakland Raiders, left football at one point to live in a California commune, saying:

> Pro football is a silly game. It dehumanizes people. They've taken the players and turned them into slabs of beef that can charge around and hit each other. But where is their esthetic soul, the feeling they can accomplish higher things? . . .
> I quit pro football because I felt I wasn't doing anything posi-tive toward making this world a better place to live. The world I

was living in, the world of making money, was leading me nowhere. . . .

In the late sixties, a new force joined in the cultural upheaval, the revolt against authority, the search for human relationships. This was the
Women's Liberation Movement, which, in a few years and on a wide
tactical front ranging from violent denunciations of male supremacy to
more moderate insistence on equal rights, made millions of Americans
conscious of the subordinate position of "the second sex." (Simone de
Beauvoir's book of that title was a pioneering statement of the issue.)

Women's Liberation pointed to the exploitation of women—
crippling their education, consigning them to the household, denying
them jobs in "men's work," paying them less than men for the same
work, leaving them to deal alone with childbirth and children as their
particular sphere, while men went off to work, or to play, or to other
women. The new feminists also pointed to the way modern culture poisons the minds of men and women, from the time they are children, so
that women are sex objects, weak, dependent, while men are leaders,
heroic, strong. Evelyn Leo described the result of this socialization:

> The course of her entire adult life, from beginning to end, is deter-
> mined by her choice of a husband because she is culturally obli-
> gated to allow him to take the lead in career, geographic location,
> friends, entertainment, interests, and her so-called comforts in life.
>   Something is terribly wrong with this dependent status of
> women. They are bound up with another human being in a closely
> intertwined relationship, yet they are carried along in a parasitic
> manner, never reaching their full potential as human beings, never
> using their own free choice or functioning as an individual within
> the marriage relationship. Something must be done to change this
> unequal, unfair, and oppressive situation in marriage.

And so women organized. They were not centrally directed. The
forms of organization, the ideology, the tactics, the emphases, differed
enormously. There seemed to be special stress on avoiding authoritarian
leadership and elitist direction, as if to illustrate in action what it meant
to be free from man's customary authority. To win reforms, to gain recognition, to make people think, women picketed Miss America contests,
formed caucuses in professional organizations, published underground
newspapers, held sit-ins and demonstrations.

A counterculture was developing in America, something more profoundly revolutionary than the political changes that followed the American Revolution and the Civil War. Along with the political struggles against racism, against war, against police brutality, there was an inchoate movement to declare for change by simply living in a different way. Some spokesmen for cultural change emphasized changing people's minds as a more fundamental act than merely engaging in political actions that could easily be absorbed by a shrewdly reformist America. Historian Theodore Roszak argued in *The Making of a Counter Culture* that "the process of weaning men away from the technocracy can never be carried through by way of a grim, hard-bitten, and self-congratulatory militancy, which at best belongs to tasks of ad hoc resistance. Beyond the tactics of resistance, but shaping them at all times, there must be a stance of life which seeks not simply to muster power against the misdeeds of society, but to transform the very sense men have of reality."

In those varied currents, although it was written in no one declaration, no one manifesto, the rough vision of some future world could be detected:

It would have to be an international society, for the nation-state—with its tight boundaries, its strangling flags, its cacophonous anthems, its armies, its hatred of others, its passports, its pledges of allegiance, its prisons, its addiction to violence—was obsolete. It was one planet; man would be embarrassed to get to Mars and explain to the green people there the Vietnam War, or the Israeli-Arab border dispute, or the Pakistani-India argument, or the Russian invasion of Czechoslovakia, or the president's latest speech on television.

The resources of the world would have to be taken away from private corporations, which exploit them for profit, and from centralized socialist states, which exploit them for political or nationalist purposes. These resources would be managed for the public good, with priority given to the production of people's most vital needs, striving for some union of social requirements and personal pleasure. Yes, socialism, some might say, but like no socialism yet seen on earth. It would retain the original socialist idea of rational use of resources for urgent needs, equitably distributed. But it would avoid national selfishness and centralized bureaucracy; it would try to give decision-making power to consumers, to those who work, with hands and brains, in the economy—to create the kind of economic democracy that has not yet existed anywhere.

Political democracy would have to go far beyond the rule of parties, whether in one-party or two-party systems, and far beyond representative government. Parliaments and congresses everywhere in the world have become a façade behind which men of power make decisions, while all other men delude themselves into thinking they control their own destiny because they go to the ballot boxes to make their puny choices, on prepared-in-advance ballots. People would have to be drawn into active, day-to-day participation in decision-making, instead of pulling a lever once in two years, or once in four or seven years, or once in a generation. People most affected by decisions would have the strongest voice in making them, and those with special knowledge would offer it to those with special interests. Administrators would be in perpetual communication with the people, and subject to immediate recall.

The circulation of ideas would have to be completely free, with no excuses of "security" to stand behind the creation of secret police, detention centers, political trials. And prisons would have to be abolished, not only because the "best" of them constitutes "cruel and unusual punishment"—unusual in the sense that the greatest perpetrators of fraud and violence, the men in charge of government and business, go unpunished—but because punishment itself is the greatest crime. No civilization worthy of respect can lock people in dungeons, deprive them of the most essential needs of human beings, and deserve to stand. It would take imagination, ingenuity, and risk to try to minimize individual acts of cruelty or violence, but that imagination and ingenuity could never come forth unless absolutely required by the elimination of imprisonment. The abolition of prisons would press Americans to speed up the transformation of the whole society—its distribution of wealth, its set of values, its human relations; it would be a good prod.

Authoritarianism in personal relations, involving blind obedience, hierarchy, arbitrary rule, control, humiliation, would have to fall away—in the family, between old and young, between man and woman, white and black, skilled and unskilled. Democracy on the personal level would be recognized as the crucial accompaniment of democracy on the social level. Americans would have to stop assigning marks of superiority to surgeons over sweepers, poets over carpenters. People would work at what most pleased them, and differences in biological or educational or cultural attributes would still leave all people equal in the most basic sense of retaining their self-respect. The ideas of cooperation, kindness, and equality would spread, by persuasion and example, firmly and vigorously.

Such, more or less, is the vision of a future society represented by the new currents of political and cultural change. How to achieve that vision, given the realities of present power and present consciousness, has been much more difficult to figure out. Many have come to believe, however, that it is not so much a matter of theorizing as of making a start. The tactics of such a change, even making a start toward change, have to be informed, both by a vision of the future and by an accurate assessment of the structure of the present. Understanding the present situation could give at least some clues to the necessary processes of change.

In postwar America it became increasingly apparent that the structure of its society differed from traditional societies—Tsarist Russia and Mandarin China, for example—not in the fact of oligarchical control, but in the mode of that control. In the traditional societies, revolution was staved off by a combination of force, tradition, and simple folk belief in obedience to authority. In the United States—as in other technologically developed societies of this century—the mode of control contained the same ingredients, but in different proportions, with different degrees of sophistication. Modern society was still held together by force—indeed, such force as could hardly be imagined in olden times—but by a much more complicated, much more effective structure of deception than in traditional societies. Control was now internalized in the masses of the citizenry by a set of beliefs inculcated from early age, by all the techniques of modern education and mass communication.

In the modern liberal scheme, there was more flexibility; partial defects could be acknowledged, so long as the whole system was considered legitimate and good. Each group that saw a tarnished side of the social structure was taught that all the other sides were clean. But most important, modern society strained the cruelties of the past through such an elaborate network of mystification as to keep the fairly educated, fairly resourceful, potentially dangerous population pacified.

Economic exploitation, for instance, has not been as obvious in liberal capitalist societies as in peasant cultures, where the lord simply took half the produce; it has been disguised by a labyrinth of contractual relationships and market interchanges that bewilder even the economists. Political tyranny has been masked by representative bodies, regular elections, and the ballyhoo of free choice. Freedom of expression, granted in theory, has been denied at crucial moments, and rationed according to wealth; the powerless have the legal right to shout into deaf ears, and the powerful have the right to pipe their message into every living room in America. Due process of law and the formalities of judicial procedure conceal inequality before the law between rich and poor, black and white, government and citizen.

All this deception is distributed through a system of compulsory education, and reinforced in home and church, so that school, church, and parents have become instruments of control. And just as the coin of the marketplace has had its value determined by powerful corporations and the government, the coin of communication, language itself, has been controlled in schools and in the mass media. Words like violence, patriotism, honor, national security, responsibility, democracy, freedom, have been assigned meanings difficult to alter.

For those seeking basic change, the main problem in liberal societies, with such a structure of control, would not be to organize military units for a violent revolution in the classical sense, but to pull apart the web of deception. What has been needed is a set of tactics aimed at exposing the gap between words and reality, a set of tactics proving that the liberal system failed to fulfill its own professed goals, that it violated its own asserted values, that it destroyed what it said it cherished, wasted what it said it revered.

The history of the postwar world demonstrated that such learning about reality did not take place in the home, the classroom, and the Sunday school, or from lecture and political platforms. Learning took place most forcefully, most dramatically, most promptly where people took direct action against an evil policy, for a desired goal. In the struggle with power that such action inevitably produced, deceptions were exposed, realities revealed, new strengths discovered. Out of such struggles, people might begin to develop new forms of working and living—the seeds of a future cooperative society. The civil rights movement, the student movement, the peace movement, the women's liberation movement revealed how rapidly Americans could learn.

Not everyone was deceived in the wealthy liberal state. Many knew that it was a rich man's society, that politics were corrupt, that justice was a farce. But they remained quiet, and played the game, because they also were very practical people; they knew they were powerless and saw the futility of rebellion. Yet for such people, organized action could give a sense of confidence, and occasional small victories could show that resistance is not always futile. Action could lay bare the potential power of the presumably powerless. It could show that money and guns are not the only ingredients of power. For whatever progress has taken place in the world, wherever revolutions or reforms have even temporarily succeeded, has it not been where some special, indefinable power was assembled out of the will and sacrifice of ordinary people?

The politics of protest in the sixties gave at least suggestions of this power. Minorities of organized blacks won gains here and there. Students drove the ROTC off fifty campuses, and changed many academic programs. Antiwar demonstrators made life impossible for Johnson and Nixon, determined the geography of their speeches, forced them to renege, if slowly, on their military policies in Asia. And there were many other examples, not always successful in attaining their immediate objectives, but showing the possibilities of action:

- In East Harlem, a group of young Puerto Rican activists, the Young Lords, seized a mobile chest X-ray unit and brought it to work in an area where the tuberculosis rate was high.
- In Boston, elderly residents organized and crowded into public hearings to get fare reductions for old people on the public transportation system.
- In Michigan, an elusive group of "billboard bandits" managed to remove 167 billboards along highways to restore the quiet beauty of central Michigan.
- In Upstate New York, a small group of volunteers guarded the home of an American Indian family being harassed by neighbors who wanted them to leave the area.
- Ten welfare mothers held a "shop-in" at Macy's department store in New York, taking clothes openly, without paying, to publicize the fact that they had no money to buy the clothes.
- An antiwar group raided a small FBI office in Media, Pennsylvania, and distributed documents to the press to publicize the way in which the FBI was acting undemocratically to suppress civil liberties.
- Poor people showed up at lavishly financed national conferences on welfare to interrupt traditional speeches and demand action.
- Protesters appeared at stockholders' meetings to ask that auto companies take measures to stop polluting the air, that banks remove investments from South Africa, that the Dow Chemical Company stop manufacturing napalm.
- Poor blacks in Greenville, Mississippi, occupied an empty air force base to demonstrate their lack of housing and their need for jobs and land.
- Doctors defied orders to close a hospital in the South Bronx, and set up voluntary clinics; residents later broke into the hospital and

reopened it to let two doctors treat patients in the emergency room.

- Indians on the West Coast occupied Alcatraz Island to dramatize neglect of their problem; Indians in South Dakota stationed themselves on top of the Mount Rushmore memorial to pressure the government to honor an 1858 treaty giving land to the Sioux.
- In Berkeley, California, radicals succeeded in getting their candidates elected to half the seats of the city council.
- In Milwaukee, members of a tenants' union invaded a housing authority meeting and succeeded in stopping evictions of two families.

The significance of these acts lay outside their immediate demands. They represented attempts to act out a fuller form of democracy, beyond the limitations of the ballot box and the political party, in which aggrieved people would make their statements directly to the public, and show directly what their needs were. Sometimes this meant bold confrontations, sometimes it meant hit-and-run tactics. One citizen, pondering the relationships of power, told a student: "No, you can't fight city hall, but you can shit on the steps and run like hell." His was one idiosyncratic approach. Significant change, however, required more permanent forms of action and organization, people moving in concert but without hierarchy. It was necessary to reach, to organize, to stir into action, large sections of the working population that had hitherto been absent from the movement of the sixties.

Some people found it necessary to act out new ways of living, to show the possibilities of cooperation. Thus, around 1970, communes became a widespread phenomenon in America, with tens of thousands of people across the country, in various living and working arrangements, trying to prove that people did not have to live competitively, that they did not have to live in small, segregated families, that a larger, warmer notion of "family" might be possible, in which children would grow up better, and adults would have a richer, freer life.

Some of these communes were based on cooperative living arrangements, with the members going off during the day to work at their regular jobs. Others were working communes, in which a group of lawyers or doctors, living where they chose, set up cooperative workforces with social need, not private profit, as the chief motivation.

In December 1970, there were at least two thousand communes across the country, but the *New York Times*, which had made the survey, acknowledged that this was a conservative estimate. Women's liberation groups set up communes. So did radical political organizers, living together in the communities where they worked. The *Times* survey found living together: Cincinnati Health Department employees campaigning for a more efficient administration; former nuns and Appalachian whites working together with mining families in the mountains of Kentucky and Tennessee; young men in Maine developing programs to save the state's open lands and shores. A common type of commune in many cities consisted of the staff of the local underground newspaper. Near a number of military bases, antiwar organizers—civilian and GI—lived and worked together, operating a local coffeeshop or a bookstore. Rural communes sprang up in Vermont, in the Rocky Mountain states, on the West Coast.

In the tactics of social change in postwar America, one problem was constant: how to work for immediate, urgent reform, without succumbing to the American system's customary way of avoiding drastic change by granting piecemeal reforms to pacify the population. No theoretical answer to this problem seemed to exist; it was a question of working hard, without losing a larger vision of change. Some were able to do this. In 1969, in Dorchester, a white working-class section of Boston, eight young people of different backgrounds—including a former student at Harvard, a local fellow just back from Vietnam, a girl who had left her high school after leading the antiwar movement—moved into a house together, opened up a storefront, and organized a food cooperative in which many local residents joined. They collected thousands of signatures on a petition to remove a particularly oppressive local judge, and they published a community newspaper. The paper was called *tpf*—the people first. It told about landlord-tenant disputes, discussed reasons why police should be hired and supervised by the community, gave special attention to the problems of women, offered practical advice to those on welfare, advertised the food co-op, explained the effects of the Vietnam War on the cost of living in Dorchester.

These eight people wanted revolutionary change in American society. They expected to get it, not by some massive military confrontation in Washington, but by groups like themselves, working all over the country to assemble the splintered power of people into forces so diverse, so widespread, so ingrained in their communities and their workplaces as to become irrepressible. The stability of the old order rested on widespread obedience. It required everyone to stay in place. Perhaps enough sensibilities could be affected, enough confidence built up, so that someday people, acting together, would refuse to obey, refuse to do their jobs on the assembly line of violence and waste, and build their own organizations, on the job and in the neighborhood. Then the government, with all its arms and money, would be impotent. Then, through free associations of people, engaged over a long period in difficult struggles with entrenched power, democracy would come into its own at last.

In postwar America, it was beginning to be recognized by a small but growing part of the population that the special qualities of control possessed by the modern liberal system demanded a long revolutionary process of struggle and example. The process would have to be long enough, intense enough, to change the thinking of people, to act out, as far as possible, the future society. To work for the great ends of the Declaration of Independence, for life, liberty, and the pursuit of happiness, did not mean looking for some future day of fruition. It meant beginning immediately to make those ends real.

PATRIOTISM

from *A Power Governments Cannot Suppress* (2007)

Throughout American history, as in recent times, no word has been used more freely to silence dissent than "patriotism," which Mark Twain once characterized as "grotesque and laughable." Those who dare to criticize the powers that be are derided as "unpatriotic," as if pride in country requires blind obedience to government or unthinking acceptance of the myths of American exceptionalism that we are spoon-fed as schoolchildren. A frequent target of such derision throughout his life, Howard had a provocative response to those who would challenge his love of country: "If patriotism means supporting your government's policies without question, then we are on our way to a totalitarian state." In this essay, he argues that if we take seriously the principles of the Declaration of Independence, then we must make "a clear distinction between the government and the people." He continues: "This principle . . . suggests that a true patriotism lies in supporting the values the country is supposed to cherish: equality, life, liberty, the pursuit of happiness. When our government compromises, undermines, or attacks those values, it is being unpatriotic." Here, Howard flips the script, arguing instead that dissent is the highest form of patriotism. He offers numerous examples from American history of how "obedience to government . . . has been disastrous for the American people." This is never more the case than during times of war. "War is almost always a breaking of that promise," he writes. "It does not enable the pursuit of happiness but brings despair and grief." To be true patriots, Howard reminds us, we must side with the people whenever the government violates its principles, betrays its promises, or abuses its power.

———

SOMETIME IN THE 1960s the folk singer Tom Paxton wrote a song called "What Did You Learn in School Today?" The song includes the following lines:

> I learned that Washington never told a lie,
> I learned that soldiers seldom die. . . .
> I learned our government must be strong,
> It's always right and never wrong.

The song is amusing—an exaggeration, of course—but not too far off the mark for all of us who grew up in the United States and were taught to have pride in our nation as soon as we entered public school. So much of our early education is filled with stories and images coming out of the Revolutionary War: the Boston Tea Party, Paul Revere, the battle of Bunker Hill, Washington crossing the Delaware, the heroism of soldiers at Valley Forge, the making of the Constitution. Our history is suffused with emotional satisfaction, glorying in the military victories, proud of our national leaders.

The march across the continent that follows the Revolution is depicted on classroom maps as the Westward Expansion. The phrase suggests a kind of natural, almost biological growth, not mentioning the military forays into Spanish Florida, the armed aggression against Mexico, and the massacres and forced removals of the indigenous peoples. Instead the maps are colored and labeled with different events using benign language: "Louisiana Purchase," "Florida Purchase," "Mexican Cession." Commercial transactions and generous gifts, rather than military occupation and conquest.

Young people learning such a "patriotic" history would easily conclude that, as Tom Paxton's song puts it, our government is "always right and never wrong." And if so, it is our duty to support whatever our government does, even to be willing to give our lives in war. But is that patriotism in the best sense of the word? If patriotism means supporting your government's policies without question, then we are on our way to a totalitarian state.

Patriotism in a democratic society cannot possibly be unquestioning support of the government, not if we take seriously the principles of democracy as set forth in the Declaration of Independence, our founding document. The Declaration makes a clear distinction between the government and the people. Governments are artificial creations, the Declaration says, established by the people with the obligation to protect certain ends: the equal rights of all to "Life, Liberty, and the pursuit of Happiness." And "whenever any form of Government becomes destructive of these ends, it is the Right of the People to alter or abolish it. . . ."

Surely, if it is the right of the people to "alter or abolish," it is their right to criticize, even severely, policies they believe destructive of the ends for which government has been established. This principle, in the Declaration of Independence, suggests that a true patriotism lies in supporting the values the country is supposed to cherish: equality, life, liberty, the pursuit of happiness. When our government compromises, undermines, or attacks those values, it is being unpatriotic.

That characterization of governments expressed in the Declaration, as "deriving their just Powers from the consent of the governed" has been understood by the most heroic of Americans—not the heroes of war, but the heroes of the long struggle for social justice. Mark Twain was one of many who distinguished between the country and the government.

Several years before he denounced the U.S. invasion of the Philippines, Mark Twain had written the novel *A Connecticut Yankee in King Arthur's Court* and put into the mouth of his main character these words:

> You see my kind of loyalty was loyalty to one's country, not to its institutions or its officeholders. The country is the real thing, the substantial thing, the eternal thing; it is the thing to watch over, and care for, and be loyal to; institutions are extraneous, they are its mere clothing, and clothing can wear out, become ragged, cease to be comfortable, cease to protect the body from winter, disease and death. To be loyal to rags, to shout for rags, to worship rags, to die for rags—that is a loyalty of unreason, it is pure animal; it belongs to monarchy, was invented by monarchy; let monarchy keep it.

The same distinction between government and country was made in the years before World War I by the feminist-anarchist Emma Goldman, who lectured in many cities on the subject of patriotism:

> What is patriotism? Is it love of one's birthplace, the place of childhood's recollections and hopes, dreams and aspirations? Is it the place where, in childlike naivety, we would watch the fleeting clouds, and wonder why we, too, could not run so swiftly? . . . Indeed, conceit, arrogance, and egotism are the essentials of patriotism. Patriotism assumes that our globe is divided into little

spots, each one surrounded by an iron gate. Those who have had the fortune of being born on some particular spot, consider themselves better, nobler, grander, more intelligent than the living beings inhabiting any other spot. It is, therefore, the duty of everyone living on that chosen spot to fight, kill, and die in the attempt to impose his superiority upon all the others.

Defining patriotism as obedience to government—as an uncritical acceptance of any war the leaders of government decide must be fought—has been disastrous for the American people. Failure to distinguish between the country and the government has led so many young people, recruited into the military, to declare that that they would be willing to die for their country. Would not those young people hesitate before enlisting if they considered that they were not risking their lives for their country, but for the government, and even for the owners of great wealth, the giant corporations connected to the government?

As a patriot, contemplating the dead GIs in Afghanistan and Iraq, I could comfort myself (as, understandably, their families do) with the thought: "They died for their country." But I would be lying to myself.

Today, the U.S. soldiers who are being killed in Iraq and Afghanistan are not dying for their country; they are dying for their government. They are dying for Cheney, Bush, and Rumsfeld. And yes, they are dying for the greed of the oil cartels, for the expansion of the American empire, for the political ambitions of the president. They are dying to cover up the theft of the nation's wealth to pay for the machines of death. As of July 4, 2006, more than 2,500 U.S. soldiers have been killed in Iraq, and almost 20,000 have been maimed or injured.

It is the country that is primary—the people, the ideals of the sanctity of human life, and the promotion of liberty. When a government recklessly expends the lives of its young for crass motives of profit and power, always claiming that its motives are pure and moral ("Operation Just Cause" in the invasion of Panama and "Operation Enduring Freedom" and "Operation Iraqi Freedom" in the present instance), it is violating its promise to the country. War is almost always a breaking of that promise. It does not enable the pursuit of happiness but brings despair and grief.

Mark Twain derided what he called "monarchical patriotism." In his words,

The gospel of the monarchical patriotism is: "The King can do no wrong." We have adopted it with all its servility, with an unimportant change in the wording: "Our country, right or wrong!" We have thrown away the most valuable asset we had—the individual's right to oppose both flag and country when he believed them to be in the wrong. We have thrown it: away; and with it, all that was really respectable about that grotesque and laughable word, Patriotism.

With the United States imposing its might in Iraq and Afghanistan, shall we revel in American military power and—against the history of modern empires—insist that the American empire will be beneficent?

Our own history shows something different. Obedience to whatever the government decides is founded on the idea that the interests of the government are the same as the interests of its citizens. However, we have a long history of government policy that suggests that America's political leaders have had interests different from those of the people. The men who gathered in Philadelphia in 1787 to draft the Constitution, while they drafted provisions for a certain degree of representative government and agreed to a Bill of Rights, did not represent the interests of people forced to be slaves, people whose enslavement was in fact legitimized by the Constitution. Nor did they represent the interests of working people, American Indians, and women of any color or class.

Nor did they represent the average white man of that time—the small farmer—for they intended to fashion a government that would be capable of putting down the kind of rebellions of farmers that had been erupting all over the country in the year before the Constitutional Convention. The very term we use, "Founding Fathers," suggests a family, with common interests. But from the founding of the nation to the present day, the government has generally legislated on behalf of the wealthy, has done the bidding of corporations in dealing with working people, and has taken the nation to war in the interests of economic expansion and political ambition.

It then becomes crucial for democracy to understand this difference of interest between government and people and to see expressions like "the national interest," "national security," "national defense" as ways of obscuring that difference and of enticing the citizens into subservience to power. It becomes important, then, to be wary of those symbols of nationhood which attempt to unite us in a false "patriotism" that works against the interests of the country and its people.

It is not surprising that African Americans, conscious of their status in a white-dominated society, would be more skeptical of such symbols.

Frederick Douglass, a former slave who became a leader of the abolitionist movement, was asked in 1852 to speak at a Fourth of July gathering in Rochester, New York. Here is a small sample of what he had
to say:

> Fellow citizens, pardon me, allow me to ask, why am I called
> upon to speak here today? What have I, or those I represent, to
> do with your national independence? Are the great principles of
> political freedom and of natural justice, embodied in that Decla-
> ration of Independence, extended to us? And am I, therefore,
> called upon to bring our humble offering to the national altar, and
> to confess the benefits and express devout gratitude for the bless-
> ings resulting from your independence to us? . . .
>
> What, to the American slave, is your 40th of July? I answer; a
> day that reveals to him, more than all other days in the year, the
> gross injustice and cruelty to which he is the constant victim. To
> him, your celebration is a sham; your boasted liberty, an unholy
> license; your national greatness, swelling vanity . . . your shouts
> of liberty and equality, hollow mockery . . . a thin veil to cover up
> crimes which would disgrace a nation of savages. There is not a
> nation on the earth guilty of practices more shocking and bloody
> than are the people of the United States, at this very hour.

African Americans have always had an ambivalent attitude toward the
idea of patriotism. They have wanted to feel patriotic in the best sense of
the term, that is, to feel at one with their fellow Americans, to feel part
of a greater community. And yet, they have resented—while they
have endured slavery, lynching, segregation, humiliation, and economic
injustice—attempts to enmesh them in a false sense of common interest.

Thus, their reaction to the nation's wars has been a troubled one.
The complexity is illustrated by the dramatically different reactions of
two boxing champions in two different wars. There was Joe Louis, who
was used by the U.S. government to build black support for World War
II, saying that whatever was wrong in this country, "Hitler won't fix
it." And there was Muhammad Ali, who refused to be drafted for the
Vietnam War and told a reporter who challenged him on the war:

"No, I'm not going 10,000 miles from home to help murder and burn
another poor nation simply to continue the domination of white slave
masters of the darker people the world over. . . . The real enemy of my
people is here. . . . So I'll go to jail, so what? We've been in jail for 400
years."

In times of war, the definition of patriotism becomes a matter of life or death for Americans and the world. Instead of being feared for our military prowess, we should want to be respected for our dedication to human rights. I suggest that a patriotic American who cares for her or his country might act on behalf of a different vision.

We need to expand the prevailing definition of patriotism beyond that narrow nationalism that has caused so much death and suffering. If national boundaries should not be obstacles to trade—some call it "globalization"—should they also not be obstacles to compassion and generosity?

Should we not begin to consider all children, everywhere, as our own? In that case, war, which in our time is always an assault on children, would be unacceptable as a solution to the problems of the world. Human ingenuity would have to search for other ways.

THE ULTIMATE POWER

from *Passionate Declarations: Essays on War and Justice* (2003)

Looking back on the twentieth century—a "century packed with history"—Howard uses this essay to highlight some of the lessons we should have learned from the "utter unpredictability" of it all. The first, he argues, is that hope should never be abandoned in the face of "apparent overwhelming power." From the American South to South Africa, El Salvador to Eastern Europe, the past century proved that "no cold calculation of the balance of power should deter people who are persuaded that their cause is just." The second lesson is that, given this "obvious unpredictability," the prevailing "excuses for war and preparation for war—self-defense, national security, freedom, justice, and stopping aggression—can no longer be accepted." In other words, Howard argues, the "traditional distinction between 'just' and 'unjust' war is now obsolete." He catalogues the truly grotesque allocation of national resources—several *trillion* dollars—for the building of American military weapons and technologies, including nuclear arms, a good number of which the United States has never actually needed or used. All of this has served a dual function: to maintain an image and to feed an addiction. "The weapons addiction of all our political leaders, whether Republican or Democrat," Howard writes, "has the same characteristic of a drug addiction. It is enormously costly, very dangerous, provokes ugly violence, and is self-perpetuating—all on a scale far greater than drug addiction." This terrifying reality presents a dilemma for those of us who want to avoid the tragic human destruction of the last century and instead "achieve justice without massive violence." To this dilemma, Howard offers historical examples of nonviolent direct action as the foundation for a vision of a new world "without war, without police states nourished by militarism, and with immense resources now free to be used for human needs. It would be a tremendous shift of resources from death to life. It would mean a healthy future for ourselves, our children, and our grandchildren." This new vision for global peace—where old terms like "defense," "security," "democracy," and "patriotism" take on distinctly different meanings—must come neither from war nor weapons, but the "ultimate power": the will of the people.

———

AS THE TWENTIETH CENTURY draws to a close, a century packed with history, what leaps out from that history is its utter unpredictability. Who could have predicted, not just the Russian Revolution, but Stalin's deformation of it, then Khrushchev's astounding exposure of Stalin, and in recent years Gorbachev's succession of surprises?

Or that in Germany, the conditions after World War I that might have brought socialist revolution—an advanced industrial society, with an educated organized proletariat, and devastating economic crisis—would lead instead to fascism? And who would have guessed that an utterly defeated Germany would rise from its ashes to become the most prosperous country in Europe?

Who foresaw the shape of the post–World War II world: the Chinese Communist revolution, and its various turns—the break with the Soviet Union, the tumultuous cultural revolution, and then post–Mao China making overtures to the West, adopting capitalist enterprise, perplexing everyone?

No one foresaw the disintegration of the old Western empires happening so quickly after the war, in Asia, Africa, and the Middle East, or the odd array of societies that would be created in the newly independent nations, from the benign socialism of Nyerere's Tanzania to the madness of Idi Amin's Uganda.

Spain became an astonishment. A million had died in the Spanish Civil War and Franco's fascism lasted forty years, but when Franco died, Spain was transformed into a parliamentary democracy, without bloodshed. In other places too, deeply entrenched regimes seemed to suddenly disintegrate—in Portugal, Argentina, the Philippines, and Iran.

The end of the war left the United States and the Soviet Union as superpowers, armed with frightening nuclear arsenals. And yet these superpowers have been unable to control events, even in those parts of the world considered to be their spheres of influence. The United States could not win wars in Vietnam or Korea or stop revolutions in Cuba or Nicaragua. The Soviet Union was forced to retreat from Afghanistan and could not crush the Solidarity movement in Poland.

The most unpredictable events of all were those that took place in 1989 in the Soviet Union and Eastern Europe, where mass movements for liberty and democracy, using the tactic of nonviolent mass action, toppled long-lasting Communist bureaucracies in Poland, Czechoslovakia, Hungary, Rumania, Bulgaria, and East Germany.

Uncertain Ends, Unacceptable Means

To confront the fact of unpredictability leads to two important conclusions:

The first is that the struggle for justice should never be abandoned on the ground that it is hopeless, because of the apparent overwhelming power of those in the world who have the guns and the money and who seem invincible in their determination to hold on to their power. That apparent power has, again and again, proved vulnerable to human qualities less measurable than bombs and dollars: moral fervor, determination, unity, organization, sacrifice, wit, ingenuity, courage, and patience—whether by blacks in Alabama and South Africa; peasants in El Salvador, Nicaragua, and Vietnam; or workers and intellectuals in Eastern Europe and the Soviet Union. No cold calculation of the balance of power should deter people who are persuaded that their cause is just.

The second is that in the face of the obvious unpredictability of social phenomena all of history's excuses for war and preparation for war—self-defense, national security, freedom, justice, and stopping aggression—can no longer be accepted. Massive violence, whether in war or internal upheaval, cannot be justified by any end, however noble, *because no outcome is sure*. Any humane and reasonable person must conclude that if the ends, however desirable, are uncertain, and the means are horrible and certain, those means must not be employed.

We have had too many experiences with the use of massive violence for presumably good reasons to willingly continue accepting such reasons. In this century there were 10 million dead in World War I, the war "to end all wars"; 40 to 50 million dead in World War II to "stop aggression" and "defeat fascism"; 2 million dead in Korea and another 1 to 2 million dead in Vietnam, to "stop communism"; 1 million dead in the Iran-Iraq war, for "honor" and other indefinable motives. Perhaps a million dead in Afghanistan, to stop feudalism or communism, depending on which side was speaking.[1]

None of those ends was achieved: wars did not end, aggression continued, fascism did not die with Hitler, communism was not stopped, there was no honor for anyone. In short (as I argued earlier in the book) the traditional distinction between "just" and "unjust" war is now obsolete. The cruelty of the means today exceeds all possible ends. No national boundary, no ideology, no "way of life" can justify the loss of millions of lives that modern war, whether nuclear or conventional, demands. The standard causes are too muddy, too mercurial, to die for. Systems change, policies change. The distinctions claimed by politicians between good and evil are not so clear that generations of human beings should die for the sanctity of those distinctions.

Even a war for defense, the most morally justifiable kind of war, loses its morality when it involves a sacrifice of human beings so massive it amounts to suicide. One of my students, a young woman, wrote in her class journal in 1985, "Wars are treated like wines—there are good years and bad years, and World War II was the vintage year. But wars are not like wines. They are more like cyanide; one sip and you're dead."

Internal violence has been almost as costly in human life as war. Millions were killed in the Soviet Union to "build socialism." Countless lives were taken in China for the same reason. A half million were killed in Indonesia for fear of communism; at least a million dead in Cambodia and a million dead in Nigeria in civil wars. Hundreds of thousands killed in Latin America by military dictatorships to stop communism, or to "maintain order." There is no evidence that any of that killing did any good for the people of those nations.

Preparation for war is always justified by the most persuasive of purposes: to prevent war. But such preparation has not prevented a series of wars that since World War II have taken more lives than World War I.

As for the claim that massive nuclear armaments have prevented World War III, that is not at all certain. World War III has certainly not taken place, but it is not clear that this is because of the massive arms race. The logic of that claim is the logic of the man, living in New York City, who sprinkled yellow powder all over his house, explaining to his friends that this was to keep elephants out, and the proof of his success was that no elephant had ever appeared in his house.[2]

There are many reasons why an all-out war between the Soviet Union and the United States has not taken place. Neither nation has anything to gain from such a war. Neither nation can possibly invade and occupy the other. Why would the Soviet Union want to destroy its great source of wheat? The atomic bombs necessary to annihilate the other superpower would create an enormous danger, through radioactivity and nuclear winter, to the attacking power. The conflicts between the United States and the USSR have, therefore, been in *other* places, and those places *have* had wars, undeterred by the arms buildup of the superpowers.

Deterrence is the favorite word of those who urge the buildup of weapons, both in the United States and in the Soviet Union. But it seems that the only thing that has been "deterred" (World War III) is deterred by other factors, which makes the enormous buildup of weapons on both sides a total waste. No politician on either side of the cold war has had the courage to make this statement, which is a matter of the most ordinary common sense.

The chief reason consistently given for spending thousands of billions of dollars on weapons has been that this prevents a Soviet invasion of Western Europe. Probably no American knows more about Soviet policy than veteran diplomat and historian George Kennan, former ambassador to the Soviet Union and one of the theoreticians of the cold war. Kennan insists that the fears of Soviet invasion of Western Europe are based on myth. This is corroborated by a man who worked for the CIA for twenty-five years, Harry Rositzke. Rositzke was at one time the CIA director of espionage operations against the Soviet Union. He wrote, in the 1980s; "In all my years in government and since I have never seen an intelligence estimate that shows how it would be profitable to Soviet interests to invade Western Europe or to attack the United States."[3]

Common sense suggests that the Soviet Union has enough problems at home, has had trouble controlling Eastern Europe, and was unable to defeat Afghanistan, a small backward nation on its border. Would it invade Western Europe and face the united opposition of 200 million people who would never submit, would make it an endless war?

It appears that the citizens of the United States have been taxed several trillion dollars because of an irrational fear. An irrational fear is, by definition, inconsolable and yet infinite in its demands.

So we have this irony. That the arms race has deterred what would not take place anyway. And it has not deterred what *has* taken place: wars all over the world, some involving the superpowers directly (Korea, Vietnam, and Afghanistan), others involving them indirectly (the Israeli-Arab wars, the Iran-Iraq war, the Indonesian war against East Timor, the contra war against Nicaragua).

While the supposed *benefits* of the arms race are very dubious, the human *costs* are obvious, immediate, and awful. In 1989 about a trillion dollars—a thousand billion dollars—were spent for arms all over the world, the United States and the Soviet Union accounting for more than half of this. Meanwhile, about 14 million children die every year from malnutrition and disease, which are preventable by relatively small sums of money.

The new-style Trident submarine, which can fire hundreds of nuclear warheads, costs $1.5 billion. It is totally useless, except in a nuclear war, in which case it would also be totally useless, because it would just add several hundred more warheads to the thousands already available. (Its only use might be to *start* a nuclear war by presenting a first-strike threat to the Soviet Union.) The $1.5 billion could finance a five-year program of universal child immunization against certain deadly diseases, preventing 5 million deaths.[4]

The B-2 bomber, the most expensive military airplane in history, approved by the Reagan and Bush administrations, and by many members of Congress in both parties, was scheduled to cost over a half billion dollars for each of 132 bombers. A nuclear arms analyst with the Congressional Budget Office estimated that the total cost would run between $70 billion and $100 billion. With this money the United States could build a million new homes.[5]

Over the past decade, several trillions of dollars have been spent for military purposes—to kill and to prepare to kill. One can only begin to imagine what could be done with the money in military budgets to feed the starving millions in Africa, Asia, and Latin America; to provide health care for the sick; to build housing for the homeless; and to teach reading, writing, and arithmetic to millions of people crippled by their inability to read or write or count.

There have been hundreds of nuclear weapons tests by the Soviet Union and the United States over the years. (News item, 1988: "The United States has concealed at least 117 nuclear explosions at its underground test site in the Nevada desert over the past quarter-century, a group of private scientists reported yesterday."[6] The $12 million used for one of these tests would train 40,000 community health workers where they are desperately needed in the Third World.

The United States spent about $28 billion to build 100 B-1 bombers, which turned out to be an enormous waste, even from the standpoint of the military, involving stupidity, greed, and fraud (critics said the B-1 would not survive a collision with a pelican).[7] Imagine what could be done for human health with that $28 billion.

Health and education in the eighties were starved for resources. But in 1985 it was disclosed that $1.8 billion dollars had been spent on sixty-five antiaircraft guns called the Sergeant York, all of which had to be scrapped as useless.[8]

Imagine what could be done to stop the most frightening fact of our time, the steady poisoning of the world's environment—the rivers, the lakes, the oceans, the beaches, the air, the drinking water, and the soil that grows our food—the depletion of the protective ozone layer that covers the entire earth, and the erosion of the world's forests. The money, technology, and human energy now devoted to the military could perform miracles in cleaning up the earth we live on.

But the cost of the arms race is not only the enormous waste of resources. There is a psychic cost—the creation of an atmosphere of fear all over the world. There is no accurate way of measuring that fear in generations of young people who have grown up in the shadow of the bomb. One can only imagine the effect on all those little schoolchildren in the United States, who, in the 1950s, were taught to crouch under their desks when they heard a siren, signifying a bombing attack.

And what is the effect on the 10 or 20 million young men (and women) who are either conscripted or enticed into the armed forces of nations, and then taught to kill, to obey orders, to stop thinking like free human beings?

These are the certainties of evil in the arms race. There are other things that are not certainties, but probabilities, and that is nuclear accidents. When thousands of nuclear weapons are stockpiled, when tests are taking place, and when bombing planes are sent aloft with hydrogen bombs, there is a strong probability that accidents will take place involving those bombs.

In fact there have been over a hundred of those accidents. The military calls them, in its quaint language, "Broken Arrows." One of the first of these was the loss of four hydrogen bombs over Spain in 1966. They didn't explode, but there was radioactive fallout. Lies were told by both the Spanish and American governments for a long time, undoubtedly to try to cool public resentment against the U.S. military presence. Nevertheless, there was a demonstration of a thousand people in front of the U.S. Embassy in Madrid. It was charged by the police, who beat demonstrators with clubs. It seems that many Spanish citizens resented the fact that hydrogen bombs were being flown, like bales of cotton, over their land.[9]

It should be noted that a *hydrogen* bomb—also called a thermonuclear bomb—is the superbomb, developed after the original atomic bomb.

Instead of *fission*, splitting a uranium atom, or a plutonium atom, to release the amounts of explosive energy that were released over Hiroshima and Nagasaki, the hydrogen bomb works by *fusion*, in which two hydrogen atoms are put together to release far more explosive energy. Indeed, 1,000 times as much, so we must imagine a bomb 1,000 times as powerful as the bomb dropped on Hiroshima.

The one dropped on Hiroshima was equivalent in its destructive power to 14 kilotons (14,000 tons) of TNT, the material used in ordinary bombs. There are hydrogen bombs with the power of 14 *megatons* (14 million tons) of TNT. And it is these bombs (called "strategic nuclear weapons" to differentiate them from the smaller "tactical nuclear weapons") of which both the United States and the Soviet Union have accumulated 10,000 each.

Two of these superbombs were involved in an accident in North Carolina in 1961. A Defense Department document obtained nineteen years later by the Reuters news agency revealed what the Pentagon at the time refused to confirm or deny. The Reuters article said:

> On January 24, 1961, a crashing B-52 bomber jettisoned two nuclear bombs over Goldsboro, North Carolina, according to the document. A parachute deployed on one bomb, while the other broke apart on impact.
>
> The bomb with the parachute was jolted when the parachute caught in a tree and five of the six interlocking safety switches were released, said the former officials. Only one switch prevented the explosion of a 24 megaton bomb, 1800 times more powerful than the one dropped on Hiroshima in 1945, they said.[10]

That should give anyone pause. The superpowers have in their arsenals the equivalent of a million Hiroshima-type bombs. Only people who were both saints and geniuses might possibly be trusted with such weapons. This does not seem an accurate description of the leaders of the United States and the Soviet Union. Consider an item like the following, shortly after Ronald Reagan took office as president:

> President Ronald Reagan and his top three aides flew to Washington yesterday aboard the so-called "Doomsday Plane", a $117-million jumbo jet equipped to serve as an airborne command post in a nuclear war. . . . Deputy White House secretary Larry Speakes quoted Reagan as saying he was highly impressed and as adding, "It gives me a sense of confidence."[11]

The very possession of nuclear weapons endangers the possessor. The chance of blowing ourselves up by accident is greater than the chance of invasion by a foreign power, just as a homeowner who keeps a rifle handy is (as statistics show) more likely to kill a member of the family with it than to shoot an outside intruder.

We would need an extraordinary faith in technology to believe that we can have 10,000 thermonuclear weapons, some of them in airplanes flying overhead, and perhaps 20,000 smaller nuclear weapons in various places, and not have accidents.

There is an even more awesome prospect than "Broken Arrow" accidents. That is, a radar error that will signal an enemy bombing attack and thus trigger off, perhaps automatically without human intervention, a genuine attack that would be the beginning of the end for everybody.

In fact, there have been many computer errors, over 100 of them in 1980–1981. One of them led to a "red alert," that is, the radar announced an imminent Soviet attack, and planes with hydrogen bombs were about to be sent aloft when the error was discovered. A news dispatch of June 18, 1980:

> On June 3 and June 6, errors in a computer at the North American Air Defense Command headquarters inside Cheyenne Mountain, near Colorado Springs, caused the system to warn erroneously that Soviet intercontinental missiles had been fired at the United States. The alert sent nearly 100 bomber crews to start their planes' engines.[12]

A few months before that incident, there was an Associated Press dispatch:

> The worldwide computer system built to warn the President of an enemy attack or international crisis is prone to break down under pressure, according to informed sources who have worked on or examined the system.
>
> A Pentagon document defending the system said that generally the "computers render effective support; the principal exception occurs in crisis situations."[13]

It will only fail in "crisis situations"!

There have been enough disasters with advanced technology to persuade us not to believe those "experts" who assure us blandly that some device is "foolproof" or "fail-safe" or has quadruple guards, or whatever. There was the near meltdown of the nuclear reactor at Three Mile Island, which came frighteningly close to a major catastrophe and which let loose enough contamination to cause sickness in humans and animals years later. Then came the even worse disaster at the Chernobyl nuclear plant in the Soviet Union. And shortly after that, the failure of the U.S. space shuttle *Challenger*, which killed all those aboard.

Those events were accompanied by official lies to cover up the true nature of what had happened. Indeed, nuclear technology, because its failures have cataclysmic consequences, encourages political leaders to deceive the public, as happened right from the beginning of the atomic tests in the Nevada desert. The Atomic Energy Commission lied to the GIs who participated in those tests and who later developed cancer far beyond the normal statistical expectations.

There is still another cost of the arms buildup, and that is the fact that the possession of superweapons tempts the possessor to use it as a threat in any international crisis. Once the threat is made, it is very difficult, given the traditional concern of political leaders with "credibility," "saving face," "maintaining our image," etc., to back down.

That is why the world came close to nuclear war during the Cuban missile crisis in the fall of 1962, when the discovery of the presence of Russian missiles on Cuba led to an American ultimatum to Khrushchev, where both nations needed to "save face" by bulling it out. As Kennedy's adviser Theodore Sorensen put it, the president "was concerned less about the missiles' military implications than with their effect on the global political balance."[14]

Only Khrushchev's decision to back down enabled an agreement on removal of the missiles, in return for a pledge not to try again to invade Cuba. President Kennedy estimated that there was a one in three chance of nuclear war in that situation and yet he went ahead with his threats.[15] And what provoked it was that the Soviets did in Cuba what the United States had already done in Turkey and other countries, to place missiles very close to the borders of the other superpower.

Recently, a researcher asked some of the top military and strategic leaders of the United States the commonsense question: Why in the world do we need tens of thousands of nuclear bombs for deterrence? Suppose we assume (what I believe to be false), that nuclear weapons are needed to deter a Soviet invasion or attack, surely a few hundred bombs—enough to destroy every major Soviet city (and which could be carried on *two* submarines)—would be a sufficient deterrent.

The answers of these policymakers were startling; they acknowledged that the weapons were unnecessary from a military point of view, but claimed they served a "political" purpose in that they conveyed a certain *image* of American power. One analyst with the Rand Corporation (a government think tank) told him:

> If you had a strong president, a strong secretary of defense they could temporarily go to Congress and say, "We're only going to build what we need. . . . And if the Russians build twice as many, tough." But it would be unstable politically. . . . And it is therefore better for our own domestic stability as well as international perceptions to insist that we remain good competitors even though the objective significance of the competition is . . . dubious.[16]

In short, hundreds of billions have been spent to maintain an *image*. The image of the United States is that of a nation possessed of a frightening nuclear arsenal. What good has that image done, for the American people, or for anyone in the world? Has it prevented revolutions, coups, wars? Even from the viewpoint of those who want to convey an image of strength—for some mysterious psychic need of their own, perhaps—what image is conveyed when a nation so overarmed is unable to defeat a tiny country in Southeast Asia, or to prevent revolutions in even tinier countries in the Caribbean?

The weapons addiction of all our political leaders, whether Republican or Democrat, has the same characteristics as drug addiction. It is enormously costly, very dangerous, provokes ugly violence, and is self-perpetuating—all on a scale far greater than drug addiction.

Aside from its uselessness for military and political purposes, its colossal waste of human resources, its dangers to the survival of us all, nuclear deterrence is profoundly immoral. It means that the United States is holding hostage the entire population of the Soviet Union—the very people it claims are suffering under communism—and stands ready to kill them all if the Soviet government makes the wrong move. And the Soviet Union is doing the same to the American population. If we think holding hostage the passengers of an airliner is unspeakably evil and call it terrorism, what name shall we give for holding hostage the entire human race?

The arms race is sustained by a fanatical righteousness that sees international conflict as total good versus total evil, and is willing to sacrifice hundreds of millions of lives in a nuclear war. William Buckley wrote in the mid-1980s:

> The suggestion that . . . no use of nuclear weapons is morally
> defensible, not even the threat of their use as a deterrent, is noth-
> ing less than an eructation in civilized thought, putting, as it does,
> the protraction of biological life as the fit goal of modern man.[17]

Not only are we supposed to feel intellectually inferior if we have to look
up the word *eructation* (which means belching, and Buckley, intent on
showing off, is not using it accurately); but we are supposed to feel morally inferior if we oppose nuclear deterrence because of some cowardly
feeling that *life* is more precious than political victory. Buckley is a
Catholic, and we might contrast his statement with that of Vatican II:
"Any act of war aimed indiscriminately at the destruction of entire
cities or of extensive areas along with their population is a crime
against God and man himself. It merits unequivocal and unhesitating
condemnation."[18]

It is sad to see how, in so many countries, citizens have been led to
war by the argument that it is necessary because there are tyrannies
abroad, evil rulers, murderous juntas. But to make war is not to destroy
the tyrants; it is to kill their subjects, their pawns, their conscripted soldiers, their subjugated civilians.

War is a *class* phenomenon. This has been an unbroken truth from
ancient times to our own, when the victims of the Vietnam War turned
out to be working-class Americans and Asian peasants. Preparation for
war maintains swollen military bureaucracies, gives profits to corporations (and enough jobs to ordinary citizens to bring them along). And
they give politicians special power, because fear of "the enemy" becomes
the basis for entrusting policy to a handful of leaders, who feel bound (as
we have seen so often) by no constitutional limits, no constraints of decency or commitment to truth.

Justice Without Violence

Massive violence has been accepted historically by citizens (but not by
all; hence desertions, opposition, and the need for bribery and coercion
to build armies) because it has been presented as a means to good ends.
All over the world there are nations that commit aggression on other nations and on their own people, whether in the Middle East, or Latin
America, or South Africa—nations that offend our sense of justice.
Most people don't really want violence. But they do want justice, and for
that sake, they can be persuaded to engage in war and civil war.

All of us, therefore, as we approach the next century, face an enormous responsibility: How to achieve justice without massive violence. Whatever in the past has been the moral justification for violence—whether defense against attack, or the overthrow of tyranny—must now be accomplished by other means.

It is the monumental moral and tactical challenge of our time. It will make the greatest demands on our ingenuity, our courage, our patience, and our willingness to renounce old habits—but it must be done. Surely nations must defend themselves against attack, citizens must resist and remove oppressive regimes, the poor must rebel against their poverty and redistribute the wealth of the rich. But that must be done without the violence of war.

Too many of the official tributes to Martin Luther King Jr. have piously praised his nonviolence, the praise often coming from political leaders who themselves have committed great violence against other nations and have accepted the daily violence of poverty in American life. But King's phrase, and that of the southern civil rights movement, was not simply "nonviolence," but *nonviolent direct action*.

In this way, nonviolence does not mean acceptance, but resistance—not waiting, but acting. It is not at all passive. It involves strikes, boycotts, noncooperation, mass demonstrations, and sabotage, as well as appeals to the conscience of the world, even to individuals in the oppressing group who might break away from their past.

Direct action does not deride using the political rights, the civil liberties, even the voting mechanisms in those societies where they are available (as in the United States), but it recognizes the limitations of those controlled rights and goes beyond.

Freedom and justice, which so often have been the excuses for violence, are still our goals. But the means for achieving them must change, because violence, however tempting in the quickness of its action, undermines those goals immediately, and also in the long run. The means for achieving social change must match, morally, the ends.

It is true that human rights cannot be defended or advanced without *power*. But, if we have learned anything useful from the carnage of this century, it is that true power does not—as the heads of states everywhere implore us to believe—come out of the barrel of a gun, or out of a missile silo.

The possession of 10,000 thermonuclear weapons by the United States did not change the fact that it was helpless to stop a revolution in Cuba or another in Nicaragua, that it was unable to defeat its enemy either in Korea or in Vietnam. The possession of an equal number of bombs by the Soviet Union did not prevent its forced withdrawal from Afghanistan nor did it deter the Solidarity uprising in Poland, which was successful enough to change the government and put into office a Solidarity member as prime minister. The following news item from the summer of 1989 would have been dismissed as a fantasy two years earlier: "Solidarity, vilified and outlawed for eight years until April, jubilantly entered Parliament today as the first freely elected opposition party to do so in a Communist country."[19]

The power of massive armaments is much overrated. Indeed, it might be called a huge fake—one of the great hoaxes of the twentieth century. We have seen heavily armed tyrants flee before masses of citizens galvanized by a moral goal. Recall those television images of Somoza scurrying to his private plane in Managua; of Ferdinand and Imelda Marcos quickly assembling their suitcases of clothes, jewels, and cash and fleeing the Philippines; of the Shah of Iran searching desperately for someone to take him in; of Duvalier barely managing to put on his pants before escaping the fury of the Haitian people.

In the United States we saw the black movement for civil rights confront the slogan of "Never" in a South where blacks seemed to have no power, where the old ways were buttressed by wealth and a monopoly of political control. Yet, in a few years, the South was transformed.

I recall at the end of the great march from Selma to Montgomery in 1965 when, after our twenty-mile trek that day, coming into Montgomery, I had decided to skip the speeches at the capitol and fly back to Boston. At the airport I ran into my old Atlanta colleague and friend, Whitney Young, now head of the Urban League, who had just arrived to be part of the celebration in Montgomery. We decided to have coffee together in the recently desegregated airport cafeteria.

The waitress obviously was not happy at the sight of us. Aside from the *integration* of it, she might have been disconcerted by the fact that the white man was still mud-splattered, disheveled, and unshaven from the march, and the black man, tall and handsome, was impeccably dressed with suit and tie. We noticed the big button on her uniform. It said "Never!" but she served us our coffee.

Racism still poisons the country, north and south. Blacks still mostly live in poverty, and their life expectancy is years less than that of whites. But important changes have taken place that were at one time unimaginable. A consciousness about the race question exists among blacks and whites that did not exist before. The nation will never be the same after that great movement, will never be able to deny the power of nonviolent direct action.

The movement against the Vietnam War in the United States too was powerful, and yet nonviolent (although, like the civil rights movement, it led to violent scenes whenever the government decided to use police or National Guardsmen, against peaceful demonstrators). It seemed puny and hopelessly weak at its start. In the first years of the war, no one in public life dared to speak of unilateral withdrawal from Vietnam. When my book *Vietnam: The Logic of Withdrawal* was published in 1967, the idea that we should simply leave Vietnam was considered radical. But by 1969 it was the majority sentiment in the country. By 1973 it was in the peace agreement, and the huge U.S. military presence in Vietnam was withdrawn.

President Lyndon Johnson had said; "We will not turn tail and run." But we did, and it was nothing to be ashamed of. It was the right thing to do. Of course, the military impasse in Vietnam was crucial in bringing the war to an end, but it took the movement at home to make American leaders decide not to try to break that impasse by a massive escalation, by more death and destruction. They had to accept the limits of military power.

In that same period, cultural changes in the country showed once again the power of apparently powerless people. Women, a century before, had shown their power and won the right to go to college, to become doctors and lawyers, and to vote. And then in the sixties and seventies the women's liberation movement began to alter the nation's perception of women in the workplace, in the home, and in relationships with men, other women, and children. The right to abortion was established by the Supreme Court against powerful opposition by religious conservatives (although that decision is still under heavy attack).

Another apparently powerless group—homosexual men and lesbian women—encouraged perhaps by what other movements had been able to accomplish against great odds, took advantage of the atmosphere of change. They demanded, and in some places received, acceptance for what had before been unmentionable.

These last decades have shown us that ordinary people can bring down institutions and change policies that seemed entrenched forever. It is not easy. And there are situations that seem immovable except by violent revolution. Yet even in such situations, the bloody cost of endless violence—of revolt leading to counterrevolutionary terror, and more revolt and more terror in an endless cycle of death—suggests a reconsideration of tactics.

We think of South Africa, which is perhaps the supreme test of the usefulness of nonviolent direct action. It is a situation where blacks have been the victims of murderous violence and where the atmosphere is tense with the expectation of more violence, perhaps this time on both sides. But even the African National Congress, the most militant and most popular of black organizations there, clearly wants to end apartheid and attain political power without a bloodbath that might cost a million lives. Its members have tried to mobilize international opinion, have adopted nonviolent but dramatic tactics: boycotts, economic sanctions, demonstrations, marches, and strikes. There will undoubtedly be more cruelty, more repression, but if the nonviolent movement can grow, perhaps one day a general strike will paralyze the economy and the government and compel a negotiated settlement for a multiracial, democratic South Africa.

The Palestinians in the West Bank and Gaza Strip, under the military occupation of the Israelis since the war of 1967, began around 1987 to adopt nonviolent tactics, massive demonstrations, to bring the attention of the world to their brutal treatment by the Israelis. This brought more brutality, as hundreds of Palestinians, unarmed (except for clubs and rocks), were shot to death by Israeli soldiers. But the world did begin to pay attention and if there is finally a peaceful arrangement that gives the Palestinians their freedom and Israel its security, it will probably be the result of nonviolent direct action.

Certainly, the use of terrorist violence, whether by Arabs placing bombs among civilians or by Jews bombing villages and killing large numbers of noncombatants, is not only immoral, but gains nothing for anybody. Except perhaps a spurious glory for macho revolutionaries or ruthless political leaders puffed up with their "power" whenever they succeed in blowing up a bus, destroying a village, or (as with Reagan) killing a hundred people by dropping bombs on Tripoli.

People made fearful by politicians but also by real historical experience worry about invasion and foreign occupation. The assumption has always been that the only defense is to meet violence with violence. We have pointed out that, with the weaponry available today, the result is only suicidal (South Korea against North Korea, Iran against Iraq, even Vietnam against the United States).

A determined population can not only force a domestic ruler to flee the country, but can make a would-be occupier retreat, by the use of a formidable arsenal of tactics: boycotts and demonstrations, occupations and sit-ins, sit-down strikes and general strikes, obstruction and sabotage, refusal to pay taxes, rent strikes, refusal to cooperate, refusal to obey curfew orders or gag orders, refusal to pay fines, fasts and pray-ins, draft resistance, and civil disobedience of various kinds.[20] Gene Sharp and his colleagues at Harvard, in a study of the American Revolution, concluded that the colonists were hugely successful in using nonviolent tactics against England. Opposing the Stamp Tax and other oppressive laws, the colonists used boycotts of British goods, illegal town meetings, refusal to serve on juries, and withholding taxes. Sharp notes that "in nine or ten of the thirteen colonies, British governmental power had already been effectively and illegally replaced by substitute governments" before military conflict began at Lexington and Concord.[21]

Thousands of such instances have changed the world, but they are nearly absent from the history books. History texts feature military heroes, lead entire generations of the young to think that wars are the only way to solve problems of self-defense, justice, and freedom. They are kept uninformed about the world's long history of nonviolent struggle and resistance.

Political scientists have generally ignored nonviolent action as a form of power. Like the politicians, they too have been intoxicated with *power.* And so in studying international relations, they play games (it's called, professionally, "game theory") with the strategic moves that use the traditional definitions of power—guns and money. It will take a new movement of students and faculty across the country to turn the universities and academies from the study of war games to peace games, from military tactics to resistance tactics, from strategies of "first-strike" to those of "general strike."

It would be foolish to claim, even with the widespread acceptance of nonviolent direct action as *the* way of achieving justice and resisting tyranny, that all group violence will come cleanly to an end. But the gross instances can be halted, especially those that require the cooperation of the citizenry and that depend on the people to accept the legitimacy of the government's actions.

Military power is helpless without the acquiescence of those people it depends on to carry out orders. The most powerful deterrent to aggression would be the declared determination of a whole people to resist in a thousand ways.

When we become depressed at the thought of the enormous power that governments, multinational corporations, armies, and police have to control minds, crush dissents, and destroy rebellions, we should consider a phenomenon that I have always found interesting: Those who possess enormous power are surprisingly nervous about their ability to hold on to their power. They react almost hysterically to what seem to be puny and unthreatening signs of opposition.

For instance, we see the mighty Soviet state feeling the need to put away, out of sight, handfuls of disorganized intellectuals. We see the American government, armored with a thousand layers of power, work strenuously to put a few dissident Catholic priests in jail or keep a writer or artist out of this country. We remember Nixon's hysterical reaction to a solitary man picketing the White House: "Get him!"

Is it possible that the people in authority know something that we don't know? Perhaps they know their own ultimate weakness. Perhaps they understand that small movements can become big ones, that if an idea takes hold in the population, it may become indestructible.

It is one of the characteristics of complex and powerful machines that they are vulnerable to tiny unforeseen developments. The disaster of the giant space vessel *Challenger* was due to the failure of a small ring that was affected by cold. Similarly, huge organizations can be rendered helpless by a few determined people. A headline in the *New York Times* in the summer of 1989 read: "Environmentalists' Vessels Sink Navy Missile Test." The story began,

> The Navy was forced to cancel a test launching of its newest missile today when four vessels manned by protesters sailed into a restricted zone 50 miles off the Atlantic coast of Florida and attached an antinuclear banner on the side of the submarine that was to fire the missile.[22]

As all-controlling a government as that in the Soviet Union must still worry about its citizens' protest, especially when large numbers of people are involved. The Soviet Union, after unilaterally halting its nuclear tests for a year and a half and finding that the United States did not respond, announced in February 1987, that it would now resume testing. And it did. But suddenly, it mysteriously halted testing for five months in 1989. Why? According to two American physicians connected with "Physicians for Social Responsibility," and in touch with Soviet doctors, the mysterious five-month absence of nuclear testing may well have been due, in their words, to "the rapid growth of a grassroots environmental movement in Kazakhstan." It seems that two underground tests had released radioactive gases into the atmosphere. This led a prominent Kazakh poet to call a meeting of concerned citizens. Five thousand people assembled and made a public appeal to close the test site in Kazakhstan. They said, "We cannot be silent. In the process of our growing democracy, the people's opinion gains power and range; Everything happening on this earth applies to all of us. Only by uniting our efforts . . . will we help ourselves survive in this still green world."[23]

Whether or not their protest stopped the testing is not certain. But the fact that in the Soviet Union such a meeting could take place and boldly call for a change in national policy was a sign of a new power developing to contest the power of the government.

Nonviolent direct action is inextricably related to democracy. Violence to the point of terrorism is the desperate tactic of tiny groups who are incapable of building a mass base of popular support: Governments much prefer violence committed by disciplined armies under their control, rather than adopt tactics of nonviolence, which would require them to entrust power to large numbers of citizens, who might then use it to threaten the elites' authority.

A worldwide movement of nonviolent action for peace and justice would mean the entrance of democracy for the first time into world affairs. That's why it would not be welcomed by the governments of the world, whether "totalitarian" or "democratic." It would eliminate the dependence on *their* weapons to solve problems. It would bypass the official makers of policy and the legal suppliers of arms, the licensed dealers in the most deadly drug of our time: violence.

It was 200 years ago that the idea of democracy was introduced into modern government, its philosophy expressed in the American Declaration of Independence: Governments derive their powers from the consent of the governed and maintain their legitimacy only when they answer the needs of their citizens for an equal right to life, liberty, and the pursuit of happiness.

It is surely time to introduce that basic democratic concept into international affairs. The terrifying events of this century make it clear that the political leaders of the world and the experts who advise them are both incompetent and untrustworthy. They have put us all in great danger.

We recall the British historian Arnold Toynbee, surveying thousands of years of human history, and despairing of what he saw in the atomic age. He cried out: "No annihilation without representation!"

The New Realism

Those of us who call for the repudiation of massive violence to solve human problems must sound utopian, romantic. So did those who demanded the end of slavery. But utopian ideas do become realistic at certain points in history, when the moral power of an idea mobilizes large numbers of people in its support. This may then be joined to the realization, by at least some of those in authority, that it would be *realistic* for them to change their policy, even perhaps share power with those they have long controlled.

It is becoming more and more clear that "military victory," that cherished goal of generals and politicians, may not be possible any more. Wars end in stalemates, as with the United States in Korea, or with Iran and Iraq, or in forced withdrawals, as the United States in Vietnam, the Soviet Union in Afghanistan. So called "victories," as Israel in the 1967 war, bring no peace, no security. Civil wars become endless, as in El Salvador, and after rivers of blood the participants must turn to negotiated settlements. The contras in Nicaragua could not win militarily, and finally had to negotiate for a political solution.

The economic costs of war and preparations for war threaten the stability of the great powers. One of the reasons the United States withdrew from Vietnam was the drain on its budget, which required the neglect of social problems at home, bringing on the black riots of 1967 and 1968, throwing a scare into the establishment. The Soviet Union undertook bold initiatives for disarmament in the mid-1980s when it recognized that its economy was overmilitarized and failing. Both superpowers must be reminding themselves more and more of all those empires in history that became arrogant with power, overburdened with armies, impoverished by taxes, and collapsed.[24]

Heads of governments become nervous when public opinion begins to veer away from their control. This happened in the 1980s, when dramatic changes took place in the public's views on war and militarism. In the United States in 1981 public opinion surveys showed that 75 percent of those polled said more money was needed for the military. But by the beginning of 1985, only 11 percent favored an increase in military spending, and 46 percent favored a decrease.[25]

When military bureaucrats worry about the growth of peace signs, the rest of the world might well be pleased. Caspar Weinberger, leaving his job as secretary of defense for seven years under Reagan, was alarmed: "A recent, rather startling poll indicated that 71% of Republicans and 74% of Democrats believe that the United States can trust the general secretary of the Soviet Union, Mikhail Gorbachev."[26]

In 1983 in West Germany, so close to the Soviet bloc, 55 percent saw the Soviet Union as a military threat; by 1988, only 24 percent saw such a threat, and half of those polled were in favor of unilateral disarmament.[27] In 1984 a quarter of a million West Germans gathered in Kassel to protest the installation of Pershing and cruise missiles. They erected ninety-six crosses in a field outside the U.S. Air Force Station, one for each cruise missile deployed there.

With both the United States and the Soviet Union facing severe economic problems—stagnation and budget deficits—there is suddenly a *realistic* incentive to cut back on military spending. Indeed, the forbidden phrase *unilateral disarmament* may become very practical.

Unilateral actions are the best way; they avoid endless negotiations, as was seen in 1963 when John F. Kennedy took the initiative to stop atmospheric nuclear testing and the Soviet Union followed suit.[28] There had been an earlier "moment of hope" (the phrase of Nobel Prize winner Philip Noel-Baker), when Khrushchev became the Soviet leader and his government withdrew Soviet forces from Austria and returned a naval base to Finland. But that didn't lead to anything significant, and, according to Soviet specialist Walter Clemens; "Washington never tested Moscow's offer to join both Germanys in a neutral and demilitarized Central Europe."[29]

The nation that takes the first initiatives to disarm will be at a great advantage. First, in world prestige, that much-desired *image*. Note how Gorbachev, after his initiatives, became the most popular political figure in West Germany, the United States' strongest ally. Second, in freeing huge resources for economic development. The obvious benefits to the nation that first disarms might well lead to a disarmament race.

Statistics indicate that, of the industrialized nations, those that spend the least for military purposes show the greatest economic progress. The United States between 1982 and 1986 spent 6 percent of its gross national product for the military while Japan spent about 1 percent. Japan's economy, everyone agreed, was more efficient, more dynamic, and healthier.

Of course, those realistic incentives are not enough by themselves to alter the habits of governments so deeply dug into old policies of militarism and war. But they create the possibility, *if* a great popular movement should develop to insist on change. Such a movement, if it became large enough and strong enough to threaten the political power of the government, would create an additional incentive for change.

A great movement must be driven by a vision, as the civil rights movement was driven by the dream of equality and the antiwar movement by the prospect of peace. The vision in this case, for people all over the world, is the most inspiring of all, that of a world without war, without police states nourished by militarism, and with immense resources now free to be used for human needs. It would be a tremendous shift of resources from death to life. It would mean a healthy future for ourselves, our children, and our grandchildren.

The vision would be of a trillion dollars (the annual military costs around the world) made available to the coming generation, to the young, who could use their energy, their talents, their idealism, and their love of adventure to rebuild the cities, feed the hungry, house the homeless, clean the rivers and lakes, refresh the air we breathe, and revitalize the arts. Imagine the 30 million young men now in uniform, imagine those several hundred million people in the world either unemployed or underemployed (the International Labor Office estimates over 400 million people in the 1980s)—imagine all that wasted energy mobilized to make their lives useful and exciting and to transform the planet.[30]

If the U.S. government can give several hundred billion dollars in contracts to corporations to build weapons, why can it not (by powerful public demand) give that valuable money to public-service corporations whose contracts will require them to employ people, young and old, to make life better for everyone? The conversion of resources requires a conversion of language. New definitions of old terms could become a part of the common vocabulary. The old definitions have misled us and caused monstrous harm.

The word *security*, for instance, would take on a new meaning: the health and well-being of people, which is the greatest strength and the most lasting security a nation can have. (A simple parable makes this clear: Would a family living in a high-crime city feel more "secure" if it put machine guns in its windows, dynamite charges in the yard, and tripwires all around the house, at the cost of half the family income and less food for the children? The analogy is not far-fetched. It is an understatement of what nations do today.)

The word *defense* would mean, not the waging of war and the accumulation of weapons, but the united actions of people against tyranny, using every ingenious device of nonviolent resistance.

Democracy would mean the right of people everywhere to determine for themselves, rather than have political leaders decide for them, how they will defend themselves, how they will make themselves secure, and how they will achieve justice and freedom.

Patriotism would mean not blind obedience to a nation's leaders, but a commitment to help one's neighbors and to help anyone, regardless of race or nationality, achieve a decent life.

It is impossible to know how quickly or how powerfully such new ways of thinking, such reversals of priorities, can take hold, can excite the imagination of millions, can cross frontiers and oceans, and can become a world force. We have never had a challenge of this magnitude, but we have never had a need so urgent, a vision so compelling.

History does not offer us predictable scenarios for immense changes in consciousness and policy. Such changes have taken place, but always in ways that could not be foretold, starting often with imperceptibly small acts, developing along routes too complex to trace. All we can do is to make a start, wherever we can, to persist, and let events unfold as they will.

On our side are colossal forces. There is the desire for survival of 5 billion people. There are the courage and energy of the young, once their adventurous spirit is turned toward the ending of war rather than the waging of war, creation rather than destruction, and world friendship rather than hatred of those on the other side of the national boundaries.

There are artists and musicians, poets and actors in every land who are ready to make the world musical and eloquent and beautiful for all of us, if we give them the chance. They, perhaps more than anyone, know what we are all missing by our infatuation with violence. They also know the power of the imagination and can help us to reach the hearts and souls of people everywhere.

The composer Leonard Bernstein a few years ago spoke to a graduating class at John Hopkins University; "Only think: if all our imaginative resources currently employed in inventing new power games and bigger and better weaponry were re-oriented toward disarmament, what miracles we could achieve, what new truths, what undiscovered realms of beauty!"[31]

There are teachers in classrooms all over the world who long to talk to their pupils about peace and solidarity among people of all nations and races.

There are ministers in churches of every denomination who want to inspire their congregations as Martin Luther King Jr. did, to struggle for justice in a spirit of joy and love.

There are people, millions of them, who travel from country to country for business or pleasure, who can carry messages that will begin to erase, bit by bit, the chalk marks of national boundaries, the artificial barriers that keep us apart.

There are scientists anxious to use their knowledge for life instead of death.

There are people holding ordinary jobs of all kinds who would like to participate in something extraordinary, a movement to beautify their city, their country, or their world.

There are mothers and fathers who want to see their children live in a decent world and who, if spoken to, if inspired, if organized, could raise a cry that would be heard on the moon.

It is, of course, an enormous job to be done. But never in history has there been one more worthwhile. And it needn't be done in desperation, as if it had to be done in a day. All we need to do is make the first moves, speak the first words.

One of the scientists who worked on the atomic bomb, who later was a scientific adviser to President Eisenhower, chemist George Kistia-kowsky, devoted the last years of his life, as he was dying of cancer, to speaking out against the madness of the arms race in every public forum he could find. Toward the very end, he wrote, in the *Bulletin of the Atomic Scientists*: "I tell you as my parting words. Forget the channels. There simply is not enough time left before the world explodes. Concentrate instead on organizing, with so many others of like mind, a mass movement for peace such as there has not been before."

He understood that it was not the bomb he had worked on, but the people he had come to work with, on behalf of peace, that were the ultimate power.

Notes

1. Statistics on war deaths from 1700 to 1987 can be found in Ruth Sivard, *World Military and Social Expenditures 1987–88* (World Priorities, 1988), 29–31.
2. John A. Osmundsen, "Elephant Repellant," *New York Times*, Jan. 2, 1988.
3. Harry Rositzke, *Managing Moscow, Guns or Words* (Morrow, 1984).

4. These comparisons of military spending and social needs come from Sivard, *World Military and Social Expenditures, 1987–88*, 35.

5. Jeffrey A. Merkeley, "The Stealth Fiasco," *New York Times*, Feb. 1, 1989.

6. *New York Times*, Jan. 17, 1988. Up to 1977 there had been over a thousand nuclear tests by the six countries possessing bombs, the overwhelming majority of these, of course, by the United States and the Soviet Union.

7. See Nick Kotz, *Wild Blue Yonder* (Pantheon, 1987), for the story of the B-1 bomber.

8. *New York Times*, Nov. 29, 1985.

9. The story of the four lost hydrogen bombs is told by Tad Szulc, *The Bombs of Palomares* (Viking, 1967).

10. *Boston Globe*, Dec. 22, 1980.

11. *Boston Globe*, Nov. 15, 1981.

12. *New York Times*, June 18, 1980.

13. *New York Times*, Mar. 10, 1980.

14. Theodore Sorensen, *Kennedy* (Harper & Row, 1965), 770.

15. Ibid., 795.

16. Steven Kull, "Mind-Sets of Defense Policy Makers," *Psycho-History Review* (Spring 1986): 21–23.

17. William Buckley, "Introduction," in *Moral Clarity in the Nuclear Age*, ed. Michael Novak (T. Nelson, 1983).

18. Walter Stein, ed., *Nuclear Weapons and Christian Conscience* (Merlon Press, 1981).

19. *New York Times*, July 5, 1989.

20. Gene Sharp, *Making Europe Unconquerable* (Ballinger, 1985).

21. Gene Sharp et al., *To Bid Defiance to Tyranny: Nonviolent Action and the American Independence Movement*, quoted by Bob Irwin, "Nonviolent Struggle and Democracy in American History," *Freeze Focus* (Sept. 1984). See also Ronald M. McCarthy, "Resistance Politics and the Growth of Parallel Government in America, 1765–1775," in *Resistance, Politics, and the American Struggle for Independence, 1765–1775*, ed. Conser, McCarthy, Toscano, and Sharp (Lynne Rienner, 1986).

22. *New York Times*, July 29, 1989.

23. Bernard Lown and Wes Wallace, "Where Do Americans Stand on Testing?" *New York Times*, July 22, 1989.

24. Paul Kennedy, *The Rise and Fall of the Great Powers* (Random House, 1987), surveys the last 500 years of history and concludes that heavy military spending has ruined the economies of great powers and ultimately hurt their security.

25. *New York Times*, Mar. 4, 1985.

26. Caspar W. Weinberger, "Arms Reductions and Deterrence," *Foreign Affairs* (Spring 1988).

27. This was a poll taken by the Allensbach Institute. *New York Times*, Jan. 21, 1988.

28. This example is cited by Russell Hardin, "Contracts, Promises and Arms Control," *Bulletin of Atomic Scientists* (Oct. 1984). Hardin calls the Kennedy unilateral initiative an example of "contract by convention," which he thinks is much preferable to endless negotiation.

29. Walter Clemens, "US and USSR: An Agenda for a New Detente," *Christian Science Monitor*, Mar. 21, 1985.

30. Sivard, *World Military and Social Expenditures 1987–88*, 22.

31. Leonard Bernstein, "War Is Not Inevitable," *Fellowship* (Jan.–Feb. 1981).

INTERLUDE: THE FUTURE OF HISTORY

Interview with David Barsamian, Cambridge, Massachusetts, 1998

from *The Future of History: Interviews with David Barsamian*

This interview with David Barsamian, the title interview of *The Future of History*, was conducted over two days in July 1998. This is perhaps the most wide-ranging of Barsamian's conversations with Howard— beginning with an assessment of the legacy of Karl Marx and ending with a discussion of Howard's own legacy as a writer, teacher, and activist. In the course of his reflections, Howard outlines what he sees as the historian's role in shaping the future: "Historians have a responsibility to point out to people several things. It's very important to point out the history of our political institutions, the history of capitalism. It's very important for historians to expose the emptiness of the promises that have been made and the emptiness behind the glorification of the past and present institutions. And at the same time to bring back into our view those events in history which show that under certain circumstances, at certain points in history, if they organize, if they risk, if they act together, if they keep an ideal in their minds, it is possible for people to change things." His familiar response highlights one of the enduring qualities that separated Howard from so many other left intellectuals: his optimism. He believed deeply in the capacity of ordinary folks to change history, and, as this interview reinforces, he devoted his life to chronicling these efforts.

———

JULY 27 AND 28, 1998

DAVID BARSAMIAN: *In* The Zinn Reader, *you write, "Important to me as I was becoming conscious of the crucial question of class was to read Karl*

Marx's The Communist Manifesto." *1998 marks the 150th anniversary of* The Manifesto. *There have been new editions and public meetings around this event. The question arises, Is Marx relevant today? If so, how?*

I decided to deal with the question of the relevance of Marx even before this 150th anniversary, to show how far in advance I am of the general culture. I decided to do that by writing a play about him. It's called *Marx in Soho*, a one-person play, which I mentioned in a previous interview. To answer your question, the reason I wanted to do something about Marx is because I think he has important things to say.

There are some things that he said in the nineteenth century that turn out to be inadequate for an understanding of what the world is like today. Clearly, he could not anticipate so much of what has happened since then. Like a lot of people on the left, he had a foreshortened view of how long it would take for a socialist revolution to come about. There was a point where he and Engels thought the revolutions in Europe of 1848 would lead to workers' revolutions. They did not. They showed their disappointment.

So he did not really figure on capitalism's ability to survive and on the ingeniousness of the system in devising obstacles to revolution and its power in suppressing revolutionary movements and its ability to wean the working class and its consciousness away from the idea of revolutionary change. The U.S. is probably the primary illustration of that, and although Marx followed events in the U.S. in the mid-nineteenth century and was a correspondent for a while of the *New York Tribune*, he could not, and I don't know that anyone could, anticipate that the American system would be able to fend off revolutionary movements by a combination of tactics. I say "tactics" as if they were deliberate, but I think that probably it's not an accurate description to call them tactics. Let's say there are a number of developments in American capitalism that made it possible for the system to survive. One of them was the fact that capitalism in the U.S., drawing upon the enormous wealth of this country, was able to respond to workers' movements by giving concessions, respond to unionism by agreeing to raise wages and lower hours. There were a lot of struggles to force the system to do that, but they did that. The system responded to economic crises by reforms, as it did in the 1930s under the New Deal. In doing so, responding with more and more reforms, it created a more satisfied section of the working class which then was not ripe for a workers' revolution, and which has remained content with the system or, when it became discontented, did not become discontented with capitalism as a system but became discontented with specific manifestations of the system. Most working people in the U.S. do not see the problems they have as systemic, but as problems which are correctable by reforms. So the system, by having the wealth sufficient to distribute more goodies to sections of the working class and yet maintain huge profits for itself, has been able to sustain itself.

At the time of World War I, W.E.B. Du Bois, certainly one of the most far-sighted of American intellectuals, saw that the American system was giving some rewards to its workers and was able to do this on the basis of its exploitation of people abroad. He saw the imperialism of World War I, of the Western powers, and he saw that the Western powers, by drawing out the wealth of the Middle East and Latin America and Asia, was able thereby to give some small part of its profits to its own working class and therefore enlist that working class in a kind of national unity which then enabled them to call this working class to war and sustain that war.

As I said, Marx did not foresee this very sophisticated ability of capitalism to create a certain degree of satisfaction among just enough of the working class, certainly not all of the working class, but just enough to give it a buffer against revolution. There's a big difference between having a working class which is eighty percent of the population and is seething with anger at the system and a working class of which half has been given enough goodies to be content, leaving a minority in desperate poverty. The minority may be an important one, in the U.S. it may be forty million people who are in desperate circumstances without health care, with a high incidence of child mortality, but still not enough to make the kind of workers' revolution that Marx and Engels were hoping for.

So Marx didn't see that kind of development. I think he also did not see, and this was pointed out by Paul Sweezy and Paul Baran when they wrote their post–World War II, post-Marxist analysis of capitalism that the economic crisis that Marxists expected to happen after the end of World War II did not take place because of the militarization of capitalism. A kind of military Keynesianism was in operation, whereby spending a huge amount of money on military contracts, the government was creating employment and was giving shots of "drugs," in the long run poisonous but in the short run sustaining the system. Baran and Sweezy saw this militarization as one of the ways in which capitalism was able to survive. And Marx did not really foresee that.

On the other hand, there were analyses that Marx made of the capitalist system which turn out to be very, very true, and very perceptive. Probably the most obvious one is the increasing concentration and centralization of capital on a worldwide scale. What we talk about now as the global economy, as globalization, Marx had foreseen. He saw the world becoming more and more interconnected economically. He saw the corporations turning into megacorporations and the mergers and the possession of the material resources of the world becoming concentrated in fewer and fewer hands. Very often it's said Marx talked about the immiseration of the proletariat and the concomitant increasing wealth of the upper classes, the polarization of wealth and poverty. And very often it's said that Marx was wrong about this. We haven't had this. In the U.S. it doesn't look that clear because of this large middle class which is not at one pole or the other. But if you look at it on a worldwide scale, world capitalism has moved exactly in that direction. If you take the wealth of the rich countries as against the wealth of the poor countries, and especially if you take the wealth of the upper income brackets in the rich countries against the ninety percent of the people in the poor countries, you have a polarization of wealth which is more stark than it was in the nineteenth century.

DB: *So in terms of looking at and understanding political economy, there is much that is relevant in Marx's analyses.*

I think his analysis of capitalism remains very relevant, and his perception that the profit motive was ruinous for the human race remains, I think, a great insight. We see that the drive of corporations for profit is done at the expense of human beings all over the world. One of the things Marx pointed out was that once money was introduced into the world economy, the pursuit of wealth became infinite. It was no longer a matter of material possessions, of land, as it was in feudal times, now there was no longer a limit to the accumulation of wealth once money was introduced. This endless pursuit of money has led to all sorts of dangerous and evil developments, because the pursuit of money has led chemical companies to pollute the air and water, has led arms manufacturers to create monstrous weapons of destruction without regard to how they will be used or against whom they will be used. His analysis of the evils of profit as a motive for production I think is more true now than it ever was.

DB: *Those who trumpet the virtues of capitalism point out that the USSR appropriated Marx and his name and the good name of socialism. Since the Soviet Union collapsed in disarray both Marx's analyses and a socialist political philosophy are therefore discredited.*

That's what's being said. Marxism would only be discredited if indeed the Soviet Union had created the kind of society that Marx and Engels foresaw as a socialist society, and then collapsed. But when Marx and Engels talked about the dictatorship of the proletariat, they had a very special conception of what that meant. It meant that the majority of the people, the working class, would be in charge of the society. They did not mean by dictatorship of the proletariat that a political party would represent itself as total spokesperson for the working class. In fact, not only would a political party not be the spokesman, but certainly not a central committee, certainly not a Politburo, certainly not one person. That kind of dictatorship was not envisioned by Marx and Engels when they talked about the dictatorship of the proletariat.

In fact, at one point, Marx was talking about the Paris Commune of 1871 and the remarkably democratic character of the Paris Commune, the *communards*, the people who gathered and legislated, made decisions in the context of endless daily, hourly, twenty-four-hours-a-day discussions in the streets of Paris by the people of Paris. Marx talked about those remarkable several months when democracy flourished in Paris, the Paris Commune. He said, You want to know what I mean by the dictatorship of the proletariat? Look at the Paris Commune. The Soviet Union certainly did not follow that. And when Marx talked about what a socialist society would look like, he certainly did not expect that a socialist society would set up gulags, would imprison dissidents and shoot not just capitalists, but fellow revolutionaries, as was done in both the Soviet Union and in China. So the police state and the totalitarian nature of the Soviet Union were very foreign to Marx and Engels. They saw the dictatorship of the proletariat as a temporary phenomenon during which the socialist character of society would become more and more communal, more and more democratic, and that the state, as they said, would become less and less necessary. Marx and Engels talked in *The Communist Manifesto* about their aim being the free development of the individual. [. . .]

To me it is very interesting that socialism in this country was at its most influential before a Soviet Union existed. Because then the people could, without the imposition of some foreign, distorted example, take a look at the ideas of socialism. It made a lot of sense to them. They could see Eugene Debs and Mother Jones and Emma Goldman and Jack London and Lincoln Steffens and see obviously admirable people in the U.S. who had turned to socialism because they saw what capitalism was doing to people. Socialism at that time represented a simple commonsense idea, that you take the wealth of the country and try to use it in a rational and humane way.

DB: *The Reaganites take credit for the collapse of the Soviet Union. They say Reagan's aggressive weapons policy, expansion of the military helped to bankrupt the USSR. What's your take on that? Do you have an alternative view on why the Soviet Union collapsed?*

I always have an alternative view. It's not just that I don't want to give Reagan credit for anything, although of course I don't want to give Reagan credit for anything. I have no doubt that the militarization of the Soviet economy was a factor in impoverishing the Soviet Union in terms of being able to do things for its people. No doubt about that. But that was a very long-term development. It didn't happen only under Reagan. It's a long-term development ever since World War II. The Soviet Union and the U.S. engaging in an arms race and both countries spending an exorbitant amount of their national wealth on the military. As a result, leaving the society impoverished, unable to use its wealth for human needs. So I don't doubt that was a factor. It also has been a factor in the U.S. in causing the U.S. to have a social service structure which is less generous to its people than, let's say, the social service sector of much poorer countries, like the countries of Scandinavia or New Zealand or France and Germany with their universal health care systems. So I don't doubt that that was a factor in causing more and more discontent in the Soviet Union.

Without pretending to know exactly and certainly what caused the Soviet Union to collapse, it seems to me that one of the truly important factors was the gradual growing discontent with the system, with the police state, with the lack of freedom. I'm thinking of the growing ties of the Soviet Union with the rest of the world, you might say the phenomenon that Marx described, that the world would become more interconnected, that people and goods would travel more and more across borders, culture would be disseminated all over the world, people would get to know about what's happening in other countries. For people in the Soviet Union, as more travel took place, as radio and television brought information to them, I think their own society became more and more distasteful to them. Restrictions on their travel, on their freedom of speech became more and more onerous. I think they developed a kind of underground of dissent. We know that there was an underground press, underground literature, *samizdat*, self-publication, literally, of things that circulated unofficially and spread subversive ideas. All of these had a kind of corrosive effect on a society that was very tyrannical. I guess I believe that tyrannies ultimately, sometimes it takes ten years and sometimes it takes forty or sixty years, must collapse. Whoever happens to be the leader of a rival country at the time the collapse takes place will take credit for it, as Reagan did in this case. [. . .]

DB: *Were you struck at all by the nonviolent transformation of the Soviet Union and its neighboring satellite states, with the exception of Rumania? Here were virtual military dictatorships undergoing a peaceful transfer of government.*

I think that's a very fascinating development and a very important piece of history for us to look at. What it does is reinforce the notion that it is possible to bring about important social change without violence, without a bloodbath. To me, it is a vindication of the notion that we should give up the idea of using military force to bring about social change. In fact, social change can come about by the actions of a great social movement. The resort to military force to bring about social change, the resort to armed insurrection or what the revolutionary movement might call armed struggle is evidence that the revolutionary movement has not built up enough support among the population. Once it builds up that mass support, if it can create among the masses of the people resistance to the ongoing government tyranny, that tyranny will not be able to stand for long. It will not be able to move. Its armed forces will not go along. Its service sectors will not serve. I think that's what happened in these countries. As soon as you have mass outpourings of people into the streets, and this happened in East Germany, too, and they could see that the resistance was overwhelming, they could not function any more. So to me this is very powerful evidence. Despite the argument that it is necessary to make war in order to overthrow tyranny, the developments in Eastern Europe reinforced the notion that war is not the way to do it. Or take the Soviet Union as an example. We came very close in the U.S. to the decision to use nuclear weapons against the Soviet Union in order to destroy it. The tyranny fell by it-self, mostly from internal causes.

Eastern Europe is not the only example of this. Spain, I think, is an-other interesting one. The Franco dictatorship lasted a long time. It seemed to a lot of observers, and certainly to people who had fought in Spain, members of the Abraham Lincoln Brigade, that Franco would not be overthrown without another bloody civil war. That civil war in Spain had cost a million lives from 1936–1939. When Franco dies years later and the regime collapses, you don't get an ideal state. You don't get a socialist state. You don't get democratic socialism. You certainly get a more liberal state. They've done away with fascism in Spain. You cre-ate openings for change to take place without a bloody civil war.

I think one of the most striking examples of the idea that important social change can take place and should take place without massive vio-lence is what happened in South Africa, where people thought that you could not get rid of apartheid without a bloody civil war. To me it was interesting that the African National Congress, which certainly was not a timid organization and was ready to engage in sabotage and even indi-vidual acts of violence, was not willing to have an all-out civil war in South Africa. They knew that it would result in millions of people being killed, most of them black South Africans. They were willing to spend more time, more energy, utilize a variety of tactics and ultimately apart-heid collapsed in South Africa. Who would have predicted that Man-dela, imprisoned on Robben Island for twenty-seven years, would become leader of the new South Africa? And while the new South Africa has not solved fundamental problems, no question about that, still, apartheid as it existed no longer exists. Black political power at least cre-ates the possibility of a change that was not possible under the old regime. It took place on the basis of a complexity of tactics that did not include armed rebellion.

DB: *You also wrote a play about Emma Goldman, entitled* Emma. *It's been performed in the U.S., Japan and England. What drew you to her?*

I knew nothing about Emma Goldman. I knew nothing about most things. Then at a certain point in our lives we learn something, and then we claim we knew those things from birth. I vaguely had heard of Emma Goldman from reading a book when I was a teenager called *Crit-ics and Crusaders,* which is long out of print but had a very important in-fluence on me. It was a book of essays on different radicals in American history. There was a chapter on each one, including Emma Goldman, the anarchist and feminist. I had read that chapter on her, but had pretty much forgotten about it, as she was forgotten by American culture for a long time. She had been a very powerful figure at the turn of the century. She was shoved into the background not just by the general culture, but by left culture, because the Communist Party was the dominant force in the U.S. in the 1930s and 1940s. Emma Goldman was anti-Communist. She had written a book, a very strong attack on the Soviet Union, as a result of her experiences. She was relegated to obscurity not just by the establishment, but by the left.

I did not know anything about her until I encountered at some meeting in Pennsylvania in the mid or late 1960s a fellow historian named Richard Drinnon who told me he had written a biography of her called *Rebel in Paradise*. You know how it is, when you meet somebody who has written a book you very often want to go and read that book. I read it. It's a wonderful book, beautifully written. Drinnon is among American historians one of the most eloquent of writers. His biography of Emma Goldman is stunning. It led me to read her autobiography, *Living My Life*, which I recommend all the time and which I have my students read. What fascinated me was that here we were in the 1960s, the New Left had distanced itself from traditional Communist Party doctrine and, without calling itself anarchist, had many of the sensibilities of the anarchist in being anti-state, anti-dogmatism and wanting to make revolutionary changes in the culture simultaneously with changes in the politics and economics. So Emma Goldman fitted, in my view, a new left conception of the universe.

I found that my students, far from seeing her as an antiquated and irrelevant figure, as I feared at one time when I began to give them her writings, were excited by her ideas and her approach to life, her powerful feminism, her anarchism, her position against the state, against capitalism, against religion, against all of the traditional rules of sexual behavior, of marriage. She was a free spirit. It fitted the freespirited culture of the 1960s. The play was a matter of the desire and the opportunity joining. When the Vietnam War was going on, I was, as so many people were, totally preoccupied with the war. In the late 1960s and early 1970s, the things that I wrote, my teaching, the talks I was giving around the country, and the teach-ins were all in one way or another connected with the Vietnam War. When the war ended in 1975, I was relieved of a lot of work. I finally saw an opening to do something I had wanted to do for some time, to write a play. The subject became Emma

Goldman and that little group of anarchists with which she was associated at the turn of the century.

DB: *What informed and influenced your play writing? Did you have any models, were you interested in Bertolt Brecht's work, for example?*

I was interested in Brecht's work. There were a number of influences in my life that led me toward play writing. First there were people in my own family who had been involved in the theater. My wife was an actress for a while in Atlanta and here in Cambridge. My daughter was in the Atlanta production of the *Diary of Anne Frank* in 1962. She played Anne Frank and won a prize as the best actress of the year in Atlanta. Our son was a musician and an actor and devoted his life to the theater, which he is still doing, running a little theater in Wellfleet on Cape Cod. So my whole family was involved in theater except me. But I was interested in theater. My wife and I, when we lived in New York, although we didn't have much money, went to see plays by Arthur Miller. We saw the first Broadway productions of *Death of a Salesman* and Tennessee Williams's *Streetcar Named Desire*. We saw Marlon Brando and Jessica Tandy, sitting in the cheapest seats possible, way up, but loving the theater.

So when the war ended I had an opportunity and more free time, and I decided I would write a play. Emma Goldman and anarchism became my theme. My son, who was at that time acting in New York, was the first director of the first production of the play in New York.

DB: *Can you give a little more detail on Brecht? He's seen as the quintessential political dramatist.*

Brecht certainly was one of the influences in my development as a playwright, if I can assume that I developed as a playwright. Brecht is important to me. I saw a number of his plays. My wife Roslyn acted in the *Caucasian Chalk Circle*, which was done when the Loeb Theater in Cambridge first opened. She had a few small parts in it, along with Jane Alexander, who also had a few small parts in it, Jane Alexander went on to become a professional actress. My wife went on to become ultimately a painter and artist. We saw here in Cambridge a production of *A Man's a Man*, a powerful antiwar play by Brecht, and *The Good Woman of Setzuan* and a number of other plays. Brecht was a brilliant playwright. Then there was *Threepenny Opera*. Brecht's politics spoke to me and his theatrical imagination spoke to me. I don't think I've ever developed that much imagination, but then, how many people have? I content myself with that thought. So yes, you might say I became hooked on the theater.

When I got involved, I had a number of very happy learning experiences. When you become a theater person, it's very different from being an academic. You immediately become part of a group project. The academy, the university, is very isolating. Presumably you're a member of a department and presumably you have colleagues, but it never works that way. You really are alone. You're writing your things alone. It's not a collective enterprise. In the theater it immediately, inevitably becomes a collective enterprise as soon as your play is taken over by the director. The director becomes equal, in fact more than equal, to you. As soon as the actors come in, the set designer and costumer and stage manager come into the picture, you have a little collective working on this project. Everybody is as eager to do this well as you are. So it was very heartwarming for me to suddenly find myself with a group of people who were all working together on this project. I had the special reward of working with my son. [. . .] We worked together beautifully. I must admit, he was the boss. It was a revelation to me. Here I was, working as an underling to my son. He said, Look, I need you to cut this out. I need you to write a few more lines here. But it was wonderful working with him, participating with him in the casting of the play.

Also, I learned a lot about the economics of the theater and about its desperate situation in a society based on profits. Sorry to get back to Marx and capitalism and the profit motive, but it pervades our entire culture. The commerce and the money element dictate what happens in the theater. It dictates that superficial plays will run on Broadway with huge budgets and be shown to huge numbers of people, and serious, important plays, because they are not going to be profitable, are not going to be funded. They're performed in small theaters and have short runs or they're never produced at all. Many of us have the experience that some of the best theater we've seen has been in small spaces by impecunious theater groups that don't have any money, where the actors do not get paid. To me people who work in the theater below the level of stars on Broadway are the most heroic people in our culture, along with poets and painters and writers and broadcasters of alternative radio, who struggle and struggle without much money to do something important in a culture. Actors and actresses rehearse for six weeks and go on stage every night for another six weeks and give their all, give their time, their heart, for nothing or for very little because they're in love with and believe in what they're doing. I have enormous admiration for these people. [. . .]

DB: [. . .] *Let's talk a bit about propaganda. Is it too charged a word to describe the U.S. media?*

Of course it is charged. We tend in the U.S. to resist using that word because we've always associated it with totalitarian states. Yet I think it's a fair word to describe a situation in which the media have some connection with the government, are influenced by the government, have a very strong connection with American corporations, whether directly on commercial television and a little less directly on public radio and television. Where the media generally tend to be nationalistic and patriotic and become unanimous in their support of military operations, then it's fair to say that they're engaging in propaganda. Where they ignore, as they do steadfastly, the dissident activities of groups in the U.S., the meetings that take place of people who belong to environmental or feminist or anti-military groups, I think that deserves to be labeled a kind of active propaganda. Propaganda is not just an act of commission, it's an act of omission.

DB: *In* Declarations of Independence, *you write, "If those in charge of our society—politicians, corporate executives, and owners of press and television— can dominate our ideas, they will be secure in their power. They will not need soldiers patrolling the streets. We will control ourselves." What are you getting at there?*

I guess I'm getting at the ingeniousness of the American political and cultural system, an ingeniousness which enables it to hold its military power and police power in reserve for special occasions, groups and events. It doesn't require wholesale police control of the entire population all the time. It can allow apertures for people to express themselves so long as those apertures don't become too great. It can afford to do this, to keep force in reserve, because by controlling our means of communication, our educational system, by keeping watch on what is done on the radio and television and the newspapers and the textbooks of our schools, it can control the information that people have and create a mind-set among a majority of the American people which then doesn't require the harsh control of police or military. If it can persuade, for instance by teaching the history of our country in a way that exalts our military heroes and makes our wars just and defensible, if it can create a population which is ready to accept the notion that any time the U.S. sends troops abroad it's for a good purpose, then it doesn't need wholesale jailings of dissidents. It can reserve that force, the military, the courts, for a relatively small number of people who have not been won over by the general indoctrination of the public. [. . .]

DB: *What then do you think of notions like "media reform," given what you are saying about the capitalist economic structures, the impulse and drive for profit? Can one talk about media reform, as some do, without talking about general economic transformation?*

I think we have to talk about both, just as in the society at large we have to talk about reforms in the economic system, health care, social security, minimum wages, day care. Let's talk about that, because those are more possibly realizable in the short term. Those are things around which you can organize people. At the same time, we need to point out that these reforms will not solve fundamental problems, and that ultimately we will need more basic changes in the system so that we don't have to keep fighting uphill again and again for small changes.

DB: *Given what you said earlier about the genius of capitalism to adopt and adapt and to coopt dissent, there will be cosmetic offerings to ameliorate any kind of opposition.*

I didn't use the word "genius," but I did use the word "ingenuity." The ingenuity of the system. And there again it's not a conspiratorial ingenuity. It's not that five people got together in a room and decided this is the way it's going to work, but they act on the basis of their immediate and long-term needs. The Founding Fathers did get together in a room. Michael Parenti is right. They did not get together on a roller coaster on Coney Island. They got together in a room in Philadelphia. They decided to satisfy their immediate needs for control of a possibly rebellious population, for control of possibly rebellious black slaves and Native Americans. They had to satisfy that immediate need by creating a constitutional structure that would set up a strong central government able to deal with rebellion and which would be flexible enough to allow for reform and change by allowing at that time at least a limited franchise. Then, although the Founding Fathers did not foresee this, their successors, that is, the people who became legislators after the Founding Fathers, again and again saw fit to enlarge the franchise and to give people certain political rights and in this way to appease their need for change while at the same time limiting the scope of that change.

DB: *You write about the Founding Fathers in* A People's History of the United States *in several chapters. In particular you discuss Shays' Rebellion in western Massachusetts in late 1786, which had a very powerful impact on the framers slated to meet in Philadelphia the next year.*

Shays' Rebellion was a series of uprisings by farmers, many of them veterans of the American Revolution. They were being beset by taxes levied on them by the general assembly of Massachusetts. The legislature was dominated by merchants and people of wealth, as legislatures generally are almost everywhere. They were levying taxes on these people which they could not afford to pay. They were falling behind in their payments. This is what happens when people fail to pay their taxes: the sheriff arrives with a writ summoning them to appear before a court and then the judge, because they failed to pay their taxes, puts up their farm for sale, as well as their land, their livestock, their possessions. This procedure of foreclosure, of evictions, seizure of property was taking place all over western Massachusetts. These farmers were not able to pay their taxes. Daniel Shays, who had been a captain in the American Revolution, became a leader of a movement to stop this. The movement consisted of armed farmers gathering before courthouses where the foreclosure proceedings were to take place and stopping these procedures from happening. A very direct, forceful, rebellious action. There were times when they would appear and block the judge from entering the courthouse. The sheriff would appear and the sheriff's deputies and they would be greatly outnumbered by the crowd. The sheriff would then call upon the local militia. The local militia would arrive and be sympathetic to the farmers. Sometimes the judge would say, Let's take a vote among the militia to see whether they want us to do this thing. They would take a vote and it would turn out that the militia would be on the side of the farmers.

You might say there was a disruption of the normal order of things in which poor people are simply deprived of their possessions because they aren't able to pay taxes. This is rebellion, revolution. This cannot be tolerated in a society that wants to maintain control and maintain the existing arrangements of property as they have been. Finally an army was put together.

DB: *Led by Hamilton?*

Hamilton was an important figure at this time in all of this, but the army that was raised was led by General Lincoln. It was financed by the merchants of Massachusetts, not by the legislature. Private merchants gathered money to pay for the army. This has happened a number of times in American history, that governments have been unable to pay for the armed forces and the rich have paid because the armed forces were going to do their bidding. The army in this case routed the rebels and defeated them. Many of them, including Shays, left the State and went to Vermont. A few were hanged. The rebellion was crushed. However, it set off great tremors among the leaders of the colonies, who at this time were bound together in the Articles of Confederation, a loose bonding in which the states had a great deal of power. There was no strong central government which could raise an army and collect taxes and create a national treasury. So Shays' Rebellion persuaded a number of people who became the Founding Fathers that a strong central government was needed to control such rebellions in the future. There's a letter that General Knox, who had been a general in the Revolutionary War serving under Washington, wrote to George Washington in which he talked about the dangers of Such rebellions. He said, These people want to equalize property. These people are envious of those who are rich and own a lot of property. Letters like this circulated back and forth. The Founding Fathers were even writing to Jefferson, who was in Paris at the time, saying, Look what's happening. Jefferson, being far from the scene and not as alarmed as they were, wrote back and said, Don't worry, a little rebellion now and then is a good thing. [. . .]

DB: *You write, "In New York, where debate over ratification was intense, a series of newspaper articles appeared, anonymously, and they tell us much about the nature of the Constitution. These articles, favoring adoption of the Constitution, were written by James Madison, Alexander Hamilton, and John Jay, and came to be known as the* Federalist Papers." *What do the Fed-*eralist Papers *tell us about the Constitution? You specifically discuss* Federalist Papers #10 *and* #63.

Federalist Paper #10 is probably the most important of all of these eighty-five articles that appeared in the New York newspapers. It was written by James Madison, who was a theoretician, a constitutional scholar. Madison lays out what is probably the fundamental political theory of the American system. He's arguing on behalf of adoption of this Constitution. But in doing so, he's not just giving immediate reasons. He's laying out a theoretical framework. He goes back as the Greeks did, as Aristotle did, in discussing the nature of societies, of politics. He talks about how societies inevitably have factions. These factions are based on who has property and who doesn't have property. There's going to be conflict among these factions on the basis of the owners of property and the non-owners of property. Therefore you need a government to control this conflict between factions. He talked about a majority and a minority faction. He said minority factions can be controlled by setting up a government in which the majority rule. A minority can be more easily controlled by such a government. But a majority faction is something to worry about. That's interesting, because we normally associate democracy with majorities. But he worries about a majority faction. Then he describes what would be the demands of a majority faction that a government would have to worry about. He says you might have "A rage for paper money," "for an equal division of property." He was talking about the fact that at that time poor farmers who were in debt wanted the state governments to issue paper money to make it easy for them to pay their debt, so anybody who was for paper money was going to be against the rich. It goes down to the present day, when the head of the Federal Reserve system says we must not have inflation because inflation will help the debtors, whereas the creditors, the bondholders do not want inflation. It's interesting that there's this continuous thread that runs from the Founding Fathers to the present-day bondholders in the American system. Madison says with these people in the majority faction there will be "A rage for paper money, for an abolition of debts, for an equal division of property, or for any other improper or wicked project." The idea is that this government will be able to control that. This is a very blunt, honest statement about what this government is being set up to prevent, a change in the property arrangements of the society, a change in the distribution of wealth. [. . .]

DB: *Why did you write about* Federalist Paper #63?

That's the one that talks about how a legislative body, a "well-constructed Senate," as I recall the phrase, would be able to be a check on what might be the temporary delusions, the temporary impetuous desires of the people. The temper of a representative body would correct the impulses of the population at large. They would be sober and careful. What was being said was that the idea of representative government is not really to represent the will of the people but to calm the anger of the people and to take the wishes of the people, which may be in any one instance powerful and angry, and subject them to the moderating influence of a representative body, to cool the passions of the multitude, to filter them through this representative body. This tells a lot about what is really the aim of representative government.

DB: *I note that you titled this chapter "A Kind of Revolution," not "A Revolution."*

Because if it were a real revolution it would replace the elite control of the colonies by Britain with democratic control by the colonists themselves. Instead, while being somewhat revolutionary in that it gets rid of the British elite, it replaces them with a domestic one. [. . .]

DB: *In the August 1998* Progressive *you have an article entitled "The Massacres of History" where you review a number of different events, primarily in American history. You write that you recently learned about the Bay View Massacre in Milwaukee, which occurred on May 5, 1886. What happened in the Bay View section of Milwaukee, and how did you find out about it?*

I found out about this massacre because I was invited by some people in Oshkosh, which is not far from Milwaukee, to attend the 100th commemoration of a strike that took place in Oshkosh in 1898, the paper workers' strike. One of the things that made the strike notable, aside from the fact that it was a strike that lasted a long time, was that at the end of the strike some of the strikers were indicted, which happens very often, and they were defended by Clarence Darrow, who gave one of his usual great speeches to the jury and they were acquitted. While being invited to that, I was also invited the next day to commemorate the Bay View Massacre of 1886, which took place right after the Haymarket event of early May 1886. The Bay View Massacre was a situation where steelworkers in this steel mill town just outside of Milwaukee were on strike. The strikers were marching toward the mill and they were simply fired at by the police. A number of them were killed, about seven. It became known at least locally as the Bay View Massacre. I had never run into the story of that. I'd read a lot of labor history and a lot of history generally and never read anything about this massacre.

I had occasion to bring that up when I was invited earlier this year to speak at historic Faneuil Hall in Boston at a symposium on the Boston Massacre of 1770. When they invited me I said to them, You want me to speak about the Boston Massacre. I'll come, so long as I don't have to speak about the Boston Massacre. I'd like to speak about other massacres in American history. To my surprise, they said OK. My point was that the Boston Massacre is much celebrated and known to schoolkids who learn about the American Revolution. They almost always learn about the Boston Massacre. One of the notable things about it was that a black or mulatto worker was killed, Crispus Attucks. I decided to try to make the point at this symposium that while it's very easy to celebrate patriotic events like the Boston Massacre because the American Revolution is one of the patriotic high moments of American history, there were other massacres, more serious in fact, that are forgotten, ignored in the telling of American history. The Bay View Massacre was just one of them.

DB: *In that article you ask, for example, why are there not symposia on things that could be called Taino Massacre or the Pequot Massacre.*

The massacre of the Taino Indians on Hispaniola by Columbus and the other *conquistadores* was a far more serious event certainly in terms of the human toll than the Boston Massacre. It was the killing of hundreds of thousands of people, a genocide, really, accompanied by torture and mutilation and starvation and overwork in the mines to the point where the indigenous population of Hispaniola, the island which is now Haiti and the Dominican Republic, was wiped out in a very short time, something that Harvard historian Samuel Eliot Morison called genocide. For him to call it genocide, considering that he was an admirer of Columbus, is quite a remarkable admission. [. . .]

DB: *You comment in* A People's History: *"My point is not to grieve for the victims and denounce the executioners. Those tears, that anger, cast into the past, deplete our moral energy for the present." I'm interested in this depletion of moral energy for the present.*

I was trying to make the point that it is very easy to become emotionally wrought up about something that happened in the past. But if it is not carried over into the present, if it doesn't become a starting point for moral indignation for things that are happening today, then there's an enormous waste of moral energy. The World War II Holocaust is an example. We've had an enormous amount of grieving over the Holocaust, and of course it deserves grieving over. But on the other hand, too much of that grieving has come as an exercise in remembering the past while blocking recognition of things that are happening in the present. I think of Elie Wiesel, who has spent so much of his literary talent dealing with the Holocaust. Yet I don't remember him speaking out on the war in Vietnam. I don't remember him speaking out against what is happening to the Palestinians in Israel. I remember once I was asked to participate in a program sponsored by Hillel House at Boston University to talk about the Holocaust. I suppose in a sense I was doing there what I did later with the Boston Massacre. I said, Let's go beyond that. Let's look at other holocausts. Otherwise, a simple remembrance of the 1940s holocaust will be of no moral value. So I talked mostly about the atrocities that were going on at that time in Central America, which the U.S. was not only overlooking but abetting by giving military aid to the military governments of El Salvador and Guatemala, giving aid to the *contras*. The U.S. was in effect responsible in the way that the people who were put on trial in Nuremberg were responsible for genocide even though they didn't actually release the gas from the chambers. The U.S. was responsible for the deaths of several hundred thousand people in Central America. So that was the gist of my talk. After that there was an angry response by a man in the audience who was a survivor of the Holocaust. He was angry because I departed from the Holocaust to talk about other things. He wanted me only to concentrate on that. To me, that concentration on a past event to the exclusion of present atrocities is an empty exercise in sentimental remembering and a moral failure.

DB: *You're Jewish. To what extent do Judaism and Jewish culture inform your intellectual development?*

I wish I knew. Shall I respond in Yiddish? A couple of months ago—I always answer these questions by going far afield, and then perhaps I come back to answer the question, it's a Jewish trait—I got a letter from a young man on the West Coast, a student who said he'd been reading my memoir, *You Can't Be Neutral on a Moving Train*, and he liked it very much. But, he said, I noticed that you just passed very lightly over your Jewishness. You don't say anything about how your Jewish background affected your values. It took me a while to answer him. It's hard to answer that question, just like it's hard to answer your question. On the one hand, I have no doubt that growing up Jewish and being aware of being Jewish, being aware of what Jews have suffered in the past and being aware even in the present of the anti-Semitism still in the world, and also growing up in the era of fascism and Hitler, inevitably had an effect on my sensitivity towards oppression and racism. It's wrong for me to say growing up Jewish meant nothing to me. On the other hand, I don't want to overemphasize the effect of growing up Jewish on the development of my attitudes towards war and peace and racism and justice because it's obvious to anyone who thinks about it that there are Jews who grew up with the same kind of Jewish heritage that I did who ended up supporting, as Kissinger did, mass murder in Southeast Asia and in Indonesia. There are Jews on both sides of the political boundary. On the other hand, I've found in my life that so many of the people who have shared exactly the same values that I have are people who did not grow up Jewish, people from all sorts of backgrounds. Armenians, for instance, but also American Anglo-Saxons. I mentioned earlier and in my memoirs write about Staughton Lynd, who was a colleague of mine who comes from a very different background from mine. But he ended up with the same values I did.

DB: *A central myth of Zionism is "a land without people for a people without a land." Does that have historical antecedents with other views of empty spaces, perhaps peopled by a few primitives?*

I have a hunch with your delicately pointed questions that you know the answer but you might be talking about the invasion of North America by Europeans into presumably an empty continent. You can say the North Americans did to the so-called empty continent what Israel did to Palestine. They turned this desert into a flowering garden, except that of course the so-called desert was peopled by human beings, and these human beings were simply overlooked. I remember when I went to school, probably in junior high school, learning about the Louisiana Purchase, when the U.S. in 1803 purchased this enormous territory from the Mississippi River to the Rockies, a huge part of what is now the U.S. I remember getting the impression that this was simply empty territory and what a wonderful thing that we now had this empty territory and

THE INDISPENSABLE ZINN

could do with it what we wanted. I was not told anything about the huge number of native tribes that lived in this area and how the acquisition of the Louisiana Territory meant the extermination of these Indian tribes in order to make that land ready for Europeans to settle.

DB: *In a talk you gave in Cambridge in late June 1998, you pointed to euphemistic terms like the Louisiana Purchase, the Florida Purchase and the Mexican Cession. Wasn't it wonderful that Mexico just ceded all this territory to the growing U.S.?*

It was all represented in classrooms by these lovely maps on the wall with different colors representing the different acquisitions. It was all called "Westward Expansion," the word "expansion" suggesting some sort of biological kind of process, benign, non-violent. The terms Mexican Cession and Florida Purchase were euphemisms for very violent forays into other areas. In the case of Florida, Andrew Jackson led military expeditions into Florida, killing people, and then Spain, in presumably a benign commercial action, "sells" Florida to the U.S. The Mexican Cession or war, was instigated by the U.S. in order to take half of Mexico, what is now the entire Southwest part of the U.S., including California. I wonder how many schoolkids in California growing up know that the territory they are on belonged to Mexico. I wonder how the Californians who now rage against Mexicans coming into California know that this once belonged to Mexico and it was the Yankees who invaded California and took it away.

DB: *You've said that George Orwell is one of your favorite writers. He wrote an essay that talks about the use of language, euphemisms, question-begging, called "Politics and the English Language." One of the terms he discusses is "pacification."*

"Pacification" is a nice word. It suggests that you're bringing peace to a warlike situation. We've had a very recent experience of pacification, and that is in the Vietnam War, where "pacification" meant the destruction of villages. I suppose it's true that when you kill somebody you pacify them. They can no longer speak, they can no longer react, they can no longer do anything, they are "peaceful" in death. The term pacification has been used by the British in building the British Empire, through a series of violent wars by the Americans, not just recently in Vietnam but before that in the Philippines. [. . .]

DB: *Talk about the use of the passive voice versus the active voice. Orwell writes about this in "Politics and the English Language" as well. I notice in* A People's History, *for example, you write, "The English landed and killed some Indians. The English went from one deserted village to the next, destroying crops." You could have just as easily written that "Indians were killed" and "crops were destroyed." Why did you choose the active voice?*

I'd like to say that I had read Orwell just the day before and deliberately chose the active voice, but I think I just naturally, unconsciously used it because it seemed a stronger and more accurate way of stating what some people did to others in the course of history. As Orwell pointed out, it does make a difference whether you use the active or the passive voice in giving power to whatever you say.

DB: *And defining agency, perhaps?*

Defining who does what to whom.

DB: *A recent example of this passive voice construction was in a* New York Times *editorial. They wrote about the 1965 period in Indonesia, when "half a million people on the country's political left were murdered." That was enlightening. One doesn't find out who did the murdering.*

The use of passive voice in that case always implies an act of God. Something happened to people and we're not going to emphasize who was responsible. That's a good example.

DB: *Let's talk about* A People's History of the United States. *When did you start writing it?*

I thought about writing it I suppose at the end of the Vietnam War, when I found myself with a little more free time. It was around 1977 that I signed a contract with Harper & Row, now HarperCollins, pushed to do it by two people, my agent, Rick Balkin, and my wife Roslyn. I went to Paris in 1978 for a four-month professorship, thinking that like all those famous writers who went to Paris to write, I would do the same. I brought my notes that I had gathered with me so that I could begin writing *A People's History* in Paris during that four-month stay. I didn't write a word. Paris was too much. So I returned to the U.S., where I went to work in 1978, finished in 1979. It took less than a year to write *A People's History*, which surprises people and sometimes makes them think I obviously did it in a hurry and didn't spend much time on it. But of course I'd been accumulating the notes and material, the data, for twenty years as a result of teaching and writing about history. So I had an enormous amount of material at hand. Once I sat down to write, I didn't use a computer yet, I had my old manual typewriter, it came very fast. I wrote very intensely and stayed up into the wee hours of every morning. [. . .]

DB: *In the course of your investigations in writing* A People's History, *what facts came out that were startling to you?*

I suppose just as the reader of my *People's History* were startled by my story of Columbus, I was startled myself. I must confess that until I began looking into it, I did not know any more about Columbus than I had learned in school. By this time I had a Ph.D. in American history. Nothing that I learned on any level of education, from elementary school through Columbia University, changed the story of the heroic Columbus and his wonderful accomplishments. It wasn't until I began to look into it myself, read Columbus's journals, read Las Casas, the great eyewitness who produced many volumes on what happened to the Indians, not until I began to read did I suddenly realize with a kind of shock how ignorant I had been and with another shock how ignorant I had been led to be by the education I had gotten in our national education system.

DB: *What about your methodology? How did you go about your task? Was it chronologically disciplined?*

At first my idea was to organize the book according to topics and issues. I thought I'd have a section on race and would carry the section on race right from the first slaves brought to Jamestown down through the present, do the same thing with labor, and so on. Then I discarded that idea. I thought I would use a more traditional approach and deal in rough chronological form with the topics that are dealt with in the orthodox American textbooks. Then it would be more obvious that I was dealing with the same topics but from a completely different point of view, and also my book would be more useful to teachers. Students could look at my book parallel to other books, go through the same chronology and find a completely different version of the events. [. . .]

DB: *You do that kind of back-announcing. You talk about Samuel Eliot Morison and what you're trying to do in terms of writing a new history from the perspective of the human impact of history on people. You also cite Henry Kissinger in his first-book,* A World Restored, *in which he writes that "history is the memory of states."*

Kissinger has always been one of my favorites. I was not surprised when I read that in his book, which is actually his doctoral dissertation. It was an exact representation of Kissinger's Machiavellian view of history. That is, you look at history and the world from the standpoint, as Machiavelli did, of the Prince. Kissinger looks at it from the standpoint of Nixon, the President or the President's advisors. My book was intended to do exactly the opposite, to look at history from the standpoint of those people who were victims of the state, those ordinary people who are not the people in power. When you look at the world from the viewpoint of the state, as Kissinger does, everything looks different. Then you can, as he did, look at the nineteenth century as an era of peace, as the great states were not at war with one another as they would be shortly thereafter in World War I. Very often that era, from 1815, the Congress of Vienna, is seen as a time when the great powers got together and established a kind of, yes, peace until 1914. From the point of view of the states, there was peace. From the point of view of ordinary people there was no peace. During that period those states were marauding in the world, conquering the Middle East and Asia. In the case of the U.S., it was conquering Latin America. Internally during that period those states were collaborating with the exploitation of their working classes by the rising industries of that time. So those are two very, very different points of view about history. [. . .]

DB: *In* A People's History *you cite Albert Camus's suggestion about victims and executioners, "It's the job of thinking people not to be on the side of the executioners."*

I was trying to make the point that we who do history, we who are scholars, we who do anything in the world should reject the notion of neutrality. As Camus said, in a world of victims and executioners, you cannot be neutral. You cannot pretend to be objective in such a world. I was suggesting that historians should take the side of the victims and not the side of the executioners.

DB: *Various groups over time have claimed, "History is on our side." You write, "I don't want to invent victories for people's movements."*

I wanted to avoid a kind of facile romanticization of the past in which the people win glorious victories. First of all, from a practical point of view, to any thinking person it obviously would be a misrepresentation of reality. But also from the point of view of historical accuracy. After all, history has been dominated by people with wealth and power. The struggles of ordinary people against that have often ended in failure. Sure, there have been successes. But to exaggerate the successes would be to minimize the obstacles that people face in overcoming their situation and creating a different world.

DB: *You talk about emphasizing new possibilities by disclosing those hidden episodes of the past.*

I think that one of the worst things about the way history is taught is that it ignores or minimizes those times in history when people who are apparently powerless have gotten together, organized themselves, and accomplished remarkable things. For instance, when I was learning about the period of slavery and the Civil War going to school, and again, this is true from elementary school up to graduate school, I was never given a full picture of the anti-slavery movement. The abolitionist movement was an absolutely extraordinary achievement, filled with heroes and heroines, something that would inspire any young person to become a fighter against injustice. We're never given a full picture of that. The person who dominates our history books in terms of the emancipation of slaves is Abraham Lincoln. But there were all of those actions taken by people against slavery. I think for instance of a set of actions that took place in the 1850s, just before the Civil War, after the Fugitive Slave Act was passed in 1850, and when the federal government was collaborating with Southern slave owners to bring escaped slaves back into captivity. People in the North, black people, white people, banded together in what were called vigilante committees. The word "vigilante" had a different connotation then. There were people who were vigilant about what was happening to other people, and when a slave was captured they would invade the courthouse, the police station, they would rescue the slave. They would send the ex-slave on the way to Canada to freedom. They did heroic things. They risked their lives, their freedom, they

risked being put in jail. Also, as part of this very inspiring set of episodes, very often when these people were put on trial for abetting the
escape of a slave and for interfering with federal authorities, the juries
acquitted them. The juries were sympathetic to them, because by the
1850s there had been a building up of the abolitionist movement. A noble
period of American history, forgotten moments, lost moments, but those
moments should be remembered because they suggest to us what is possible for apparently powerless people to accomplish in the face of overwhelming odds. We've seen that again and again.

DB: *Do you think the question, Whose side is history on? is the wrong
question?*

There's no real answer to that question. If you answer that question,
you will be declaring a determinist view of history, like inevitably history must be on the side of the oppressor or the oppressed. I think
history is open. If we think of history as closed I think it depletes our
energy. If we think it's closed against us, then we are left in a state of
helplessness. If we think it's for us, then we think we don't have that
much to do.

DB: *After the collapse of the Soviet Union in the early 1990s, Francis
Fukuyama proclaimed "the end of history." In an age of capitalist triumpha-
lism and U.S. hegemony, does history have any future?*

I think it does. I don't think it has come to an end. That was wishful
thinking on his part. It's a Hegelian notion, really. Hegel also saw history reaching an end at a certain point. Actually, the end being the supremacy of the German state. Fukuyama sees it as the end being the
victory of capitalism. It's very clear, and should be clear to him, I hope,
that he was speaking too soon. Capitalism has not triumphed. It's true
that the Soviet Union has disintegrated, but capitalism has only revealed
itself since then more and more as incapable of solving the problems of
the world. The intrusion of a capitalist ethic into Russia these past years
has been disastrous, leaving many people to harken back romantically
even to the era of Stalin. With all of the terrible things that happened
under Stalin, people remember that they had jobs, they had food. . . .

DB: *Health care. . . .*

It was a welfare state. This very happy export of capitalism to other countries has obviously resulted in disaster. We're a long way from the end of history because we have something very important yet to do. Michael Moore in his latest film, *The Big One*, meaning the United States, has a last line I thought was classic: One evil empire down, one to go.

DB: *What role do you see, then, for historians in shaping the future?*

Historians have a responsibility to point out to people several things. It's very important to point out the history of our political institutions, the history of capitalism, the suffering that has gone on under capitalism. It's very important for historians to expose the emptiness of the promises that have been made and the emptiness behind the glorification of past and present institutions. And at the same time to bring back into our view those events in history which show that under certain circumstances, at certain points in history, if they organize, if they risk, if they act together, if they keep an ideal in their minds, it is possible for people to change things.

DB: *Who among current historians do you admire?*

In England we just had recently the passing of E.P. Thompson, I think he is one of the most extraordinary of contemporary historians, who wrote the classic work, *The Making of the English Working Class*. To me he was exemplary not just because he was a historian who unearthed the history of class struggle and class conflict and the awakening of working class consciousness in England, but because he acted out his beliefs in his personal life. In his last years he became one of the important voices in England speaking against the nuclear arms race. I see him as a model of a scholar-activist. In this country, there are a number of admirable historians. Staughton Lynd is one of them, although he's not officially a historian. Of course, many of our best historians are not officially historians. He was once, then he became a labor lawyer when he was drummed out of the profession. He and his wife, Alice Lynd, have put together a remarkable compendium of documents of nonviolent resistance in American history, *Nonviolence in America*. To me it is an absolutely essential work. Talking about people who are not officially historians but have done marvelous history, Noam Chomsky comes immediately to mind. He's given us all sorts of history, of the Middle East, Central America, America and foreign relations, history of the last five hundred years of capitalism in the world. I know of no one who is officially a historian who can match him. There are others. Eric Foner has done a great book on the Reconstruction period, the best book that's been written since W.E.B. Du Bois's *Black Reconstruction*. I think of Richard Drinnon, who has written some remarkable books. I mentioned at some other point his biography of Emma Goldman, which affected me greatly, but I also think of his book *Facing West*, a brilliant survey of American expansionism, using the word "expansionism" now in a much more critical way, in this country against the Indians, abroad in Vietnam and against the Philippines, an absolutely remarkable synthesis of history and literature, beautifully written. Drinnon also wrote a very good account of our incarceration of the Japanese in concentration camps during World War II. It is the story of Dillon Myer, the commandant of those concentration camps.

We now have in the U.S. a whole generation of new historians. I think of Gerda Lerner, who has brought to light women's history. I think of Rosalyn Baxandall and Linda Gordon and Susan Reverby who did a book on the history of working women, *America's Working Women*. I shouldn't ignore the Marxist historians who did pioneering work which enabled so many of us to go on from there. Philip Foner. No more prolific historian exists in the U.S. He died a few years ago. Herbert Aptheker, whose *A Documentary History of the Negro People in the U.S.* is still the most valuable single source book for black history. Very often people ask me, Where can I get information? I tell them, Go to the library. [. . .]

DB: *Turning to your writing style, which is fluid, fluent, straightforward and direct. I'm wondering to what extent you've been influenced by literature, novels for example. You've mentioned* The Death of Ivan Illich, *by Leo Tolstoy and James Joyce's* A Portrait of the Artist as a Young Man. *We've talked about Dickens and Orwell and others.*

I guess I've always been aware that fiction can often represent history more accurately than nonfiction. As I mentioned in a previous interview, John Steinbeck's *The Grapes of Wrath* can represent the Depression more realistically than a dry set of statistics about how many people were unemployed and how many people were hungry during the 1930s. I've always been aware of that because it has always seemed to me that the representation of reality is not simply a matter of telling about a past event on a flat surface, but that by going beneath that surface and by exploring something in detail and by making it more vivid, by writing about it in a literary way, you are bringing that event to life much more importantly than by a simple prosaic description. So I've always been interested in literature for that reason. When I read Upton Sinclair's novel about the Sacco and Vanzetti case, *Boston*, I had read other things about the case, but I thought, This brings those events into our imagination, into our vision, much more powerfully than any non-fiction account could do, and without doing an injustice to the facts. [. . .]

DB: *You had something in mind in a lecture when you mentioned Tolstoy's* Death of Ivan Illich *and Joyce's* Portrait of the Artist as a Young Man. *What was that?*

I think what I had in mind was that young people, especially when thinking about their whole future lying ahead of them, should try to imagine what Ivan Illich went through when at the end of his life, Tolstoy is giving young people an opportunity to see forty or fifty years ahead and ask, How will I think back upon my life forty or fifty years from now. For them to see that Ivan Illich, this successful man, this man who did everything right, looks back at his life and says, This is not the kind of life I wanted to lead, is something very instructive for young people, who are being captivated, being pressured on all sides to get money, to get success, to do the right things, all of them superficial, evanescent, the kinds of things that at the end of one's life will evaporate immediately. I very often talk about *The Death of Ivan Illich* because I want young people to think about the question of, What am I living my life for? What can I be proud of when I go? What will my grandchildren be proud of when they think of my life? Similarly with James Joyce, who said, I want to live my life freely. I don't want to be hampered by authority. I want to decide for myself how I want to think and what I want to do.

DB: *Clearly, it's too soon to talk about a Zinn legacy, but I was wondering if you could speculate on that.*

I don't think it's too soon to talk about a legacy. I think we should have started talking about it a long time ago, maybe when I was ten years old. A Zinn legacy. What do I leave? I think the best legacy one can leave is people. I can say, I would like to leave a legacy of books, and yes, there are writings that have an effect on people and it's good to think that you've written something that has made people think, and think about their lives. When I say legacy is people, I guess I mean people have been affected by reading, by your life, or people you've encountered. The best kind of legacy you can leave is a kind of example of how one should live one's life, not that I've lived my life in an exemplary way, but let's put it this way, people should be very selective about what they look at in my life. If I were to single out, as I would be prone to do, only the good things, I would think of the necessity to work at changing the world and at the same time maintain a kind of decency towards all the people around you. So that what you are striving for in the future is acted out in the present in your human relations. [. . .]

DB: *In the mid-1990s you updated* A People's History. *What did you add, and did you subtract or delete anything from the previous body of work?*

I didn't subtract or delete anything, because, as you know, everything I write is precious. It would be an act of cruelty to delete anything that I had written. But I did add because the original edition ended in the 1970s, and I wanted to bring the story up into the 1990s. I had actually gone into the Carter administration in the 1970s, but I wanted to go into Reagan and Bush. I deliberately wrote a chapter in which I combined my discussion of Carter, Reagan, and Bush. I wanted to make the point that, although they differ in detail, in general the policies of the liberal Carter and the conservative Reagan and Bush fell within the framework of American tradition. That tradition is capitalist and nationalist. Carter, even though he was among this triumvirate the liberal of the three, still maintained the military budget and a fundamentally nationalist foreign policy. Carter simply went along with what Indonesia was doing to the people in East Timor. In his domestic policy he did not make any really important changes in the direction of distributing the wealth of the country in a more equitable way. So the class issues and the nationalist issues were dealt with in roughly the same way by these three Presidents. I wanted in that one chapter which I added to make that point. I quoted Richard Hofstadter in *The American Political Tradition*, to me by far the best book that Hofstadter wrote, where he said that as he went through American history, there was a consistent American political tradition based upon nationalism, upon the idea of private property, the latter being a euphemism for capitalism. Then I wanted to also add a chapter on the resistance to the policies of these Presidents. I did a chapter called "The Unreported Resistance." That adjective "unreported" could be applied to resistance throughout American history. But in this particular case I wanted to bring out the fact that for instance the policies of Reagan did not go without opposition throughout the country. Reagan's policies in Central America brought about protests and demonstrations all over the country. Here in Boston we had 550 people sit in at the federal building in Boston to protest against Reagan's declaration of a blockade on Nicaragua. 60,000 people in the country signed a pledge of resistance that if Reagan invaded Nicaragua these people would act in some way against that.

In the early Reagan years there was a great anti-nuclear movement in which several million people participated, calling for a freeze on nuclear arms by the Soviet Union and the U.S. In 1982 there was a huge demonstration, close to a million people, in Central Park in New York. All over the country, city councils and state legislatures and even Congress passed resolutions calling for a nuclear freeze. Those were also the years when the policy of being nice to the white government of South Africa was opposed on hundreds of college campuses, with rallies that called for the divestment by American corporations and universities of their South African–connected holdings.

Maybe the most vivid example of underreported resistance was what happened in the Bush administration during the Gulf War, where the impression was given of near-unanimous support of the Gulf War by the American people. I tried in that chapter to tell something of the widespread protests against the Gulf War that took place, even though it was a very short war and there was very little time to organize protests. It was a protest that was much greater than there had been in the early months of the Vietnam War.

DB: *How many copies of* A People's History *have been sold?*

About 500,000. The interesting thing about the publication history is that the sales have gone up each year. The usual situation with books is that they sell the greatest number in the first year and then they go down. My editor at HarperCollins took me to lunch one day in New York. He told me how surprised he and the other people at Harper were that the sales of the book kept increasing. Harper had not really advertised the book. Not a single ad in the *New York Times*. Word of mouth, it's as simple as that. I guess I was just lucky in that I produced this history at a time, 1980, 1981, when all those people who had been influenced by the movements of the sixties and seventies were looking for a new, unorthodox view of American history. I just happened to write it at that moment. [. . .]

DB: *Rupert Murdoch's News Corporation owns HarperCollins, the publisher of* A People's History. *It also controls Fox TV and 20th Century Fox. Murdoch's Fox TV network may turn* A People's History *into a miniseries. What light can you shed on this, as the pundits like to ask?*

I could say that Murdoch is repaying me for the cookies I used to give him. But frankly, I'm baffled by it. But it's a possibility. Fox TV seems to be interested in turning *A People's History* into a ten-hour dramatized miniseries. I've been out to Los Angeles twice for meetings with Fox executives and joining me in this enterprise have been Matt Damon and Ben Affleck. The three of us, along with Chris Moore, who was one of the producers of *Good Will Hunting*, are slated to be executive producers of this miniseries. We're in the early stages, and I can't say definitely that it will happen. But it's moving in that direction.

DB: *Clearly you recognize that if this project is consummated the potential audience is huge.*

Television is seen by millions of people. If it's well done it will be seen by many millions of people. If it remains true to the point of view of the book, which we will try to ensure, then I would feel that something important has been accomplished. I think it would be a dramatic high point in American culture, without exaggerating the importance of my book, to take any kind of radical view of American society and place it before millions of people, just as Michael Moore did in his work. It's a rare thing in our society. [. . .]

DB: *you did a [recent] benefit talk in Cambridge for Revolution Books, not exactly the Barnes & Noble or Borders of the Boston metropolitan area. You talked about Antonio Gramsci and the importance of culture. Paraphrasing Gramsci,* Politics can be controlled but at the cultural level people and ideas can change. *Do you believe that?*

Yes, in fact, probably the culture has a better chance of changing than the political structure, because the political structure is very tightly controlled. The economic system is very tightly controlled. In the culture of a society there are more openings and possibilities and in the realm of ideas it is possible for people to begin to think new ideas before they have the opportunity to change their institutions. But if a culture changes enough, if the ideas of people change enough, then beneath the surface of politics and economics there's a bubbling that takes place, an energy that grows and finally breaks through the surface and then you see political and economic institutions change. I think that very often social change takes place in that sequence, the quiet changes beneath the surface and the culture becoming more and more powerful and breaking through.

DB: *Another Italian writer you've been quoting and you write about in the* Progressive *article is Ignazio Silone and his novel* Fontamara. *What did you find in* Fontamara *of value?*

First of all Ignazio Silone is one of my heroes, a brilliant novelist under Mussolini's Italy, in exile for a long time, a member of the Communist Party for a while but who left the party in disillusionment, as many people did. He retained his radical humanism. In *Fontamara*, which is a novel about peasants in this little village in Italy under fascism, what struck me was when these peasants were organizing an underground resistance, again talking about changing the culture, before they could overtly resist, create partisan groups, they circulated underground newspapers. They had this newspaper in which they simply reported things that were going on, things that had been done to people. So-and-so has been arrested. This woman has been abused. So-and-so has had land taken away. They would recite these facts, telling people what was going on. Then at the end of it they would simply say, "*che fare?*" What should we do? They wouldn't tell people what to do. They would simply give them the information and suggest by their question that something should be done and leave it to the people to figure out what they could best do. To me that was a marvelous example of how to resist and how to do it in a way that is sensitive to what people can do. [. . .]

DB: *Are we seeing some ferment in the U.S.? I'm thinking about the very successful and widely supported UPS strike, the defeat of fast-track legislation, the derailment of the Multilateral Agreement on Investment, the stopping of the Iraq bombing, and even the victory on organic food labeling.*

Again, going back to the title I gave that chapter, "The Unreported Resistance," yes, there are things that are unreported or underreported or passed over quickly every day that I think are indications of progress being made.

DB: *This is like taking to heart something Marlin Fitzwater once said. He was George Bush's press secretary. You conclude* A People's History *with this particular incident in 1992: "The Republican Party held a dinner to raise funds at which individuals and corporations paid up to $400,000 to attend. Fitzwater told reporters, 'It's buying access to the system, yes.' When asked about people who didn't have so much money, he replied, 'They have to demand access in other ways.'"*

I hope Fitzwater is honored by my mention of him at the end of my book. I thought that was a very telling statement, that people will have to find access in other ways if they don't have that kind of money. He's giving us good advice, telling us that if we are going to change the system we are going to have to organize, we're going to have to create power, we're going to have to do it without that wealth and without the military force that the government has at its command. I suppose I wanted to end the book with that kind of warning and lesson given by somebody in the Establishment who knows how things happen.

DB: *I think by your work and your spirit of solidarity, your* People's History of the United States, *that you've done much to provide access to many people. Thanks very much.*

Thank you.

Part 4
ON WAR AND PEACE

HIROSHIMA

from *The Politics of History* (1970)

Howard's experience as a young Air Force pilot during World War II made a deep impression on him about the horrors of war that helped to inspire and sustain a lifetime of opposing war and advocating for peace. In this stirring essay, he draws on archival war records and his own personal history to show "that great moral crusades, whether carried on by nations or revolutionary movements, often bring atrocities committed by the crusaders." Here, Howard focuses on the infamous (and unnecessary) bombing of Hiroshima and Nagasaki in August 1945. Connecting this tragic episode to Vietnam (napalm was first used during World War II), Howard writes: "The bombing of villages by American planes in the Vietnam war has been accompanied by similar claims, in military accounts, that only military targets are aimed at. But the nature of bombing from high altitudes, saturation style, makes this a lie, whatever the intention of the spokesman. Atrocities in modern warfare need not be deliberate on the part of the fliers or their superiors; they are the inevitable result of warfare itself. This fact does not exculpate the bombardiers; it implicates the political leaders who make the wars in which bombardiers fly, and all the rest of us who tolerate those political leaders." In describing these atrocities—both large and small—Howard levels a devastating critique of war as "immoral," a special kind of hell created by those who separate the decision-makers from the bomb-droppers, who follow orders without questioning them, who turn a blind eye to civilian casualties, who value certain kinds of human life over others, and who tolerate different standards of accountability for "democratic" and "totalitarian" regimes who wage the same kind of wars. When it comes to matters of war and peace, Howard reminds us, we must commit ourselves to "acting on what we feel and think, here, now, for human flesh and sense, against the abstractions of duty and obedience."

———

WITH ROBERT BUTOW'S RESEARCH on the Japanese side, Robert Jungk's exploration of the minds of the atomic scientists concerned, Herbert Feis's study of State Department files, and the old records of the U.S. Strategic Bombing Survey—we can approach from four sides the moral question: should we have dropped the atomic bomb on Japan? More important, perhaps we can pull together the evidence, and draw some conclusions to guide us in this frightening time when hydrogen bombers are ready all over the world.

First, let me describe my four sources:

The U.S. Strategic Bombing Survey was set up in November of 1944 to study the effects of bombing on Germany. On August 15, 1945, Truman asked the Survey to do the same for Japan, and one result was its report, *Japan's Struggle to End the War*. The Survey (Paul Nitze and John Kenneth Galbraith worked on it, among others) interrogated seven hundred Japanese officials, later turned the files over to the CIA.

In 1954, an American scholar named Robert Butow, having gone through the papers of the Japanese Ministry of Foreign Affairs, the records of the International Military Tribunal of the Far East, and the interrogation files of the U.S. Army, personally interviewed many of the Japanese principals, and wrote *Japan's Decision to Surrender*. This is the most detailed study from the Japanese side.

Robert Jungk, in a book first published in German, studied the making and dropping of the bomb from the standpoint of the atomic scientists, and in 1958 the American edition was published: *Brighter Than a Thousand Suns*. This book is based largely on personal interviews with the people who played a leading part in the construction and dropping of the bombs.

In 1961, Herbert Feis, who has had unique access to the files of the State Department and to part of the Department of the Army's records on the Manhattan Project, published *Japan Subdued*, which gives us the view from Washington.

What follows now is a compressed chronology of those events which, speeding along in blind parallel on both sides of the Pacific, culminated on August 6th and August 9th of 1945 in the obliteration by blast and fire of the Japanese cities of Hiroshima and Nagasaki.

As early as the spring of 1944, top Japanese admirals anticipated ultimate defeat and began discussing ways of ending the war. In July, the Tojo government fell. In September, the Navy was ready to call a halt, while the Army stood firm. In February of 1945, the Emperor was told by a group of senior statesmen that defeat was certain and peace should be sought at once, and by March a specific peace overture was under cabinet discussion. That month, Tokyo was hit by American fire bombs, and there were eighty thousand killed.

In April of 1945, American forces landed on Okinawa, within close striking distance of Japan, and often considered the southernmost island in the Japanese chain. The Koiso government was replaced by Suzuki, who took office with the specific idea of ending the war as quickly as possible and who undertook approaches to Russian Ambassador Malik about interceding for peace. In this same month, President Roosevelt died, Truman took office, and Secretary of War Stimson told him about the Manhattan Project. In this month too, within that Project, an Interim Committee of distinguished civilians, with an advisory scientific committee of Oppenheimer, Fermi, Arthur Compton, and E.O. Lawrence, was set up to study use of the bomb.

In June of 1945, Okinawa was taken, the Emperor of Japan told a new Inner War Council to plan to end the war, and the Interim Committee advised Truman to use the bomb as quickly as possible, on a dual civilian-military target and without warning. That same month, the report drawn up by atomic scientists James Franck, Leo Szilard and Eugene Rabinowitch, urging that we not drop the bomb on Japan, was referred by Stimson to the scientific committee of four and was rejected.

On July 13, 1945, the United States intercepted Foreign Minister Togo's secret cable to Ambassador Sato in Moscow asking him to get the Soviets to end the war short of unconditional surrender. On July 16th, the test bomb exploded at Alamogordo, New Mexico, and word was sent to Truman at the Potsdam Conference, which began the next day. The Potsdam Declaration of July 26th called for unconditional surrender, not mentioning the Emperor, whose status was of primary concern to the Japanese.

The Japanese cabinet was divided on unconditional surrender, and while it continued to discuss this, the bomb was dropped August 6th on Hiroshima. While the Japanese were meeting and moving towards acceptance of the Potsdam terms, the Russians declared war August 8th, and the second bomb was dropped on Nagasaki August 9th. Washington's ambiguity about the Emperor delayed final acceptance by the Japanese, but that came August 14th.

Here are the conclusions reached by our four close students of the affair:

The U.S. Strategic Bombing Survey: "Based on a detailed investigation of all the facts and supported by the testimony of the surviving Japanese leaders involved, it is the Survey's opinion that certainly prior to 31 December 1945, and in all probability prior to 1 November 1945, Japan would have surrendered even if the atomic bombs had not been dropped, even if Russia had not entered the war, and even if no invasion had been planned or contemplated."*

Robert Jungk, referring to our interception of the Japanese cables: "But Truman, instead of exploiting diplomatically these significant indications of Japanese weakness, issued a proclamation on July 26 at the Potsdam Conference, which was bound to make it difficult for the Japanese to capitulate without 'losing face' in the process."

Robert Butow, referring to Prince Konoye, special emissary to Moscow who was working on Russian intercession for peace: "Had the Allies given the Prince a week of grace in which to obtain his Government's support for acceptance of the proposals, the war might have ended toward the latter part of July or the very beginning of the month of August, without the atomic bomb and without Soviet participation in the conflict."

Referring to the intercepted cables, Butow says: "The record of what occurred during the next two weeks . . . indicates that Washington failed to turn this newly won and unquestionably vital intelligence data to active and good account."

And: "The mere fact that the Japanese had approached the Soviet Union with a request for mediation should have suggested the possibility that Japan, for all of her talk about 'death to the last man,' might accept the Allied demand for unconditional surrender if only it were couched in more specific terms than those which Washington was al-

---

*This conclusion is supported by the statements of virtually every top military leader of that period: Eisenhower, MacArthur, Marshall, Leahy, LeMay, etc. After this essay first appeared, Gar Alperovitz published his brilliant study, *Atomic Diplomacy*. His final chapter summarizes the evidence for the argument that political considerations, not military ones, were paramount in dropping the bomb.

ready using to define its meaning." ("Specific," Butow means, in relation to the Emperor, for former Ambassador Joseph Grew had been pounding away at the White House with the idea that this question of the Emperor was supremely important, but to no result.)

Herbert Feis: ". . . the curious mind lingers over the reasons why the American government waited so long before offering the Japanese those various assurances which it did extend later." These reasons, Feis says, are a complex of personal motives and national psychology. Truman was influenced by the desire of the Joint Chiefs of Staff to whip Japan further, by the desire of Secretary of State Byrnes for joint action with our allies, by the desire of Secretary of War Stimson to test the bomb, and by domestic criticism of less than unconditional surrender. Also by "the impetus of the combat effort and plans, the impulse to punish, the inclination to demonstrate how supreme was our power. . . ."

Feis sees two questions: was the bombing essential; and was it justified as a way of bringing early surrender. "The first of these, and by far the easiest to answer, is whether it was essential to use the bomb in order to compel the Japanese to surrender on our terms within a few months. It was not. That ought to have been obvious even at the time of decision, but . . . it does not seem to have been." On the second question, Feis is uncertain. He notes the tremendous desire to end the war as quickly as possible, concern that a demonstration bomb would fail. Yet he thinks it probable that such a demonstration, plus Soviet entry, would have brought victory as soon, or a few weeks later.

After rummaging through this mess of death and documents, I have some random ideas which may be worth thinking about:

1. The question of *blame* should be ignored. I can think of two ways in which blame-saying might be useful: in assessing persons who are still alive and about whom a choice might need to be made in the granting of crucial responsibility (for instance if we were picking a head for the Atomic Energy Commission, we would feel safer with Leo Szilard than with Robert Oppenheimer on the basis of experience with the Manhattan Project); and in puncturing illusions about nations whose behavior has often been idealized, like our own. But in general, our concern should be to see what we can learn for the handling of our present situation, not to settle dead arguments. Also, blame-placing sets up psychological blocks to the creation of rapport with people who have made mistakes in the past.

2. One wonders about our easy generalizations as to the difference in decision-making between "democratic" and "totalitarian" countries when we learn of the incredible number of deliberations and discussions that went on in the Japanese higher councils in days when everything was quite literally crashing around their ears—and when we recall, on the other hand, Truman's quick decisions on Korea, and Kennedy's on Cuba.

3. Making sure our military-minded men do not make top political decisions seems very important after seeing how the military in Japan delayed surrender until the bombs were dropped and how military men played such a large part in our decision to drop the bomb. (General Groves, though not an official member of the crucial Interim Committee, attended all its meetings and played a leading part in its decisions. Truman, too, seemed much influenced by the military.) Yet I believe now, after reading the evidence presented by Gar Alperovitz in *Atomic Diplomacy* that this emphasis on the special guilt of the military men is wrong. High civilian officials—Truman, Stimson, Byrnes—seem to have been the crucial decision-makers on the dropping of the bomb. It is a long chain of responsibility, and we need to concentrate on those links which we can ourselves affect.

4. While a decision-making process may seem to thunder along like a diesel truck, a firm touch by any one of a number of people can often send it in a different direction. Truman could certainly have applied that touch. Groves could have. Stimson as head of the Interim Committee could have. James Byrnes, carrying to Potsdam a State Department memo stressing the Emperor question, might have affected the final Declaration in such a way as to bring Japanese response if only he himself had believed in the memo. Oppenheimer or Fermi or Compton (since Lawrence already seemed to have objections to the policy) might have turned the tide by a specific recommendation from the scientific advisors to the Interim Committee. Lower down in the pyramid of power, the probability of any one man changing a crucial decision decreases, but it does not disappear. Szilard and his buried petition *might* have brought results, if joined by others. The point is: no human being inside an organizational apparatus should become overwhelmed by it to the point of immobility. He needs to play the probability statistics coolly, exerting his own pressure to the utmost even in the face of complete uncertainty about what others may be doing at the same time.

5. The impulse to "win the war, and as fast as possible" seems to have dominated everyone's thinking, to the exclusion of rational and humane

judgments. The most advanced thinkers in the West, its greatest liberals (and radicals), were more sold on this war than on any in history; never were the moral issues more clear in a great conflict, and the result was simplistic thinking about the war. (I recall August 6, 1945, very clearly. I had served as a bombardier in the Eighth Air Force in Europe, flew back to the States for a thirty-day furlough before a scheduled move to the Pacific, and while on furlough picked up a newspaper telling of the bomb dropped on Hiroshima. I felt only gladness that the end of the war was imminent.)

6. Oppenheimer has said that he did "not know beans about the military situation in Japan" when he and his committee decided to reject the Franck report. General Groves and the atom bomb people did not know about the messages the State Department had intercepted, while the State Department did not know the bombing was imminent. This suggests the importance of the free flow of information. But it would be naive to think that evil acts are only the result of poor communications. Some people can simply change their minds on the basis of new information; with others, a drastic revision of their sense of right and wrong is needed. If Oppenheimer and Fermi and others had only known how close Japan was to surrender, and known that an invasion was not necessary to defeat Japan, their decision would probably have been different. With others, like Groves—and probably Truman—the question would still remain: can we save *any* American lives (or gain *any* political advantage) by killing 100,000 Japanese? With them, the nationalistic morality which equates one American life with one thousand foreigners' lives seems to have obtained; or more likely, as the Stimson-Byrnes-Truman views disclosed by Alperovitz indicate, it was not even American lives, but national power that was the supreme value. Values have little to do with quantities of data; they are not necessarily changed by the mere increase of information. For some people on the verge of change this may not be true, but for most others it takes something beyond mere information: it takes direct experience, psychological convulsion, or irresistible pressure—a general assault on the emotions.

7. All this has implications for those interested in social change. It indicates, I think, that we need to distinguish, in the tactics of ideological conflict, between different kinds of human obstacles, and concentrate carefully on the type of technique needed to deal with each. For some, this means information. For others, we had better not assume that their value-system will be revolutionized in the short run. Instead, our disappointed recognition of the solidity of peoples' value-systems

can urge upon us the realistic tactic of playing values against one another. A particular cherished value is not likely to be destroyed, but it
can be shunted aside in favor of another which is even more desired.
The supreme value of survival has often been the only bulwark against
the almost supreme value of power. In the past, such value-clashes have
been accidental. Perhaps men can begin to use them deliberately.

8. People must be willing to make decisions "out of their field." Oppenheimer and the other three scientists on his committee felt that the
dropping of the bomb was really out of their province as scientists. We
should lose our awe of the specialists and stop assuming the "expert"
knows his stuff. There is a certain incompatibility between specializa-
tion and democracy.

9. The effort made to change a decision not-of-one's-own in a particular situation should match the dimensions of the peril involved. Ordinary and routine methods of protest may not be enough today, when
the entire human race is at the mercy of a handful of decision-makers.
More is required than calm and reasoned action. Or, to be more exact,
we need to think calmly and reasonably about taking extreme measures.
In C.P. Snow's novel, *The New Men*. British scientists, fearful that the
United States will drop the atomic bomb on a helpless city, hold a meeting. They reject the wild and irrational plan advanced by one of them
to reveal the entire secret to the public in an effort to stop the bombing.
They decide instead to do the sane, sensible thing. They appoint a committee to visit the United States and to impress their ideas on top American officials. The committee departs. The other scientists wait for its
return, and while waiting, they hear on the radio that the bomb has
been dropped on Hiroshima. So much for their sane, sensible decision.

VIETNAM: THE MORAL EQUATION
from *The Politics of History* (1970)

Though consistently antiwar for most of his life, Howard was never a purist when it came to the use of violence. He begins this essay, published in the midst of his own opposition to the Vietnam War, with the supposition that "it is logically indefensible to hold to an absolutely nonviolent position, because it is at least theoretically conceivable that a small violence might be required to prevent a larger one." Seeking to "create a rational basis for moral denunciation of our government's actions in Vietnam," Howard outlines "four tests" for evaluating when violence might be used as a "means to achieve just ends": first, *self-defense*, when a limited degree of violence is required to repel "outside attackers or a counterrevolutionary force within"; second, *revolution*, when violence is used for the purpose of overthrowing a "deeply entrenched oppressive regime"; third, *innocent civilians*, toward whom the use of violence is never morally justified; and fourth, *relative cost*, where violence should be avoided if the losses incurred during self-defense or revolution are simply too great to justify its use to achieve victory. In establishing a "moral calculus" for evaluating the war, Howard explains the appeal of communism for the Vietnamese and seeks to dismantle the faulty "Munich analogy," which political elites used to compare Cold War anticommunism with attempts to halt Hitler's expansion in Europe during World War II. "One touches the Munich analogy and it falls apart," he writes. "This suggests something more fundamental: that American policy makers and their supporters simply do not understand either the nature of communism or the nature of the various uprisings that have taken place in the postwar world. They are not able to believe that hunger, homelessness, oppression are not sufficient spurs to revolution . . . just as Dixie governors could not believe that Negroes marching in the streets were not led by outside agitators." In the end, Howard sees the Vietnam War as a classic struggle for self-determination: "The road to freedom is stony, but people are going to march on it. What we need to do is improve the road, not blow it up."

———————

WHEN THOSE OF US who would make an end to the war speak passionately of "the moral issue" in Vietnam, only our friends seem to understand. The government continues to bomb fishing villages, shoot women, disfigure children by fire or explosion, while its policy brings no outcry of opposition from Hubert Humphrey, Oscar Handlin, Max Lerner, or millions of others. And we wonder why.

The answer, I suggest, involves the corruption of means, the confusion of ends, the theory of the lesser evil, and the easy reversibility of moral indignation in a species which is aroused to violence by symbols. To explain all this, however, is to get involved in a discussion of dangerous questions, which many people in the protest movement avoid by talking earnestly and vacantly about "morality" in the abstract, or by burrowing energetically into military realities, legal repartee, negotiating positions, and the tactics of "broad coalition." Yet it is only by discussing root questions of means and ends—questions such as violence, revolution, and alternative social systems—that we can understand what it means to say there is "a moral issue" in Vietnam.

To start with, we ought to recognize the escalation of evil means during this century—a process in which few of us can claim innocence. What Hitler did was to extend the already approved doctrine of indiscriminate mass murder (ten million dead on the battlefields of World War I) to its logical end, and thus stretch further than ever before the limits of the tolerable. By killing one-third of the world's Jews, the Nazis diminished the horror of any atrocity that was separated by two degrees of fiendishness from theirs. (Discussing with one of my students Hochhuth's *The Deputy*, I asked if we were not all "deputies" today, watching the bombing of Vietnamese villages; she replied, no, because this is not as bad as what Hitler did).

The Left still dodges the problem of violent means to achieve just ends. (This is not true of Herbert Marcuse and Barrington Moore Jr. in the book they have done with Robert Paul Wolff: *A Critique of Pure Tolerance*. But it was so true of the Communists in the United States that the government, in the Smith Act trials, had to distort the facts in order to prove that the Communists would go as far as Thomas Jefferson in the use of revolutionary violence.) To ignore this question, both by avoiding controversy about comparative social systems as ends, and foregoing discussion of violence as a means, is to fail to create a rational basis for moral denunciation of our government's actions in Vietnam.

I would start such a discussion from the supposition that it is logically indefensible to hold to an absolutely nonviolent position, because it is at least theoretically conceivable that a small violence might be required to prevent a larger one. Those who are immediately offended by this statement should consider: World War II; the assassination attempt on Hitler; the American, French, Russian, Chinese, Cuban revolutions; possible armed revolt in South Africa; the case of Rhodesia; blacks in America. Keep in mind that many who support the war in Vietnam may do so on grounds which they believe similar to those used in the above cases.

The terrible thing is that once you stray from absolute nonviolence you open the door for the most shocking abuses. It is like distributing scalpels to an eager group, half of whom are surgeons and half butchers. But that is man's constant problem—how to release the truth without being devoured by it.

How can we tell butchers from surgeons, distinguish between a healing and a destructive act of violence? The first requirement is that our starting point must always be nonviolence, and that the burden of proof, therefore, is on the advocate of violence to show, with a high degree of probability, that he is justified. In modern American civilization, we demand unanimity among twelve citizens before we will condemn a single person to death, but we will destroy thousands of people on the most flimsy of political assumptions (like the domino theory of revolutionary contagion).

What proof should be required? I suggest four tests:

1. Self-defense, against outside attackers or a counterrevolutionary force within, using no more violence than is needed to repel the attack, is justified. This covers the Negro housewife who several years ago in a little Georgia town, at home alone with her children, fired through the door at a gang of white men carrying guns and chains, killing one, after which the rest fled. It would sacrifice the Rhineland to Hitler in 1936, and even Austria (for the Austrians apparently preferred not to fight), but demands supporting the Loyalist government in Spain, and

defending Czechoslovakia in 1938. And it applies to Vietnamese fighting against American attackers who hold the strings of a puppet government.

2. Revolution is justified, for the purpose of overthrowing a deeply entrenched oppressive regime, unshakable by other means. Outside aid is permissible (because rebels, as in the American Revolution, are almost always at a disadvantage against the holders of power), but with the requirement that the manpower for the revolution be indigenous, for this in itself is a test of how popular the revolution is. This could cover the French, American, Mexican, Russian, Chinese, Cuban, Algerian cases. It would also cover the Vietcong rebellion. And a South African revolt, should it break out.

3. Even if one of the above conditions is met, there is no moral justification for visiting violence on the innocent. Therefore, violence in self-defense or in revolution must be focused on the evildoers, and limited to that required to achieve the goal, resisting all arguments that extra violence might speed victory. This rules out the strategic bombing of German cities in World War II, the atom bombing of Hiroshima and Nagasaki; it rules out terrorism against civilians even in a just revolution. Violence even against the guilty, when undertaken for sheer revenge, is unwarranted, which rules out capital punishment for any crime. The requirement of focused violence makes nonsensical the equating of the killing of village chiefs in South Vietnam by the Vietcong and the bombing of hospitals by American fliers; yet the former is also unjustified if it is merely an act of terror or revenge and not specifically required for a change in the social conditions of the village.

4. There is an additional factor which the conditions of modern warfare make urgent. Even if all three of the foregoing principles are met, there is a fourth which must be considered if violence is to be undertaken: the costs of self-defense or social change must not be so high, because of the intensity or the prolongation of violence, or because of the risk of proliferation, that the victory is not worth the cost. For the Soviets to defend Cuba from attack—though self-defense was called for—would not have been worth a general war. For China and Soviet Russia to aid the Vietcong with troops, though the Vietcong cause is just, would be wrong if it seriously risked a general war. Under certain conditions, nations should be captive rather than be destroyed, or revolutionaries should bide their time. Indeed, because of the omnipresence of the great military powers—the United States and the USSR (perhaps

this is not so true for the countries battling England, France, Holland, Belgium, Portugal)—revolutionary movements may have to devise tactics short of armed revolt to overturn an oppressive regime.

The basic principle I want to get close to is that violence is most clearly justified when those whose own lives are at stake make the decision on whether the prize is worth dying for. Self-defense and guerrilla warfare, by their nature, embody this decision. Conscript armies and unfocused warfare violate it. And no one has a right to decide that someone else is better off dead than Red, or that someone else should die to defend his way of life, or that an individual (like Norman Morrison immolating himself in Washington) should choose to live rather than die.

It would be foolish to pretend that this summary can be either precise or complete. Those involved in self-defense or in a revolution need no intellectual justification; their emotions reflect some inner rationality. It is those outside the direct struggle, deciding whether to support one side or to stay out, who need to think clearly about principles. Americans, therefore, possessing the greatest power and being the furthest removed from the problems of self-defense or revolution, need thoughtful deliberation most. All we can do in social analysis is to offer rough guides to replace nonthinking, to give the beginnings of some kind of moral calculus.

However, it takes no close measurement to conclude that the American bombings in Vietnam, directed as they are to farming areas, villages, hamlets, fit none of the criteria listed, and so are deeply immoral, whatever else is true about the situation in Southeast Asia or the world. The silence of the government's supporters on this—from Hubert Humphrey to the academic signers of advertisements—is particularly shameful, because it requires no surrender of their other arguments to concede that this is unnecessary bestiality.

Bombings aside, none of the American military activity against the Vietcong could be justified unless it were helping a determined people to defend itself against an outside attacker. That is why the administration, hoping to confirm by verbal repetition what cannot be verified by fact, continually uses the term "aggression" to describe the Vietnamese guerrilla activities. The expert evidence, however, is overwhelming on this question:

1. Philippe Devillers, the French historian, says "the insurrection existed before the Communists decided to take part. . . . And even among the Communists, the initiative did not originate in Hanoi, but from the

grass roots, where the people were literally driven by Diem to take up arms in self-defense."

2. Bernard Fall says "anti-Diem guerrillas were active long before infiltrated North Vietnamese elements joined the fray."

3. The correspondent for *Le Monde*, Jean Lacouture (in *Le Viet Nam entre deux paix*) confirms that local pressure, local conditions led to guerrilla activity.

4. Donald S. Zagoria, a specialist on Asian communism at Columbia University, wrote recently that "it is reasonably clear that we are dealing with an indigenous insurrection in the South, and that this, not Northern assistance, is the main trouble."

One test of "defense against aggression" is the behavior of the official South Vietnamese army—the "defenders" themselves. We find: a high rate of desertions; a need to herd villagers into concentration-camp "strategic hamlets" in order to control them; the use of torture to get information from other South Vietnamese, whom you might expect to be enthusiastic about "defending" their country; and all of this forcing the United States to take over virtually the entire military operation in Vietnam.

The ordinary people of Vietnam show none of the signs of a nation defending itself against "aggression," except in their non-cooperation with the government and the Americans. A hundred thousand Vietnamese farmers were conducting a rebellion with mostly captured weapons (both David Halberstam and Hanson Baldwin affirmed this in the *New York Times*, contradicting quietly what I. F. Stone demolished statistically—the State Department's White Paper on "infiltration"). Then they matched the intrusion of 150,000 American troops with 7,500 North Vietnamese soldiers (in November 1965, American military officials estimated that five regiments of North Vietnamese, with 1,500 in each regiment, were in South Vietnam). Weapons were acquired from Communist countries, but not a single plane to match the horde of American bombers filling the skies over Vietnam. This adds up not to North Vietnamese aggression (if indeed North Vietnamese can be considered outsiders at all) but to American aggression, with a puppet government fronting for American power.

Thus, there is no valid principle on which the United States can defend either its bombing, or its military presence, in Vietnam. It is the factual emptiness of its moral claim which then leads it to seek a one-piece substitute, that comes prefabricated with its own rationale, surrounded by an emotional aura sufficient to ward off inspectors. This transplanted fossil is the Munich analogy, which, speaking with all the passion of Churchill in the Battle of Britain, declares: to surrender in Vietnam is to do what Chamberlain did at Munich; that is why the villagers must die.

The great value of the Munich analogy to the Strangeloves is that it captures so many American liberals, among many others. It backs the Vietnamese expedition with a coalition broad enough to include Barry Goldwater, Lyndon Johnson, George Meany, and John Roche (thus reversing World War II's coalition, which excluded the far Right and included the radical Left). This bloc justifies the carnage in Vietnam with a huge image of invading armies, making only one small change in the subtitle: replacing the word "Fascist" with the word "Communist." Then, the whole savage arsenal of World War II—the means both justified and unjustifiable—supported by that great fund of indignation built against the Nazis, can be turned to the uses of the American Century.

To leave the Munich analogy intact, to fail to discuss communism and fascism, is to leave untouched the major premise which supports the present policy of near genocide in Vietnam. I propose here at least to initiate such a discussion.

Let's refresh our memories on what happened at Munich. Chamberlain of England and Daladier of France met Hitler and Mussolini (this was September 30, 1938) and agreed to surrender the Sudeten part of Czechoslovakia, inhabited by German-speaking people, hoping thus to prevent a general war in Europe. Chamberlain returned to England, claiming he had brought "peace in our time." Six months later, Hitler had gobbled up the rest of Czechoslovakia; then he began presenting ultimatums to Poland and by September 3, 1939, general war had broken out in Europe.

There is strong evidence that if the Sudetenland had not been surrendered at Munich—with it went Czechoslovakia's powerful fortifications, 70 percent of its iron, steel, and electric power, 86 percent of its chemicals, 66 percent of its coal—and had Hitler then gone to war, he would have been defeated quickly, with the aid of Czechoslovakia's thirty-five well-trained divisions. And if he chose, at the sign of resistance, not to go to war, then at least he would have stopped his expansion.

And so, the analogy continues, to let the Communist-dominated National Liberation Front win in South Vietnam (for the real obstacle in

the sparring over negotiations is the role of the NLF in a new government) is to encourage more Communist expansion in Southeast Asia
and beyond, and perhaps to lead to a war more disastrous than the present one; to stop communism in South Vietnam is to discourage its expansion elsewhere.

We should note, first, some of the important differences between the
Munich situation in 1938 and Vietnam today:

1. In 1938, the main force operating against the Czech status quo
was an outside force, Hitler's Germany; the supporting force was the
Sudeten group inside led by Konrad Henlein. Since 1958 (and traceable
back to 1942), the major force operating against the status quo in South
Vietnam has been an inside force, formed in 1960 into the NLF; the chief
supporter is not an outside nation but another part of the same nation,
North Vietnam. The largest outside force in Vietnam consists of American troops (who, interestingly, are referred to in West Germany as *Ban-
denkampfverbande*, Bandit Fighting Units, the name used in World War II
by the Waffen-S.S. units to designate the guerrillas whom they special-
ized in killing). To put it another way, in 1938, the Germans were trying
to take over part of another country. Today, the Vietcong are trying to
take over part of their own country. In 1938, the outsider was Germany.
Today it is the United States.

2. The Czech government, whose interests the West surrendered
to Hitler in 1938, was a strong, effective, prosperous, democratic
government—the government of Beneš and Masaryk. The South Vietnamese government which we support is a hollow shell of a government,
unstable, unpopular, corrupt, a dictatorship of bullies and torturers, disdainful of free elections and representative government (recently they
opposed establishing a National Assembly on the ground that it might
lead to communism), headed by a long line of tyrants from Bao Dai to
Diem to Ky, who no more deserve to be ranked with Beneš and Masaryk than Governor Wallace of Alabama deserves to be compared
with Thomas Jefferson. It is a government whose perpetuation is not
worth the loss of a single human life.

3. Standing firm in 1938 meant engaging, in order to defeat once and
for all, the central threat of that time, Hitler's Germany. Fighting in
Vietnam today, even if it brings total victory, does not at all engage
what the United States considers the central foes—the Soviet Union and
Communist China. Even if international communism *were* a single or-
ganism, to annihilate the Vietcong would be merely to remove a toenail

from an elephant. To engage what we think is the source of our difficulties (Red China one day, Soviet Russia the next) would require nuclear war, and even Robert Strange McNamara doesn't seem up to that.

4. There is an important difference between the historical context of Munich, 1938, and that of Vietnam, 1966. Munich was the culmination of a long line of surrenders and refusals to act: when Japan invaded China in 1931, when Mussolini invaded Ethiopia in 1935, when Hitler remilitarized the Rhineland in 1936, when Hitler and Mussolini supported the Franco attack on Republican Spain 1936–39, when Japan attacked China in 1937, when Hitler took Austria in the spring of 1938. The Vietnam crisis, on the other hand, is the culmination of a long series of events in which the West has on occasion held back (as in Czechoslovakia in 1948, or Hungary in 1956), but more often taken firm action, from the Truman Doctrine to the Berlin blockade to the Korean conflict, to the Cuban blockade of 1962. So, withdrawing from Vietnam would not reinforce a pattern in the way that the Munich pact did. It would be another kind of line in that jagged graph which represents recent foreign policy.

5. We have twenty years of cold war history to test the proposition derived from the Munich analogy—that a firm stand in Vietnam is worth the huge loss of life, because it will persuade the Communists there must be no more uprisings elsewhere. But what effect did our refusal to allow the defeat of South Korea (1950–53), or our aid in suppressing the Huk rebellion in the Philippines (1947–55), or the suppression of guerrillas in Malaya (1948–60), have on the guerrilla warfare in South Vietnam which started around 1958 and became consolidated under the National Liberation Front in 1960? If our use of subversion and arms to overthrow Guatemala in 1954 showed the Communists in Latin America that we meant business, then how did it happen that Castro rebelled and won in 1959? Did our invasion of Cuba in 1961, our blockade in 1962, show other revolutionaries in Latin America that they must desist? Then how explain the Dominican uprising in 1965? And did our dispatch of the Marines to Santo Domingo end the fighting of guerrillas in the mountains of Peru?

One touches the Munich analogy and it falls apart. This suggests something more fundamental: that American policy makers and their supporters simply do not understand either the nature of communism or the nature of the various uprisings that have taken place in the postwar world. They are not able to believe that hunger, homelessness,

oppression are sufficient spurs to revolution, without outside instiga-
tion, just as Dixie governors could not believe that Negroes marching
in the streets were not led by outside agitators.

So, communism and revolution require discussion. They are sensitive
questions, which some in the protest movement hesitate to broach for
fear of alienating allies. But they are basic to that inversion of morality
which enables the United States to surround the dirty war in Vietnam
with the righteous glow of war against Hitler.

A key assumption in this inversion is that communism and Nazism are
sufficiently identical to be treated alike. However, communism as a set of
ideals has attracted good people—not racists, or bullies, or militarists—
all over the world. One may argue that in Communist countries citizens
had better affirm their allegiance to it, but that doesn't account for the
fact that millions, in France, Italy, and Indonesia are Communist party
members, that countless others all over the world have been inspired by
Marxian ideals. And why should they not? These ideals include peace,
brotherhood, racial equality, the classless society, the withering away of
the state.

If Communists behave much better out of power than in it, that is a
commentary not on their ideals but on weaknesses which they share
with non-Communist wielders of power. If, presumably in pursuit of
their ideals, they have resorted to brutal tactics, maintained suffocating
bureaucracies and rigid dogmas, that makes them about as reprehensi-
ble as other nations, other social systems which, while boasting of the
Judeo-Christian heritage, have fostered war, exploitation, colonialism,
and race hatred. We judge ourselves by our ideals; others by their actions. It is a great convenience.

The ultimate values of the Nazis, let us recall, included racism, elit-
ism, militarism, and war as ends in themselves. Unlike either the Communist nations or the Capitalist democracies, there is here no ground
for appeal to higher purposes. The ideological basis for coexistence
between Communist and Capitalist nations is the rough consensus of
ultimate goals which they share. While war is held off, the citizens on
both sides—it is to be hoped and indeed it is beginning to occur—will
increasingly insist that their leaders live up to these values.

One of these professed values—which the United States is trying
with difficulty to conceal by fragile arguments and feeble analogies—
is the self-determination of peoples. Self-determination justifies the over-

throw of entrenched oligarchies—whether foreign or domestic—in ways that will not lead to general war. China, Egypt, Indonesia, Algeria, and Cuba are examples. Such revolutions tend to set up dictatorships, but they do so in the name of values which can be used to erode that same dictatorship. They therefore deserve as much general support and specific criticism as did the American revolutionaries, who set up a slaveholding government, but with a commitment to freedom which later led it, *against its wishes*, to abolitionism.

The easy use of the term "totalitarian" to cover both Nazis and Communists, or to equate the South Vietnamese regime with that of Ho Chi Minh, fails to make important distinctions, just as dogmatists of the Left sometimes fail to distinguish between Fascist states and capitalist democracies.

This view is ahistorical on two counts. First, it ignores the fact that, for the swift economic progress needed by new nations today, a Communist-led regime does an effective job (though it is not the only type of new government that can). In doing so, it raises educational and living standards and thus paves the way (as the USSR and Eastern Europe already show) for attacks from within on its own thought-control system. Second, this view forgets that the United States and Western Europe, now haughty in prosperity, with a fair degree of free expression, built their present status on the backs of either slaves or colonial people, and subjected their own laboring populations to several generations of misery before beginning to look like welfare states.

The perspective of history suggests that a united Vietnam under Ho Chi Minh is preferable to the elitist dictatorship of the South, just as Maoist China with all its faults is preferable to the rule of Chiang, and Castro's Cuba to Batista's. We do not have pure choices in the present, although we should never surrender those values which can shape the future. Right now, for Vietnam, a Communist government is probably the best avenue to that whole packet of human values which make up the common morality of mankind today: the preservation of human life, self-determination, economic security, the end of race and class oppression, that freedom of speech which an educated population begins to demand.

This is a conclusion which critics of government policy have hesitated to make. With some, it is because they simply don't believe it, but with others, it is because they don't want to rock the boat of "coalition."

Yet the main obstacle to United States withdrawal is a fear that is real—that South Vietnam will then go Communist. If we fail to discuss this honestly, we leave untouched a major plank in the structure that supports U.S. action.

When the jump is made from real fears to false ones, we get something approaching lunacy in American international behavior. Richard Hofstadter, in *The Paranoid Style in American Politics*, writes of "the central preconception of the paranoid style—the existence of a vast, insidious, preternaturally effective, international conspiratorial network designed to perpetuate acts of the most fiendish character."

Once, the center of the conspiracy was Russia. A political scientist doing strategic research for the government told me recently with complete calm that his institute decided not too long ago that they had been completely wrong about the premise which underlay much of American policy in the postwar period—the premise that Russia hoped to take over Western Europe by force. Yet now, with not a tremor of doubt, the whole kit and caboodle of the invading-hordes theory is transferred to China.

Paranoia starts from a base of facts, but then leaps wildly to an absurd conclusion. It is a fact that China is totalitarian in its limitation of free speech, is fierce in its expression of hatred for the United States, that it crushed opposition in Tibet, and fought for a strip of territory on the Indian border. But let's consider India briefly: it crushed an uprising in Hyderabad, took over the state of Kerala, initiated attacks on the China border, took Goa by force, and is fierce in its insistence on Kashmir. Yet we do not accuse it of wanting to take over the world.

Of course, there is a difference. China is emotionally tied to and sometimes aids obstreperous rebellions all over the world. However, China is not the source of these rebellions. The problem is not that China wants to take over the world, but that various peoples want to take over their parts of the world, and without the courtesies that attend normal business transactions. What if the Negroes in Watts really rose up and tried to take over Los Angeles? Would we blame that on Castro?

Not only does paranoia lead the United States to see international conspiracy where there is a diversity of Communist nations based on indigenous Communist movements. It also confuses communism with a much broader movement of this century—the rising of the hungry and harassed people in Asia, Africa, Latin America (and the American South). Hence we try to crush radicalism in one place (Greece, Iran,

Guatemala, the Philippines, etc.) and apparently succeed, only to find a revolution—whether Communist or Socialist or nationalist or of indescribable character—springing up somewhere else. We surround the world with our navy, cover the sky with our planes, fling our money to the winds, and then a revolution takes place in Cuba, ninety miles from home. We see every rebellion everywhere as the result of some devilish plot concocted in Moscow or Peking, when what is really happening is that people everywhere want to eat and to be free, and will use desperate means and any one of a number of social systems to achieve their ends.

The other side makes the same mistake. The Russians face a revolt in Hungary or Poznan, and attribute it to bourgeois influence, or to American scheming. Stalin's paranoia led him to send scores of old Bolsheviks before the firing squad. The Chinese seem to be developing obsessions about the United States; but in their case we are doing our best to match their wildest accusations with reality. It would be paranoid for Peking to claim that the United States is surrounding China with military bases, occupying countries on its border, keeping hundreds of thousands of troops within striking distance, contemplating the bombing of its population—if it were not largely true.

A worldwide revolution is taking place, aiming to achieve the very values that all major countries, East and West, claim to uphold: self-determination, economic security, racial equality, freedom. It takes many forms—Castro's, Mao's, Nasser's, Sukarno's, Senghor's, Kenyatta's. That it does not realize all its aims from the start makes it hardly more imperfect than we were in 1776. The road to freedom is stony, but people are going to march along it. What we need to do is improve the road, not blow it up.

The United States government has tried hard to cover its moral nakedness in Vietnam. But the signs of its failure grow by the day. Facts have a way of coming to light. Also, we have recently had certain experiences which make us less naive about governments while we become more hopeful about people: the civil rights movement, the student revolt, the rise of dissent inside the Communist countries, the emergence of fresh, brave spirits in Africa, Asia, Latin America, and in our own country.

It is not our job, as citizens, to point out the difficulties of our military position (this, when true, is quite evident), or to work out clever bases for negotiating (the negotiators, when they *must*, will find a way), or to dissemble what we know is true in order to build a coalition (coalitions grow naturally from what is common to a heterogeneous group, and require each element to represent its colors as honestly as possible to make the mosaic accurate and strong). As a sign of the strange "progress" the world has made, from now on all moral transgressions take the form of irony, because they are committed against officially proclaimed values. The job of citizens, in any society, any time, is simply to point this out.

WITHDRAWAL

from *Vietnam: The Logic of Withdrawal* (1967)

Describing the Vietnam war as "a theater of the absurd," Howard was among the first American intellectuals to call for the full and immediate withdrawal of American troops. Arguing that there is "no necessary relationship between liberalism in domestic policy and humaneness in foreign policy," he published his slim yet explosive volume *Vietnam: The Logic of Withdrawal* in 1967. In it, he called on ordinary Americans to protest the actions of their government: "The citizen's job, I believe, is to declare firmly what he thinks is right. To compromise with politicians from the very start is to end with a compromise of a compromise." Howard lays out a clear case for withdrawal based on both practical and political concerns. He asks, "Which is more terrible: to have people in the world say that the United States withdrew from an untenable situation, or to have it said, as is now being said everywhere, that the United States is acting foolishly and immorally in Vietnam?" Howard's argument culminates with a fictional "Speech for LBJ," wherein he imagines an alternative pathway for the President. In Howard's imagination, LBJ concludes by saying: "I need not tell you how long I have waited for this moment—and how happy I am to be able to say that now, after so much pain, after so much sacrifice, our boys will be coming home. My fellow Americans, good night and sleep well. We are no longer at war in Vietnam." Of course, President Johnson never gave such a speech, and his political career—to say nothing of the nation's moral standing—was ruined as a result. We have yet to recover.

SENATOR HICKENLOOPER OF IOWA was questioning George Kennan at the Senate Foreign Relations Committee Hearings in early 1966:

> Hickenlooper: Now, there are problems facing us and others. . . . How we disengage ourselves without losing a tremendous amount of face or position in various areas of the world.
>
> Kennan: Senator, I think precisely the question, the consideration that you have just raised is the central one that we have to think about; and it seems to me, as I have said here, that a precipitate, sudden, and unilateral withdrawal would not be warranted by circumstances now.

A bit later in the questioning:

> Hickenlooper: Do you think the rather immediate withdrawal of the United States forces and our activity in South Vietnam from that country could be used effectively as a propaganda tool and weapon in Africa and in the emerging nations of Africa?
>
> Kennan: Senator, it would be a six months' sensation, but I dare say we would survive it in the end, and there would be another day. Things happen awfully fast on the international scene, and people's memories are very short. . . .

Kennan's testimony on the matter of withdrawal is important because it is representative of a large body of influential opinion which says flatly we must not withdraw, but then cannot really give persuasive reasons why we should not. Prestige, Kennan says, is the "central question" if we withdraw, but then he adds that it would be a "six months' sensation" and "we would survive it in the end."

In *Triumph or Tragedy*, Richard Goodwin argues that withdrawal "would damage the confidence of all Asian nations, and of many other nations, in the willingness and the ability of the United States to protect them against attack." But it seems that most Asians and "many other nations" disagree completely with Goodwin; they would like us to leave Vietnam. And one can readily see why: We are "protecting" Vietnam by killing its people and destroying its land. Who else would want such protection?

Toward the end of his book, Goodwin makes an odd statement. He says: "In the South we have no choice but to continue the war. We are under attack and withdrawal is impossible and unwise." Are we not "under attack" because we are *there*, and is it not true that if we withdrew we would no longer be under attack?

General Gavin, who preceded Kennan as a major witness before the Fulbright Committee, had an exchange with Senator Frank Church of Idaho:

> Church: Now, if we had not intervened in the interim since . . . and if we had not made the pledges that have been made to the Saigon government, and committed American presence and prestige there; in other words, if you were again faced with the same question . . . would you still be of the same opinion that the vital security interests of the United States from a military standpoint do not require the deployment of American troops in Indochina?
>
> Gavin: Yes, sir. I would say so. "Vital" is the key word there.

It turns out that a remarkable number of high-placed officials agree that the United States should never have become involved in military intervention in Vietnam. But now that she has done so, they feel an important matter of "prestige" is involved. For instance, in a roundup of opinion in the Senate which *New York Times* reporter E.W. Kenworthy made in the summer of 1965, he found that "many of these silent Senators" told reporters off-the-record that they wished the United States "had never gone into Vietnam; they would like to get out, even at the cost of a political compromise amounting to defeat, but they will not advocate military withdrawal under fire."

We are dealing here with an odd logic: that it was wrong for the United States to get involved in the first place, because Vietnam is simply not "vital" for American security, but that we must not withdraw from a move that was both wrong and costly because now our "prestige" is involved. This must mean that the stake in prestige is enormously important. It was so important to Senator Frank Church that when Gavin said he *still* felt no vital United States interests were at stake, Church immediately said:

> I wanted to get that on the record, General, because there has been so much discussion of withdrawal, and I do not know anyone around this table, certainly no member of the Foreign Relations Committee, that has advocated a withdrawal . . . under the

> present circumstances . . . in Vietnam. But . . . we have made a
> very great commitment of American prestige and a very solemn
> political commitment that has to be thrown into the balance. . . .

Not one member of the Senate Foreign Relations Committee would
advocate withdrawal, even those as critical of United States policy as
Fulbright, Morse, Church, Gore, and Clark. The "solemn political commitment" to General Ky could hardly be considered more solemn than the
nation's commitment to the Geneva Accords, to the United Nations Charter, to the Constitution of the United States, all of which have been ignored by United States policy in Vietnam. What is left is "prestige," and it
must be that even for the Senators criticizing the administration this
weighed so heavily in "the balance" Church spoke of that none would call
for withdrawal. The factor of "prestige" would then have to outweigh all
else that stemmed from the admitted original error of engagement in Vietnam: billions of dollars, thousands of lives, and also, untold dollars, lives,
and dangers in the future. To balance all *that* the prestige factor would
need to be of overwhelming significance. Let us see.

Kennan himself, in his testimony, talked about "the damage being
done to the feelings entertained for us by the Japanese people" by the
present policy and said "the confidence and good disposition of the Japanese is the greatest asset we have had and the greatest asset we could
have in East Asia." Does not the loss of United States prestige in Japan—
"the greatest asset . . . in East Asia" rank at least equal to the "six
months' sensation" that Kennan said would be the cost of our withdrawal? And if to Japan we add England, France, indeed, most of
Western Europe, as well as Africa and Latin America, where our prestige has suffered badly as a result of the Vietnam policy, does it not
seem likely that the result of withdrawal would be a net *gain* in prestige?

History does not show that a nation which liquidates a bad venture
suffers a serious loss of prestige where it can compensate in other ways.
Proud, powerful England surrendered to the ragtag thirteen American
colonies, removed her armed forces ignominiously, and did not suffer
for it. More recently, and more pertinently, France moved out volun-
tarily from Algeria and from Indochina; today she has more prestige
than ever before. The Soviet Union pulled her missiles out of Cuba; her
prestige has not suffered, and many people who feared World War III
was coming feel a certain gratitude for her prudence. Hans Morgenthau,
who has spent a good part of his scholarly career analyzing international

relations and who made his reputation as a hard-headed "realist," not as an "idealist," has written:

> Is it really a boon to the prestige of the most powerful nation on earth to be bogged down in a war which it is neither able to win nor can afford to lose? This is the real issue which is presented by the argument of prestige.

So far I have been talking only about prestige as a flat, one-dimensional quantity. But more important is its *quality*. There is a kind of prestige this nation should not worry about losing—that which is attached to sheer power, to victory by force of arms, devoid of moral content. Which is more terrible: to have people in the world say that the United States withdrew from an untenable situation, or to have it said, as is now being said everywhere, that the United States is acting foolishly and immorally in Vietnam?

For George Kennan, there is no vital reason for the United States to stay in Vietnam, even knowing its withdrawal would probably lead to a Communist-dominated Vietnam, *except* for prestige. As he told the Committee:

> If it were not for the considerations of prestige that arise precisely out of our present involvement, even a situation in which South Vietnam was controlled exclusively by the Vietcong, while regrettable and no doubt morally unwarranted, would not, in my opinion, present dangers great enough to justify our direct military intervention.

And if, upon examination, this "prestige" turns out to be empty (using Kennan's own example of Japan, plus what else we know), there is hardly anything left to support our "direct military intervention."

Then why, instead of simply urging immediate withdrawal, do Kennan, Gavin, and Morgenthau advance the "enclave" theory: that United States forces should stop bombing and retire to a few strong positions on the coast? All of them, not believing that a United States presence in Vietnam is vital, are really suggesting this as a halfway step to withdrawal. The presumption is that holding on to enclaves would also hold on to a bit of prestige, and unlike "precipitate, sudden, unilateral" withdrawal, would give us time to negotiate our way out of Vietnam.

This proposal, however, comes too late in the history of the conflict in

Vietnam. By now, the war against the Vietcong is mainly an American war; by September 1966, United States forces were larger than the regular forces of the Ky government. With American bombings ended and troops withdrawn, the Saigon government would collapse. Would it serve American "prestige" to stand by in enclaves while the Ky government fell apart to be replaced by a government which—whether Buddhist-neutralist or Vietcong—would ask or tell the United States to leave?

It would be far less ignominious for the United States to decide to leave on its own—before it is asked by a new government in South Vietnam. Speedy withdrawal need not be shameful; this is not a Dunkirk situation where decimated troops, harassed on ground and air, scramble into boats and flee. The United States controls the air, the ports, the sea; it can make the most graceful, the most majestic withdrawal in history. Of course it could not do this in a day or a week; it would need to pull its troops from the interior to the coast (so that *temporarily* there would be something like "enclaves"), and then transport them away from Vietnam as quickly as ships and planes can carry them.

The enclave proposal comes too late in another sense. The supposition is that United States troops could be concentrated in enclaves while negotiations proceeded, at the end of which they would come home. But what would be the point of this? At one time, it might have been argued that this would create the show-of-force on the spot which would enable the United States to negotiate from a position of some strength. But this implies there is something to negotiate *for*. If there once was, that time is past. Earlier in the war, the National Liberation Front might possibly have settled for some solution less than a dominant position in South Vietnam. For instance, right after Diem's assassination in November 1963 (according to the *New York Times* and the *Manchester Guardian*, and cited in the American Friends Service Committee's *Peace in Vietnam*), Hanoi was willing to discuss a coalition, neutralist government in South Vietnam. But at that time Rusk turned down a French proposal for a neutral, independent South Vietnam, and the following July the United States rejected a suggestion by U Thant, accepted by France, the USSR, Peking, and Hanoi, to reconvene the Geneva Conference. On July 24, 1964, responding to DeGaulle's plea to reconvene at Geneva, President Johnson told the press: "We do not believe in conferences called to ratify terror, so our policy is unchanged." (See Schurmann, et al., *The Politics of Escalation in Vietnam*.) By April 1965, the negotiating position of Hanoi had become hardened into four points which included settling Vietnam affairs "in accordance with the program of the National Liberation Front."

It is an old story in the history of rebellion. The American colonists would have been ready to accept some solution less than independence in early 1775, but by January 1776 they were committed to no less than independence. Negroes in Montgomery, Alabama were ready at one point in the 1955 campaign, on bus desegregation to accept merely a modified form of desegregation; but by the time their movement had crystallized they would accept nothing less than total integration. Richard Goodwin points (in *Triumph or Tragedy*) to the increasing militancy of the other side, despite our ferocious bombing, and says:

> We cannot know the will of men we do not understand. From Thermopylae to the Japanese-infested islands of the Pacific and Hitler's Berlin bunker, history is full of individuals and fighting forces who chose to fight against impossible odds and accept certain death.

Goodwin points to the dilemma of negotiations *at this stage*: the Vietcong will not accept any settlement that does not give them "a role in the political life of the country"; and at the same time, "it is unlikely we will permit any government to come to power which would inflict on us what some would see as the 'humiliation' of requesting our withdrawal."

By now, the Vietcong (and their friends in the North) have sacrificed too much to settle for anything less than a South Vietnam in which the NLF plays the major role, and from which United States troops completely withdraw. And if this is the only possible successful outcome of negotiations with a determined revolutionary foe, what is the point of negotiating? It might be argued that such a settlement might be made in effect, but tied with enough pretty bows and frills to make it *look* as if the United States had gained something from it. The world will hardly be deceived; the deception will last a short time, and there will be a much longer time—no matter what we do—for other countries to contemplate the fact that the United States had, whatever the niceties, departed from Vietnam.

True, there are certain developments to be hoped for when the present government and its American military support are gone. But none of these—except one—depends on the presence of United States soldiers. That one positive thing which the United States can do, as it departs, is to take with it those government officials, army officers, and others who fear for their lives when a new government comes in. These people could be resettled in any of a dozen places. Are we required to stay in Vietnam, as some have suggested, in order to "meet our pledges" to the present officialdom, when this seems to require killing their fellow countrymen in large numbers in order to keep them alive? Surely our job is not to go around the world protecting semifeudal dictatorships from the wrath of revolutionaries. It is a historical fact that revolutionaries, after victory, are merciless with those of the old regime. After World War II, Frenchmen executed—without benefit of trial— thousands of former Nazi collaborators. (We might note that the United States government, which seems very concerned with what might happen to Vietnamese officials, was silent when 250,000 Indonesians, said to be Communists, were massacred.) With a bit of inconvenience, we can save many of those in Vietnam who are in danger.

The other desirable developments cannot be guaranteed, indeed can only be thwarted, by United States military presence. One of these is the establishment of a government in which not only the NLF, but Buddhist, Montagnard, and other elements play a role. This we will have to leave to the Buddhists and others to work for; they are quite militant and capable of pressing for their rights. The United States cannot negotiate, for any future component of government in South Vietnam, a strength which does not exist. If it does exist, then the Vietnamese must negotiate it for themselves. The presence of the United States can only distort the true balance of forces, and only a settlement which represents this balance can be stable.

What was fundamentally wrong with the Geneva Agreement was that the great powers dominated it and falsified the real relationship of forces. All the North and half the South were under Vietminh control, and the division of the country into two equal parts was bound to fail. Not only the United States, but also the Soviet Union and China, were responsible for this development, because their own national ambitions required a peaceful settlement, even at the expense of the Vietminh. Neither Communism nor capitalism, it seems, can be depended on to look out for the interests of *other* nations.

We say we want economic well-being for Vietnam. But this, too, is more likely to be hurt than helped by our military occupation. We can be quite sure that an independent South Vietnam, first alone, and then in union with the North, will engage in the kind of economic experimentation and development that Communist countries in different parts of the

world have done, and quite successfully. This is part of the moderniza-
tion process that other, non-Communist nations of Asia and Africa are
going through. It will be hard, progress will be uneven, and there will
be sacrifices, unjustly distributed perhaps. But that is how it was in the
West in its period of swift industrial growth.

What else would we presumably like to get out of staying and negotiating: political freedom? This is hard to come by in any part of the economically undeveloped world, whether Communist or non-Communist.
We have not been very successful in developing this in those parts of the
world dominated by the United States, though we fondly include them
in "the free world." Vietnam will probably have to go through a long evo-
lutionary struggle for this, as have most countries in the world, whether
Communist or not.

There is a good deal of evidence to show that political liberty is related to economic security. As nations grow less desperate in the struggle for necessities, as education spreads, as young people speak out,
society becomes more open; this has been happening in the Soviet
Union and in Eastern Europe. This means that the best way we can
show our concern for both the economic well-being and the political
freedom of the Vietnamese is to take the billions that have gone for
death and turn them to the service of life. We should offer several billions in economic aid to North and South Vietnam, with no strings attached; or, better still, we can put that money into a United Nations fund
which will then go to Vietnam under international sponsorship.

A United States military presence is a danger to the Vietnamese and
to us. Its withdrawal is neither "abdication of responsibility" nor "iso-
lationism." Our bombing and shooting are irresponsible. In the future,
we can show our responsibility by giving economic aid, when invited.
We can be isolationist in the military sense; we can be internationalist
in the economic and cultural fields.

The United States, thus, cannot gain anything for Vietnam by negotiating, and it *should not gain anything for itself.* Since this country does
not belong in Vietnam it has no moral basis for negotiating any status
for itself—certainly not military bases or troops; Vietnam has had
enough of that.

There is something intrinsically wrong in the idea that the United
States should participate in negotiations to decide the future of Vietnam. We are an outside power, and the fact that we have inundated the
country with combat soldiers does not thereby give us any moral right

to decide its fate. Perhaps might makes right, as a historical fact, but it *should not* make right; and it is the duty of citizens to assert the "shoulds," however statesmen behave.

This is true also for China, the Soviet Union, England, and all other great powers. To have the future of Vietnam decided by these outside powers at an international conference is as much a violation of self-determination as was the settlement of Czechoslovakia's fate by Hitler, Mussolini, Daladier, and Chamberlain in 1938 at Munich. Whatever negotiation goes on should be among the Vietnamese themselves, each group negotiating from its own position of strength, undistorted by the strength of the great powers. This would give the present government virtually no voice in the future of the country, because it has—without United States backing—virtually no strength. It would give the Buddhist groups an important voice, because they represent significant numbers of people, whose support any future government must have. And it would undoubtedly give the National Liberation Front the major voice. (In September 1966, the NLF reasserted its willingness to work with other Vietnamese groups in a future government, and to desist from reprisals against former foes. This has been a basic part of its program, as Staughton Lynd and Tom Hayden point out in the book reporting their trip to Hanoi, *The Other Side*.)

In this light, to ask whether the United States will be willing to negotiate with the Vietcong seems strange. Rather, the question is: Should the Vietcong be willing to negotiate with the United States? From a standpoint of moral principle it should not; from the standpoint of military reality it may have to. But it is the oppressive power of *our* country which forces this violation of moral principle, and it is the duty of American citizens—whatever the reality of power—to try to bend the power of government toward what is *right*.

For the United States to withdraw unilaterally, leaving the negotiating to the various groups in Vietnam, would avoid the present impasse over negotiations. This impasse is founded on a set of psychological realities which protract the war. The National Liberation Front, imbued with the spirit of patriots driving off an invading army, is willing to continue its guerrilla tactics until the United States is worn down. Besides, the Geneva experience taught it to distrust international agreements; it is confident of its skill in the jungles of Vietnam, not so confident it can outmaneuver great powers at conference tables. The United States government appears divided in its intentions, between its spokesmen for peace (like Goldberg at the United Nations) and its military minds bent on victory. (The same day that Goldberg proposed peace talks at the United Nations—September 28, 1966—McNamara announced an increase in bomber production for Vietnam.)

To wait until all of the sensitive and stubborn elements are fitted together in that intricate mechanism of negotiation—the NLF, its sympathizers and advisers in Hanoi, the split personalities of the Johnson administration, plus its client government in Saigon—is to consign thousands more each month to injury or death. Does it really absolve us of guilt to say that "they" won't talk with us, and so we must continue killing? Does "their" stubbornness end *our* responsibility? No actor in this complex situation has more freedom to act, has less to lose by so acting, has greater resources to fall back on, than the United States. The sanity of unilateral withdrawal is that it makes the end of the war independent of anyone's consent but our own. It is clean-cut, it is swift, it is right.

Some say that the administration, even if it decided on such a move, could not do it, because it is not feasible "politically"; that is, the American public would not accept it. According to this argument, the "prestige" that everyone talks about our losing by withdrawal is really prestige at home.

But the argument is weak. The Johnson administration has *not* gained prestige from its Vietnam actions. The national polls show that the public has gradually, steadily lost faith in this administration. In September 1966, less than half of those polled throughout the country voiced support for the administration's Vietnam policy. It is true that the polls do not show a substantial number of Americans in favor of withdrawal. But it is also true that most Americans are tired of the war and wish we would get out, one way or another. Many think this is best done by military escalation; others by de-escalation; but the idea of *ending the war* is the most common feeling.

Withdrawal has not drawn large support, because it has not been put forward either by the administration or by its most prominent critics. And so the public has been forced to choose within a limited set of respectable alternatives. If the administration were to advance a new alternative, it would soon gain the respectability that *any* proposal gets which is made by the leaders of government.

In the 1966 elections, one American city—Dearborn, Michigan—confronted its citizens directly with the issue of withdrawal, by asking on the ballot: "Are you in favor of an immediate cease-fire and withdrawal of U.S. troops from Viet Nam so the Vietnamese people can settle their own problems?" Of those voting (34,791) 41 percent voted for withdrawal. The issue had been put on the ballot by the Mayor, an ex-Marine, who said: "I think the war is illegal. If I were a young fellow, I certainly wouldn't go to Viet Nam. I'd rather spend three years on a rock pile than to fight some poor little barefoot guys who have never done anything to us."

What is remarkable, it seems to me, is that in spite of a barrage of arguments from the nation's leaders *against* withdrawal, with no one high in government and no one in the national mass media arguing for withdrawal, 41 percent of the citizens of Dearborn (a rather conservative city, traditionally) should vote for such a solution. What might the result have been if, for just one week, national political leaders and the press had been giving the arguments *for* withdrawal?

It may be sad to note, but the American public (and probably, *any* public anywhere) is extremely changeable and open to suggestion, especially when the suggestion comes from on high. When Woodrow Wilson said the United States was too proud to fight in World War I, the public went along. When he then said the United States must fight in World War I, the public again went along. FDR said he would keep the nation out of war and was reelected. He took aggressive steps toward the Axis and we became involved in the war; he was reelected again. When Truman got us into the Korean war, the American public supported him. When Eisenhower got us out, the public was even more enthusiastic.

The President is the most powerful molder of national opinion; he has access to television, radio, the press. Everything he says carries the weight of tradition and patriotism with it—even when he changes his policy, as so many presidents have done in the past. Political sociologist Seymour Lipset (in *Transaction*, September–October 1966, "The President, the Polls and Vietnam") analyzed the national poll results: "Though most Americans are willing to keep fighting in Vietnam, they clearly would prefer not to be there and are anxious and willing to turn over the responsibility to someone else. . . . The President makes opinion, he does not follow it."

The memory of the public is short; it takes little time to adjust to new realities. It accepted American toughness toward the Soviet Union. It also accepted American agreements with the Soviet Union on nuclear testing. The President has it within his power to *make* a policy politically feasible; the nation tends to rally around him, especially in foreign affairs, *whatever* his policy is. We must remember, too, that President Johnson, running on a platform of peace in Vietnam, defeated Goldwater by an overwhelming majority when Goldwater was asking military escalation in Vietnam. That constituency for peace still exists, waiting for Johnson to give the word.

Of course it takes courage to change a policy, to withdraw suddenly from a situation in which one has become more and more involved. It takes courage to fight off the snipers, the critics, the militarists, the fanatics. It requires either open or implied admission of error. But this is what genuine leadership is.

President Johnson has repeatedly asked his critics: "What do *you* suggest?" I am suggesting that the President should appear on national television one evening, announcing beforehand that he will make a major policy speech on Vietnam. If he goes before the nation, announces the withdrawal of American military forces from Vietnam, and states cogently, clearly, the reasons for this withdrawal, the American people will unite behind him, the editorials of support will blossom everywhere, and the angry cries of the fanatics will be drowned in an immense and overwhelming national sigh of relief.

Many critics of our policy, who know very well that the United States should leave Vietnam, do not want to ask for immediate and unilateral withdrawal. This is not because they find powerful reasons against it, but because it is not a good "tactic," not "popular," not acceptable to the President and his staff.

I believe this is based on a false notion of how political decisions are made—the notion that citizens must directly persuade the President by the soundness of their arguments. This makes two assumptions which I think are unfounded. One is that the interests of the citizens and the President are the same, so that if they both think straight, they will be led to the same conclusions. Robert Michels (*Political Parties*) long ago made the classic case for the fact that once we elect our representatives, they develop a special interest of their own; the history of human misery under government does much to support this. The number of Americans and Vietnamese already sent to their deaths by decisions made in the quiet offices of President Johnson is further evidence.

The other assumption is that the President is a rational being who can be persuaded by rational arguments. We have seen—and our recent foreign policy illustrates it—how our highest officials have become the victims of myths which they themselves help to perpetuate.

The so-called "realists" who urge us to speak softly and so persuade the President are working against the reality, which is that the President responds to self-interest rather than to rational argument. Citizens can create a *new* self-interest for the President by persuading enough of their fellow citizens, who will then make enough of a commotion to "persuade" the President that he had better make a change. This cannot be effectively done by a citizenry which says only half of what it believes, which dilutes its passion and surrenders its moral fervor. If enough people speak for withdrawal, it can *become* politically feasible. Scholars, newspaper editors, congressional critics fail the public when they do not speak their full mind.

Wendell Phillips, a shrewd student of the relationship between the politician and the citizen, once wrote: "We must ask for the whole loaf, to get the half of it." Johnson may make a different kind of speech; he may negotiate his way out, waiting longer, letting more die in the interim, but getting out. He may "arrange" for the Saigon government to fall. (He may also drown the world in blood, because delay and escalation invite dangerous, uncontrollable developments.)

The pressures of concerned citizens will not by themselves change a major policy. Ultimately, a combination of factors will probably end the war: military impasse in Vietnam, criticism from other countries, dissatisfaction at home. Because it will be a combination, every citizen must put his full moral weight, his *whole* argument, into the balance.

When we urge Johnson to do exactly how much we *want* him to do, and not just that little which we *expect* him to do, we are engaging in the true politics of the citizen in a democracy, not the sham politics of the citizen who thinks he is The Prince. Politics is not the art of the probable. It is the art of the possible. And it is our job to insist that the politicians expand their narrow view of what is possible.

But let us listen to the President of the United States.

THE CASE AGAINST WAR IN IRAQ

from *The Boston Globe* (2002), reprinted in *The Zinn Reader:*
Writings on Disobedience and Democracy (2009)

Having spent half a century protesting American wars abroad, Howard
was a major voice of opposition to U.S. involvement in Afghanistan
and Iraq until his death in 2010. In the following editorial, published
in the *Boston Globe* in 2002, Howard makes the case that the "Bush administration's plan for preemptive war in Iraq so flagrantly violates both
international law and common morality that we need a real national
debate." This debate, of course, never really occurred, notwithstanding
the millions of citizens throughout the globe who took to the streets
between 9/11 and the spring of 2003 to protest this latest manifestation
of American imperialism. Howard makes a strong case that Iraq's possession of "weapons of mass destruction"—a "fact" we now know to
have been fabricated—"does not constitute a clear and present danger
justifying war." A grave warning to Americans, this essay has a certain
prophetic quality: "A war against Iraq has no logical connection to the
tragic events of September 11. Rather than diminishing terrorism, such
an attack would further inflame anger against the United States and
may well lead to more terrorist attacks. . . . A preemptive war against
Iraq, legally impermissible, morally unpardonable, would be cause for
shame for future generations." Cause for shame indeed.

———

THIS ESSAY WAS PUBLISHED in the Boston Globe *in August 2002, when
the United States was already heavily involved in a war in Afghanistan and
the Bush administration began talking of a preemptive war on Iraq. The arguments I make are the same ones that were made repeatedly and more*

frequently by the growing number of people who eventually opposed the war in Iraq. I've added it here not for its tragic prescience, but as a testament to how clear the case was even then, and how strong it remains.

The Bush administration's plan for preemptive war against Iraq so flagrantly violates both international law and common morality that we need a real national debate.

The discussion should begin with the recognition that an attack on Iraq would constitute an attack on the Charter of the United Nations, since the United States would then be in violation of several provisions, beginning with Article 1, Section 4, which states: "All members shall refrain in their international relations from the threat or use of force against the territorial integrity or political independence of any state."

But let us suppose that international law should not stand in the way when extraordinary circumstances demand immediate violent action. Such circumstances would exist if there were, in the language of our own Supreme Court, a "clear and present danger" represented by the Iraqi regime of Saddam Hussein.

There are facts and there are conjectures about Iraq. The facts: this regime is unquestionably tyrannical; it invaded a neighboring country twelve years ago; it used chemical weapons against Kurdish rebels fifteen years ago. The conjectures: Iraq may have biological and chemical weapons today. It may possibly be on the way to developing one nuclear weapon.

But none of these facts or conjectures, even if true, make Iraq a clear and present danger. The fact that Iraq is a tyranny would not, in itself, constitute grounds for preemptive war. There are many tyrannies in the world, some kept in power by the United States. Saudi Arabia is only one example. That Iraq has cruelly attacked its Kurdish minority can hardly be a justification for war. After all, the United States remained silent, and indeed was a supporter of the Iraqi regime, when it committed that act. Turkey killed thousands of its Kurds, using US weapons.

Furthermore, other nations which killed hundreds of thousands of their own people (Indonesia, Guatemala) not only were not threatened with war, but received weapons from the United States.

Iraq's history of invading Kuwait is matched by other countries, among them the United States, which has invaded Vietnam, Cambodia, Grenada, and Panama. True, Iraq may possess, may be developing "weapons of mass destruction." But surely the possession of such weapons, if not used, does not constitute a clear and present danger justifying war.

Other nations have such weapons. Israel has nuclear weapons. Pakistan and India have nuclear weapons and have come close to using them. And what country has by far the largest store of weapons of mass destruction in the world? And has used them with deadly consequences to millions of people: in Hiroshima, Nagasaki, Southeast Asia?

There is the issue of weapons inspection. Iraq insists on certain conditions before it will allow inspections to resume. Secretary of State Colin Powell told the Senate Foreign Relations Committee earlier this year that "inspectors have to go back in under our terms, under no one else's terms." One might ask if the United States would ever allow its biological, chemical, and nuclear facilities to be inspected, under any terms. Is there one moral standard for Iraq and another for the United States?

Before September 11 there was not the present excited talk about a strike on Iraq. Why would that event change the situation? There is no evidence of any connection between Iraq and that act of terrorism. Is it possible that the Bush administration is using the fear created by September 11 to build support for a war on Iraq that otherwise has no legitimate justification?

The talk of war has raised the question of American casualties, and rightly so. Are the lives of our young people to be expended in the dubious expectation that the demise of Saddam will bring democracy to Iraq? And what of the inevitable death of thousands of Iraqis, all of them made doubly victims, first of Saddam, then of Bush? Shall we add a new death toll to the hundreds of thousands of Iraqis (the figures are from the UN) who have died since the application of sanctions?

A war against Iraq has no logical connection to the tragic events of September 11. Rather than diminishing terrorism, such an attack would further inflame anger against the United States and may well lead to more terrorist attacks. We have a right to wonder if the motive for war is not stopping terrorism but expanding US power and controlling Mideast oil.

A preemptive war against Iraq, legally impermissible, morally unpardonable, would be a cause for shame to future generations. Let the debate begin, not just in Congress, but throughout the nation.

INTERLUDE: RESISTANCE AND THE ROLE OF ARTISTS

Interview with David Barsamiam, Cambridge, Massachusetts, 2004

from *Original Zinn: Conversations on History and Politics*

Anyone who knew Howard appreciated his deep love of literature and the arts. A playwright himself, he was a frequent theatergoer, and his son, Jeff Zinn, directs the Wellfleet Harbor Actors Theater on Cape Cod. On February 6, 2004, just before the first anniversary of George W. Bush's war on Iraq, David Barsamian interviewed Howard about the role of artists in a time of war. Arguing that "artists play a very special role in relation to social change," Howard says, "I thought art gave them a special impetus through its inspiration and through its emotional effect that couldn't be calculated. Social movements all through history have needed art in order to enhance what they do, in order to inspire people, in order to give them a vision, in order to bring them together, make them feel that they are part of a vibrant movement." In this interview, conducted in Cambridge, Massachusetts, Howard reflects on the influence of a variety of artists, including poets Percy Bysshe Shelley and Langston Hughes; folklorist Zora Neale Hurston; musicians Bob Dylan, Pearl Jam's Eddie Vedder, and the Dixie Chicks; political humorist Molly Ivins; and novelists Graham Greene and Dalton Trumbo.

DAVID BARSAMIAN: *You often bring up the role of artists in a time of war. Why?*

The reason I do is because artists play a very special role in relation to social change. This came to me when I was a teenager and becoming politically interested for the first time. It was people in the arts who perhaps had the greatest emotional effect on me. Singers such as Pete Seeger, Woody Guthrie, and Paul Robeson. Writers like Upton Sinclair and Jack London. I was reading the newspapers and Karl Marx. I was reading all sorts of subversive matter. But there was something special about the effect of what artists did.

And by artists I mean not only singers and musicians but poets, novelists, people in the theater. It always seemed to me that there was a special power that artists had when they commented, either in their own work or outside their work, on what was going on in the world. There was a kind of force that they brought into the discussion that mere prose could not match. Part of it had to do with a passion and an emotion which comes with poetry, which comes with music, that comes with drama, which is rarely equaled in prose, even if it is beautiful prose. I was struck by that at an early age.

Later, I came to think about the relative power of people in charge of society and the powerlessness of most people who become the victims of the decision makers. I thought about the possibility of people without the ordinary attributes of power, that is, money and military equipment, resisting those who have a monopoly on that power, and I thought how can they possibly resist it? I thought art gave them a special impetus through its inspiration and through its emotional effect that couldn't be calculated. Social movements all through history have needed art in order to enhance what they do, in order to inspire people, in order to give them a vision, in order to bring them together, make them feel that they are part of a vibrant movement.

DB: *You quote the poet Shelley in* A People's History. *There's an interesting intersection with the American labor movement, where workers at the turn of the twentieth century were organizing, but they were also reading to other workers to inform them, to impart literature to them.*

It's interesting how very often people who are not acquainted with the workplace, people who have not worked in factories or mills, think that working people are not interested in literature, that they don't read, that they are not part of the reading public. But it has always been true that working people had a life outside of their workplace. And outside of their workplace they would read, and they would become self-educated. Sometimes in their workplace they would take whatever opportunity they had to talk to one another, to read to one another. They would take whatever opportunity they had to draw upon the great voices in literature. And that's what I was referring to in *A People's History*, when I was talking about the struggles of garment workers in the early part of the twentieth century. I was referring to the fact that they would read poetry to one another. One worker in her memoir talked about how they would read Shelley's poem "The Mask of Anarchy" and quote those inspiring lines:

> Rise like lions after slumber
> In unvanquishable number!
> Shake your chains to earth, like dew
> Which in sleep had fallen on you—
> Ye are many; they are few!

What a remarkable affirmation of the power of people who seem to have no power. Ye are many, they are few. It has always seemed to me that poetry, music, literature, contribute very special power.

DB: *Shelley wrote "The Mask of Anarchy" after a massacre in Manchester, England, in 1819 when eleven peaceful demonstrators were killed and hundreds wounded. They were protesting against the deplorable economic conditions at the time. He also wrote one about hubris and the arrogance of great emperors in "Ozymandias" which is Greek for Ramses, the ancient pharaoh of Egypt. "'My name is Ozymandias, King of Kings: / Look on my works, ye Mighty, and despair!' / Nothing beside remains. Round the decay / Of that colossal wreck, boundless and bare / The lone and level sands stretch far away."*

I remember in school reading that poem, but a lot of its meaning was lost to us. I don't think the teacher drew the full meaning of that poem, the transient nature of power. Power is temporary; it comes into being and it goes out. Great monuments and great works that look as if they will stand forever decay and they fall. Shelley was certainly a very politically aware person and had a connection to some of the anarchists of that time, including William Godwin, whose daughter he was involved with. Shelley had a certain connection with the anarchist idea, and the anarchist idea is based on, for one thing, the ephemeral nature of power and the fact that if enough people assemble their meager resources, they can together overcome the most powerful force.

DB: *You like the work of Langston Hughes. He wrote a poem entitled "Columbia." What draws you to him?*

Langston Hughes is one of my favorite poets, and I suppose that's why he got into trouble. Not because he was one of my favorite poets but because he wrote the kind of poetry that would get him in trouble with the establishment. I remember he wrote a very short poem once called "Good Morning Revolution." But this particular poem you are referring to I chose because I see it as a forerunner, decades earlier, of Martin Luther King's speaking out against the Vietnam War. Hughes is speaking out here against the hubris of the United States as a new imperial power in the world. He's very skeptical of the claims of the United States to innocence in its forays in the world. He addresses the United States in this poem, saying, "My dear girl, / You haven't been a virgin so long." And goes on to say that the United States is "one of the world's big vampires." So, he asks:

> Why don't you come on out and say so
> Like Japan, and England, and France,
> And all the other nymphomaniacs of power. . . .

Langston Hughes also leads me to think of Zora Neale Hurston. Zora Neale Hurston was a magnificent African American writer. Very southern and unclassifiable. Nobody could put her in any kind of slot and categorize her. Very often she offended other black people by the things she would say. She was a totally honest person; she just spoke her mind. She wasn't afraid of going against the conventional so-called wisdom of the day. So when World War II broke out and everyone was supposed to jump on the bandwagon and support the war, Zora Neale Hurston would not go along with that. She saw the war as not simply a war between democratic, liberty-loving nations against fascist nations; she saw it as a war of one set of empires against another set of empires. She wrote her autobiography in 1942, shortly after Pearl Harbor. In *Dust Tracks on a Road* she said that she could not get teary-eyed, as everyone was doing, over what the Japanese and Germans were doing to their subject peoples. It's not that she was supporting what they were doing or that she approved of what they were doing. But she said they're doing what the Western powers, now supposedly on the good side of the war, are doing. They're doing what the Dutch have done in Indonesia, what the English have done in India, what the Americans have done in the Philippines. They are doing the same thing. Her publisher cut that out of her autobiography. It wasn't put back until many, many years after World War II when a new edition of *Dust Tracks on a Road* came out. When the United

States bombed Hiroshima and destroyed several hundred thousand human beings, Zora Neale Hurston wrote about Truman as the Butcher of Asia. Nobody else was speaking that way about Harry Truman.

But I bring her up because of this tradition of black writers, poets, intellectuals going beyond the issue of race. Of course, not totally beyond because they are watching people of color around the world being brutalized by the white imperial nations of the world, but going beyond the racial question in the United States to talk about what happens to people in other parts of the world.

DB: *Let's jump a little chronologically to Bob Dylan and his "Masters of War."*

Dylan is the great folksinger of the sixties, of the civil rights movement, of the movement against the war in Vietnam. There is probably no voice, no music more powerful than his in expressing the indignation of that generation against racism and against war. He was a genius with words and with music, speaking with such power that his words echo today. Not only do they echo today in relation to what happened then, but they echo because they are so relevant to today.

I chose to quote "Masters of War" because I thought, well, of course, he was talking about that time, and about the Vietnam War, but he could just as well be talking about the wars we have fought since Vietnam, and particularly the war of today, of the United States against Iraq. "Masters of War" is still being sung, not just by Dylan but by many other singers. I was at a concert not long ago here in Boston and heard Eddie Vedder of Pearl Jam sing "Masters of War." The huge and appreciative audience consisted mostly of young people. Pearl Jam is one of the most popular musical groups in the country. Eddie Vedder and Pearl Jam are bringing the Dylan sensibility to a whole new generation. Dylan's song must be heard to convey the full measure of its power, but I will spare you by not singing it. All I can do is faintly suggest its impact. He addresses himself to "You that build big guns, / You that build the death planes. . . ." He says to them that they play with the world as if it's their little toy. And he asks the "Masters of War": "Is your money that good? / Will it buy you forgivness, do you think that it could?"

DB: *Another artist who has achieved widespread popularity is filmmaker and writer Michael Moore. He's had several bestselling books. At the Seventy-fifth Academy Awards ceremony in March 2003, he received the Oscar for his documentary* Bowling for Columbine, *and with a global audience of perhaps a billion people watching he said "Shame on you, Mr. Bush," and he denounced the war. A bit later the Spanish filmmaker Pedro Almodóvar also made a very strong antiwar statement, albeit a little low-key.*

I think it's admirable when artists use an occasion to do what they're not supposed to do, that is, speak out on what's going on in the world. They are just supposed to immerse themselves in the spectacle of the moment, of the Oscars, of this Hollywood extravaganza. They are supposed to shut out the world and just feast on the glitter of what people are wearing and what trophies people are taking away. It is impolite and unprofessional to say that people are dying in other parts of the world while we are sitting here in our resplendent dress and giving out and receiving prizes. I admire the people who break out of the rule that you must be silent and be what they call a professional.

This rule of not going outside the boundaries is a rule that is welcomed very strongly by people in power. They want all of us to stay within the boundaries set by our professions. I have faced this myself as a historian. As a historian, I am supposed to just do history, and if I show up at the meeting of the American Historical Association in 1969 and propose a resolution that the historians should speak out against the war in Vietnam, well there's shock. We're historians; we're supposed to be here to talk about history and present our papers and leave matters of life and death to politicians. Rousseau had something to say about that. Back in the late eighteenth century, Rousseau said we have all sorts of specialties—we have engineers, we have scientists, we have ministers—but we no longer have a citizen among us. Somebody who will go beyond our professional prison and take part in the combat for social justice.

The people who break out of that, like Michael Moore, I think deserve an enormous amount of credit. You talk about Michael Moore being able to reach a huge number of people. People in the entertainment world have a possibility of reaching larger numbers of people than we do, and if they miss out on an opportunity to reach huge numbers of people, then they are depriving all of us of the very special opportunity.

So the Dixie Chicks speak out, as they did, using words similar to Michael Moore. One of the Dixie Chicks said I am ashamed that I come from Texas, which is George Bush's state. This was a wonderful thing to do.

One of the valuable things about big stars speaking out is that they may be condemned for speaking out on social issues, but their talents are powerful enough to overcome that. People don't stop going to their concerts. People didn't stop going to hear the Dixie Chicks. And people didn't stop reading Michael Moore's books; in fact, they sold even more after that event. And people aren't going to stop seeing Jessica Lange's movies. I think all these opportunities should be seized.

A friend of mine who was in Spain wrote to me. He pointed out that in the American Academy Awards, it was only a rare person like Michael Moore who would speak out and declare his political views. But in Europe that's accepted. The Spanish equivalent of the Oscars are called Goyas. That is interesting in itself, since Goya is the great anti-war painter, depicting the horrors of the Napoleonic wars. This friend was telling me that the recipients of the Goyas in Spain, almost every single one of them that year at the beginning of Bush's war on terrorism, almost every single one of them who got up to the microphone wore an antiwar button or banner on their clothes.

DB: *Molly Ivins, the syndicated columnist and author of the bestseller* Bushwhacked, *reports on citizens who say they are not interested in politics and have this sense of resignation and hopelessness. What do you say to people who feel there is no use in getting involved?*

Well, like Molly Ivins, I hear those cynical comments a lot. It's interesting because I may be speaking to a college audience or an audience of community people, fifteen hundred people, and someone gets up from the audience and says, What can I do? We're really helpless. And I say, Look around. There are fifteen hundred people sitting here. These fifteen hundred people have just applauded me very enthusiastically for speaking out against the war or for speaking out against the monopolization of power and wealth. That's just in this small community. There are fifteen hundred people or two thousand people everywhere in the United States who feel the way you do, who feel the way I do, and in fact not only are they feeling that way but more and more of them are acting on behalf of their feelings. Very often you don't know what they are doing because in the United States we are so fragmented. It is a very big country. The media do not report what is happening in other parts of the country. You may not even know what's happening in your part of the country. Maybe you may know what's happening in your neighborhood but not even in another part of your city, the newspapers, the media, do not report the activities of ordinary people. They will report what the president ate yesterday, but they will not report the gathering of a thousand or two thousand people on behalf of some important issue. So keep in mind that all over this country there are many, many people who add up to the millions of people who care about the same things you do.

Now whether their caring can have an effect is something you can't judge immediately. Here is where history comes in handy. If you look back at the development of social movements in history, what do you find? You find that they start with hopelessness. They start with small groups of people meeting, acting in their local communities and looking at the enormous power of the government or the enormous power of corporations and thinking, we don't have a chance—there is nothing we can do. And then what you find at certain points of history is that these small movements become larger ones, they grow, they grow. There's a kind of electronic vibration that moves across from one to the other. This is what happened in the sit-in movements in the sixties. This is how the civil rights movement developed. It developed out of the smallest of actions taken in little communities—in Greensboro, North Carolina, or Albany, Georgia—and moved and moved and grew until it became a force that the national government had to recognize. And we've seen this again and again. So at any early point in the development of a movement, things look hopeless, and if you are so intimidated by this hopelessness that you don't act, then those small groups will never become large ones.

DB: *John Lewis on the fortieth anniversary of the March on Washington reminded people that they were able to do that without the Internet, without cell phones, without faxes, just simply going door-to-door and phones calls. And there were no answering machines in those days. If you didn't get some-one, there was no way to leave a message. But they were able to organize an enormous event.*

That's an interesting point that John Lewis made because we tend to think now that what we have now is indispensable. My God, what did people do? I mean, how could Tolstoy write without a computer? But human beings have enormous capabilities. It's the nature of human beings to be ingenious and inventive. To figure out means of communication. To learn how to take whatever advantage they have, whatever small openings there are in a controlled system, and reach out to one another and communicate with one another. And so, yes, the civil rights movement grew as a result of people doing the most elemental things, of going into little towns and going door-to-door and holding meetings in churches and talking to people. During the Vietnam War people set up community newspapers and underground newspapers and organized teach-ins and rallies and GI coffeehouses. GIs could come and meet with one another and share antiwar views and be encouraged by learning that there were other GIs who felt the same way. So social movements have always been able to overcome the limits of communication. Now that we have the Internet, we have more tools at our command.

DB: *In a recent column in* The Progressive, *you write that "We are at a turning point in the history of the nation . . . and the choice will come in the ballot box."*

I'm a little embarrassed that I said it, since it is always said. Everyone thinks they are at a turning point in history. But I actually believe that today, in the United States, we are at a special turning point. We have an administration in power that is more ruthless, more tied to corporate power, more militaristic, more ambitious in its desire to seize control and influence in all parts of the world, even in space, to militarize space. We have an administration that I believe is more dangerous than any administration we've ever had in American history. It has the capacity to send its armed forces all over the world, to kill large numbers of people; it has the capacity to use nuclear weapons. And these are people who seem unconstrained by the democratic idea that they should listen to other voices. It's an administration that won 47 percent of the popular vote in the last election, was put into office by a 5-10-4 vote of the Supreme Court in a very shady and tainted election. It immediately seized 100 percent of the power and began to use that power to control the wealth of the country and to assert military power abroad. We have a government that has so far been unrestrained in its use of power. It feels that there are no countervailing forces, that the United States, with ten thousand nuclear weapons, with more than a hundred military bases all over the world, is in a position to do whatever it wants. This makes this a very special time. And the reason I said so much hinges on the next election—and this is an unusual statement for me because I rarely think that that much hinges on elections—is that I believe we need to defeat George Bush in the next election because this is an especially cruel and ruthless administration. To beat George Bush should be a very high priority, an indispensable priority for anybody who wants to see a different kind of country. I don't think that electing another person other than George

Bush is going to really solve the fundamental problems that we have because our experience has been that both Democratic and Republican administrations have been aggressive in foreign policy and have been tied to corporate power and corporate interests. But I think that another president coming into power after George Bush, a president who necessarily comes into power distinguishing himself from the policies of George Bush and criticizing the policies of George Bush, will be in a position where he has to in some sense answer to his constituency. And the constituency that will elect the next president, other than George Bush, will be a constituency that is antiwar and wants to change the priorities of the country from using the enormous wealth of the country for a military budget and tax breaks for corporations to using the great wealth for the needs of ordinary people.

DB: *We live in a country where in some places it is easier to buy a gun than to vote. Why are elections on Tuesday, a workday? Why not have them on the weekend? And why do we have a winner-take-all electoral college system rather than one-person-one-vote majority rule?*

Those are very good questions. Why do we have the election on Tuesday when working people are at work? Executives of corporations and big business people can take time out any time they want. It's no surprise then that 50 percent of Americans don't vote in a presidential election. And many of them are working people. Many of them probably do find it hard to get away from their jobs on a Tuesday and go to vote.

Why don't we have one person one vote? Why do we have this absurd system of the electoral college? It was something that was set up in the eighteenth century, and we are still using it in the twenty-first century. One reason we have the system is that it is easily manipulated by powerful political groups, and it creates the possibility that very small manipulation of votes can win all of the electoral votes in a state. By doing enough chicanery to move your vote from 49.9 percent to 50.1 percent, you then get 100 percent of the state's electoral votes. It is a system that lends itself to corruption.

We saw this most blatantly in the 2000 presidential election. By giving Bush, in a very shady way, a 500-vote plurality, he got all of the electoral votes of Florida, enough to give him, in the eyes of the Supreme Court, the presidency. So we do not have a very democratic system. We have a democratic system when you compare it to totalitarian systems. We have a democratic system when you compare it to dictatorships, where you don't have elections. But we would be deceiving ourselves if we thought that because we don't have a totalitarian system and because we don't have a military dictatorship that therefore we have a democracy, that we have free elections. It's hypocritical of the United States to demand very haughtily that other countries should have free elections and then we will declare them democracies, when we ourselves have elections that are not free.

They are not free in the sense that money is involved. Money dominates our election process. Huge sums of money are expended for one candidate or another. Both candidates, Democrats and Republicans, need to amass enormous sums of money in order to win. Those sums of money do not come from ordinary people. They come from the big business interests. So it's not a free election in that sense.

And it's not a free election in the sense that people have the freedom to choose whatever candidate they want because the Democratic and Republican parties dominate the entire system. Third parties don't have an opportunity. If you have a presidential debate on television, third party candidates are not allowed to appear. All the people see are the Democratic and Republican parties. It's hardly a free choice. It is a very limited choice that people have.

DB: *Another aspect is that citizens who commit crimes and serve the time come out and then are denied the right to vote for the rest of their lives.*

One of the really scandalous things that happened in the 2000 election in Florida is that they went through the rolls, and where they found people who had criminal records, they removed them from the voting rolls. Many thousands were removed. Since the people in the prisons in the United States are disproportionately people of color, it was people of color who were denied to right to vote.

DB: *Going back to literature, talk about Graham Greene's* Quiet American, *which was also made into a film. Why do you like Greene's novel?*

It's refreshing to find a novelist who doesn't simply concentrate, as so many contemporary novelists do today, on the relationship of two people, three people, or four people. It's refreshing to find a novelist who looks outside of them and sees what the larger society is doing and gives the reader a kind of social consciousness, who does something more than say something about the romantic involvement of these two or three or four people. We have so many novels these days that simply deal in a very microscopic way with what is called relationships. You wouldn't know that there is anything else going on in the world.

I think the really important novels deal with personal stories, but they also put these personal stories in a social context, like *The Grapes of Wrath* and *Native Son*. *The Quiet American* is a very personal story. It has the anguish of a love story, a triangle of people are involved, an American, a British, a Vietnamese woman, but it is a story that goes beyond that. The setting is Vietnam, and it is the time when the United States is getting involved in Vietnam in a very insidious way. *The Quiet American* refers to an American who appears innocent but who really is working secretly for the American government. In the guise of stopping communism, he is engaging in atrocious acts that kill men, women, and children in Saigon. This is the social setting for this personal story of love.

It's interesting that when this film was recently released, Miramax, a giant in the film industry, held it back and was afraid to release it because it would be considered unpatriotic. It's unpatriotic to suggest that the United States in its policy in Vietnam was doing something immoral. Commentary and criticism on the morality of government policy is considered outside the pale, this in a supposedly democratic country. So they held the film for a while. It took the influence and power of its star, Michael Caine, brought to bear on Miramax, that finally caused the film's release. However, I noticed that it has not been given an enormous amount of attention or advertising as other films have. It's been consigned to a certain small number of theaters in the country. They've tried to limit the audience for a film that would dare to make a statement about the United States.

DB: *Dalton Trumbo wrote* Johnny Got His Gun. *He was blacklisted and went to jail in the McCarthy era. He couldn't find work under his own name for years. Why did you assign this book to students?*

I chose the book because I've always believed that a work of art can bring a point home better than any prosaic exposition. I could give ten lectures about war and give them in such a way as to express my passionate feelings against war, and they would not have the impact that a student reading *Johnny Got His Gun* for one evening would feel.

Dalton Trumbo took the cruelty of war to the most extreme point: to take a soldier who is found on the battlefield barely alive but without arms, without legs, blind, deaf, the senses gone, really just a torso with the heart beating and a brain. This thing, this strange human being is picked up from the battlefield and brought into a hospital and put on a cot. The book consists of this person's brain operating and thinking.

There are two stories going on simultaneously. One is the thinking of this human being. All he can do is think: think about his past, his life, his small town, his girlfriend, the mayor of the town sending him off with great ceremony, going off to fight for democracy and liberty. He brings this all back and thinks about all of this.

At the same time, in the hospital ward he is trying to figure out how to communicate with the outside world. He can't speak. He can't hear. He can only sense vibrations. He can sense sunlight. He can feel the warmth of the sun and the cool of the evening. That's a way he can build up a calendar in his mind. He figures out a way of communicating with a nurse who is empathetic and ingenious enough to figure out what he is trying to do by using his head to tap against a piece of furniture. He taps out messages in code and the nurse deciphers them, and they communicate that way.

The climax comes when the big brass comes in to give him a medal. Through this nurse, they ask him, what do you want? And he thinks, what do I want? He taps out his response. The response, in the language of this generation, blows you away. He tells them what he wants. What he wants they cannot give him, of course. They cannot give him his arms, his legs, his sight. He asks them to take him into the school houses, classrooms, churches, wherever there are people, where there are young kids. He says, point to me and say, this is war. Their response is, this is beyond regulations. That's their answer. They want him to be forgotten.

This is a metaphor for our time. They want us to forget about the GIs. They want to forget about the guys who come back from war with legs gone, with arms gone, or blinded. No one may be as total a catastrophe as the character in *Johnny Got His Gun*, but there are people who in one way or another represent what he represents: the horrors of war.

But the government—we see this with the Bush administration— does not want people to be conscious of the fact that there are thousands and thousands of veterans of this war in Iraq who have come back blinded or without limbs. They've completely hidden that fact from the public. Only occasionally does a glimpse of that come through. There was a story in the *New York Times* not long ago about a GI who was blinded in Iraq. He was a young guy who was hit by shell fragments.

His mother visits him in the hospital. When she visits him, she passes the cots of other young people without arms, without legs. She sees a young woman soldier who is back from Iraq without legs, crawling on the floor with her little child crawling behind her. This is the picture that the present administration wants to hide from the American people. A novel like *Johnny Got His Gun* can awaken its readers to an understanding of what war is like and how the government wants to hide the reality of war, the reality of what happens to our people, and certainly of what happens to people on the other side.

Part 5

MARX IN SOHO:
A PLAY ON HISTORY

MARX IN SOHO: A PLAY ON HISTORY

Marx in Soho is the last of three plays Howard wrote during his lifetime (the first, *Emma*, was first performed in 1977; the second, *Danghter of Venus*, in 1985). Subtitled "A Play on History," Howard's one-man *Marx in Soho* imagines Karl Marx's return to earth in an attempt to clear his name from more than a century of misrepresentation. Indeed, the play's protagonist describes his return—full irony intended—as a "second coming." At the opening of the play, Marx appears and assures his audience that "those idiots who said: 'Marx is dead' " are, well, dead wrong. We learn that the nineteenth century revolutionary has negotiated a temporary exception to the ban on travel in the afterlife, but due to a bureaucratic snafu, has been sent to New York City's Soho, as opposed to his former London home. Described by journalist Amy Goodman as "hilarious and informative," the play is both a postmodern (and late-capitalist) primer on Marx's life and ideas, and a powerful critique of the manic culture of consumption and corporate greed that has driven America to the brink of ruin—or revolution.

———

HOUSE LIGHTS UP part of the way. Light on center stage, showing a bare stage, except for a table and several chairs. Marx enters, wearing a black frock coat and vest, white shirt, black floppy tie. He is bearded, short, stocky, with a black mustache and hair turning gray, wearing steel-rimmed spectacles. He is carrying a draw-sack, stops, walks to the edge of the stage, looks out at the audience, and seems pleased, a little surprised.

Thank God, an audience!

He unloads his supplies from the draw-sack: a few books, newspapers, a bottle of beer, a glass. He turns and walks to the front of the stage.

Good of you to come. You weren't put off by all those idiots who said: "Marx is dead!" Well, I am . . . and I am not. That's dialectics for you.

He doesn't mind joking about himself or his ideas. Perhaps he's mellowed over all these years. But just when you think Marx has grown soft, there are bursts of anger.

You may wonder how I got here . . . *smiles mischievously* . . . public transportation.

His accent is slightly British, slightly continental, nothing to draw attention, but definitely not American.

I did not expect to come back *here* . . . I wanted to return to Soho. That's where I lived in London. But . . . a bureaucratic mix-up. Here I am, Soho in New York . . . *Sighs.* Well, I always wanted to visit New York. *Pours himself some beer, takes a drink, puts it down.*

His mood changes.

Why have I returned?

He shows a little anger.

To clear my name!

He lets that sink in.

I've been reading your newspapers . . . *Picks up a newspaper.* They are all proclaiming that my ideas are dead! It's nothing new. These clowns have been saying this for more than a hundred years. Don't you wonder: why is it necessary to declare me dead again and again?

Well, I have had it up to here. I asked for the right to come back, just for a while. But there are rules. I told you: it's a bureaucracy. It is permissible to read, even to watch. But not to travel. I protested, of course. And had some support . . . Socrates told them: "The untraveled life is not worth living!" Gandhi fasted. Mother Jones threatened to picket. Mark Twain came to my defense, in his own strange way. Buddha chanted: Ommmm! But the others kept quiet. My God, at this point, what do they have to lose?

Yes, there too I have a reputation as a troublemaker. And even there, protest works! Finally, they said, "All right, you can go. You can have an hour or so to speak your mind. But remember, *no agitating!*" They do believe in freedom of speech . . . but within limits . . . *Smiles.* They are liberals.

You can spread the word: Marx is back! For a short while. But understand one thing—I'm not a Marxist. *Laughs.* I said that once to Pieper and he almost croaked. I should tell you about Pieper. *Takes a drink of beer.*

We were living in London. Jenny and I and the little ones. Plus two dogs, three cats, and two birds. Barely living. A flat on Dean Street, near where they dumped the city's sewage. We were in London because I had been expelled from the continent. Expelled from the Rhineland, yes, from my birthplace.

I had done dangerous things. I was editor of a newspaper, *Der Rheinische Zeitung*. Hardly revolutionary. But I suppose the most revolutionary act one can engage in is . . . to tell the truth.

In the Rhineland, the police were arresting poor people for gathering firewood from the estates of the rich. I wrote an editorial protesting that. Then they tried to censor our paper. I wrote an editorial declaring that there was no freedom of the press in Germany. They decided to prove me right. They shut us down. Only then did we become radical— isn't that the way it is? Our last issue of the *Zeitung* had a huge headline in red ink: "Revolt!" . . . That annoyed the authorities. They ordered me out of the Rhineland.

So, I went to Paris. Where else do exiles go? Where else can you sit all night in a café and tell lies about how revolutionary you were in the old country? . . . Yes, if you are going to be an exile, be one in Paris.

Paris was our honeymoon. Jenny found a tiny flat in the Latin Quarter. Heavenly months. But the word was out, from the German police to the Paris police. It seems that the police develop an internationalist consciousness long before the workers . . . So, I was expelled from Paris, too. We went to Belgium. Expelled again.

We came to London, where refugees come from all over the world. The English are admirable in their tolerance . . . and insufferable in their boasting about it.

He coughs, which he will do from time to time. Shakes his head.

The doctors told me the cough would go away in a few weeks. That was in 1858.

But I was telling you about Pieper. You see, in London, the political refugees from the continent marched in and out of our house. Pieper was one of them. He buzzed around me like a hornet. He was a flatterer, a sycophant. He would station himself six inches from me, to make sure I could not evade him, and he would quote from my writings. I would say: "Pieper, please don't quote me to myself."

He had the audacity to say, thinking I would be pleased, that he would translate *Das Kapital* into English. Ha! The man could not speak an English sentence without butchering it. English is a beautiful language. It is Shakespeare's language. If Shakespeare had heard Pieper speak one sentence of English, he would have taken poison!

But Jenny felt sorry for him. She liked to invite him to our family dinners. One evening, Pieper came and announced the formation of "The Marxist Society of London."

"A Marxist society?" I asked. "What's that?"

"We meet every week to discuss another of your writings. We read aloud, examine sentence by sentence. That's why we call ourselves Marxists—we believe completely and wholeheartedly in everything you have written."

"Completely and wholeheartedly?" I asked.

"Yes, and we would be honored, Herr Doktor Marx"—he always called me Herr Doktor Marx—"if you would address the next meeting of the Marxist society."

"I cannot do that."

"Why?" he asked.

"Because *I am not a Marxist." Laughs heartily.*

I didn't mind his bad English. Mine was not that perfect. It was his way of thinking. He was an embarrassment, a satellite encircling my words, reflecting them to the world but distorting them. And then he defended the distortions like a fanatic, denouncing anyone who interpreted them differently.

I once said to Jenny: "Do you know what I fear most?"

And she said: "That the workers' revolution will never come?"

"No, that the revolution *will* come, and it will be taken over by men like Pieper—flatterers when out of power, bullies and braggarts when holding power. Dogmatists. They will speak for the proletariat and they will interpret my ideas for the world. They will organize a new priesthood, a new hierarchy, with excommunications and indexes, inquisitions and firing squads.

"All this will be done in the name of Communism, delaying for a hundred years the Communism of freedom, dividing the world between capitalist empires and Communist empires. They will muck up our beautiful dream and it will take another revolution, maybe two or three, to clean it up. That's what I fear."

No, I wasn't going to have Pieper translate *Das Kapital* into English. It represented fifteen years of work—in the conditions of Soho. Walking every morning past beggars sleeping amidst the sewage, making my way to the British Museum and its magnificent library, working there until dusk, reading, reading. . . . Is there anything more dull than reading political economy? *He thinks.* Yes, writing political economy.

Then, home through the darkening streets, listening to the vendors calling out the prices of their wares, and the veterans of the Crimean War, some blind, others without legs, begging for a penny in the noxious air. . . . The poor-smell of London, yes.

My critics, trying to minimize what went into *Das Kapital*, would say, as they always say about radical writers, "Oh, he must have had some dreadful personal experience." Yes, if you want to make much of it, that walk home through Soho fueled the anger that went into *Das Kapital*.

I hear you saying, "Well, of course, that's how it was *then*, a century ago." Only *then?* On my way here today, I walked through the streets of your city, surrounded by garbage, breathing foul air, past the bodies of men and women sleeping on the street, huddled against the cold. Instead of a lassie singing a ballad, I heard a voice in my ear . . . *plaintively*: "Some change, sir, for a cup of coffee?"

Angry now: You call this progress, because you have motor cars and telephones and flying machines and a thousand potions to make you smell better? And people sleeping on the streets?

He picks up a newspaper and peers at it. An official report! the United States' Gross National Product (yes, gross!) last year was seven thousand billion dollars. Most impressive. But tell me, where is it? Who is profiting from it? Who is not? *Reads from the newspaper again.* Less than five hundred individuals control two thousand billion dollars in business assets. Are these people more noble, more hard-working, more valuable to society than the mother in the tenement, nurturing three children through the winter, with no money to pay the heating bill?

Did I not say, a hundred and fifty years ago, that capitalism would enormously increase the wealth of society, but that this wealth would be concentrated in fewer and fewer hands? *Reads from newspaper:* "Giant merger of Chemical Bank and Chase Manhattan Bank. Twelve thousand workers will lose jobs . . . Stocks rise." And they say my ideas are dead!

Do you know Oliver Goldsmith's poem "The Deserted Village"?

Recites: "Ill fares the land to hastening ills a prey/Where wealth accumulates and men decay." Yes, *decay.* That's what I saw as I walked through your city this morning. Houses decaying, schools decaying, human beings decaying. But then I walked a bit farther, and I was suddenly surrounded by men of obvious wealth, women in jewels and furs. Suddenly I heard the sound of sirens. Was violence being done somewhere nearby? Was a crime being committed? Was someone trying to take part of the Gross National Product, illegally, from those who had stolen it legally?

Ah, the wonders of the market system! Human beings reduced to commodities, their lives controlled by the super-commodity, money.

Lights flash threateningly. Marx looks up, confides to audience: The committee doesn't like that!

His tone softens, reminiscing. In that little flat in Soho, Jenny made hot soup and boiled potatoes. There was fresh bread from our friend the baker down the street. We would sit around the table and eat and talk about events of the day—the Irish struggle for freedom, the latest war, the stupidity of the country's leaders, a political opposition confining itself to pips and squeaks, the cowardly press . . . I suppose things are different these days, eh?

After dinner, we would clear the table and I would work. With my cigars handy, and a glass of beer. Yes, work until three or four in the morning. My books piled up on one side, the parliamentary reports piled up on another. Jenny would be at the other end of the table, transcribing—my handwriting was impossible, and she would rewrite every word of mine—can you imagine a more heroic act?

Occasionally, a crisis. No, not a world crisis. A book would be missing. One day I could not find my Ricardo. I asked Jenny: "Where is my Ricardo?"

"You mean *Principles of Political Economy*?" Well, she thought I was finished with it and she had taken it to the pawnshop.

I lost my temper. "My Ricardo! You pawned my Ricardo!"

She said: "Be quiet! Last week didn't we pawn the ring my mother gave me?"

That's how it was. *Sighs.* We pawned everything. Especially gifts from Jenny's family. When we ran out of those gifts, we pawned our clothes. One winter—do you know the London winters?—I did without my overcoat. Another time, I walked out of the house and my feet began to freeze on the snow, and then I realized: I was not wearing shoes. We had pawned them the day before.

When *Das Kapital* was published, we celebrated, but Engels had to give us some money so we could go to the pawnshop and retrieve our linens and dishes for the dinner. Engels . . . a saint. There's no other word for him. When they cut off our water, our gas, and the house was dark, our spirits low, Engels paid the bills. His father owned factories in Manchester. Yes . . . *smiling* . . . capitalism saved us!

He did not always understand our needs. We had no money for groceries and he would send us crates of wine! One Christmas, when we had no means to buy a *Weihnachtsbaum*—a Christmas tree—Engels arrived with six bottles of champagne. So, we imagined a tree, formed a circle around it, drank champagne, and sang Christmas songs. *Marx sings, hums a snatch of a Christmas carol:* "Tannenbaum . . ."

I knew what my revolutionary friends were thinking: Marx, the atheist, with a Christmas tree!

Yes, I did describe religion as the opium of the people, but no one has ever paid attention to the full passage. Listen. *He picks up a book and reads:* "Religion is the sigh of the oppressed creature, the heart of a heartless world, the soul of soulless conditions, it is the opium of the people." True, opium is no solution, but it may be necessary to relieve pain. *Shakes his head.* Don't I know that from my boils? And doesn't the world have a terrible case of boils?

I keep thinking about Jenny. *He stops, rubs his eyes.* How she packed all our possessions and brought our two girls, Jennichen and Laura, across the Channel to London. And then gave birth three times in our miserable cold flat on Dean Street. Nursed those babies and tried to keep them warm. And saw them die one by one . . . Guido, he had not even begun to walk. And Francesca, she was one year old . . . I had to borrow three pounds to pay for her coffin . . . As for Moosh, he lived for eight years, but something was wrong from the start. He had a large handsome head, but the rest of him never grew. The night he died, we all slept on the floor around his body until the morning came.

When Eleanor was born, we were fearful. But she was a tough little thing. It was good that she had two older sisters. They had barely survived themselves. Jennichen was born in Paris. Paris is marvelous for lovers, but not for children. Something about the air. Laura was our second, born in Brussels. No one should be born in Brussels.

In London, we had no money. But we always had Sunday picnics. We would walk an hour and a half into the countryside, Jenny and I, the children, and Lenchen (oh, I'll tell you about her . . .). Lenchen would make a roast veal. And we would have tea, fruit bread, cheese, beer. Eleanor was the youngest, but she drank beer.

No money, but children need a vacation. Once, I took the rent money and sent them to the Atlantic coast of France. Another time, with our groceries money, I bought a piano, because the girls loved music.

A father is not supposed to have favorites among his children. But Eleanor! I would say to Jenny: "Eleanor is a strange child." And Jenny would reply: "You expect the children of Karl Marx to be normal?"

Eleanor was the youngest, the brightest. Imagine a revolutionary at the age of eight. That's how old she was in 1863. Poland was in rebellion against Russian rule, and Tussy wrote a letter (that's what we called her: Tussy)—she wrote to Engels about "those brave little fellows in Poland," as she called them. When she was nine, she sent a letter to America, advice to President Lincoln, telling him how to win the war against the Confederacy!

Also, she smoked. And drank wine. Still, she was a child. She would dress her dolls . . . while sipping from a glass of wine! She played chess with me when she was ten, and I could not easily defeat her. At fifteen, she suddenly became furious against the law about observing the Lord's Day. No activity on Sunday was permitted. So, she organized "Sunday Evenings for the People" at St. Martin's Hall, brought musicians there to play Handel, Mozart, Beethoven. The hall was packed. Two thousand people. It was illegal, but no one was arrested. A lesson. If you are going to break the law, do it with two thousand people . . . and Mozart.

I used to read Shakespeare and Aeschylus and Dante aloud to her and her sisters, which she loved. Her room was a Shakespeare museum. She memorized *Romeo and Juliet* and insisted that I read, over and over, those lines of Romeo, when he sees Juliet for the first time:

> *The brightness of her cheek would shame those stars*
> *As daylight doth a lamp; her eyes in heaven*
> *Would through the airy region stream so bright*
> *That birds would sing and think it were not night.*

Tussy was not easy to live with. Oh, no! Do you know how embarrassing it is to have a child who finds flaws in your reasoning? She would argue with me about my writings! For instance, my essay "On the Jewish Question." Not easy to understand, I admit. Well, Eleanor read it, and immediately challenged me: "Why do you single out the Jews as representatives of capitalism? They are not the only ones poisoned by commerce and greed."

I tried to explain: I wasn't singling out the Jews, just using them as a vivid example. Her answer was to start wearing a Jewish star. "I'm a Jew," she announced. What could I say? I shrugged my shoulders and Eleanor said: "*That's a very Jewish gesture.*" She could be very annoying!

Tussy knew my father had converted to Christianity. It was not practical to be a Jew in Germany . . . Is it ever practical to be a Jew, anywhere? He had me baptized at the age of eight. This fact intrigued Eleanor. She asked: "Moor"—the family called me Moor because of my dark complexion—"I know you were baptized. But first you were circumcised, weren't you?" Nothing embarrassed that girl!

At such times she was impossible. Listen to this. Alongside her Jewish star, she wore her crucifix. No, she was not enamored of Christianity, but of the Irish, and their rebellion against England. She learned about the Irish struggle from Lizzie Burns, Engels's love.

Lizzie was a mill girl and could not read. Engels spoke nine languages. You might think this would make it hard for them to communicate. But they loved one another. Lizzie was active in the Irish movement. Tussy would visit and the two of them would sit on the floor and drink wine together and sing Irish songs until they fell asleep.

There was that terrible night, the night the English government hanged two young Irishmen, right there in Soho, with a drunken crowd cheering . . . Those genteel English with their afternoon tea and their public hangings! I understand you don't hang people anymore—only gas them, or inject poison into their veins, or use electricity to burn them to death. Much more civilized. Yes, they hanged two young Irishmen for wanting freedom from England. Eleanor wept and wept.

I would say to her: "Tussy, you don't have to get involved so soon with the horrors of the world. You're fifteen." And she would answer: "That's the point, Moor. I'm not thirteen. I'm not fourteen. I'm *fifteen*."

Yes, she was fifteen, and she became infatuated with any dashing, handsome man who visited our flat. I could draw up a list. For all the rest of her life, Eleanor was clever in politics, idiotic in love. She was mad about the hero of the Paris Commune, Lissagaray. Well, at least he was a Frenchman.

Jennichen's fellow was English. English men are like English food. Need I say more? And there was Laura's lover, LaFargue. His public displays of ardor were absurd. He would put his hand on her ass, in public, as if it were the most natural thing. And Jenny defended him. "It's his Creole background," she said. "You know his family came to France from Cuba." As if in Cuba everyone went around with their hands on somebody's ass!

Sighs. Jenny was always trying to calm me down. Well, she might calm *me*, but she was unsuccessful with my boils. *Grimaces.* Did you ever have boils? There is no sickness more odious. They plagued me all my life. And led to stupid attempts to analyze me via my boils. "Marx is angry at the capitalist system because he has boils!" What imbeciles! How do they account for all the revolutionaries who don't have boils?

Of course, they always find something: this one was beaten by his father; this one was nursed by his mother until he was ten; that one had no toilet training—as if one must be abnormal to resent exploitation. Every explanation except the obvious one, that capitalism, by its nature, its attack on the human spirit, breeds rebellion . . .

Oh yes, they say capitalism has become more humane since my time. Really? Just a few years ago—it was in the newspapers—factory owners locked the doors on the women in their chicken factory in North Carolina. Why? To make more profit. There was a fire, and twenty-five workers were trapped, burned to death.

Perhaps my anger did inflame my boils. But try working, try sitting and writing, with boils on your ass! And don't tell me about doctors. The doctors knew less than I did. Much less, because the boils were mine. *Takes another drink of beer.*

I could not sleep. Then I discovered something miraculous—water. Yes, as simple as that. Cloths soaked in warm water. Jenny would apply them patiently, hour after hour. She would wake up in the middle of the night when I cried out, and apply those soothing wet cloths. . . . Sometimes, when Jenny was away, Lenchen would do that.

He stops to reflect. Yes, Lenchen. Here we are, living in poverty in Soho, and Jenny's mother decides to send us Lenchen, to help with the babies. We had pawned our furniture, but suddenly we had a servant girl. That's how it is when you marry into aristocracy. Your in-laws don't send you money, which you desperately need. They send you fine linens and silverware. And a servant. Actually, not a bad idea. The servant can take the linens and silverware to the pawnshop and get some money. Lenchen did that many times . . .

But she was never a servant. The children adored her. And Jenny had tremendous affection for her. When Jenny was ill, Lenchen was with her, tending to every need.

But, yes, her presence created a great tension between Jenny and me. I remember a scene. Jenny said: "This morning, I saw you looking at Lenchen."

"Looking? What do you mean?"

"I mean the way a man looks at a woman."

"I still don't know what you mean." *Shakes his head sadly.* It was one of those conversations which cannot possibly come to any good.

There was all this going on inside our flat on Dean Street. And out-side was London. . . . Can you imagine the streets of London in 1858? The coster girls, trying to sell a few rolls for a few pennies. The organ grinder with his monkey. The prostitutes, the magicians, the fire-eaters, the street vendors bellowing trumpets, ringing bells, the hurdy-gurdies, the organs, the brass bands, the fiddlers, the Scottish pipers, and always a beggar girl singing an Irish ballad. That's what I saw and heard, walking home every evening from the British Museum, under the gas lamps that had just been lit, until I got to Dean Street and made my way through the mud and sewage, thinking about the care they took in pav-ing streets of the wealthy neighborhoods. *Sighs.* Well, I suppose it was only fitting that the author of *Das Kapital* should slog through shit while writing his condemnation of the capitalist system . . .

Jenny did not sympathize with my complaints about wading through the mud on the street. She would say: "That's how it feels to me reading *Das Kapital*!" She was always my severest critic. Unsparing. Honest, you might say. Is there anything more outrageous than an honest critic?

The book troubled her. Yes, *Das Kapital*. *Picks up the book.* She wor-ried that I would bore people from the start with my discussion of com-modities, use value, exchange value. She said the book was too long, too detailed. She used the word "ponderous." Imagine!

She reminded me what our trade union friend Peter Fox said when I gave him the book. "I feel like a man who has been given an elephant as a gift."

Yes, Jenny said, it *is* an elephant. I tried to tell her this is not the *Communist Manifesto*, which was intended for the general public. It is an analysis.

"Let it be an analysis," she said. "But let it cry out like the *Manifesto*."

"A spectre is haunting Europe—the spectre of Communism! Yes," she said, "that excites the reader . . . *A spectre is haunting Europe!"*

And then she read to me the first words of *Das Kapital*, to torment me, of course. *Marx picks the book from the table, and reads:* "The wealth of those societies in which the capitalist mode of production prevails presents itself as an immense accumulation of commodities."

She said, "That will put readers to sleep."

I ask you, is that boring? *He thinks.* Maybe it is a little boring. I admitted that to Jenny. She said, "There's no such thing as *a little* boring."

Don't misunderstand. She did see *Das Kapital* as a profound analy-sis. It showed how the capitalist system must, at a certain stage in history, come into being and bring about a colossal growth of the productive forces, an unprecedented increase in the wealth of the world. And then how it must, by its own nature, distribute that wealth in such a way as to destroy the humanity of both laborer and capitalist. And how it must, by its nature, create its own gravediggers and give way to a more human system.

But Jenny always asked, "Are we reaching the people we want to reach?"

One day, she said to me: "Do you know why the censors have allowed it to be published? Because they cannot understand it and assume no one else will."

I reminded her that *Das Kapital* was receiving favorable reviews. She reminded me that most of the reviews were written by Engels. . . . I told her that perhaps she was being critical of my work because she was unhappy with me.

"You men!" she said. "You cannot believe that your work *deserves* criticism and so you attribute it to something personal. Yes, Moor, my personal feelings are there, but this is separate."

Yes, her personal feelings. Jenny was having a terrible time then. I suppose I was responsible. But I did not know how to ease her anguish. You must understand, Jenny and I fell in love when I was seventeen and she was nineteen. She was marvelous looking, with auburn hair and dark eyes. For some reason, her family took a liking to me. They were aristocrats. Aristocrats are always impressed with intellectuals. Jenny's father and I would have long discussions about Greek philosophy. I had done my doctoral thesis on Democritus and Heraclitus. I was beginning to realize that up to now the philosophers had only interpreted the world. But the point was to *change* it!

When I was expelled from Germany, Jenny followed me to Paris and there we married and she gave birth to Jennichen and Laura. We were happy in Paris, living on nothing, meeting our friends in a café. They also lived on nothing. What a bunch we were! Bakunin, the huge, shaggy anarchist. Engels, the handsome atheist. Heine, the saintly poet. Oh, Stirner, the total misfit. And Proudhon, who said, "Property is theft!" . . . but wanted some!

Being poor in Paris is one thing. Being poor in London is another. We moved there with two children, and soon Jenny was pregnant again. Sometimes I felt she blamed me for having to bring up our children in a cold, damp flat where someone was sick all the time.

Jenny came down with smallpox. She recovered, but it left pockmarks on her face. I tried to tell her she was still beautiful, but it didn't help.

I wish you could know Jenny. What she did for me cannot be calculated. And she accepted the fact that I could not simply get a job like other men. Yes, I did try once. I wrote a letter of inquiry to the railway for a position as clerk. They responded as follows: "Dr. Marx, we are honored with your request for a position here. We have never had a doctor of philosophy working for us as a clerk. But the position requires a legible handwriting, so we must regretfully decline your offer." *He shrugs.*

Jenny believed in my ideas. But she was impatient with what she considered the pretensions of high-level scholarship. "Come down to earth, Herr Doktor," she would say.

She wanted me to describe the theory of surplus value so ordinary workers could understand it. I told her, "No one can understand it without first understanding the labor theory of value, and how labor power is a special commodity whose value is determined by the cost of the means of subsistence and yet gives value to all other commodities, a value which always exceeds the value of labor power."

She would shake her head: "No, that won't do. All you have to say is this: your employer gives you the barest amount in wages, just enough for you to survive and work; but out of your labor he makes far more than what he pays you. And so he gets richer and richer, while you stay poor."

All right, let us say only a hundred people in world history have ever understood my theory of surplus value. *Gets heated.* But it is still true! Just last week, I was reading the reports of the United States Department of Labor. There you have it. Your workers are producing more and more goods and getting less and less in wages. What is the result? Just as I predicted. Now the richest one percent of the American population owns forty percent of the nation's wealth. And this in the great model of world capitalism, the nation that has not only robbed its own people, but sucked in the wealth of the rest of the world . . .

Jenny was always trying to simplify ideas that were, by their nature, complex. She accused me of being a scholar first and a revolutionary second. She said: "Forget your intellectual readers. Address the workers."

She called me arrogant and intolerant. "Why do you attack other revolutionaries more vehemently than you attack the bourgeoisie?" she asked.

Proudhon, for instance. The man did not understand that we must applaud capitalism for its development of giant industries, and then take them over. Proudhon thought we must retreat into a more simple society. When he wrote his book *The Philosophy of Poverty*, I replied with my own book, *The Poverty of Philosophy*. I thought this was clever. Jenny thought it was insulting. *Sighs.* I suppose Jenny was a far better human being than I could ever be.

She encouraged me to get off my behind and get involved in the cause of the London workers. She came with me when I was invited to address the first meeting of the International Working Men's Association. It was the fall of 1864. Two thousand people were packed into St. Martin's Hall. *Steps forward, extends his arm as if to a great crowd as he speaks very deliberately, powerfully:*

"The workers of all countries must unite against foreign policies which are criminal, which play upon national prejudices, which squander, in wars, the people's blood and treasure. We must combine across national boundaries to vindicate the simple laws of morals and justice in international affairs. . . . Workers of the world, unite!" *Pauses . . .*

Jenny liked that . . . *Takes a drink.*

She kept the family going, with the water cut off, the gas cut off. But she never tired of the subject of female emancipation. She said that the vitality of women was being sapped by staying at home and darning socks and cooking. And so she refused to stay at home.

She accused me of being theoretically an emancipationist but practically ignorant of the problems of women. "You and Engels," she said, "write about sexual equality, but you do not practice it." Well, I won't comment on that . . .

She supported with all her heart the Irish struggle against England. Queen Victoria had said, "These Irish are really abominable people—not like any other civilized nation." Jenny wrote a letter to the London newspapers: "England hangs Irish rebels, who wanted nothing but freedom. Is England a civilized nation?"

Jenny and I were powerfully in love. How can I make you understand that? But we went through hellish times in London. The love was still there. But, at a certain point, things changed. I don't know why. Jenny said it was because she was no longer the great beauty I had wooed. That made me angry. She said it was because of Lenchen. That made me even more angry. She said I was angry because it was true. That made me furious!

He sighs, takes a swallow of beer, looks over the newspapers on the table, picks one up. They claim that because the Soviet Union collapsed, Communism is dead. *Shakes his head.* Do these idiots know what Communism is? Do they think that a system run by a thug who murders his fellow revolutionaries is Communism? *Scheisskopfen!*

Journalists, politicians who say such things—what kind of education did they have? Did they ever read the *Manifesto* that Engels and I wrote when he was twenty-eight years old and I was thirty?

He reaches for a book on the table and reads: "In place of the old bourgeois society, with its classes and class antagonisms, we shall have an association, in which the free development of each is the condition for the free development of all." Do you hear that? An *association*! Do they understand the objective of Communism? Freedom of the individual! To develop himself, herself, as a compassionate human being. Do they think that someone who calls himself a Communist or a socialist and acts like a gangster understands what Communism is?

To shoot those who disagree with you—can that be the Communism that I gave my life for? That monster who took all power for himself in Russia—and who insisted on interpreting my ideas like a religious fanatic—when he was putting his old comrades up against the wall before firing squads, did he allow his citizens to read that letter I wrote to the *New York Tribune* in which I said that capital punishment could not be justified in any society calling itself civilized? . . . *Angry.* Socialism is not supposed to reproduce the stupidities of capitalism!

Here in America, your prisons are crowded. Who is in them? The poor. Some of them have committed violent and terrible crimes. Most of them are burglars, thieves, robbers, sellers of drugs. They believe in free enterprise! They do what the capitalists do, but on a much smaller scale . . .

He picks up another book. Do you know what Engels and I wrote about prisons? "Rather than punishing individuals for their crimes, we should destroy the social conditions which engender crime, and give to each individual the scope which he needs in society in order to develop his life."

Oh, yes, we spoke of a "dictatorship of the proletariat." Not a dictatorship of a *party*, of a central committee, not a dictatorship of one man. No, we spoke of a temporary dictatorship of the working class. The mass of the people would take over the state and govern in the interests of all—until the state itself would become unnecessary and gradually disappear.

Bakunin, of course, disagreed. He said that a state, even a workers' state, if it has an army, police, prisons, will become a tyranny. He loved to argue with me.

Do you know about him? Bakunin, the anarchist? If a novelist invented such a character, you would say the existence of such a person is not possible. To say Bakunin and I did not get along is a great understatement.

Listen to what he said at the time Engels and I were in Brussels, writing the *Manifesto*. *Marx picks up a document from the table and reads:* "Marx and Engels, especially Marx, are ingrained bourgeois."

We were ingrained bourgeois! Of course, compared to Bakunin, everyone was bourgeois, because Bakunin chose to live like a pig. And if you did not live like a pig, if you had a roof over your head, if you had a piano in your sitting room, if you enjoyed some fresh bread and wine, you were a bourgeois.

I grant the man courage. He was imprisoned, sent to Siberia, escaped, wandered the world trying to foment revolution everywhere. He wanted an anarchist society, but the only anarchism he ever succeeded in establishing was in his head. He tried to start an uprising in Bologna, and almost killed himself with his own revolver. His revolutions failed everywhere, but he was like a man whose failure with women only spurs him on to more.

Did you ever see a photograph of Bakunin? A giant of a man. Bald head, which he covered with a little gray cap. Massive beard. Ferocious expression. He had no teeth—scurvy, the result of his prison diet. He seemed to live not in this world but in some world of his imagination. He was oblivious to money. When he had it, he gave it away; when he didn't have it, he borrowed without any thought of returning it. He had no home, or, you might say, the world was his home. He would arrive at a comrade's house and announce: "I'm here—where do I sleep? And what is there to eat?" In an hour he was more at home than his hosts!

There was that time in Soho. We were having dinner, and Bakunin burst in. Didn't bother to knock. It was his habit to arrive at dinnertime. We were surprised; we thought he was in Italy. Whenever we heard about him, he was in some far-off country organizing a revolution. Well, he almost knocked the door off its hinges, came in, looked around, smiled his toothless smile, and said, "Good evening, comrades." And without waiting for a response, sat down at the table, and began devouring sausage and meat in enormous chunks, stuffing in cheese, too, and glass after glass of brandy.

I said to him: "Mikhail, try the wine, we have plenty of that; brandy is expensive."

He drank some wine, spit it right out. "Absolutely tasteless," he said. "Brandy helps you think more clearly."

He then began his usual performance, preaching, arguing, ordering, shouting, exhorting. I was furious, but it was Jenny who spoke up. "Mikhail," she said, "Stop! You're consuming all the oxygen in the room!" He just roared with laughter and went on.

Bakunin's head was full of anarchist garbage, romantic, utopian nonsense. I wanted to expel him from the International. Jenny thought this ridiculous. Why, she asked, do revolutionary groups with six members always threaten someone with expulsion?

He had a hundred disguises, because the police were looking for him in every country in Europe. When he came to us in London, he was disguised as a priest. At least he thought so. He looked ridiculous!

Well, he was with us a week. Once we stayed up the whole night, drinking and arguing and drinking some more, until neither of us could walk. In fact, I fell asleep in the midst of one Bakunin's perorations. He shook me until I woke up, saying, "I haven't finished my point."

It was that glorious time in the winter of 1871, when the Commune had taken power in Paris. . . . Yes, the Paris Commune. Bakunin leaped, with his full bulk, into that revolution. The French understood him. They had a saying: "On the first day of a revolution, Bakunin is a treasure. On the second day, he should be shot."

Do you know about that magnificent episode in human history, the Paris Commune? The story starts with stupidity. I am speaking of Napoleon the Third. Yes, the nephew of Bonaparte.

He was a buffoon, a stage actor smiling to the crowd while sixteen million French peasants lived in blind dark hovels, their children dying of starvation. But because he kept a legislature, because people voted, it was thought they had democracy. . . . A common mistake.

Bonaparte wanted glory, so he made the mistake of attacking Bismarck's armies. He was quickly defeated, whereupon the victorious German troops marched into Paris and were greeted by something more devastating than guns—silence. They found the statues of Paris draped in black, an immense, invisible, silent resistance. They did the wise thing. They paraded through the Arc de Triomphe and quickly departed.

And the old French order, the Republic. Liberals, they called themselves. They did not dare come into Paris. They were trembling with fear because, with the Germans gone, Paris was now taken over by the workers, the housewives, the clerks, the intellectuals, the armed citizens. The people of Paris formed not a government, but something more glorious, something governments everywhere fear, a commune, the collective energy of the people. It was the *Commune de Paris*!

People meeting twenty-four hours a day, all over the city, in knots of three and four, making decisions together, while the city was encircled by the French army, threatening to invade at any moment. Paris became the first free city of the world, the first enclave of liberty in a world of tyranny.

I said to Bakunin: "You want to know what I mean by the dictatorship of the proletariat? Look at the Commune of Paris. That is true democracy." Not the democracy of England or America, where elections are circuses, with people voting for one or another guardian of the old order, where whatever candidate wins, the rich go on ruling the country.

The Commune of Paris. It lived only a few months. But it was the first legislative body in history to represent the poor. Its laws were for them. It abolished their debts, postponed their rents, forced the pawnshops to return their most needed possessions. They refused to take salaries higher than the workers. They lowered the hours of bakers. And planned how to give free admission to the theater for everyone.

The great Courbet himself, whose paintings had stunned Europe, presided over the federation of artists. They reopened the museums, set up a commission for the education of women—something unheard of—education for women. They took advantage of the latest in science, the lighter-than-air balloon, and launched one out of Paris to soar over the countryside, dropping printed papers for the peasants, with a simple, powerful message, the message that should be dropped to working people everywhere in the world: "*Our interests are the same.*"

The Commune declared the purpose of the schools—to teach children to love and respect their fellow creatures. I have read your endless discussions of education. Such nonsense! They teach everything needed to succeed in the capitalist world. But do they teach the young to struggle for justice?

The Communards understood the importance of that. They educated not only by their words, but by their acts. They destroyed the guillotine, that instrument of tyranny, even of revolutionary tyranny. Then, wearing red scarves, carrying a huge red banner, the buildings festooned with sheets of red silk, they gathered around the Vendôme Column, symbol of military power, a huge statue surmounted by the bronze head of Napoleon Bonaparte. A pulley was attached to the head, a capstan turned, and the head crashed to the ground. People climbed on the ruins. A red flag now floated from the pedestal. Now it was the pedestal not of one country but of the human race, and men and women, watching, wept with joy.

Yes, that was the Commune of Paris. The streets were always full, discussions going on everywhere. People shared things. They seemed to smile more often. Kindness ruled. The streets were safe, without police of any kind. Yes, *that* was socialism!

Of course that example, the example of the Commune, could not be allowed. And so the armies of the Republic marched into Paris and commenced a slaughter. The leaders of the Commune were taken to Père Lachaise cemetery, put against the stone wall, and shot. Altogether, thirty thousand were killed.

The Commune was crushed by wolves and swine. But it was the most glorious achievement of our time . . . *Walks, takes some more beer.*

Bakunin and I drank and argued, drank and argued some more. I said to him: "Mikhail, you don't understand the concept of a proletarian state. We cannot shake off the past in one orgasmic moment. We will have to remake a new society with the remnants of the old order. That takes time."

"No," he said. "The people, overthrowing the old order, must immediately live in freedom or they will lose it."

It began to get personal. I was getting impatient and I said, "You are too stupid to understand."

The brandy was having an effect on him, too. He said: "Marx, you are an arrogant son of a bitch, as always. It is you who don't understand. You think the workers will make a revolution based on your theory? They care not a shit for your theory. Their anger will rise spontaneously, and they will make a revolution without your so-called science. The instinct for revolution is in their bellies." He was aroused. "I spit on your theories."

As he said this, he spat on the floor. What a pig! This was too much. I said: "Mikhail, you can spit on my theories, but not on my floor. Clean it immediately."

"There," he said. "I always knew you were a bully."

I said, "I always knew you were a eunuch."

He roared. It sounded like a prehistoric animal. Then he leaped on top of me. You must understand, the man was enormous. We wrestled on the floor, but were too drunk to really hurt one another. After a while, we were so tired that we just lay there, catching our breath. Then

Bakunin rose, like a hippopotamus rising out of a river, unbuttoned his trousers, and began to urinate out the window! I could not believe what I was seeing. "What in hell are you doing, Mikhail?"

"What do you think I'm doing? I'm pissing out your window."

"That is disgusting, Mikhail," I said.

"I'm pissing on London. I'm pissing on the whole British Empire."

"No," I said, "You're pissing on my street."

He didn't reply, just buttoned his pants, lay down on the floor, and began to snore. I lay down on the floor myself, and was soon unconscious.

Jenny found us both like that, hours later, when she woke with the dawn. *Stops to take a swallow of beer.*

No, they could not allow the Commune to live. The Commune was dangerous, too inspiring an example for the rest of the world, so they drowned it in blood. It still happens, does it not, that whenever, in some corner of the world, the old order is pushed aside and people begin to experiment with a new way of living—people innocent of ideology, just angry about their lives—it cannot be permitted. And so they go to work—you know who I mean by *they*—sometimes insidiously, covertly, sometimes directly, violently, to destroy it.

Reading in the newspaper. So, they keep saying: "Capitalism has triumphed." Triumphed! Why? Because the stock market has risen to the sky and the stockholders are even wealthier than before? Triumphed? When one-fourth of American children live in poverty, when forty thousand of them die every year before their first birthday?

Reads from the paper: A hundred thousand people lined up before dawn in New York City for two thousand jobs. What will happen to the ninety-eight thousand who are turned away? Is that why you are building more prisons? Yes, capitalism has triumphed. But over whom?

You have technological marvels, you have sent men into the stratosphere, but what of the people left on earth? Why are they so fearful? Why do they turn to drugs, to alcohol, why do they go berserk and kill? *Holds up the newspaper.* Yes, it's in the newspapers.

Your politicians are bloated with pride. The world will now move toward the "free enterprise system," they say.

Has everyone become stupid? Don't they know the *history* of the free enterprise system? When government did nothing for the people and everything for the rich? When your government gave a hundred million acres of land free to the railroads, but looked away as Chinese immigrants and Irish immigrants worked twelve hours a day on those railroads, and died in the heat and the cold. And when workers rebelled and went on strike, the government sent armies to smash them into submission.

Why the hell did I write *Das Kapital* if not because I saw the misery of capitalism, of the "free enterprise system"? In England, little children were put to work in the textile mills because their tiny fingers could work the spindles. In America, young girls went to work in the mills of Massachusetts at the age of ten and died at the age of twenty-five. The cities were cesspools of vice and poverty. That is capitalism, then and now.

Yes, I see the luxuries advertised in your magazines and on your screens. *Sighs.* Yes, all those screens with all those pictures. You see so much and know so little!

Doesn't anyone read history? *He is angry.* What kind of shit do they teach in the schools these days? *Flashing lights, threatening. Looks up.* They are so sensitive!

I miss Jenny. She would have something to say about all this. I watched her die, sick and miserable at the end. But surely she remembered our years of pleasure, our moments of ecstasy, in Paris, even in Soho.

I miss my daughters . . .

Picks up newspaper again, reads: "Anniversary of Gulf War. A victory, short and sweet." Yes, I know about these short, sweet wars, which leave thousands of corpses in the fields and children dying for lack of food and medicine. *Waves the newspaper.* In Europe, Africa, Palestine, people killing one another over boundaries. *He is anguished.*

Didn't you hear what I said a hundred and fifty years ago? Wipe out these ridiculous national boundaries! No more passports, no more visas, no more border guards or immigration quotas. No more flags and pledges of allegiance to some artificial entity called a nation. Workers of the world, unite! *He clutches his hip, walks around.* Oh, God, my backside is killing me . . .

I confess: I did not reckon with capitalism's ingeniousness in surviving. I did not imagine that there would be drugs to keep the sick system alive. War to keep the industries going, to make people crazed with patriotism so they would forget their misery. Religious fanatics promising the masses that Jesus will return. *Shakes his head.* I know Jesus. He's not coming back . . .

I was wrong in 1848, thinking capitalism was on its way out. My timing was a bit off. Perhaps by two hundred years. *Smiles.* But it will be transformed. All the present systems will be transformed. People are not fools. I remember your President Lincoln saying that you can't fool all of the people all of the time.

Their common sense, their instinct for decency and justice, will bring them together.

Don't scoff! It has happened before. It can happen again, on a much larger scale. And when it does, the rulers of society, with all their wealth, with all their armies, will be helpless to prevent it. Their servants will refuse to serve, their soldiers will disobey orders.

Yes, capitalism has accomplished wonders unsurpassed in history— miracles of technology and science. But it is preparing its own death. Its voracious appetite for profit—more, more, more!—creates a world of turmoil. It turns everything—art, literature, music, beauty itself— into commodities to be bought and sold. It turns human beings into commodities. Not just the factory worker, but the physician, the scientist, the lawyer, the poet, the artists—all must sell themselves to survive.

And what will happen when all these people realize that they are all workers, that they have a common enemy? They will join with others in order to fulfill themselves. And not just in their own country, because capitalism needs a world market. Its cry is "Free trade!" because it needs to roam freely everywhere in the globe to make more profit— more, more! But in doing so, it creates, unwittingly, a world culture. People cross borders as never before in history. Ideas cross borders. Something new is bound to come of this. *Pauses, contemplatively.*

When I was in Paris with Jenny in 1843, I was twenty-five, and I wrote that in the new industrial system people are estranged from their work because it is distasteful to them. They are estranged from nature, as machines, smoke, smells, noise invade their senses—progress, it is called. They are estranged from others because everyone is set against everyone else, scrambling for survival. And they are estranged from their own selves, living lives that are not their own, living as they do not really want to live, so that a good life is possible only in dreams, in fantasy.

But it does not have to be. There is still a possibility of choice. Only a possibility, I grant. Nothing is certain. That is now clear. I was too damned certain. Now I know—anything can happen. But people must get off their asses!

Does that sound too radical for you? Remember, to be radical is simply to grasp the root of a problem. And the root is *us*.

I have a suggestion. Pretend you have boils. Pretend that sitting on your ass gives you enormous pain, so you must stand up. You must move, must act.

Let's not speak anymore about capitalism, socialism. Let's just speak of using the incredible wealth of the earth for human beings. Give people what they need: food, medicine, clean air, pure water, trees and grass, pleasant homes to live in, some hours of work, more hours of leisure. Don't ask who deserves it. Every human being deserves it.

Well, it's time to go.

Picks up his belongings. Starts to go, turns.

Do you resent my coming back and irritating you? Look at it this way. It is the second coming. Christ couldn't make it, so Marx came . . .

AFTERWORD

Alice Walker

We have lost a gift, which having received it, all of us might become.

On hearing the news of his death.

Me: Howie, where did you go?

Howie: What do you mean, where did I go? As soon as I died, I went back to Boston.

I met Howard Zinn in 1961 my first year at Spelman College in Atlanta, Georgia. He was the tall, rangy, good-looking professor that many of the girls at Spelman swooned over. My African roommate and I got a good look at him everyday when he came for his mail in the post office just beneath our dormitory window. He was always in motion but would stop frequently to talk to the many students and administrators and total strangers who seemed attracted to his energy of non-hesitation to engage. We met formally when some members of my class were being honored and I was among them. I don't remember what we were being honored for, but Howard and I ended up sitting next to each other. He remembered this later; I did not. He was the first white person I'd sat next to; we talked. He claimed I was "ironic." I was surprised he did not feel white.

I knew nothing of immigrants (which his parents were) or of Jews. Nothing of his father's and his own working-class background. Nothing of his awareness of poverty and slums. Nothing of why a white person could exist in America and not feel white: i.e., heavy, oppressive, threatening, and almost inevitably insensitive to the feelings of a person of color. The whole of Georgia was segregated at that time; in

Originally appeared in the *Boston Globe*, January 31, 2010.

coming to Spelman, I had had a run-in with the Greyhound bus driver (white as described above), who had forced me to sit in the back of the bus. This moment changed my life, though how that would play out was of course uncertain to a seventeen-year-old.

One way it did play out was that the very next summer I was on my way to the Soviet Union to see how white those folks were and to tell as many of them as I could, even if they were white, that I did not agree to my country's notions of bombing them. I didn't see a lot of generals, but children and women and men and old people of both sexes were everywhere. They were usually smiling and offering flowers or vodka. There was no "iron curtain" between us, as I'd been told to expect by Georgia media. I love to tell the story of how I was so ignorant at the time I didn't have a clue why folks were queuing up to see in Lenin's tomb; nor did I even know what "The Kremlin" was. I also didn't speak a word of Russian.

Coming back to Spelman, I discovered Howard Zinn was teaching a course on Russian history and literature and a little of the language. I signed up for it, though I was only a sophomore and the course was for juniors (as I recall). I had loved Russian literature since I discovered Tolstoy and Dostoyevsky back in the school library in Putnam County, Georgia. As for the Russian language, as with any language, I most wanted to learn to say hello, good-bye, please, and thank you.

Howard Zinn was magical as a teacher. Witty, irreverent, and wise, he loved what he was teaching and clearly wanted his students to love it also. We did. My mother, who earned $17 a week working twelve-hour days as a maid, had somehow managed to buy a typewriter for me and I had learned typing in school. I said hardly a word in class (as Howie would later recall), but, inspired by his warm and brilliant ability to communicate ideas and conundrums and passions of the characters and complexities of Russian life in the nineteenth century, I flew back to my room after class and wrote my response to what I was learning about these writers and their stories that I adored. He was proud of my paper, and, in his enthusiastic fashion, waved it about. I learned later there were those among other professors at the school who thought that I could not possibly have written it. His rejoinder: "Why, there's nobody else in Atlanta who *could* have written it!"

It would be hard not to love anyone who stood in one's corner like this.

Under the direction of SNCC (Student Nonviolent Coordinating Committee), many students at Spelman joined the effort to desegregate

Atlanta. Naturally, I joined this movement. Howie, taller than most of us, was constantly in our midst, usually somewhere in front. Because I was at Spelman on scholarship, a scholarship that would be revoked if I were jailed, my participation caused me a good bit of anxiety. Still, knowing Howard and other professors of ours—the amazingly courageous and generous Staughton Lynd, for instance, my other history teacher—supported the students in our struggle, made it possible to carry on. But then, while he and his family were away from campus for the summer, Howard Zinn was fired. He was fired for "insubordination."

Yes, he would later say, with a classic Howie shrug, *I was guilty.*

For me, and for many poorer students in my position, students on scholarship who also worked in the Movement to free us of centuries of white supremacy and second-class citizenship, it was a disaster. I wrote a letter to the administration that was published in the school paper pointing out the error of their decision. I wrote it through tears of anger and frustration. It was these tears, which appeared unannounced whenever I thought of this injustice to Howard and his family—whom I had met and also loved—that were observed by Staughton Lynd, who realized instantly that (a) there was every chance I was headed toward a breakdown; and (b) the administration would quickly find a reason to expel me from school. Added to the stress, which nobody knew about, was the fact that I was working for a well-respected older man who, knowing I had to work in order to pay for everything I needed as a young woman in school, was regularly molesting me. Lucky for me he was very old, and his imagination was stronger than his grasp. As a farm girl and no stranger to manual labor, I could type his papers with one hand while holding him off with the other. What rankled so much, then as now, is how much others respected, even venerated him. Perhaps this was one of many births of my feminism. A feminism/womanism that never seemed odd to Howard Zinn, who encouraged his Spelman students, all of them women, to name and challenge oppression of any sort. This encouragement would come in handy, when writing my second novel, *Meridian,* years later, I could explore the misuse of gender-based power from the perspective of having experienced it.

With Staughton Lynd's help, and after he had consulted with Howie (I did not know this), I was accepted to finish my college education at Sarah Lawrence College, a place I had never heard of before. I went off in the middle of winter without a warm coat or shoes, and ice and snow greeted me. But also Staughton's mother, Helen Lynd, who immediately provided money for the coat and shoes I needed, as well as a blanket that had been her son's. In my solitary room, knowing no one on campus, I hunkered down to write. Letters to the Zinns, first of all. To inform them I had been liberated from Spelman, as they had been, and had landed.

I was Howard's student for only a semester, but in fact I have learned from him all my life. His way with resistance: steady, persistent, impersonal, often with humor, is a teaching I cherish. Whenever I've been arrested, I've thought of him. I see policemen as victims of the very system they're hired to defend, as I know he did. I see soldiers in the same way. In some ways, Howie was an extension of my father, whom he never met. My father was also an activist as a young man and was one of the first black men unconnected to white ancestry or power to vote in our backwoods county; he had to pass by three white men holding shotguns in order to do this. By the time I went off to college, the last of eight children, he was exhausted and broken. But these men were connected in ways clearer to me now as I've become older than my father was when he died. They each saw injustice as something to be acknowledged, confronted, and changed if at all possible. And they looked for signs of humanity in their opponents and spoke to that. They both possessed a sense of humor and love of a good story that made them charismatic teachers. I recently discovered—and it amuses me—that their birth dates are remarkably close, though my father was thirteen years older.

Howie and I planned to rendezvous in Berkeley in March, when he would come out to spend a few weeks with his grandchildren. In April we planned to be on a panel with Gloria Steinem and Bernice Reagon at an event in New Orleans for Amnesty International. I had decided not to go, but Howie said if I didn't come he would "sorely miss" me. I wrote back that in that case I would certainly be there as "soreness of any sort" was not to be tolerated.

Over the years I've been in the habit of sending freshly written poems to Roz and Howie. After her death, I continued to send the occasional poem to Howie. Last week, after the Supreme Court's decision to let corporations offer unlimited funding to political candidates, I wrote a poem about what I would do if I were president, called "If I Was President: 'Were' for Those Who Prefer It." My first act as president, given that corporations may well buy all elections in America from now on, would be to free Mumia Abu-Jamal and Leonard Peltier, both men accused of murders I've felt they did not commit, both men in prison for sadistically long periods of time.

Howie's response, and the last word he communicated to me, was "Wonderful." I imagined him hurriedly typing it, then flying, even at eighty-seven, out the door.

The question remains: where do our friends and loved ones go when they die?

They can't all go back to Boston, or wherever they've lived their most intense life.

I fell asleep, after leaking tears for Howie most of the day: my sweetheart's shirt was luckily absorbent and available to me, and after tossing and turning almost all night, I had the following dream: we (Someone and I) were looking for the place we go to when we die. After quite a long walk, we encountered it. What we saw was this astonishingly gigantic collection of people and creatures: birds and foxes, butterflies and dogs, cats and beings I've never seen awake, and they were moving toward us in total joy at our coming. We were happy too. But there was nothing to support any of us: no land, no water, nothing. We ourselves were all of it: our own earth. And I woke up knowing that this is where we go when we die. We go back to where we came from: inside all of us.

Good-bye, Howie. Beloved. Hello.

PERMISSIONS